Dr. William H. Brannen is Associate Professor of Marketing at Creighton University. In addition to consulting and case writing, the author has been active in both the American Marketing Association and the International Council for Small Business.

SUCCESSFUL MARKETING FOR YOUR SMALL BUSINESS

WILLIAM H. BRANNEN

A SPECTRUM BOOK

PRENTICE-HALL, INC., *Englewood Cliffs, New Jersey 07632*

Library of Congress Cataloging in Publication Data

Brannen, William H.
    Successful marketing for your small business.

    (A Spectrum Book)
    Includes bibliographies and index.
    1. Marketing management.   2. Marketing.
3.   Small businesses.   I. Title.
HF5415.13.B676   658.8   78-1116
ISBN 0-13-863399-1
ISBN 0-13-863381-9 pbk.

© 1978 by Prentice-Hall, Inc., Englewood Cliffs, New Jersey 07632

A Spectrum Book

10   9   8   7   6   5   4   3   2   1

Printed in the United States of America

PRENTICE-HALL INTERNATIONAL, INC., *London*
PRENTICE-HALL of AUSTRALIA PTY. LIMITED, *Sydney*
PRENTICE-HALL of CANADA, LTD., *Toronto*
PRENTICE-HALL of INDIA PRIVATE Limited, *New Delhi*
PRENTICE-HALL of JAPAN, INC., *Tokyo*
PRENTICE-HALL of SOUTHEAST ASIA PTE. Ltd., *Singapore*
WHITEHALL BOOKS LIMITED, *Wellington, New Zealand*

Dedicated to HOWARD BRANNEN,
my father and a very successful small business marketer

Contents

I

INTRODUCTION
TO SMALL BUSINESS
MARKETING
MANAGEMENT

1

2

3

II

MARKETS AND SB MARKETING OPPORTUNITIES

III

THE SBMM ENVIRONMENT

IV

THE MARKETING MIX OF THE SBMM

V

THE PEC MANAGEMENT PROCESS IN SBMM

Preface

This book is for everyone interested in small business marketing. The basic theme is that the marketing management concept that has proven so successful for big business can and should be *adapted* to provide for success in small business. Each present and potential small marketer is offered a framework for successfully applying the marketing management concept to an individual business.

Just as basic principles of navigation apply to both aircraft carriers and canoes or as basic principles of aeronautics apply equally well to jumbo jets and small aircraft, so also do basic principles of management and marketing apply to businesses of all sizes. However, many important differences exist between big businesses and smaller businesses that make it necessary to *adapt* such principles if they are to be applicable to small and medium-size firms. Such adaptations have been based on the best thoughts and research available on the subject of small business marketing. With these adapted principles, the small business marketer is invited to use the provided framework to plan, execute, and control a marketing strategy directed toward fulfilling the needs of his specific target markets at a profit.

An outstanding feature of the book is its organization. Each part of the book (and chapters within each part) relates to other parts in a systematic manner that visualizes the book outline or table of contents into a total picture or model of small business marketing strategy. The overall big picture is shown in Figure 3–1 of Chapter 3. Portions of the visual model are shown at appropriate locations throughout the book. A simple, eight-step conference method of marketing strategy planning is described in detail. By using this conference method, each small marketer can best utilize product, place, price, promotion, and people to build a successful marketing program that best fits his individual situation. The organization of the book is also flexible in that any portion may be read or reviewed to shed light on specific problem areas in small business marketing.

You, the reader, are asked to remember that this book is different by design. The research and writing tasks were enjoyable as well as educational for the author. Reading and studying should produce similar enjoyment and education for the reader. However, the real payoff for us all is in helping to create more and better successful small business marketers. Yes, you may judge the book, and your feedback to the author will be appreciated. Ultimately, the market will judge us both.

Although I accept the responsibilities of authorship, I also wish to acknowledge others for their help. In addition to the many sources and authors cited in the text, I also wish to thank my teaching colleagues, graduate students, and undergraduate students. Creighton University is thanked for providing me both time and resources used to complete this book. I thank Professor C. Glenn Walters for suggestions on the consumer behavior chapter. Thomas Kirsch is thanked for making finished line drawings from my rough sketches. For an excellent job of typing the manuscript, I thank Mary Jo Steffensmeier Schmid. For her editorial assistance, encouragement, and many other ways of helping, I thank my wife, Kathy. Finally, to my children, Julie and Patrick, I say thank you for wating so long for the book to be finished.

I

INTRODUCTION TO SMALL BUSINESS MARKETING MANAGEMENT

Success in small business marketing management (SBMM) requires a definite commitment. Much external assistance is available, but success is very unlikely without the necessary commitment. This book, as a form of external assistance, also requires a commitment on the part of the reader if the book is to be of maximum benefit to future successful small business marketers.

The organization of the book is such that it all fits together in a systematic manner. Chapter 1 introduces small business by highlighting both the qualitative

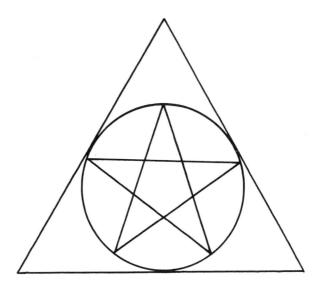

and quantitative differences between small business and big business. Chapter 2 adds the marketing management perspective to our study of small business. After these two chapters have introduced the field of study, our systematic method of study, the small business marketing management (SBMM) model, is presented in overview and pictorial form in Chapter 3. These first three chapters (especially Chapter 3) are extremely important to a better understanding of the remainder of the book because these chapters outline the marketing management philosophy in the small business environment. A casual scanning through the remainder of the book will reveal additional drawings of portions of our SBMM model. Plan to use these drawings later on as an aid to studying the relationships among the various subsystems in the model. Also, plan to refer back to Chapter 3 on occasion to review the total model.

1

What Is Small Business?

Some college freshmen were sitting around the snack bar during "Freshman Week." Kathy asked Bob where he was from, to which he very loudly and proudly replied, "Chicago!"

"Oh!" she said, "I've been there visiting my cousin several times. It's a fun town."

"No, not a town," said Bob, "Chicago is a city!" Then Bob asked Kathy where she was from. Kathy's reply and Bob's "put down" were not heard by Lois, her roommate, who was thinking what Bob might call her home community of 300 people after he finished with a name for Kathy's home town of 14,000 people.

Whether a particular community is considered to be a village, suburb, town, city, metropolis, or megalopolis quite often depends on the perspective of the person who is attempting to fit that particular community into a neat classification. The assigned classification varies with the individual and the purpose. In addition to different individual perspectives and purposes, a large amount of confusion can result from a lack of standard definitions for such terms as *village, suburb,* and so forth. A somewhat analogous situation exists when one attempts to determine if a particular business is a *small business.* Here also, the task is complicated by the lack of standard definitions of *small business.*

In this book, we won't solve this seemingly impossible definitional dilemma. We also won't add to the dilemma by adding another definition. Our approach will be to offer some accepted definitions for the reader's consideration and to point out some limitations of these. Then the chapter will focus on differences between small and big business, on some subtypes of small business, on the importance of people in small business, on the overall importance of small business, and on a discussion of success and failure. After exposure to the above topics, the reader will be asked to decide for himself how small business should be defined. At the end of the chapter, the reader should plan to:

(1) formulate his own simple definition and criteria for *small business.*

3

(2) implement his definition by determining in what ways and to what extent any particular business falls inside or outside his definition.

In formulating and implementing his definition, the reader is reminded that (1) there is room for considerable variability within a single definition, and (2) that the basic distinctions between small business and big business are distinctions of kind as well as of degree.

SOME DEFINITIONS

Many definitions of *small business* have originated with the federal government. And, as is often the case with our federal bureaucracy, there are considerable differences among the various federal agencies. In a 1972 article, Dr. Carolyn N. Hooper discusses some of the changing government concepts of *small* business.[1] Dr. Hooper states:

In 1953, Congress established the Small Business Administration (SBA) and instructed it to develop a detailed working definition of small business which would account for the variations in size of business from industry to industry. According to the 1953 act: ". . . a small business concern shall be deemed to be one which is independently owned and operated and which is not dominant in its field of operation. In addition to the foregoing criteria the Administrator, in making a detailed definition, may use these criteria, among others: Number of employees and dollar volume of business. Where the number of employees is used as one of the criteria in making such definition for any of the purposes of this act, the maximum number of employees which a small business concern may have under the definition shall vary from industry to industry."[2]

Changes have occurred, and will continue to occur in the SBA definition. The latest SBA definition can be obtained from the local SBA office. We should note that the major purpose of the SBA definition is to determine a firm's eligibility for participation in government programs.

Authors of small business management textbooks have wrestled with the definitional problem. In an excellent book, Dan Steinhoff says:

Of the various definitions of a small firm used for different purposes, perhaps the most useful one has been developed by the Committee for Economic Development (CED). This important research organization based its definition on the characteristics of the individual firm. To qualify as a small business under this definition, a firm must possess at least two of the following four key factors:

1. Management of the firm is independent. Usually the managers are also the owners.

2. Capital is supplied and the ownership is held by an individual or a small group.

3. The area of operations must be mainly local, with the workers and owners living in one home community. However, the markets need not be local.

4. The relative size of the firm within its industry must be small when compared

[1]Carolyn N. Hooper, "Defining 'Small Business' In Government Programs," *Journal of Small Business Management,* 10 (October 1972), 28–34.

[2]Hooper, 31–32. Dr. Hooper footnotes the U. S. Congress, *Reconstruction Finance Corporation Liquidation Act; Small Business Act of 1953,* Public Law 163, 83d Cong., 1st Sess., 1953.

with the biggest units in its field. This measure can be in terms of sales volume, number of employees, or other significant comparisons.[3]

Another recent contribution to the literature of small business management discusses definitions according to size and according to the intentions of managers or owners. These authors, after stating that there is no generally accepted definition of *small business,* offer one which is certainly acceptable for many purposes. They define *small business* as "an organization with a name, a place of operations, an owner, and one or more workers other than the owner." The different philosophies between small business owners and large enterprise managers are also brought out by Tate et al.[4] Before getting into a detailed discussion of these very important differences, let's take a brief break to agree on some terminology among ourselves. We will also find some abbreviations convenient to use.

TERMINOLOGY AND ABBREVIATIONS

The following list of terms that could be used in describing people involved in small business is probably very incomplete:

1. entrepreneur
2. entrepreneur-manager
3. family-operated business
4. family-owned business
5. independent
6. independent businessman
7. independent operator
8. owner-manager
9. owner-operator
10. small business entrepreneur
11. small business manager
12. small business owner
13. small business operator
14. small businessman.

These terms have different connotations and slightly different meanings. At least two of the above may suggest incorrectly that small business is for "men only." While all of the above terms will be used in this book when appropriate, our major term which will be most often used is *small business marketer.* This seems most appropriate for our purposes. Quite often we will abbreviate this term, along with some other terms, as follows:

$$SB = \text{small business}$$
$$SBM = \text{small business marketer}$$
$$SBMM = \text{small business marketing management}$$
$$BB = \text{big business.}$$

[3]Dan Steinhoff, *Small Business Management Fundamentals* (New York: McGraw-Hill Book Company, 1974), p. 7.
[4]Curtis E. Tate, Jr. et al., *Successful Small Business Management* (Dallas, Texas: Business Publications, Inc., 1975), p. 4.

DIFFERENCES BETWEEN SMALL BUSINESS
AND BIG BUSINESS

In the most comprehensive study of its kind, *How Management Is Different In Small Companies,* Cohn and Lindberg clearly show the importance of exploiting size-related opportunities by small business (SB) through the knowledge of size-related differences in management practice.[5] With the firm belief that the common body of general management principles is based upon large company experience, these pioneer researchers state, "Managerial competence in small firms is often seriously diluted by uncritical adherence to the belief that the principles of management are applicable in companies of every size. When this belief extends beyond managerial generalizations of the broadest scope, serious problems often arise."[6]

Cohn and Lindberg have partially based their conclusions on a survey of presidents of small companies (defined by them to have annual sales of from $2 million to $10 million) and large companies (annual sales of from $80 million to $600 million). The great wealth of this study is highlighted by their two dozen conclusions:

1. Small and big firms must differ deliberately in many of the ways they administer their businesses.
2. Small firms should focus on achieving managerial excellence; they tend to underestimate the need for and the difficulty in attaining such excellence because of the protections offered by their abilities to live in small markets and to profit from short production runs.
3. Where the small businessman does consciously attend to administration, he tends to adopt the methods and practices used in larger firms rather than to develop techniques and applications that are more specific to his needs. This form of imitation usually brings about operating and procedural inefficiencies. Techniques copied from large firms are, in small companies, more often brought in as unrelated bits of administrative magic than as part of an integrated process.
4. Small companies should not try to skimp on management staff; many of the problems of small businesses can be traced to shortages of top personnel.
5. Planning is the most difficult function to perform well in a small company. Therefore, small companies should take pains to see that the effectiveness of planning is raised to the highest level.
6. The poorest part of the planning job done in small firms is the setting of overall goals. Conceptualizing a firm's mission or goals in terms of externals (markets served or aimed at, product needs identified or to be exploited) is much more difficult for the small company than it is for a large firm, even though it is equally necessary in both. The small firm's financial, production, and marketing limitations force it to deal with more factors in less stable environments than large firms must deal with.
7. Small companies should strive to excel in shortterm planning. Detailed planning beyond the clearly seen future can induce rigidities that may largely offset or destroy the advantages of a small firm's innate flexibility and maneuverability. The smaller quantities of goods produced, fewer salesmen, lower inventory levels, smaller outlays for advertising and promotion, and similar characteristics of small businesses seldom justify the risks or costs imposed by long-range plans.

[5]Theodore Cohn and Roy A. Lindberg, *How Management Is Different in Small Companies,* An AMA Management Briefing, 32 pp.

[6]Reprinted by permission of the publisher from Theodore Cohn and Roy A. Lindberg, *How Management Is Different in Small Companies,* An AMA Management Briefing, © 1972 by American Management Association, Inc. p. 1.

8. Nothing a small company does in planning should be allowed to impair, even temporarily, customer services and product customization capabilities (which are critical to survival of the small business).

9. Next to the provision of wanted products, keeping costs low is the most important advantage a small firm can possess. Not having the advantages that stem from high capitalization and commodity markets, the profitability of a small firm rests largely on the tighter control that top management close to operations can exercise over the costs of making the products or providing the services it offers.

10. Small companies should seek to automate data processing as soon as technically and economically feasible. Small companies, which in the past did not have the resources to operate on the basis of the best available knowledge, can now afford the information they need (and have hitherto lacked) to manage their affairs on an informed basis. (For example, product profitability analysis, projections, and decision-making aids are available through time-sharing computer terminals and service bureaus at $25–$100 a month.)

11. The manager in a small company can afford less to be a specialist than his big-company counterpart, but he should not try to be all things to his firm. He must be able to contribute to tight control of costs and key resources and be aware of his firm's progress, but he should rely on others (inside or outside the firm) to perform the tasks for which he is not qualified.

12. An inexpensive, proven method of broadening the basis of key decision making in the small firm is through the formation of a carefully chosen and authoritative board of directors or management (advisory) committee with at least a 40 percent outside membership (nonequity).

13. Small companies cannot always afford to make decisions mainly on the basis of the relevant facts or sound reasoning. At certain times and in certain circumstances, the smaller and more personal environment of a small company requires consensus rather than a decision that is objectively arrived at.

14. Although the small company is a more natural habitat for entrepreneurs than the large company, it offers a poorer environment for the radical individualist. The small company is less hierarchical, systematized, and compartmentalized than the large company and is, therefore, more readily disrupted by persons with deficient interpersonal interests and skills.

15. The skills and personal characteristics of executives exert a more powerful influence on the fortunes of small companies than they do on large, and should weigh heavily in determining the kinds of methods and procedures adopted. Methods and procedures in small firms should be designed not only to offset personal deficiencies but also to utilize strengths.

16. Small companies should seek to employ high-potential (entrepreneurial or otherwise gifted) people by emphasizing the special attractions of small businesses. Current shifts in cultural values increasingly favor working in small firms.

17. Small companies lose employees more often for dollars than do large. Small firms should review compensation against the cost of replacing and training key people and make adjustments as needed to attract and keep effective people.

18. Small companies should look for people skilled in handling a big volume of detail and making varied decisions. Ironically, an increasingly important source of such persons is large business.

19. Growth, when it becomes a self-contained objective, exposes the small company to extraordinary hazards. A high percentage of small companies which make a primary aim of getting bigger, and which succeed in greatly increasing sales volume, lose control over costs and strangle on their growth.

20. Small companies can improve their performance by upgrading the quality of directive

elements (plans, policies, procedures, and so forth); the advantages of relatively smaller scales of activities in small firms are often lost by failure to employ methods and tools that can significantly reduce the need for information transference and repetitive decision making.

21. Small firms should not make a fetish of keeping organization as simple as possible; they can often benefit from structural arrangements (for example, centralized purchasing) that in large firms create handicaps which exceed the benefits received.

22. Because the risks of failure of original products is great and can cause more serious losses for small companies than for large companies, small firms should lean more toward evolution than invention in product development.

23. When small firms must risk their future on new products (not externally available), they should aim at radical development; many of the greatest product innovations have come from small firms.

24. Small firms have more problems in creating sales than in managing people. The problems of large firms are more the opposite.[7]

MARKETING-RELATED ADVANTAGES AND DISADVANTAGES OF SB

The advantages and disadvantages of anything are not automatic. Although some may tend to be unique or inherent to a particular phenomenon such as small business marketing, other advantages may go unrealized while disadvantages are unnecessarily self-imposed. The smart SBM will want to capitalize on all the possible advantages while recognizing the disadvantages only in order to avoid them. Although it is possible for a firm of any size to be, unnecessarily, at the mercy of some self-imposed disadvantages, it is impossible for a firm to enjoy at the same time the advantages of both small business (SB) and big business (BB).

Small business marketers should also remember that much of the activity of big business (BB), such as coordinating the efforts of various departments, is more critical for BB because of its size in order to simulate a somewhat more natural state which is possible in SB. It is the quantitative differences to some extent, but even more so, it is the qualitative differences (i.e., differences in kind) that make for a different set of advantages and disadvantages for small business marketing management (SBMM) and big business marketing management. In the overall planning, execution, and control of marketing, the differences between SBMM and BB marketing management are evident at both the strategic and tactical levels. Small business marketers may employ combinations of marketing strategies and tactics, in comparison to BB, as follows:

1. Strategies similar, tactics similar.
2. Strategies similar, tactics different.
3. Strategies different, tactics similar.
4. Strategies different, tactics different.

The specific marketing strategies and tactics employed in various areas of the SB marketing mix will depend on to what extent the following advantages and disadvantages

[7]Cohn and Lindberg, pp. 2–3.

are apparent to the SBM. A list of small business marketing-related advantages (and conditions under which the SBM can advantageously operate) follows:

1. Less goal conflict should take place in SB. The overall company goals of the SB are (or should be) very compatible with the marketing goals of the SB. By contrast, in BB, the overall company goals are very likely to be interpreted differently at the different levels of management and in the various functional areas. Also, in BB, the overall company goals as well as the marketing goals are very likely to be in conflict with the personal goals of many managers. The probability of conflict among overall company goals, marketing goals, and personal goals is less for SB.

2. Limited markets are opportunities for SB but not for BB. Markets may be limited by geographic area, by the demographics of consumers, or by any of the other dimensions discussed in a later chapter (chapter 4) on markets and market segmentation. The point is that either because of existing natural size limitations or because of purposeful and successful market segmentation, the SBM may profitably serve markets that are too limited to be of interest to BB. The lack of interest on the part of BB is due to a certain minimum scale of operations necessary to support the overhead of the bureaucracy before the BB can, from a "return on investment" point of view, become interested in a market opportunity. More simply stated, some markets are "not worth the bother" to BB.

3. Product characteristics sometimes favor SB. For example, perishable products and individualized or customized products are more attractive opportunities to SB than BB. Products (or product-service combinations) requiring a significant amount of personal service (especially skilled service) are often good for SB. A product which has a rather short product life-cycle, such as a fad or fashionable merchandise, is often handled more advantageously by SB than BB.

4. Flexibility is often listed as one of the advantages of SB. However, this term is not always sufficiently explained. What is usually meant by *flexibility* is the ability to change rapidly with changing market situations. If SB is, in fact, to have a greater amount of flexibility than BB, it must be by design. Like all advantages, it is not automatic. For example, if the SB firm wishes to be able to take advantage of a developing new market opportunity, it will be possible to do so only if the firm is not saddled with overextended financial commitments. This may suggest that marketing flexibility can be enhanced by maintaining a low ratio of fixed costs to variable costs.

5. Closer customer contact is possible in SB. Informal organization and personal communications make it possible (but do not guarantee) for the SBM to better know the needs and wants of and to better satisfy the customer. This is an extremely important advantage of the SBM and should never be taken lightly. Simply assuming that this advantage is working for the SB does not make it so. The SBM must take positive action to make it work.

A list of small business marketing-related disadvantages (and conditions under which the SBM might operate at a disadvantage) follows:

1. Competing head-on with mass marketers for mass markets is very difficult. Such a strategy is even difficult for many large businesses. While economies of scale are not to be ignored by SB, the advantages of mass production and mass marketing usually tend to favor BB.

2. A lack of coordination or balance between production and marketing may exist in SB. For example, because products and markets are not unique, the SBM may feel that he is losing sales because his product line is too narrow. On the other hand, he knows that if he gets into product diversification at too rapid a rate his finances will be strained, his

production and marketing costs will rise, his manpower needs will not be met, and his flexibility for taking advantage of future market opportunities will be lost.

3. Some discrimination against small size does exist in the competitive marketplace. At the retail level, for example, shopping center developers do tend to favor large national chains as tenants. Tradesmen do give quantity discounts. Discount structures of advertising media may make it very difficult for a new firm or product to become known in the marketplace. Even beyond this, high advertising budgets are often required to receive brand acceptance and loyalty. The successful SBM must either cope with or adapt to monopolistic market practices.

4. Certainly a major disadvantage is the lack of effective marketing techniques employed by SB. This is true of advertising, personal selling, marketing research, and virtually all areas of marketing. Lack of functional specialization in SB results in less internal staff expertise. The often suggested remedy to this disadvantage is to acquire such expertise from outside consultants, trade associations, bankers, accountants, and other professionals.

SUBTYPES OF SB

Although it is clear, from the above discussion of advantages and disadvantages, that SB is certainly not the same as BB, we can also note that small businesses are not all alike. Mentioned here are two kinds of differences found among small businesses. Many other differences exist. Size differences can be substantial within most definitions of SB. Sizes range from the "very small" or "too small" to the "rather substantial," with some sort of "medium" to the range. The mere recognition of size differences is more important than the actual divisions into subclasses by size. All are small businesses.

Steinhoff classifies small firms on the basis of activity area into manufacturing, mining, wholesaling, retailing, and service.[8] Small manufacturers and miners often employ middlemen to perform a part of the marketing functions. This is also true of other raw materials producers. Small wholesalers, whether merchants or agents, perform marketing functions for both their suppliers and customers. Retailing probably represents the largest percentage of SB. Retailers market to ultimate consumers. Service firms, serving both the industrial and consumer markets, represent a growing segment of SB. All of the above five activity areas are marketers. All perform some or all of the marketing functions: buying, selling, transporting, storing, standardizing and grading, financing, risk taking, and market information. The success of these small businesses is dependent in large measure on the extent to which they recognize and carry out their roles as marketers. Throughout this book, we will emphasize the fact that all subtypes of SB are (or should be) small business marketers in order to enjoy maximum success.

PEOPLE IN SB

People are an important ingredient to the success of a business of any size. However, in SB, the people who make up the business are of special importance to the customers of that business. The lack of hierarchy and formal bureaucratic organization places special

[8]Steinhoff, pp. 8–9.

emphasis on the *people* element in SB. A concept closely related to the people element is entrepreneurship. Entrepreneurship is by no means synonomous with SB marketing or management. It is also not exclusively within the domain of SB. People differences are often found when comparing owners, managers, employees, outside consultants, and so forth from SB and BB.

In later chapters, the importance of people in the SB marketing mix will be shown. *People* will join the traditional "4 P's" of marketing (*product, place, price,* and *promotion*) to form the "5 P's" of small business marketing. Our SB marketing strategy will involve the right people, marketing the right products, at the right place and price, by using the right promotion.

For the above overall SB marketing strategy to work effectively, the SBM must employ an effective people strategy. Such a people strategy must recognize the differences that exist between SB and BB. After briefly reviewing some of these differences, one researcher suggests, "Given these factors, a number of smaller firms have in fact failed to develop personnel strategies of any kind."[9] Although this "no choice" strategy is not surprising, it certainly does not facilitate the successful achievement of marketing goals. The lack of a people strategy is an unnecessary, self-imposed disadvantage for some small business marketers.

IMPORTANCE OF SB

SB is and historically has been very important to the economy. The diversity of definitions makes for some disagreement as to exactly how important SB is. Comments from multiple sources indicate that:

1. There are more small businesses today, both in absolute numbers and as a percentage of population, than there were at the turn of the century.
2. About 95 per cent of all businesses are small.
3. Statistics which show a decline in "self-employment" should be adjusted for the decline in numbers of farms due to the larger average size of farms in order to reflect the small business (SB) situation more accurately.
4. Although small businesses usually employ fewer than 100 persons per firm, collectively they account for approximately half of our total employment.
5. The *"Fortune 500"* and other BB firms are very interdependent with SB, both as sources of supply and as members of distribution channels.
6. Many big businesses started as successful small businesses that expanded by providing innovations to our society.

The future for SB appears to be bright. The important role of SB seems to be supported by several market trends favoring SB. Baumback cites the following trends as being favorable for SB because SB is especially suited to serving the needs of segmented markets:[10]

[9]John B. Miner, "Personnel Strategies In The Small Business Organization," *Journal of Small Business Management,* 11 (July 1973), 14.
[10]Clifford M. Baumback et al., *How to Organize and Operate a Small Business* (Englewood Cliffs, New Jersey: Prentice-Hall, Inc., 1973), pp. 42–45.

1. Increasing consumer affluence.
2. Increased leisure time.
3. The "do-it-yourself" trend.
4. Antimaterialism, or the "counterculture."
5. Environmental concern or ecology.
6. Technological development.

SB SUCCESS AND FAILURE

To be successful, study success. That is one of the major themes of this book. Success and failure in any activity are often measured by whether or not, and the extent to which, the goals and objectives are achieved.

In the following paragraphs, we will look briefly at the traditional "failure message" found in books on SB. Then the whole subject of failure and all its warnings will be dropped throughout the rest of the book. Our discussion here will also focus briefly on SB goals, growth, and rewards. We are interested in why the SBM succeeds and what he does to achieve this success.

The Traditional Failure Message to SB

Many books and articles on SB begin by quantitative and/or qualitative discussions of failure. A primary information source for such discussions is Dun & Bradstreet. For example, in 1975, as in other years, D & B gives causes along with percentages for over 11,000 "business failures." Percentage figures are supplied for manufacturers, wholesalers, retailers, construction, commercial services, and all (total). The broad categories of underlying causes for all business failures are further subdivided into apparent causes. Table 1–1 shows percentages for the all (totals) columns only.[11]

Dun & Bradstreet, in another publication, lists the major pitfalls of starting and owning your own business:[12]

> Lack of experience
> Lack of capital
> Poor location
> Too much inventory, particularly of the wrong kind
> Excessive purchase of fixed assets
> Poor credit granting practice
> Personal expenses too high
> Unplanned expansion
> What might be called faulty attitudes.

Other businesses, both SB and BB, did not succeed in terms of their own goals, but they do not appear in the Dun & Bradstreet statistics. These "limited successes" simply did not reach their goals, but did perhaps come closer to doing so than most of the Dun &

[11]Dun & Bradstreet, Inc., *The Business Failure Record 1975,* A Report Prepared by the Business Economics Department. (New York, 1976), pp. 12–13.
[12]W. H. Kuehn, *The Pitfalls In Managing A Small Business,* A Dun & Bradstreet Publication (New York, 1973).

Table 1-1 Causes of 11,432 Business Failures in 1975

All	Underlying Causes	Apparent Causes		All
1.1	Neglect	Due to …………	Bad Habits	0.4
			Poor Health	0.3
			Marital Difficulties	0.1
			Other	0.3
0.5	Fraud	On the part of the principals, reflected by ………	Misleading Name	0.0
			False Financial Statement	0.1
			Premeditated Overbuy	0.1
			Irregular Disposal of Assets	0.2
			Other	0.1
16.9	Lack of Experience in the Line	Evidenced by inability to avoid conditions which resulted in ……	Inadequate Sales	51.3
13.7	Lack of Managerial Experience		Heavy Operating Expenses	15.9
21.1	Unbalanced Experience		Receivables Difficulties	9.5
41.2	Incompetence		Inventory Difficulties	8.3
			Excessive Fixed Assets	2.5
			Poor Location	3.4
			Competitive Weakness	22.3
			Other	1.8
1.0	Disaster	Some of these occurrences could have been provided against through insurance ………	Fire	0.4
			Flood	0.0
			Burglary	0.0
			Employees' Fraud	0.0
			Strike	0.0
			Other	0.6
4.5	Reason Unknown			
100.0	Total		Percent of Total Failures	100.0

Source: Dun & Bradstreet, Inc. Adapted and reprinted by permission.

Bradstreet statistics. Our question, and the important positive question of the book, is why and how SB succeeds. But first, one last flirtation with failure is suggested in an interesting book called *Mismarketing*. This book suggests that successful marketers have learned to avoid these following problems in specific areas of marketing:

Failures and Decision Making—Arthur Nielsen, Jr., President of A. C. Nielsen Company, once recorded what he termed "the 13 most common marketing errors." They are:

1. *Failure to keep product up-to-date*—first you must have a good product—suited to the market.
2. *Failure to estimate the market potential accurately*—to temper enthusiasm with regard to prospects of future sales.
3. *Failure to guage the trend of the market*—to guide adjustments in the marketing program—either up or down.
4. *Failure to appreciate regional differences in market potential and in trend of market*—to make sound distribution of sales and advertising efforts.
5. *Failure to appreciate seasonal difference in your buyers' demand*—not only nationally but for various types of market breakdowns.
6. *Failure to establish the advertising budget by the job to be done*—any company which continues to set its advertising budget based upon sales alone is asking for trouble.
7. *Failure to adhere to policies established in connection with long-range goals*—to allow time for a significant trend to develop.
8. *Failure to test-market new ideas*—there is a big difference in what people say they will do—and what they actually will do.
9. *Failure to differentiate between short-term tactics and long-range strategy*—special promotions are no substitute for advertising.
10. *Failure to admit defeat*—to learn from our errors, and to change.
11. *Failure to try new ideas while a brand is climbing*—all too often, changes are made only after a competitor forces the change.
12. *Failure to integrate all phases of the marketing operation into the over-all program.* Coordination is the key word.
13. *Failure to appraise objectively your competitors' brands*—the tendency to (a) underestimate the resources and ingenuity of your competitors; while at the same time (b) overestimating the position or reputation of your own brand.[13]

Goals and Growth in SB

Consider the following two propositions:

1. The overall *goal* or *objective* of business (SB or BB) is profit. The goal may be expressed as maximum profit in the long run, satisfactory profit, target return on investment (ROI), and so forth. The means for achieving the goal is satisfying customers.

2. The overall purpose of business, that is, the goal or objective for which society permits business to justify its existence, is to satisfy customers. The incentive to business for performing its functions is the profit motive.

Business practitioners and academicians cannot agree among themselves whether or not the above statements (a) are conflicting statements, only one of which is possibly correct; (b) are compatible statements taken from different perspectives; or (c) are essentially similar statements with mere differences in semantics. In terms of social

[13]From *Mismarketing: Case Histories of Marketing Misfires* by Thomas L. Berg. Copyright © 1970 by Thomas L. Berg. Used by permission of Doubleday & Company, Inc., p. 11.

responsibility and the marketing practices of SB, some have suggested that SB should be socially responsible (in such things as pricing, products, promotion, etc.) only to the extent that (a) they are legally compelled to do so and (b) that such socially responsible practices enhance the goal of maximizing profits.

The above issues are by no means settled. The reader should begin to examine his own positions.

Among more specific overall company goals of SB, *growth* may or may not play a dominant role. Growth or the absence of growth should probably be considered when stating goals. Thus, growth as an indicator of success would be determined by the importance of growth in the stated goals of the SB. Despite much thinking to the contrary, growth for its own sake is not an essential ingredient for success.

An article on venture management begins by stating that the one thing successful small businesses all have in common is a comparative advantage over their giant competitors.[14] The two forms of such an advantage are (1) to fill a limited local need; and, (2) through innovation, to exploit a new product or market opportunity not yet recognized by BB. Growth may be destructive of success to the firm relying primarily on the first advantage, but growth may be very important to the SB relying on the second advantage. In fact, the second type of advantage, called a venture, may be unable to prevent its market from growing.[15]

If growth is to be important in the overall goals, a unique set of problems will be encountered by the SB. Other specific goals will be affected. For example, product and pricing strategies may differ considerably. The chief executive will find it necessary to "lengthen his shadow" by gradually beginning to adopt more and more of the organizational and managerial characteristics of BB. Of course, the attainment of such a growth goal is always predicated on the true desires of the top executive. Does he really want the company to grow?[16]

Specific marketing goals and subgoals will be discussed in later chapters.

Rewards of SB

The rewards for success and the punishments for failure are different in SB and BB. At this point, let us consider only the economic incentives on both the plus and minus sides. Let's also look at the extremes, that is, the best and the worst. For the successful manager in BB, the best is quite often a promotion or other form of advancement either within or outside his present company. This is usually accompanied by a larger salary and more fringe benefits. Rewards are also quite often moderated so as not to get out of line with the rewards of others. The unsuccessful manager in BB (possibly only if he is very unsuccessful) will lose his job. He will be fired. At the same time, he may lose some unprotected fringe benefits. He may even find it difficult to find another job. For the successful small business marketer, who often has an ownership interest, the best reward is a fortune limited only by the amount of success. On the negative side, the SBM, if unsuccessful, may not only lose his job (or self-employment), along with the accompany-

[14]Donald C. King and Robert L. Thornton, "Venture Management And The Small Businessman," *Journal of Small Business Management,* 12 (October 1974), 30.

[15]King and Thornton, p. 30.

[16]O. G. Dalaba, "Lengthening Your Shadow—The Key To Small Business Growth," *Journal of Small Business Management,* 11 (July 1973), 18.

ing fringes; but he may also lose his entire capital investment, along with substantial borrowed funds.

Undoubtedly the economic rewards are not the only ones, and they are possibly not even the most important ones for many persons in SB. To conclude this discussion on the incentives of SB, I am reminded of the chase between the dog and the rabbit. In this story, Fido was hanging around with some of his fellow dogs when a rabbit appeared. It was agreed that the rabbit belonged to Fido. His companion dogs eagerly watched as Fido began the chase. After some time and several near misses, the rabbit had escaped and had clearly beaten Fido. Upon coming back to the group of companion dogs with his tail between his legs, Fido was at first quite embarrassed. Then he suddenly began wagging his tail with a smile and said, "Winning that chase was more important to the rabbit than it was to me. He was running for his life and I was simply out for the good time and fun of the chase." The rabbit in the above story is similar to SB. Although SB sometimes cooperates as well as competes with BB, the SB does have much more to lose (negative incentive) if he is overtaken and gobbled up by a BB. It should also be remembered that while small business rabbits cooperate in many ways among themselves, they are sometimes their own greatest competition—especially when they out-multiply the customer supply.

IN CONCLUSION

Now that some of the highlights of SB have been briefly presented, the reader should decide whether or not, and if so, how, to define SB for his own purposes. This chapter could be considered a very lengthy descriptive definition of SB. In Chapter 2, we will discuss marketing management. Then, in Chapter 3 we will combine small business (SB) and marketing management (MM) into a small business marketing management (SBMM) model to be used throughout the book.

BIBLIOGRAPHY

Books

BAUMBACK, CLIFFORD M., LAWYER, KENNETH, AND KELLEY, PEARCE C. *How to Organize and Operate a Small Business.* Englewood Cliffs, New Jersey: Prentice-Hall, Inc., 1973.

BAUMBACK, CLIFFORD M. AND MANCUSO, JOSEPH R. *Entrepreneurship and Venture Management.* Englewood Cliffs, New Jersey: Prentice-Hall, Inc., 1975.

BERG, THOMAS L. *Mismarketing: Case Histories of Marketing Misfires.* Garden City, New York: Doubleday & Company, Inc., 1970.

KOPMEYER, M. R. *Success Is As Easy As ABC/C.* Los Angeles: Sherbourne Press, Inc., 1968.

MANCUSO, JOSEPH R. *How to Start, Finance, and Manage Your Own Small Business.* Englewood Cliffs, New Jersey: Prentice-Hall, Inc., 1978.

STEINHOFF, DAN. *Small Business Management Fundamentals.* New York: McGraw-Hill Book Company, 1974.

TATE, CURTIS E., JR., MEGGINSON, LEON C., SCOTT, CHARLES R., JR., and TRUEBLOOD, LYLE R. *Successful Small Business Management.* Dallas, Texas: Business Publications, Inc., 1975.

Periodicals

BRERETON, PHILIP R. "The Qualifications For Entrepreneurship," *Journal of Small Business Management,* 12 (October 1974), 1–3.

DALABA, O. G. "Lengthening Your Shadow—The Key To Small Business Growth," *Journal of Small Business Management,* 11 (July 1973), 17–21.

HENDERSON, RICHARD IVAN. "The Best Of Two Worlds: The Entrepreneural Manager," *Jour-*

nal of Small Business Management, 12 (October 1974), 4–7.

HOOPER, CAROLYN N. "Defining 'Small Business' In Government Programs," *Journal of Small Business Management,* 10 (October 1972), 28–34.

KING, DONALD C., AND THORNTON, ROBERT L. "Venture Management and the Small Businessman," *Journal of Small Business Management,* 12 (October 1974), 30–34.

KLINE, JOHN B. "Personal Strategy Guidelines To Avoid Business Failure," *Journal of Small Business Management,* 12 (July 1974), 10–14.

MINER, JOHN B. "Personnel Strategies In The Small Business Organization," *Journal of Small Business Management,* 11 (July 1973), 13–16.

VESPER, KARL H. "Entrepreneurship, A Fast Emerging Area In Management Studies,"

Journal of Small Business Management, 12 (October 1974), 8–15.

Reports

BERGHASH, ROBERT. *Investment in People: A Small Business Perspective.* An AMA Management Briefing, 1974.

COHN, THEODORE, AND LINDBERG, ROY A. *How Management Is Different in Small Companies.* An AMA Management Briefing, 1972.

DUN & BRADSTREET, INC. *The Business Failure Record 1975.* A Report Prepared by the Business Economics Department. New York, 1976.

KUEHN, W. H. *The Pitfalls in Managing A Small Business.* A Dun & Bradstreet Publication, 1973.

2

What Is Marketing
Management (MM)?

This chapter builds from a definitional consideration of *marketing* to a discussion of marketing management in the small business enterprise and the organizational implications of such. Building blocks along the way include (1) utility and the marketing functions, (2) the concept of the marketing mix, (3) the marketing concept and its application for SB, and (4) a short digression on *strategy*.

WHAT IS MARKETING?

Since the committee on Definitions of the American Marketing Association published the following definition in 1960, a popular (and somewhat productive) sport of marketing practitioners and academicians has been to point out the shortcomings of the definition. The AMA Committee defined *marketing* as "the performance of business activities that affect the flow of goods and services from producer to consumer or user."[1] In order to show the changes that have been made in the above definition, the following definitions are quoted from two of today's most popular marketing textbooks. McCarthy, after considering both *macro* and *micro* levels, gives the following definition from the marketing manager (*micro*) viewpoint: *"Marketing is the performance of business activities which direct the flow of goods and services from producer to consumer or user in order to satisfy customers and to accomplish the company's objectives."*[2] The systems definition of Stanton states that marketing is " . . . a total system of interacting business activities designed to plan, price, promote,

[1]Committee on Definitions, Reprinted from *Marketing Definitions: A Glossary of Marketing Terms* published by the American Marketing Association, Chicago, 1960, p. 15.
[2]E. Jerome McCarthy, *Basic Marketing: A Managerial Approach* (Homewood, Illinois: Richard D. Irwin, Inc., 1975), p. 19.

and distribute want-satisfying products and services to present and potential customers."[3] Both of the above generally accepted definitions add important dimensions to the original AMA definition.

Marketing is a twentieth century creation. While some of the functional elements of marketing such as sales and advertising have existed and have been the subjects of study for some time, the practice and study of *marketing* began to evolve only in the current century. The Industrial Revolution in North America provided the mass production which was interdependent with mass marketing. Such trends have probably favored BB more than SB, but later trends such as target marketing have also greatly favored SB.

In recent years, two viewpoints (*macro* and *micro*) on the study of marketing have received much emphasis. The *macro* viewpoint is that of the entire society or economy. Of interest here is how well the entire marketing system meets the needs of the entire economy. The concepts are analogous to *macroeconomics* and *microeconomics*. *Micromarketing* is from the point of view of the individual firm. Although both points of view are certainly important for SBMM, our vantage point for most of this book is micromarketing; that is, the viewpoint of the marketing manager of the SB firm. However, keep in mind that the alert SBM will be constantly aware of the so-called *micro-macro dilemma:* that what is good for the individual firm may not necessarily be good for the total marketing system and *vice versa.* For example, many issues of consumerism have directly affected and been affected by SB marketing.

Among the several approaches to the study of marketing have been the commodity, functional, institutional, managerial, systems, societal, and nonbusiness approaches. For our purposes, the managerial approach seems to make sense. This approach to marketing does not necessarily exclude materials found in the other approaches; rather, it views such materials and issues from the perspective of the marketing manager. In our case, this means from the perspective of the SB marketing manager. The focus is on the planning, execution, and control of marketing programs involving strategies and tactics for marketing. The management differences between SB and BB set forth in Chapter 1 will be used to formulate an appropriate managerial approach to SB marketing.

UTILITY AND MARKETING FUNCTIONS

Economic utility has traditionally been somewhat artificially divided into *form* utility, created by production; and *time, place,* and *possession* utilities, created by marketing. Marketing creates utility by the performance of business activities. The terms "activities" and "functions" can be used to mean quite different things, as is illustrated by saying that the activity of the human heart is to beat or pulsate while its function is to pump blood. Some marketers have also argued that the traditional "functions of marketing" are really activity areas rather than functions.[4] In any event, a listing of the marketing functions might be as follows:

1. The transaction functions of (a) buying and (b) selling.
2. The physical distribution functions of (a) transportation and (b) storage.

[3]William J. Stanton, *Fundamentals of Marketing* (New York: McGraw-Hill Book Company, 1975), p. 5.
[4]For a complete discussion see Richard J. Lewis and Leo G. Erickson, "Marketing Functions and Marketing Systems: A Synthesis," *Journal of Marketing,* 33 (July 1969), 10–14.

3. The facilitating functions of (a) standardizing and grading, (b) financing, (c) risk taking, and (d) market information.

In order to create utility, the marketing functions must all be performed by someone. As the old saying goes, "You can eliminate the middleman, but you can't eliminate the functions he performs." Marketing functions can, however, be shifted among the various members of the channel of distribution (including the consumer). Such shifting may or may not result in more efficient performance of marketing functions. Likewise, highly integrated big businesses may or may not perform various marketing functions more efficiently than marketing channel systems involving significant numbers of SB marketers.

THE MARKETING MIX

The concept of the marketing mix (not the same as the marketing concept) was developed by Neil H. Borden.[5] Since its development, most marketing books, including the present one (Chapter 3), have used some variation of the concept of the marketing mix. Borden's generalized concept includes (a) a list of the important elements or ingredients making up marketing programs and (b) a list of forces bearing on the firm's marketing operations to which the marketing manager must adjust in search of a successful program. Borden suggests the following twelve major classifications (along with subclassifications) as the elements of the marketing mix of manufacturers:[6]

1. Product Planning
2. Pricing
3. Branding
4. Channels of Distribution
5. Personal Selling
6. Advertising
7. Promotions
8. Packaging
9. Display
10. Servicing
11. Physical Handling
12. Fact Finding and Analysis

As Borden suggests, other marketers do break down the classifications differently. For example, Lazer and Kelley, in looking at a marketing mix for retailers rather than manufacturers, stated, "the retailing mix, as such, is composed of three sub-mixes: a goods and services mix, a communications mix, and a distribution mix. Customer satisfaction is achieved through optional sub-mix blending. It is through the achievement of a high customer satisfaction that a store prospers and grows."[7]

[5]Neil H. Borden, "The Concept Of The Marketing Mix," *Journal of Advertising Research*, 4, No. 2 (June 1964), 2–7.
[6]Borden, p. 4.
[7]William Lazer and Eugene J. Kelley, "The Retailing Mix: Planning and Management," *Journal of Retailing*, 37, No. 1 (Spring 1961), 37.

The forces which govern the mixing of marketing elements are listed by Borden under four categories: the behavior of consumers, the trade, competitors, and government.[8] Here again, other marketers use different categories. Borden points out, by using SB as an example, that marketing managers must fashion their mixes to fit their respective resources:

> If his firm is small, he must judge the response of consumers, trade, and competition in light of his position and resources and the influence that he can exert in the market. He must look for special opportunities in product or method of operation. The small firm cannot employ the procedures of the big firm. Though he may sell the same kind of product as the big firm, his marketing strategy is likely to be widely different in many respects. Innumerable instances of this fact might be cited. For example, in the industrial goods field, small firms often seek to build sales on a limited and highly specialized line, whereas industry leaders seek patronage for full lines. Small firms often elect to go in for regional sales rather than attempt the national distribution practiced by larger companies. Again, the company of limited resources often elects to limit its production and sales to products whose potential is too small to attract the big fellows. Still again, companies with small resources in the cosmetic field not infrequently have set up introductory marketing programs employing aggressive personal selling and a "push" strategy with distribution limited to leading department stores. Their initially small advertising funds have been directed through these selected retail outlets, with the offering of the products and their story told over the signatures of the stores. The strategy has been to borrow kudos for their products from the leading stores' reputations and to gain a gradual radiation of distribution to smaller stores in all types of channels such as often comes from the trade's follow-the-leader behavior. Only after resources have grown from mounting sales has a dense retail distribution been aggressively sought and a shift made to place the selling burden more and more on company signed advertising.
> Many additional instances of the varying strategy employed by small versus large enterprises might be cited.[9]

THE MARKETING CONCEPT IN SB

Is, and if so, *how* is the marketing concept (not the same as the concept of the marketing mix) appropriate for SB? What is the marketing concept?

The marketing concept was born as a concept for BB. Historically the production orientation of the late nineteenth century led to the sales orientation of the early twentieth century which began to give way to the marketing orientation in the 1950s. Not all firms have moved through these orientations at the same pace. This is discussed further in the following paragraphs. Some elements of the marketing concept (such as customer satisfaction or orientation) are renewed rather than being entirely new. Once having adopted the marketing concept, it is not impossible (and in fact it may even be easy to do so) to slide back into a production-oriented way of business thinking. This is so because the production orientation with its self-centered logic is much simpler than the other-centered marketing concept.

Few precise formal definitions of the marketing concept exist, but descriptions are

[8]Borden, pp. 2–7.
[9]Borden, p. 5.

numerous. Among the descriptive statements often made about the marketing concept are the following:

1. It is a philosophy, that is, a way of business thinking that permeates the entire business.
2. Customer satisfaction at a profit is most important.
3. The whole firm (and extended channel of distribution members) is a marketing organization.
4. Profitable sales volume replaces maximum sales volume as an objective.
5. The marketing activities are organizationally integrated into a total system of action.
6. Broad company decisions are made on the basis of marketing implications.

Some differences between the production-oriented and marketing-oriented business are obvious. The marketing-oriented business will make only what will sell, after determining this by extensive marketing research aimed at determining customer needs, style and design preferences, customer-oriented packaging, preferred customer services, place and method of purchasing, and so forth. In short, the customer-orientation dominates and the marketing-oriented firm prospers by being innovative rather than by simply being competitive.

Not all firms (both BB and SB) have successfully adopted the marketing concept. Many have not even attempted to do so. Rememeber, the production-orientation seems more logical and is certainly easier to follow. If all marketers had adopted the marketing concept and had been even moderately successful in carrying it out, it is very doubtful that consumerism would be a household word today. Who has, and who has not, adopted the marketing concept?

A study by McNamara began with the following two major hypotheses:

1. Consumer goods corporations have tended to accept the marketing concept to a greater degree than have industrial corporations.
2. Large corporations (over $150 million annual sales) have tended to accept the concept to a greater degree than have small ($10 to $19 million) and medium-sized ($20 to $150 million) corporations.[10]

The methodology of this study distinguished between two major dimensions of the marketing concept: (1) *adoption* of the concept, which referred to embracing the philosophical implications for business management, and (2) *implementation* of the concept, which referred to specific organizational methods for using the philosophy in actual business practice. The results of the study supported the hypotheses quoted above.[11] Breaking down the *acceptance* of the marketing concept into *adoption* and *implementation* may be very meaningful for SB. Management principles apply differently to BB and SB. Just as basic principles of navigation apply to both battleships and row boats or as basic principles of aeronautics apply equally well to jumbo jets and small aircraft, so also do basic principles of management and basic principles of marketing apply to both big business and small business. However, such principles must be *adapted* according to the size of the firm. Such differences also exist in the *acceptance* of the marketing concept by SB versus BB. This is true in both the *adoption* and the specific methods of *implementation*.

[10]Carlton P. McNamara, "The Present Status of The Marketing Concept," *Journal of Marketing,* 36 (January 1972), 51.
      [11]McNamara, pp. 50–57.

However, the major difficulties have been with implementation. The SBM needs to know exactly how to adapt and apply the marketing concept to his particular business. The reader should be able to answer this "how to" question upon completing this book.

At this point, some suggestions from an article which appeared many years ago seem appropriate. Before presenting a four-step logical sequence for implementing the marketing concept, the author warned that the implementation must be personalized to fit the particular company, that the concept and the reason for it must be understood by everyone in the business, and that the move to marketing should be a gradual one.[12] The four steps are (1) the "do it" decision, (2) the assessment decision, (3) the "what to be" decision, and (4) the "how to be" decision.[13] Step 1 simply refers to actually making the decision to adopt the marketing concept. This decision must be made by the top executive of the firm and then communicated down to all others. Step 2 is a situation analysis of how well the company organization is presently operating in a customer-oriented manner. Step 3 relates to objectives; and Step 4 deals with both organization structure and people decisions.

Some readers may feel that we have not been asking the right questions. A young marketing instructor recently remarked to the author, "I didn't know small business did any marketing." In fact, many small businesses don't. It may even be possible that some SB firms, because of some resource limitation such as unadaptable people, would find it impossible to move from their present orientation to a marketing orientation. However, for that vast number of firms who do not suffer from such limitations, the acceptance (both adoption and implementation) of the marketing concept offers great rewards.

THE CONCEPT OF STRATEGY

Strategy is a central concept of marketing management. It is introduced here and is explained more fully in the following pages. The important relationship between strategy and objectives is illustrated in the following example, which relates four characteristics of strategy (a, b, c, and d in the quotation below) to strategy objectives:[14]

> The four characteristics are thus complementary, rather than mutually exclusive. We will call them, therefore, the *components of strategy.* In conjunction with its objectives the firm may choose one, two, or all of the strategy components. For example, a chemical firm may specify the following:
>
> 1. Objectives: ROI: Threshold 10%, goal 15% Sales Growth Rate: Threshold 5%, goal 10%
> 2. Strategy
> a. Product-market scope: Basic chemicals and pharmaceuticals
> b. Growth vector: Product development and concentric diversification
> c. Competitive advantage: Patent protection, superior research competence
> d. Synergy: Use of the firm's research capabilities and product technology

[12]Charles E. St. Thomas, "A Basic Guide To Marketing For The Smaller Company," *Industrial Marketing,* 44 (July 1959), p. 12, insert.

[13]St. Thomas, pp. 12–14.

[14]H. Igor Ansoff, "Concept of Strategy," *Marketing Management and Administrative Action,* ed. Steuart Henderson Britt and Harper W. Boyd, Jr. (New York: McGraw-Hill Book Company, 1975), p. 104. For a comprehensive look at Market Strategy, see David J. Luck and Arthur E. Prell, *Market Strategy* (New York: Appleton-Century-Crofts, 1968).

Thus strategy and objectives together describe the concept of the firm's business. They specify the amount of growth, the area of growth, the directions for growth, the area of growth, the directions for growth, [sic] the leading strengths, and the profitability target. Furthermore, they are now stated operationally: in a form usable for guiding management decisions and actions.

Firms who do not employ strategy may enjoy such advantages as (1) not having to commit resources to strategic planning, (2) an unlimited (or at least undefined) field of potential opportunities, and (3) being able to delay commitments. The strategy approach also boasts several advantages. Essentially, the alternative to strategy is to have no rules. Five specific consequences of ignoring strategy are (1) in the absence of strategy, there are no guides in searching for new opportunities; (2) poorer quality project decisions exist in firms without strategy; (3) in the absence of strategy, the firm will have no formal provision for partial ignorance; (4) the information from periodic strategy appraisal will be lost; and (5) without strategy, the firm will lack an internal ability to anticipate change.[15]

The need for strategy in marketing management and the importance of good strategy planning is summarized by McCarthy, who says, "This leads to what we will call the *General Foods hypothesis*: Good strategy planning may be more important to the profitable operation of a business than good execution and control."[16] The above quote is a generalization based upon research which shows that some well-managed stores were destined ·to have poor profit results due to initial planning decisions while other strategically well-located stores were doing well in spite of their operating management.

As is clearly stated by McCarthy, "A marketing strategy consists of two distinct and yet interrelated parts:

1. *A target market*—A fairly homogeneous group of customers to whom a company wishes to appeal.
2. *A marketing mix*—the controllable variables which the company combines in order to satisfy this target group."[17]

Before temporarily leaving our discussion of marketing strategy, two suggestions are made here. First, a strategy which is not effectively communicated to the lowest operating level of the firm may as well not exist. In too many cases, it is the lower level operating people whose decisions determine the future of the firm. Secondly, for SB, marketing strategy is important. However, differences will exist between SB and BB. For example, in order to retain its flexibility, SB will emphasize short-range marketing strategy more than long-range marketing strategy.

MARKETING MANAGEMENT IN SB

The division of the management task or management process into its component parts has been performed in several ways by management experts. For purposes of SBMM, a three-way breakdown, similar to that used in popular basic marketing texts, seems most appropriate.[18] The management process in marketing (SB or BB) consists of the following

[15]Ansoff, pp. 104–105.
[16]McCarthy, p. 38.
[17]McCarthy, p. 35.
[18]For examples, see McCarthy, p. 33 or Stanton, p. 33.

three tasks: (1) planning, (2) execution, and (3) control. The continuous job of management in these three areas of activity is necessary for success. Too often in SB, the planning and control functions are neglected in favor of the execution function. Planning means the creation of a marketing strategy, based upon specific company and marketing objectives, involving marketing mixes which are specifically designed to meet the needs of selected target markets, and doing all this in an environment of uncontrollable external forces. Once the basic strategy has been planned, management can begin to execute or implement the plan. Modifications will also be continuously made in the plan. The execution phase involves the actual carrying out of operations. Some managers would say that what we are calling *execution* is really a shorthand for *organizing, directing,* and *staffing.* "Getting things done" is the time-consuming task of actually putting the marketing plan (along with the plans for the elements of the marketing mix such as product, place, price, and promotion) into action. Control is the feedback phase of marketing management in which the manager attempts to measure, analyze, and evaluate how well and in what ways the plan worked in actual operations in the marketplace.

The framework of marketing management, or the marketing management system, is quite often shown in pictorial form by using concentric circles as shown in Figure 2–1. Since the satisfaction of the customer is so important in the marketing orientation, the center circle or bull's-eye is reserved for the customer. Ring 2 in Figure 2–1 surrounds the customer with the firm's marketing mix. The controllable variables or elements of the firm's marketing mix are usually stated in marketing texts today to be (1) *product,* (2) *place* (sometimes called *distribution* or *channel* strategy), (3) *price,* and (4) *promotion.* The outside ring (numbered 3 in Figure 2–1) shows those external variables of the environment over which marketing management usually has very little or no control, at least in the short run. Marketing educators are not in complete agreement on how to break down the uncontrollable variables. Among the items listed as uncontrollable factors by various authors, the following are typical:

1. Economic environment
2. Competition or competitive environment
3. Political and legal environment, that is, government
4. Societal environment and culture
5. Science or technology

The marketing manager plans, executes, and controls the elements of the marketing mix (ring 2) toward the satisfaction of the target customers (ring 1) within the limitations of the environment (ring 3). This management job is done with the profit objectives of the firm in mind. In Chapter 3, the marketing management model pictured in Figure 2–1 and briefly described here will be adapted to SBMM. At that point, all parts of the management model will be described in more detail. Later chapters will simply be expansions and more detailed explanations of the model in Chapter 3.

ORGANIZATIONAL IMPLICATIONS OF MARKETING MANAGEMENT FOR SB

The organization structure of a business is only a means to an end. Therefore, organization structure by itself does not insure that the marketing concept is in operation. However, organization is a necessary condition for proper implementation of the

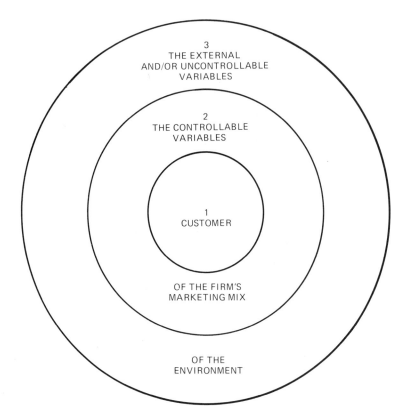

Figure 2-1   Typical Framework for Marketing Management

philosophy of the marketing concept. It is unlikely that the marketing concept will be fully implemented in the absence of favorable organizational structure. The importance of organization is stated by Stanton:

> For a business enterprise to realize the full fruits of the marketing concept, the philosophy must be translated into practice. This means that (1) the marketing activities in a firm must be better organized, coordinated, and managed, and (2) the chief marketing executive must be accorded a more important role in total company planning and policy making than has been generally true in the past. As these two changes take place, we see emerging in American business the idea of marketing management. *Marketing management* is the marketing concept in action.[19]

Thus, two organizational implications of the marketing concept are (1) the better organization, coordination, and management of the marketing activities and (2) according more importance to the chief marketing executive in the management of the total company. For SB, this second implication must certainly be somewhat different in format if, as is sometimes the case, the company president and the chief marketing executive are

[19]Stanton, p. 14.

the same person. Thus, an organization structure which reflects the change to the marketing orientation will vary from BB to SB. Some of the differences between SB and BB discussed in Chapter 1 are at work here. Before viewing organization charts, let's look at some organizational implications:

1. Since SB organizations tend to be built around people more than BB hierarchies are, changes to the marketing orientation must be made through people. This can be accomplished by (1) changing the attitudes and philosophies of present people, (2) changing organizational relationships and duties among present people, and (3) in some cases, changing the actual people involved. In any event, SB marketers should concentrate their efforts on high potential people.

2. Since organization structure is less of a problem for SB than the creation of sales, all organizational efforts and resulting structures should not dilute the inherent advantages that SB possesses—such as closeness to its customers by all parts of the SB organization and an ability to rely more heavily on informal organization than would be possible in a BB.

3. Although SB should not make a fetish of organizational simplicity by refusing to take advantage of warranted specialization of effort, such specialization may emerge in different organizational forms. For example, consensus decision-making from committees (*ad hoc* or standing) may replace objective decision-making by line and staff groups in BB. Therefore, in SB, the membership and leadership of key committees may take on additional importance. Another example involves the use of outside consultants or advisory committees for SB. This may be a way to add specialized expertise to the management of the SB firm. The choice of which types of outsiders to solicit and exactly how such outsiders are to participate in the management of the SB will affect the extent to which such outsiders help the SB to implement the marketing concept. Perhaps such "outsiders" should be shown on the organization chart of the SB.

4. The short-range planning emphasis of SB as opposed to the long-range emphasis of BB suggests that the organizational problems of implementing the marketing management concept will differ in SB and BB. The SB flexibility and informality may even make it more difficult at times to bring about such a change. This is true because of the less tangible nature of flexibility and informality when compared to rigid methods and procedures as spelled out in a BB operating manual.

The above are undoubtedly only a few of the more important organizational implications of marketing management for SB. Let's now, somewhat superficially, show how organization charts may differ for the "before" and "after" implementation of the marketing concept by SB management. Remember, the chart is not the organization.

Figure 2–2 shows the organization chart of a small firm that has not implemented the marketing concept. Although the organization chart by itself does not show how the organization operates, you are asked to draw an "after" chart incorporating some or all of the suggestions below in order to implement the marketing management concept for this small firm.

1. Change the name "sales manager" to "marketing manager" and have additional functions such as credit, physical distribution, product design, and service under his direction.

2. Appoint the marketing manager to chair the committee on new products.

3. Solicit (from outside the firm) an advisory board composed of a good representation of marketing and other executives. This board would meet with the president, marketing manager, production manager, and other top executives concerning major goals and strategies.

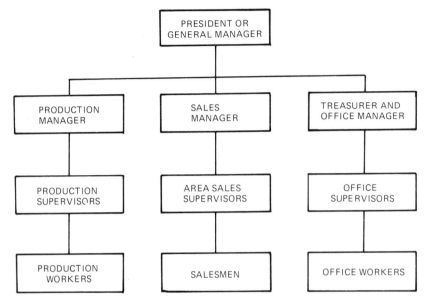

Figure 2–2. Organization Chart Before Implementation of the Marketing Management Concept

4. Hire staff expertise such as marketing research to assist the marketing manager. This may have to be on a part-time basis in the beginning.

5. Hire a sales manager to manage the sales force now that your former sales manager is now functioning as a marketing manager.

6. Make some additional or alternate changes of your own choosing. In all changes, please remember that both the "before" and "after" charts are simply illustrative. The ideal would depend on the particular situation. Also, the chart is not complete: It does not describe duties or persons. You may wish to draw your SB organization chart showing that one individual occupies more than one position. This is often the case in SB.

BIBLIOGRAPHY

Books

ANSOFF, H. IGOR. "Concept of Strategy," *Marketing Management and Administrative Action.* Ed. Steuart Henderson Britt and Harper W. Boyd, Jr. New York: McGraw-Hill Book Company, 1975.

LUCK, DAVID J., AND PRELL, ARTHUR E. *Market Strategy.* New York: Appleton-Century-Crofts, 1968.

MCCARTHY, E. JEROME. *Basic Marketing: A Managerial Approach.* Homewood, Illinois: Richard D. Irwin, Inc., 1975.

STANTON, WILLIAM J. *Fundamentals of Marketing.* New York: McGraw-Hill Book Company, 1975.

Periodicals

BORDEN, NEIL H. "The Concept of The Marketing

Mix," *Journal of Advertising Research,* 4, No. 2 (June 1964), 2–7.

LAZER, WILLIAM, AND KELLEY, EUGENE J. "The Retailing Mix: Planning and Management," *Journal of Retailing,* 37, No. 1 (Spring 1961), 34–41.

MCNAMARA, CARLTON P. "The Present Status of The Marketing Concept,"*Journal of Marketing,* 36 (January 1972), 50–57.

ST. THOMAS, CHARLES E. "A Basic Guide To Marketing For The Smaller Company," *Industrial Marketing,* 44 (July 1959), 1–14, insert.

Reports

Committee on Definitions. *Marketing Definitions: A Glossary of Marketing Terms.* American Marketing Association. Chicago, 1960.

3

The Small Business Marketing Management (SBMM) Model

The diagram of the SBMM model involves many shapes. The entire model is shown in Figure 3–1. The specific shapes involved are:

1. The *outside triangle,* showing the continuous functions of marketing management: the planning, execution, and control of the marketing program.
2. The *circle,* encompassing the environmental variables which are beyond the control of the SBM, but within which he must formulate his marketing mix.
3. The five-pointed *star* (which we will call the pentastar rather than pentacle or pentagram), showing the five elements (controllable variables) of the SB marketing mix: product, place, price, promotion, and people.
4. The *five triangles,* each of which represents one of these controllable variables of the SB marketing mix and for each of which the management functions of planning, execution, and control are shown and will be performed.
5. The *pentagon* at the center of the diagram, which represents the target customer and which will be viewed in two ways: as the consumer market for SB and as the intermediate market for SB, with accompanying attempts to explain buyer behavior in each of these two market types.

The above description of the overall SBMM model is, of course, a backwards description. It began from the larger outside shapes and worked in toward the customer in the middle. Logically, all marketing strategy planning begins with an understanding of the target market customer. After a description of the separate parts of our SBMM model and after showing how the parts fit together, we'll consider some of the "how to" questions of marketing strategy planning by using the model as a framework for our thinking. Our expansion of the overview presented in this chapter will then logically turn to a consideration of markets in Chapters 4 and 5.

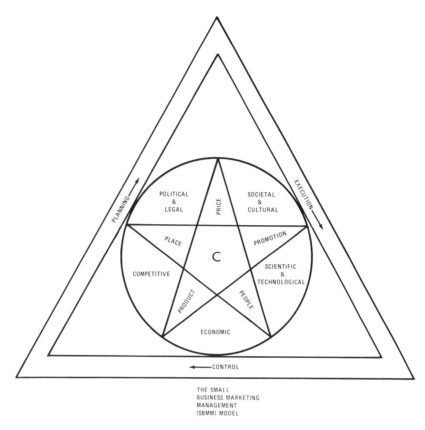

Figure 3–1   **The Small Business Marketing Management (SBMM) Model**

THE OVERALL SBMM MODEL

Attempting to explain the SBMM model is somewhat like attempting to explain the modern automobile or any other complex system composed of several subsystems. Our approach in this chapter will be to first explain the major functions of the various subsystems and how they relate to each other. These subsystems (or components of the overall SBMM system) were named above. They are (a) the marketing management functions of planning, execution, and control; (b) the environmental (or uncontrollable) variables; (c) the SB marketing mix composed of its five "P's"—product, place, price, promotion, and people; and (d) the customer. In following sections of this chapter we'll consider each of the subsystems individually in much the same manner as an auto mechanic considers in detail the suspension system at one time and then the electrical system at another time.

The model diagrammed in Figure 3–1 has motion, as is indicated by the various arrows. It works something like this. The center focus of the whole system is the target customer, represented by a "C" inside a pentagon at the center of our diagram. This "C" acts as a center around which the whole system moves. Two types of movement are present: rotation and revolution. The pentastar rotates in a clock-wise direction around the "C" and within the circle. This represents the movement of the marketing mix around the object customer and within the confines of the marketing environment. This rotation takes place simultaneously with the revolving of the PEC (planning, execution, and control) process of marketing management. The operation of this process is shown at the overall level of the big triangle (or triangular route) and at the level of the five marketing mix variables by the five triangles which make up the star. At either level, this PEC process can be pictured in the mind as a continuous belt similar to that found surrounding the wheels of a bulldozer or an army tank. Marketing is the active agent which sets the whole process in motion. The system as pictured in Figure 3–1 runs smoothly. However, such may not always be the case.

The triangle of planning, execution, and control is the continuous management process of the marketing manager. For the SBM, this planning, execution, and control (PEC) takes place at two levels: at the overall marketing level and at the level of each of the five "P's" of the SB marketing mix. Let us first consider the overall marketing level, that is, the outside triangle of Figure 3–1. Here a tip from the management-by-objective (MBO) advocates may be helpful. The first thing to do is to set the overall objectives for the SB firm. These objectives should be specifically stated. For example, the objectives of "increasing sales" or "earning maximum profits" are probably desirable but are stated in very vague terms. The planning portion of our PEC process might get rolling much better if objectives were stated more specifically—in such terms as "increasing sales of product XYZ by a minimum of 5% and a desired maximum of 20% in target markets currently being served." Such a sales objective may be one of several objectives of the SBM. Another objective might be to enter a new target market and capture a stated share of that market within a stated time period. Once these several overall marketing objectives have been specifically stated by the SBM, an overall or grand marketing strategy can begin to be formulated.

In formulating his overall marketing strategy, the SBM operates within the framework of the controllable variables (the 5 P's) and the uncontrollable variables. However, his central focus is always the objective(s) to be achieved. These objectives can usually also be stated in terms of the target markets (customers) to be served. And for each target market, the SBM will want to plan, execute, and control a separate marketing mix. The combination of all the firm's marketing mixes for all the target markets served will ideally form an integrated grand marketing strategy with some plus benefits of the synergetic effect (the whole is greater than the sum of the parts). For example, let's suppose that the marketing objectives as stated during the marketing planning process involve three distinct markets. During the PEC management processes, the SBM would want to first plan three separate but integrated strategies, one for each of the three markets. He might do this by using three separate and distinct versions of our SBMM model as shown in Figure 3–1. Secondly, he would *execute* or implement his plans. Then he would perform the *control* function of evaluating the actual against the plan. Even many small marketers have several overall objectives and serve several target markets. Pictorially, this may be shown as in Figure 3–2. We could also, of course, complicate Figure 3–2 by showing the different marketing mixes necessary to reach each of these target markets. A further complication which the SBM is likely to face is the varying strengths of the uncontrollable variables in different target markets. But let's save some of these complications for individual attention later on.

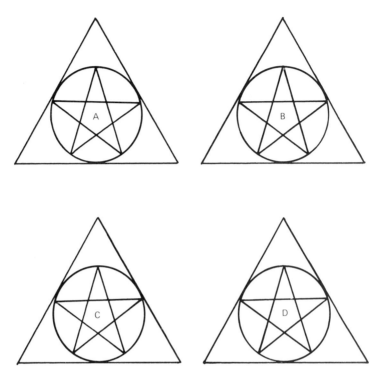

Figure 3–2   The PEC Marketing Management Process for the SBM Serving Four Target Markets

To recap, planning means the creation of a marketing strategy, based upon specific company and marketing objectives, involving marketing mixes which are specifically designed to meet the needs of selected target markets, and doing all this in an environment of uncontrollable external forces. Once the basic marketing strategy has been planned, the SBM can begin to *execute* the plan. This organizing, directing, and staffing will involve much of the time and effort of the SBM. This is the continuous task of putting the plans into action. In the control process, the SBM attempts to measure, analyze, and evaluate how well and in what ways the plan worked.

Now that you have been able to conceptualize your thinking somewhat by studying the aids presented in this chapter, let's explore some other parts of our SBMM model. Remember that this is a *model*. It's supposed to be a bit abstract. It is also supposed to be a useful tool for looking at some very practical and important SB marketing questions throughout the rest of the book.

THE ENVIRONMENT OF SBMM

The large circle in Figure 3–1 encompasses the field of the environmental or so-called uncontrollable variables. Remember, these are variables. That means that they *do* change. In fact, most SB marketing managers will tell us that the environment is constantly changing. These variables are called uncontrollable because, at least in the short run, they are beyond the control of the SBM. (In our discussion, the terms uncontrollable variables, environmental variables, and external variables are used interchangeably.)

Do BB and SB face the same set of environmental variables? Probably not. Or, even if the general categories are similar, it is very likely that particular variables differ both in relative importance and in the ways which these variables are faced by SB. For example, these uncontrollable variables are generally said to be uncontrollable (for BB)—at least in the short run. It is suggested here that if variables are uncontrollable in the short run, for SB they are in fact always uncontrollable since SB lives in the short run. Thus while BB may exert some control over such variables in the long run, these variables turn out to be uncontrollable in both the short *and* long runs for SB. It is therefore necessary for SB to adapt constantly to changing external variables (i.e., uncontrollable variables) in planning marketing strategy.

In our SBMM model, the environmental variables are classified under the headings of (a) the economic environment, (b) the competitive environment, (c) the political and legal environment, (d) the societal and cultural environment, and (e) the scientific and technological environment. These five categories are undoubtedly not all-inclusive or mutually exclusive. They do, however, seem to cover the major environmental forces with which the SBM is faced. We'll describe each beiefly here and will devote Chapter 8 to a more complete discussion.

The *economic* environment refers to the economic conditions of the markets in which the SBM is marketing. Such factors as depression, recession, inflation, tight money, interest rate levels, employment levels, and general levels of economic expectation can affect the success of a particular marketing strategy. The SBM tends to be more specialized and sometimes more localized than BB in the markets served. Therefore, specialized and localized economic conditions may be of more importance to SB than to BB. For example, if the unemployment rate is very high in the city where a small retailer is located, that retailer is not cheered much by the national news announcement that the nation's unemployment rate continued to fall toward an all-time low.

The *competitive* environment refers to the nature and intensity of those firms who are seeking to satisfy the wants and needs of the same target markets. The SBM must plan his marketing strategy around such questions as: How strong is the competition? Which competitive tools, such as low price or extra services, are likely to be used by various competitors? Is the industry monopolistic, oligopolistic, highly competitive, or what? What is the indirect competition? What new competition can be expected as a result of innovations in technology or distribution? The answers to these and other questions will be important to the SBM in formulating his marketing strategies and tactics. For example, a small marketer who knows that a long price war would drive him out of business would want to investigate carefully the pricing policies of his larger and financially stronger competitors before actively promoting a low price campaign. Otherwise, short-lived gains may result in retaliation of disastrous proportions.

The *political* and *legal* environment refers to government relations with SB. In this country, government at most levels is big government. Therefore the relationship of SB to government is usually one of unequal size. The political and legal climate has been both favorable and unfavorable to SB. At any given time, both plus and minus points can be found. For example, the same SBM who has recently been aided by the federal government through the Small Business Administration (SBA) may feel that he has been put at a competitive disadvantage by the seemingly arbitrary standards of the Occupational Safety and Health Act (OSHA). In local markets, small businesses are probably somewhat effective in dealing with local governing bodies. At times, local SB may even be able to use local politics to its advantage against nonlocal competition. The large number of laws affecting marketing usually requires the SBM to seek outside help from attorneys, trade associations, and others in order to adjust his marketing strategy to the changing political and legal environment.

The *societal* and *cultural* environment affects the SBM most directly in the behavior of the firm's customers. Consumer behavior is the major topic of Chapter 6. SB is also affected by the general attitudes of the public toward SB and BB. In recent years, such public attitudes have tended to improve for SB. However, businesses of all sizes have a long way to go on improving the public image of business. Items of specific interest to the SBM in formulating his marketing strategy include changing life styles, the redefinition of traditional roles of men and women, cultural values of ethnic groups, shifting populations, increased leisure time, increased discretionary income, and so forth.

The *scientific* and *technological* environment tends to make old marketing opportunities obsolete while creating new ones for SB. However, to take advantage of these new opportunities, the SBM must possess both the willingness and the required flexibility to change. For example, the SBM which is locked into old technology due to long-term financing has lost a considerable amount of flexibility in his ability to take advantage of new technological developments. The SB can both affect and be affected by technological change. In other words, the SB could help to market a new technology or could use a new technology in its own marketing efforts. The results of science and technology will affect both SB and BB, but the effects may often be felt more dramatically by SB. All of the above environmental variables tend to act as constraints within which the SBM must formulate and operate his strategy. However, the alert SBM will find them to be much less restricting than his mediocre competitors.

In Figure 3–1, we have pictured the environmental field as circular in shape. For the purposes of our conceptualization let's assume (as any economist might say) that this circle of exactly the right size represents an equilibrium environment. In such a perfect circle environment, our marketing mix (the pentastar in Figure 3–1) will rotate freely in order to carry out our marketing strategy effectively. However, environmental change is always taking place. The equilibrium state is seldom, if ever, reached. To picture some of the many possible different changes which may be taking place in the environment, let's look at Figure 3–3. Here we see (a) an "egg-shaped" environment, (b) a "knobby or bumpy" environment, (c) one with a "cavern," (d) one which is circular but too small, and (e) one which is circular but too large. Let's describe briefly what each of these five shapes demonstrates. The egg-shaped environment displays a situation in which the circle (even though its size is more or less the same) has been bent out of shape by the dominance of one or more of the environmental variables and compensating adjustments by other environmental variables. Such dominance has tended to decrease the relative and absolute importance of the remaining environmental variables. In such a situation, the SBM must adapt his marketing mix constantly in order to fit the noncircular environment. The SBM might choose to do this by having a marketing mix with great flexibility, especially at the outside tips of the pentastar. Such flexibility would permit the SBM to force the rotation of the marketing mix. Although such a forced rotation might be somewhat rough, it would work. Even so, this "rubber-tipped star" is likely to have a tough time centering exactly on satisfying the target customer. Also, an uneven pressure will be placed on various elements of the SB marketing mix at different times. For example, government regulation may at times be excessive to the point that the SBM must adjust product, place, price, promotion, and/or people in the marketing mix in such a way that the overall resulting marketing mix is off-center in satisfying target customers. (Note: *Excessive* government regulation is not necessarily the same thing as restrictive government regulation. Government regulation tends to be either prescriptive, that is, *do this;* or prohibitive, that is, *do not do this.* When we say *excessive* in our example, we mean that government has gone far beyond the needs of both business and customers to create an artificial portion of the environment. Upon occasion, SB has been exempted from certain forms of excessive government regulation.) The same off-centered result could be caused by any number of relative imbalances of the environment.

Parts B and C of Figure 3–3 show two limited cases of that situation pictured in part A of Figure 3–3 as described above. Part B of Figure 3–3 shows a "knobby or bumpy" environment in which one element of the environment has become large or tended to bulge beyond the circle. Our example of excessive government regulation would also fit here. However, in this case, we note that the remainder of the environment ignored the excess rather than compensate for it. Thus in part B, we are assuming that the "knob or bump" of excessive (not restrictive) government regulation had little or no effect on other areas such as the economic or competitive environments, for example. This may suggest that the SBM may also wish to ignore the "bump." His marketing program may be able to

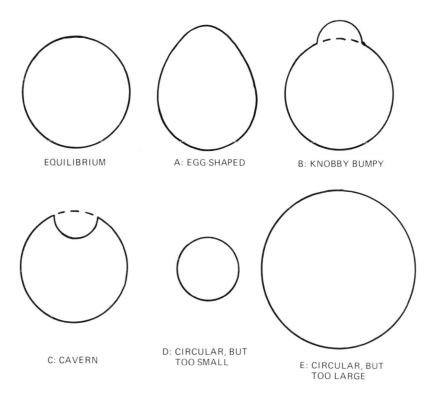

Figure 3–3   Shapes of Other Small Business Marketing Environments at Various States of Disequilibrium

operate effectively for quite some time without straying into the area of the excess or "bump." In plain language, this particular SBM may not get caught by this particular excessive governmental regulation. However, a contingency plan may be advisable, especially if the bump is sizable.

Part C of Figure 3-3 shows a "cavern" or an environmental area in which a void exists. That is, the environment is lacking in some way. Now that we're well down the road to conceptualization, let's tackle this one. As our marketing mix rotates, each point of the star will strike this restrictive (not excessive) cavern. However, with sufficient flexibility in each area of our marketing mix, the marketing program can still be carried out—probably at a slower pace. An example of the cavern might be a lack of regulation (by government or industry) in a particular aspect of marketing activity. Such a lack may create so many unknowns that some marketers, including SB marketers, will hesitate to serve certain target markets for fear of extremely large liability.

Part D of Figure 3-3 shows an environment which is circular, but which is simply too small in total size. In such an environment, the pentastar won't even fit—let alone rotate. If this environment is not too much too small, and if the marketing mix is very flexible, we may be able to make it work at reduced efficiency. However, simply getting our marketing mix, flexible as it may be, into such a restrictive (not excessive) environment may be quite a job. Low profits will probably be our most optimistic projection in such a situation. For example, could we expect anything else if we tried to market in a restrictive *economic* climate, with extremely severe *competition,* under adverse *political* and *legal* constraints, in an unfriendly and unfamiliar *society* and *culture,* without the benefit of *scientific* and *technological* advances?

Part E of Figure 3-3 portrays a marketing environment which is circular, but which is also too large. Operating our marketing program here is similar to trying to insert a small bolt into a large nut. It fits into the nut, but it doesn't fasten. Likewise, our pentastar will fit into this very large circle. It will even rotate. But it won't stay on course at the center. It will rotate aimlessly throughout the available excessive space. Occasionally, it may be centered on the target customer, but most often the pentastar will be bouncing from one edge of the circle to another as it rotates haphazardly. Such haphazard movement is not likely to satisfy target customers at a profit to the SBM. When the marketing environment appears to be so lacking in structure, the SBM himself must attempt to define structure as best he can. This is probably an extreme situation which does not occur very often.

After all that conceptualizing, hopefully we can see that a balanced marketing strategy in a balanced environment will optimally satisfy the target customer at a profit to the SBM. As an additional point, we might insert here a lengthy conceptual discussion of the effects of these odd-shaped "circles" of environment on the efficiency and effectiveness of the PEC process at both levels as shown by the triangles in Figure 3-1. Now that you are an old hand at conceptualization, why not try that one on your own?

In this section and in Figure 3-3, we have briefly shown five of the broad types of disequilibrium environmental situations which the SBM may face. Undoubtedly, many other types and subtypes could be shown. Any experienced SBM will readily attest to the great variety in the marketing environment. It is the job of the SBM to know his environment (which he cannot control) in order that his market mixes will best achieve his objectives. In the planning stage, the SBM must allow sufficient flexibility in his marketing strategy to adjust for rapid environmental change. He may even decide to relegate certain decisions from the strategic level to the tactical level in order to maintain the required flexibility.

THE MARKETING MIX OF THE SBM

For purposes of explanation at this point, we are going to afford ourselves a luxury which is unavailable to the practicing SBM. However, we can afford the luxury in this chapter because we are conceptualizing. The luxury is that in this section we are going to assume that the SB marketing environment is balanced, that is, at equilibrium. In spite of the realism of all those odd-shaped "circles" of the previous section, we are temporarily assuming that the SB environment is a perfect circle of the proper size. Now let's see how much perfection exists in the SB marketing mix.

As shown in Figure 3-1, the SB marketing mix is the five-pointed star composed of the five "P's" centered around the target customer. The pentastar is balanced with all five points of equal size. This represents the coequal force of each in the overall marketing strategy. This doesn't necessarily mean that twenty percent of the dollar budget goes into each of the five "P's." Rather, it means that each of the five is present in the marketing mix in the *ideal* manner and that the five taken together form a unified and integrated total marketing strategy. This *ideal* is determined by (a) the target markets or customers to be served at a profit and (b) the environmental variables. Since we've already assumed the environment to be balanced, let's refer back to Figure 3-2 at this time. In that figure, four separate SBMM models were illustrated, one for each target market being served. In actual practice, both target markets and marketing mixes tend to have considerable overlap. However, for simplicity and for planning purposes, it may be easier to speak here of one target market only. By repetition, our discussion could apply to several target markets. These could then be combined in an overall SBMM model.

Now let's look at some odd-shaped "stars" in Figure 3-4, but first we must briefly describe each of our five "P's." The five "P's" represented by the star are product, place, price, promotion, and people. By *product* we mean the goods and services combination to be marketed by the SBM. Product strategy develops around such questions as product development, product line additions and deletions, and product features such as branding and packaging. *Place* is the controllable variable dealing with the channel of distribution decisions of where, when, and by whom products will be marketed. Physical distribution systems involving the transportation and storage functions are also a part of place strategy. *Price* is that which the SBM receives in exchange for the goods and services combinations he markets. The price variable probably most directly affects the profits of the SBM. Strategic questions in pricing are how much, in what form, when, and with what variations—such as discounts and so forth. *Promotion* is the variable used by the SBM to communicate information and to persuade the target customers concerning the total product offering of the firm. Complementary components of promotion strategy are categorized as advertising, personal selling, and sales promotion. *People* is the controllable variable of the marketing mix which may be unique to SB. People are also present in BB, but as a part of a bureaucratic hierarchy. In SB, employing and managing the right people is every bit as important as promoting the right amount of the right product at the right place at the right time at the right price. *People* refers to all the employees of the SBM. It may even be extended to include a portion of the channel of distribution used by the SBM. People strategies include such areas as investment in people and their development, organization, motivation, and other "personnel" matters that can, if viewed as a part of marketing strategy, give the alert SBM a differential advantage. Now, let's conceptualize some more.

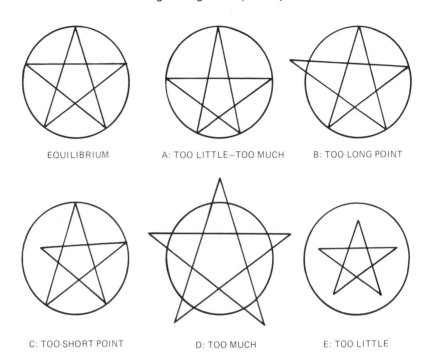

EQUILIBRIUM   A: TOO LITTLE–TOO MUCH   B: TOO-LONG POINT

C: TOO-SHORT POINT   D: TOO MUCH   E: TOO LITTLE

Figure 3–4   Shapes of the Small Business Marketing Mix at Various States of Disequilibrium

The odd-shaped stars in Figure 3–4 are (a) the too little-too much, (b) the too long point, (c) the too short point, (d) the too much, and (e) the too little. The reader may, by now, be able to construct a few odd shapes not shown in Figure 3–4.

The "too little-too much" figure represents the marketing mix of the SBM who has strayed from the ideal blending. Although this marketer has remained at all points a proper relationship with the environment (all five points touching the circle), some components of the mix are short of the ideal proportion while others are present to excess. Both plus and minus deviations from the ideal tend to lessen the effectiveness of the marketing strategy. Thus our first figure might represent a marketing strategy which is about half as effective as it could be if all elements of the mix were present in the ideal proportions. In this case, we have only partially satisfied our target market and will have done so by poor utilization of resources, which may result in a very small profit or even in a loss. An example would be a firm which invested too little in *product* development and *people* development, had a poorly conceived *place* strategy in regard to the channels of distribution used, and which then tried to compensate for these weaknesses by excessive advertising *(promotion)* at extremely competitive *prices.* Numerous other combinations are possible.

The "too long point" figure depicts a marketing mix one portion of which attempts to operate beyond the support of the available environment. Obviously, this star won't rotate on center unless the too long point has flexibility; and even then this too long point will probably act as a drag on the whole system. In marketing terms, this marketing strategy won't work. That is, it doesn't center on satisfying the target customer at a profit unless the overdone element of the marketing mix has sufficient flexibility. Even then, this overdone "P" will probably be a burden to the whole marketing effort. An example of this would be an otherwise sound marketing strategy whose effectiveness was diminished by a promotional program which went beyond the norms of our culture and was therefore thought to be in bad taste.

The star with the "too short point" illustrates a marketing strategy that is simply lacking in some respect. For example, our marketing mix might have everything except a good product. Or we may have a great product, good distribution, the right price, and superb people; but nobody knows about us because our tiny promotional budget produces minimal amounts of advertising of very poor quality.

The "too much" star has mechanical problems of not being able to rotate unless all five points have sufficient flexibility to be crammed into the environment. If, in a marketing sense, this could be done, we would have a highly flexible marketing strategy which would be of too large a total size. Such a strategy would likely result in over-kill rather than profit. The marketing program is too large because the SBM has viewed the target market (the pentagon) as larger than it actually is. Thus, the SBM has a marketing strategy which, if the environmental conflict can be avoided through sufficient flexibility, may satisfy the real smaller target market. However, the likelihood of doing so at a profit is not too great.

The "too little" star shows a marketing strategy based on the underestimation of the size of the target market and a lack of appreciation of the realities of the marketing environment. Such a naive strategy may be balanced enough to survive for a short time, but the competitive forces of the environment will soon point out to this marketer that "too little" and/or "too late" are not successful marketing mixes. An example would be a firm that let a marketing opportunity go by because they didn't recognize the true size of the target market and/or felt constrained by the environment where in fact these constraints were partially imagined.

Let's now conceptualize in a slightly different way with our marketing mix. By using some numbers in a simple example (grade school mathematics), we can see the interdependence of the five marketing mix variables—product, place, price, promotion, and people. In true mathematical notation, we'll call these P_1, P_2, P_3, P_4, and P_5. The statement which we'll express as an equation is: The effectiveness of the marketing mix is equal to the product (mathematical) of the effectiveness of all five marketing mix variables. Now, if a variable such as price or promotion is exactly at the *ideal* level, we say it is 100% effective and we give it a value of 1. That is, 100% effectiveness equals 1. A variable could be either plus or minus the ideal. Any deviation (plus or minus) from the ideal will be subtracted from 1 in order to show the value of that variable to the marketing mix. Thus if we've done a poor job of advertising, for example, the promotional variable (P_4) would be assigned some value of less than 1. How *much* less would depend on how bad our advertising was. If our advertising was about 75% effective in terms of our ideal, we would assign .75 (that is, the decimal equivalent of 75%) as our value for P_4.

The effectiveness of the
SB marketing mix $\quad = (P_1)(P_2)(P_3)(P_4)(P_5).$

The effectiveness of the
ideal SB marketing mix $\quad = (1.0)(1.0)(1.0)(1.0)(1.0)$
$\quad\quad\quad\quad\quad = 1 \text{ or } \underline{100\%}.$

For an example of less than ideal effectiveness, let's assume the following:

| *Variable* | *Symbol* | *Effectiveness* | |
		%	*Decimal*
Product	P_1	80%	.8
Place	P_2	90%	.9
Price	P_3	100%	1.0
Promotion	P_4	100%	1.0
People	P_5	70%	.7

By substituting the above P values into our formula, we have:

$$(.8)\ (.9)\ (1.0)\ (1.0)\ (.7)\ =\ .504\ =\ 50.4\%.$$

Thus we see that the cumulative effect of our ineffectiveness has reduced our marketing strategy to the point of being about 50% effective as compared to how effective the ideal SB marketing strategy would be. This is so even though, taken individually, our lowest strategic variable rated at the 70% level. Let's run this through again to see what would happen if by good management we could raise the level of effectiveness for P_5 from 70% to 80%.

We have:

$$(.8)\ (.9)\ (1.0)\ (1.0)\ (.8)\ =\ .576\ =\ 57.6\%.$$

Thus an increase in one variable raises the overall effectiveness of the total marketing strategy. Unfortunately, this also works in reverse for decreases in the effectiveness of any one variable. Note that the effectiveness of the overall marketing strategy cannot exceed the level of the most ineffective variable. Of course, the old cliché about the chain and the weakest link immediately comes to mind.

In concluding our overview of the marketing mix of the SBM, let us remember that the elements (variables) designed to satisfy the target market(s) can be combined in many ways. Experience has demonstrated that there is more than one way to accomplish the marketing objectives.

THE TARGET CUSTOMER

Just as the Pentagon near Washington, D.C. is the center of the military system in the United States, so also is a pentagon the center of our SBMM model. In Figure 3–1, this pentagon is labeled "C" to designate the target customer. This collective target customer may be called the target market. It is composed of *people* with *money* and a *willingness* to buy that which offers satisfaction. In a customer-oriented economic system such as ours we often hear such phrases as "the customer is king." Thus we have a decentralized economic system with many "kings" rather than a single Pentagon with a few generals.

Markets may be classified as *consumer* markets or as *industrial* (or intermediate) markets. Consumer markets are also known as household, ultimate, or final consumer markets. The consumer market removes goods and services from the marketing system in order to provide for personal or family satisfaction. The industrial or intermediate market, composed of business, government, and nonprofit institutions, purchases for resale in one form or another. The terms *consumer* and *customer* are often distinguished in specific ways. We'll skip that discussion until Chapter 6.

Alternate strategies, based upon production orientation vs. customer orientation, are available to the marketer. Under a production orientation, the marketer assumes the market to be a mass homogeneous total. The strategy followed here is typically mass production, with slight product differentiation, promoted heavily to this aggregate mass market. Under a customer orientation, the total market is assumed to be heterogeneous in total, but consisting of many submarkets which are each internally homogeneous in significant marketing aspects. Market segmentation techniques are used to identify these submarkets or segments. Management may then determine which of these segments it wishes to pursue as target markets. Appropriate strategies are then developed for each target market. Naturally, the target marketing approach based upon the customer orientation is favored by the author. Although BB uses target marketing very often, it is almost always the appropriate strategy approach for SB as well. The competitive advantages of scale do not often lie with the SBM in either mass production or mass marketing.

Now, let's take a look at one approach to attempting to understand the customer. We'll center our efforts here on the consumer market only. Both the consumer market and the industrial market will be treated in more detail in Chapters 4 and 5. Before presenting this portion of the model, a word of warning is in order. Understanding the customer (the "C" in our pentagon) is about as difficult as turning the five-sided nut on a fire plug with a conventional wrench. The model of consumer market behavior is adapted from Walters and Paul.[1] Our description here will be brief, but a more detailed description of consumer and market behavior is the subject of Chapter 6.

The consumer, like the SBM, is also a strategist. His (or her) strategy formulation is affected by individual influences and by environmental influences. The purchase strategy used by the consumer to find solutions to consumption problems involves two types of purchase decisions:

1. *Assortment Decisions.* These are a group of decisions necessary to determine the particular group of products and services that the consumer desires to consume.
2. *Market-related Decisions.* These are a group of decisions concerning the specific actions taken by the consumer in the market place in order to provide products for the assortment.[2]

The purchase strategy, which results in purchase action, and eventually in consumer satisfaction, is affected by two sets of variables. The basic determinants or variables internal to the individual are needs, motives, perception, and attitudes. The environmental or external variables of influences are categorized as family influences, social influences, business influences, cultural influences, and economic influences. The whole process of consumer behavior is a dynamic one with change constantly taking place in all the variables. This suggests that we could graphically demonstrate some "odd shapes" *within* our consumer behavior pentagon. Let's do that mentally only at this point

---

[1]C. Glenn Walters and Gordon W. Paul, *Consumer Behavior: An Integrated Approach* (Homewood, Illinois: Richard D. Irwin, Inc., 1970), see Chapter 1. This book has since been revised under the sole authorship of Walters. The revision contains a somewhat different model of consumer behavior. The model of the prior edition seems more suited to our brief description.

[2]C. Glenn Walters, *Consumer Behavior* (Homewood, Illinois: Richard D. Irwin, Inc., 1974), p. 10.

so we can return to the pentagon itself for a brief look at some markets. We'll try to understand more about the consumer behavior of these target markets later.

Figure 3–5 shows some shapes of the target customer (market) as correctly and incorrectly viewed by the SBM. Pentagon A shows the actual target customer, which, taken collectively, is the actual target market. It is the right size and shape by the market's own definition. If the SBM correctly perceives the target market, he will see it as shown in pentagon A.

In pentagon B of Figure 3–5, the SBM has incorrectly perceived the target market to be smaller than it actually is. If the SBM formulates and implements a marketing strategy on his mistaken underestimate of the size of the target market, several outcomes might be possible. Both good and bad elements could be contained in these outcomes. Some possible outcomes are: (1) The SBM will give up a part of the target market to present and potential competition simply because he failed to recognize the existence of that portion of the market; (2) the SBM will forego available economies of scale in both production and marketing; (3) the SBM may have high marketing costs per target customer served; (4) the SBM may become very entrenched in his underestimated target market but competitively unable to expand; (5) the SBM may decide to forego entering the market at all since he underestimates its size; and (6) the SBM may make inappropriate strategic and tactical decisions in such operational areas as selecting specific

Figure 3–5   Shapes of the Target Customer As Correctly and Incorrectly Viewed by the SBM

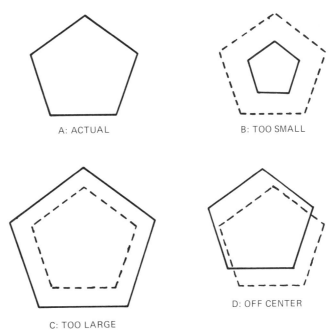

A: ACTUAL

B: TOO SMALL

C: TOO LARGE

D: OFF CENTER

*The Dotted Line Is The Actual Size And Shape Of The Target Market And The Solid Line Is The Perception Of The Target Market By The SBM.

advertising media, developing sales territories, determining extent of the product line, or the optimum price level, and so forth. Of course, speaking mechanically, as in our SBMM model, we would say that this "too small" pentagon could not properly serve as an anchor point around which a balanced marketing mix could rotate.

What if, as in pentagon C of Figure 3–5, the pentagon is too large? Well, mechanically it will overwhelm the points of our pentastar to the degree that the rotation of the pentastar will be more or less uncontrolled by the action of the points. In marketing terms, this means that the target market (as incorrectly overestimated by the SBM) is of such a magnitude that it requires a large marketing mix. That is, in order to satisfy this target market, the SBM incorrectly plans, executes, and controls in "too large" a way. The target market isn't as large as he thought it was. Sales and profits will very likely be less than expected. The various strategies and tactics will be inappropriate in operation. For example, production runs will be too long, inventories may be too large, sales territories may be too small, advertising media may involve wasted circulation, and so forth.

Pentagon D in Figure 3–5 shows the actual and perceived pentagons to be of the same size but not in the same place. Mechanically, the pentagon is "off center." As such, it will not serve as a properly located pivot around which the balanced points of the star will rotate. In a marketing sense, the SBM has somehow properly estimated the size of the target market, but he has made a considerable error as to which "customers" are and are not a part of the target market. In short, except for the area of overlap in pentagon D of Figure 3–5, the marketing strategy is being misdirected. This results in wasting marketing efforts where no potential exists while at the same time placing no marketing efforts in what should be the properly defined target market.

Many other shapes of target markets could be illustrated. However, let's not test our patience at this point. Using the preceding conceptualizations presented in this chapter, let's get to some of the "how to" of marketing strategy planning. Reality often presents some odd-shaped target markets served by odd-shaped marketing strategies operating in odd-shaped environments.

THE "HOW TO" OF MARKETING STRATEGY PLANNING FOR SB

The foreword of an article in the prestigious *Harvard Business Review* states:

> While many sophisticated concepts of formulating corporate strategy are being studied with interest by large corporations, they hold little promise for medium-sized and smaller companies—at least in the foreseeable future. For the latter, strategic planning is still more of an art than a science.[3]

The step-by-step approach to marketing strategy planning for SB outlined below recognizes the inherent differences between BB and SB. Also, what we have below is a skeleton or outline. Each individual SBM must "put the flesh on" in order to make the outline meaningful for his particular SB. No one else can do it for him (you). Our method is not the only one, but it does work. Adaptation to specific needs of the particular SB firm

[3]Frank F. Gilmore, "Formulating Strategy In Smaller Companies," *Harvard Business Review,* 49 (May 1971), 71.

can make it work best. Our approach is patterned after Gilmore's "simple, practical method" as applied to our SBMM model.[4]

Our method is not complex, although it could be used with complex techniques, if desired. The basic tools are a note pad, a conference room, good leadership, and a good marketing management team. Get your note pad ready! You and the members of your marketing team have many questions to discuss and answer.

The eight steps in planning our marketing strategy are:

1. Record the current marketing strategy.
2. Identify strategic marketing problems.
3. Divide current strategic marketing problems into core strategy areas and supporting strategy areas.
4. Formulate alternative strategies at both core and support levels.
5. Evaluate these alternatives in various combinations.
6. Choose the new marketing strategy.
7. Plan the details of implementation of the new strategy.
8. Set performance standards and monitor feedback.

Step 1—Record the current marketing strategy.   Don't try to short-cut the process at this point (or at any later point) by saying, "Well, I guess we all know what our current marketing strategy is, so I guess we can go right on to the next step." The chances are pretty good that even in the very small firm, the firm's marketing strategy is very fuzzy in the minds of most of the management.

Recording of the current (and past) marketing strategy serves as an important foundation. If the SBM is operating according to a well-defined strategy, the recording job will be easy. However, many SB firms probably have a more difficult job here because of the informality of past and current strategies. Even in such cases it is possible to infer from company actions and from the activities of marketing management pretty much what the marketing strategy has been.

Overall company objectives should be made clear in the process of recording the current marketing strategy. In fact, the statement of overall objectives in specific terms is the only framework which can give meaning to the marketing strategy. You must ask yourself, "Just what kind of firm do we want to be?" A very specific answer to this question of objectives is required. Once the objectives are stated, then the SBM should attempt to state and record the current strategy by answering such questions as the following:

1. What *target market(s)* are involved in our objectives? To what extent are we and are we not currently serving these target markets? What have the trends been within these markets? What have been our successes and failures in these target markets? What core strategies and supporting strategies have been successful?

2. What environmental conditions have existed in each of the five areas of environment during the implementation of the past and current marketing strategies? What trends are evident? What environmental factors have favored or impaired our past and current strategies? How have past and current marketing strategies been adjusted for the environment?

3. How, and how effectively have we combined the five "P's" of our marketing mix in past and current marketing strategies? How about the elements of each submix?

[4]Gilmore, pp. 76–81.

4. In what areas of the marketing management process (planning, execution, and control) is the company doing a good job?

Once the above information is down on paper, we have a basis for moving on. Some of the above information will be less than ideal. This is normal. Management is always operating with less than one hundred percent information. However, let's fill the vacuum as well as possible.

Step 2—Identify strategic marketing problems. Unless the current marketing strategy is perfect (an unlikely situation), some strategic marketing problems exist. Let's now identify them. These are *strategic* rather than *tactical* marketing problems. They may exist in either or both the *core* strategy and the *supporting* strategies. Now, let's take a minute to discuss these four terms.

Strategic marketing problems are those problem areas which are keys to overall success. Decisions in the strategy areas are more basic, tend to be made more infrequently (i.e., they last longer), and tend to be more critical than *tactical* decisions. The terms derive from the military usage of the words "strategy" and "tactics," and the examples to illustrate the differences are well known. Some further observations about strategies and tactics are:

1. Tactical decisions are those made on an *ad hoc* or by default basis.
2. The more you know about your target market, the more decision making you can do as strategic decision making.
3. A point can be reached when a tactical decision becomes so repetitive that it should be considered as part of the strategic plan.
4. If marketing SB management abdicates setting strategy, then lower level employees will in fact set strategy: Each will implement his own strategy.
5. The SBM should determine very carefully which problems are strategic and which are tactical, for each will be treated as defined.

The *core* strategy is the basic strategy from which all other planning flows. It is based on the firm's differential advantage and is the central focus for competitive and/or innovative success. As Luck and Prell state:

> Core strategy is the crux of the accumulated intelligence, insight, and ingenuity of the firm, focused on the particular element in the market that appears to promise success. Its identification is reached through the firm's understanding of its market and of how the consumer or business buyer is likely to act in the market. Since this concept is the nucleus from which the firm's whole strategic position and plans are to evolve, its statement must be precise and in a form that can be spelled out operationally.[5]

In distinguishing between *core* and supporting strategies, Luck and Prell go on to say:

> One might consider that core strategy actually tends to be a set of interrelated strategies that each relate to a different aspect of the firm's operations. However, since one strategy in this set tends to be the principal one, we feel justified in

[5]David J. Luck and Arthur E. Prell, *Market Strategy* (New York: Appleton-Century-Crofts, 1968), p. 32.

identifying it as the *"core"* strategy and those relating to other aspects as the *"supporting"* strategies. No rule can be suggested regarding the number of supporting strategies that may be desirable to maximize the effectiveness of a core strategy. This depends on how many areas or functions of operations are so crucial to the core scheme's success that there also should be special strategies conceived and selected.[6]

Thus, the SBM may formulate a core strategy around the differential advantage he holds in one area such as product. The differential advantage held in the product area means that the starting point in formulating the strategy will necessarily be in the area of product strategy. The core strategy will be supported by integrating strategies in the areas of place, price, promotion, and people.

Now, we're attempting to identify strategic—(not tactical)—marketing problems. We are also attempting to identify which of these strategic marketing problems in our current marketing strategy are *core* and which are *supporting*. We must ask, "Given the changes that have taken place and that will take place, how valid is our strategy?" We are looking both for weaknesses and unrealized strengths. In doing so, we must be careful to distinguish between symptoms of problems and the actual problems themselves. The latter are usually more deep-seated and more difficult to identify.

If our investigation discloses the existence of strategic marketing problems, we must determine and precisely define the elements of these problems. If no major *problems* exist, we may look only to the positive side of strategy planning by asking the question, "Do any unrealized opportunities exist?"

Step 3—Divide current strategic marketing problems into core strategy areas and supporting strategy areas.　　Assuming that some strategic marketing problems (or opportunities) exist, we should determine whether such problems are in the core strategy and/or in the supporting strategies. A problem in the core strategy will usually be the result of a very significant change in either target market or environment. Such problems may call for more complete revisions of the marketing strategy than do problems found in the supporting strategy areas. For example, if our core strategy was built around the differential advantage of a product which was both unique and of superior quality, what would happen if this differential advantage disappeared by the introduction of a superior competitive product? We would need a new core strategy built around a new or, at least, adjusted differential advantage. However, if, in this example, the problem was in one area of the supporting strategies such as the advertising strategy or the pricing strategy, our new strategy will probably resemble the current strategy as regards the core area since our differential advantage remains. Whatever modifications are made are likely to be in one or several of the supporting strategy areas.

Up to this point we have (1) recorded the current marketing strategy, (2) identified strategic marketing problems, and (3) determined whether such problems are with the core strategy and/or the supporting strategies. At this point, we know where we stand. Since we now know where we are, we can "look at the map" to see where we might want to go. In fact, in some cases we may even be able to go where no one has been before.

Step 4—Formulate alternative strategies at both core and support levels.　　Once the problems have been determined, the SBM can begin the creative and integrative process of formulating new alternative strategies. Such strategy formulations should go on at both

---

[6]Luck and Prell, p. 41.

the core and supporting levels even though problems were identified at only one level. This is usually necessary in order to arrive at combinations which are internally consistent.

In this step, the SBM should be restricted only by the broadest of boundaries. Such items as company objectives, management values, and some reasonable ideas of resource limitations are warranted. However, the SBM should eagerly pursue the investigation of all alternatives that show promise for success. It is in the next step, not this one, that we will evaluate alternatives. First we must gather the alternatives.

Alternative strategies are found by looking. You must look! The number of possible combinations available to the SBM is almost unlimited. How do we find a few meaningful strategies with so many from which to choose? The process is basically this: (1) Look for a differential advantage; (2) derive the core strategy from the differential advantage; and then (3) support the core with appropriate supporting strategies. Of course, the seeking of marketing strategies is based on company objectives with respect to target markets. Repeat the above process until it is seemingly exhausted. Creative thinking can be enjoyable, but also try to be realistic.

The differential advantage may come in several forms, such as technical knowledge, exclusive product features, excess production or marketing capacity, market contacts, strong customer franchise, and so forth. If the SBM has absolutely no differential advantage for the markets he is currently serving, success is likely to be very limited. However, most often some differential advantage does exist. In many small firms it may be personalized service, customized products, and so on. If a differential advantage is difficult to find as regards a particular target market, perhaps the SBM should consider serving different target markets.

Once the differential advantage is determined, the SBM should derive a core strategy that will put that advantage to work. As was stated in the first chapter: "Advantages and disadvantages of anything are not automatic." An example of the advantage at work in a core strategy follows. Suppose the SBM had a differential advantage in the form of a high quality product with excellent reputation within a limited geographic region. His core strategy should be one which will exploit the advantage. Quality deterioration in times of rising materials costs would clearly be a route by which this SBM could give away his differential advantage by such a shift in core strategy. Likewise, in the areas of supporting strategy, the SBM would insist on selling through quality outlets using well-trained people and appropriate prices.

Now, see how many alternative strategies you can find to exploit the differential advantage in the above example or in the SB with which you are familiar. Spell out details of your various strategies at both the core and support levels.

Although we are seeking strategies that can be made operational, it is important not to be too limiting. We need at least several good alternative strategies in order to truly evaluate their relative attractiveness in the next step.

Step 5—Evaluate these alternatives in various combinations.   In this step we are simply evaluating. We are not yet making a selection. What we want to do here is take a look at both the positive and negative aspects of each alternative. We'll be looking at each alternative in terms of both core strategy and supporting strategies. Thus if we had three core strategies, which we'll call A, B, and C, and if each core strategy had various supporting strategy combinations, we might have the following total number (9) of alternatives to evaluate:

A_1, A_2, A_3, B_4, B_5, B_6, B_7, C_8, C_9, and so on.

We have used different subscript numbers in order to show that the supporting strategies are likely to be different for each core strategy. In rare cases, this may not be so.

As we are seeking the optimum marketing strategy for our particular SB, several questions must be answered regarding alternative strategies. Some of these are:

1. What is a realistic sales and profit projection for this strategy?
2. What competition and competitive reaction can be expected during and beyond the implementation of this strategy?
3. What will be the relative effectiveness of alternative strategies in solving the strategic marketing problems identified in previous steps?
4. To what extent will each strategy impair or enhance the differential advantage of the firm?
5. To what extent will each proposed strategy create or minimize the creation of new problems in both marketing and nonmarketing areas of the SB firm?

The above short list of questions suggests that the evaluation of alternative strategies is not going to be easy. An interim approach of first evaluating core strategies and then evaluating supporting strategies may make the job easier. However, if such an approach is used, it should not act as a substitute for the final evaluation of each combination of core strategies and its supporting strategies. Thus, if the interim approach were used, we would first evaluate core strategies A, B, and C without considering the merits of alternate supporting strategies. We would then evaluate supporting strategies 1, 2, and 3 for core strategy A; 4, 5, 6, and 7, for core strategy B; and 8 and 9 for core strategy C. Our point is that this by itself is not sufficient, although it may be helpful. We must then evaluate the alternate combinations of core and supporting strategies:

A_1, A_2, A_3, B_4, B_5, B_6, B_7, C_8, C_9, and so on.

Step 6—Choose the new marketing strategy. The SBM does have to eventually make a decision; hopefully, it will be the right one. The newly selected marketing strategy will be a combination of a core strategy and its supporting strategies. Its implementation will call for tactical adjustments from time to time. The strategy selected by the SBM is very likely going to be the one which reflects some important subjective elements unique to that SB and to that SBM. For this reason, it is most unlikely that any two groups or businesses would choose identical strategies. However, this does not mean that there is only one right answer. There are several good, workable marketing strategies that could be successful for a single business or for different small businesses. The one best strategy for a particular SB will depend on unique factors. Hence, it is almost impossible to plan a marketing strategy for the SB without the active leadership of the SBM. Also, there may be several good marketing strategies for a particular SB. This suggests that we take a tip from the space age by providing for a back-up strategy. This back-up would probably be our "second-best" marketing strategy. We would go to the back-up only if a major flaw developed in our primary marketing strategy and if the flaw were of such a nature that it could not be handled by tactical marketing adjustments. An example of such a flaw would be a sudden move by competition which could not have been anticipated and which would have a great positive or negative effect on our strategy implementation. Since much hard work will go into the formulation of our back-up strategy, it should be fairly sound.

Step 7—Plan the details of implementation of the new strategy. Up to this point, we've been concentrating on *what* it is we are going to do. Now it's time to spell out the details of exactly *how* we're going to do this, and also *when, where,* and *by whom.* Although these areas have been implicitly covered in our previous steps, we need to consider explicitly the details of the implementation of the strategy. Items to be considered here are specific assignment of tasks, scheduling and sequencing, locating outside assistance, planning sources of supply, and so forth.

Step 8—Set performance standards and monitor feedback. Our marketing strategy is directed toward the accomplishment of certain specific objectives. The first question we are asking in this step is: In what ways (qualitative) and to what extent (quantitative) are we accomplishing the objectives? We do not answer this question in the planning of our marketing strategy. That answer is for the control phase of our PEC marketing management process. However, in this step we do determine the criteria by which we can later measure our degree of success. Thus, in this step, we say to ourselves: These are the specific criteria against which we will later judge our performance. Such a statement at this time gives us a concrete standard of performance to use later and prevents us from later drawing up the performance criteria which make us "look good" after the fact.

Our second question in this final step is to ask constantly: How are we doing? Such feedback to the SBM is necessary for determining what tactical adjustments may be necessary in order to improve the strategy implementation of the current strategy and in order to improve the strategy planning of the SBM for the future.

In conclusion, the steps outlined above are an outline or guide for marketing strategy planning by the SBM and his management team. Filling in the outline for a particular SB takes much hard work. This work is probably required in direct proportion to the expected results. If the SBM doesn't plan his marketing strategy, no one else will plan it for him. In effect, he will have no strategy. To achieve success with such a self-imposed disadvantage would be fortuitous indeed in today's highly competitive markets.

BIBLIOGRAPHY

Books

LUCK, DAVID J., AND PRELL, ARTHUR. *Market Strategy.* New York: Appleton-Century-Crofts, 1968.

WALTERS, C. GLENN. *Consumer Behavior: Theory and Practice.* Homewood, Illinois: Richard D. Irwin, Inc., 1974.

WALTERS, C. GLENN, AND PAUL, GORDON W. *Consumer Behavior: An Integrated Framework.* Homewood, Illinois: Richard D. Irwin, Inc., 1970.

Periodicals

GILMORE, FRANK F. "Formulating Strategy In Smaller Companies," *Harvard Business Review,* 49 (May 1971), 71–81.

MARKETS
AND SB MARKETING
OPPORTUNITIES

For most small businessmen, the fact that the total U.S. consumer market is composed of more than 200 million people is a rather unusable statistic. Equally useless statistics regarding the total size of the intermediate market are available. What the SBM really wants, in most cases, is a much more detailed picture of smaller target markets.

In the next few chapters we will investigate markets, both consumer and industrial, from the perspective of the SBM. Buyer behavior, especially in the

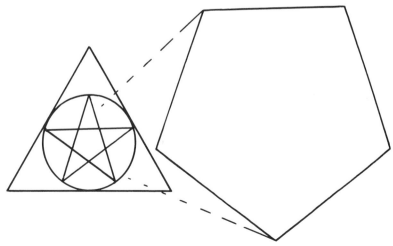

PART II—MARKETS AND SB MARKETING OPPORTUNITIES

consumer market, will also be viewed from the SB perspective. In Chapter 7, our focus will turn to marketing information (including market information) for SBMM. In short, this part of the book attempts to answer four basic questions:

1. What consumer markets are of greatest interest to the SBM?
2. What intermediate (industrial) markets are of greatest interest to the SBM?
3. What should the SBM know about consumer and market behavior?
4. What marketing information (research) can be used by the SBM to plan, execute, and control the marketing program?

4

Consumer Markets
For SB

WHAT IS A MARKET?

Is a market a place such as Wall Street where stocks and bonds are sold? Is it a place such as Omaha where hogs and cattle are made ready for the packing houses? Is it a thing the housewife does on her weekend shopping trip for groceries? Or, the expression, "What's the market doing?" may refer to the price rather than the place. Numerous other meanings and shades of meaning for the term *market* will readily come to mind. We did our conceptualizing in Chapter 3. In this chapter, we want to begin using the model we have developed. So let's get to the task by concretely defining what we mean by a *market.*

A market is composed of (1) *people* with (2) *money* and (3) a *willingness* to spend that money for satisfactions. These three elements may take slightly different forms. In the consumer market, the *people* element may be referred to more concisely as people with needs. In the industrial market, the *people* element is a business firm, a governmental unit, or a private institution such as a school or church. *Money*, in our definition, may be actual cash or some other form of purchasing power. Likewise, in place of *willingness* to spend, some marketers will talk about inclination or authority to spend or about the wide spectrum of buyer behavior. Thus, some definitional differences do exist. But most marketers basically agree that a market is composed of people, with money, and with a willingness to spend it.

Implied in our definition of a market is what the economist would refer to as *demand.* This is a demand for products, both goods and services, which are capable of satisfying needs. The sovereignty of the customer, especially in the consumer market, is a fundamental of the market system. That is, the customer decides which products to buy and from which firms to buy them.

In discussing markets, some other terms are commonly used. A *potential market* is one that is not yet actual or realized, usually because the willingness to buy is lacking. *Market potential* usually refers to the expected sales of a product or service for an entire industry during a given time period. That portion of the market potential which one firm or product might expect is referred to as *sales potential.*

A simple definition of the term *market* would be the collective customer. Customers, individual and collective, exist in both the *consumer* market and the *industrial* market. By making this division into consumer and industrial, we have just *segmented* the market. We'll go into market segmentation much deeper later on in this chapter. The *consumer* market is also known as the household, ultimate, or final consumer market. The consumer market— that is, the market for consumer goods and services—removes goods and services (consumer products) from the marketing system in order to provide for personal or family satisfaction. The *industrial* market is also known as the intermediate market. The industrial market—the market for industrial goods and services—is composed of business, government, and nonprofit institutions. It purchases goods and/or services for resale in one form or another to some other member of the industrial market or to the consumer market. The industrial market for SB will be considered separately in the next chapter. Our present chapter focuses on the consumer market as it relates to the SBM.

Many marketing texts distinguish between the terms *customer* and *consumer.* After such distinctions are made, it is not uncommon to later use the terms interchangeably. This text will probably be no exception. In this and the following chapter, we will speak of customers in both the consumer and industrial markets. In Chapter 6, on consumer behavior, we'll examine some of the fine points between consumers and customers in the consumer market. These distinctions can sometimes be very important to the marketer.

Good marketing strategy is based upon the selection of a target market. In fact, probably the *most* basic and *most important* strategic marketing problem facing the SBM is the proper definition of each of his target markets. Even for large marketers, the existence of a single, national, mass market is thought by most marketers to be a myth. Certainly for most SB marketers, there is neither a single national market nor a mass market of any other dimension. Most SB marketers are, and inherently should be, target marketers rather than mass marketers.

Defining a target market(s) is a subjective process, or an art. However, the process can be improved considerably by an understanding of markets, of how they work, and of current information on what changes are taking place. To aid in the selection of targets and the understanding of these target markets, let's first look at the big picture. We'll view the U.S.A. consumer market profile very briefly; we shall also take a look at more limited markets before getting into market segmentation. Keep in mind that the SBM is usually interested in more limited markets and that he usually should aim at target markets. Another important point to keep in mind is the definition of a market. It is the needs of customers and not the products that can satisfy them that is important here. If we are to avoid the myopic view, we will talk about the market for transportation, not the market for railroads; about the market for home air conditioning, not the market for home air conditioners; and so on. Markets are customer-based, not product based. The SBM is often in an advantageous position to profit from this fact.

CONSUMER MARKET PROFILES

Markets can be described in many ways. Here we will list some of the various characteristics used to describe markets. Then we'll look at some more limited markets, particularly since the SBM is quite often most interested in limited markets.

Characteristics Used to Describe Markets

Some agreement exists among professional marketing researchers as to the appropriate characteristics to be used to describe markets. (For example, the American Association of Advertising Agencies has published a recommended standard breakdown for demographic characteristics to be used in surveys of consumer advertising media analysis.) In spite of such agreement, practitioners tend to devise their own descriptions to fit individualized needs. Of course, the SBM should also individualize his market profile descriptions. The categories given below in Table 4–1 are for illustrative purposes only. The items listed may be subdivided and cross-classified in many ways in order to serve specific data needs.

Although we cautioned above that markets are based on needs, that is, that they are customer based, it is often a shorthand convenience to speak of markets in terms of products. We tend to speak not simply of a market, but of a market for *something*. This shorthand is fine so long as we do not become myopic, as mentioned above. One author states:

> Once the market has been identified by *generic product class, subclass*, or *brand*, purchasers may be described by a number of means: (1) size of the market; (2) geographical locations of purchasers; (3) demographic descriptions of purchasers; (4) social-psychological characteristics; (5) reasons why products are purchased; (6) who makes the actual purchases, and who influences the purchaser; (7) when purchases are made; (8) how purchasing is done. Even more descriptive classifications could be added, such as methods of distribution, effects of pricing changes, or results of sales promotion. But those numbered above are the most common.[1]

Table 4–1   Some Typical Characteristics Used to Describe Markets

People
　　Total population
　　Regional or geographic distribution of population by area
　　Rural, urban, and suburban distribution
　　Sex distribution
　　Age distribution
　　Family, total number
　　Family life cycle or stage
　　Family size
　　Households
　　Ethnics such as race, religion, and nationality
　　Educational level
　　Occupational group
Income
　　Total income
　　Income distribution
　　Disposable income
Consumer Behavior
　　Expenditure patterns
　　Savings patterns

---

[1] Jack Z. Sissors, "What Is a Market?" *Journal of Marketing*, 30 (July 1966), 17–18.

Some of the above descriptions of a market will appear later in this chapter when we discuss market segmentation. These same characteristics can be used to describe more limited markets. Such markets, as we have said, are often of more interest to the SBM.

More Limited Markets

What the SBM wants to know is: What is the profile for my specific target market? Such target markets tend to be limited by such dimensions as geography, sex, age, and the other characteristics listed in Table 4–1. Let's consider only geographically limited markets. Among the geographic units which may be used to describe markets and for which data are readily available are census tracts, ZIP code areas, cities and towns, counties, standard metropolitan statistical areas (SMSA's), retail trading areas, wholesale trading areas, states, and so forth. The smallest unit for which much data is available is the census tract. The SBM may rather easily define his market geographically and find data about this geographic area. However, such a geographic description is not a workable profile for the SBM. Several dimensions, not just one such as the geographic dimension, of market segmentation must be skillfully combined in order to define a market meaningfully.

A consumer market profile, of whatever size market, is a static picture. It is a starting point, but it is not an analysis of the market. Additional insight into market analysis for the SBM can be gained by first introducing the idea and process of market segmentation. This discussion will give us an opportunity to see how the many dimensions of markets can be combined to define profitable market opportunities for SB. We have not yet defined our market. Market segments with internal homogeneity and external heterogeneity do exist and can be identified.

MARKET SEGMENTATION—A CONSUMER-ORIENTED APPROACH TO SB MARKET SELECTION

As was stated above, the most basic and most important strategic marketing problem facing the SBM is the proper definition or selection of each of his target markets. Market segmentation is a process that facilitates the solution of this problem. *Market segmentation* as a marketing concept was introduced into the marketing literature in 1956 by Wendell R. Smith.[2] Since that time, much research and controversy have taken place over exactly how the market segmentation concept should be implemented. Our remarks here are directed toward the implementation of market segmentation by the SBM, although much evidence shows that market segmentation (along with the marketing concept) has been primarily a concept of BB. Quite often, when the SBM has practiced market segmentation, he has done so unknowingly and perhaps unwillingly rather than as a planned basis for a sound marketing strategy.

Market segmentation is the process of dividing the heterogeneous total market into smaller groups of customers, each of which internally possesses rather homogeneous characteristics of significance to the marketer. Such smaller groups of customers are referred to as *market segments*. In turn, if these market segments are determined to be the ones to be served by a marketer, they may be called *target markets*.

[2]Wendell R. Smith, "Product Differentiation and Market Segmentation as Alternative Marketing Strategies," *Journal of Marketing,* 20 (July 1956), 3–8.

Markets are, in fact, segments. As one marketer stated:

> Segmented markets are created by segmented attitudes held by significant numbers of people who choose to spend their lives, their time and their money in a similar way. They have been with us practically forever. Shakespeare wrote about the many roles a man plays in his lifetime. Solomon wrote of a time for everything. Thoreau wrote of those who march to a different drum.[3]

The market segmentation process is often viewed as a process of dividing. An alternate approach is to begin with individual customers, rather than dividing the total market, and then aggregate these individuals into market segments. The logic and practicality of each approach may be argued. In slightly different terminology, McCarthy describes the aggregation approach as market gridding. He states:

> A target marketer starts out with the assumption that everyone is an individual and does have unique needs. He does not mechanically break down the whole market into sub-markets using one or a few "hopefully" relevant dimensions. Instead, he aggregates. He assumes that each individual has his own set of relevant dimensions and tries to aggregate together those persons who happen to have somewhat homogeneous sets of relevant dimensions.[4]

In the terminology of the economist, market segmentation is a way of viewing the market as composed of several demand curves (one for each segment) rather than a single demand curve. With such a perspective, even the SBM may at times be able to act with some monopoly power, within a given segment.

Historically, markets were probably first segmented on the basis of geography. This was due to the lack of development of "national" channels of communication and distribution. Much geographic segmentation exists today. However, as a strategic marketing tool, the recent history of segmentation begins in the late 1950s with the acceptance of the mass consumer market possessing increased discretionary spending power and with the attempts of marketers to satisfy the so-called "average" consumer. Then, as Peterson notes, "If the 1950s ushered in the idea of one ideal product as the dominant strategy, the 1960s ushered in the idea of segmenting the market to try to find products that one group of customers would like better than any other product on the market."[5] This product expansion or product proliferation policy of the 1960s was probably more advantageous for large marketers than for small ones; but even for many large marketers the return on investment decline indicates the need for a new market segmentation strategy. For the SBM, extensive product line expansion has always been a strategy involving many difficulties and competitive disadvantages. For the future, market segmentation will undoubtedly take new forms. The development of radically new and innovative ideas will likely be linked to market segmentation analysis.

In addition to product development and product-line expansion, market segmentation can serve other purposes. Segmentation can direct all types of marketing efforts in the most profitable direction. For example, the selection of both advertising messages and

[3]James C. Arthur, "Every Marketing Target Has a Bull's-Eye," *The Conference Board Record,* 11, No. 9 (September 1974), 58.

[4]E. Jerome McCarthy, *Basic Marketing: A Managerial Approach* (Homewood, Illinois: Richard D. Irwin, Inc., 1975), p. 112.

[5]James R. Peterson, "Market Fragmentation Reconsidered," *Marketing Strategies,* ed. Earl L. Bailey (New York: The Conference Board, Inc., 1974), p. 4.

media can be aided by segmentation. Better channels of distribution can be determined. And all elements of the marketing mix can be determined in a more effective manner.

The bases of market segmentation, or the dimensions which are used to segment markets, are items similar to those listed in Table 4–1. While marketing theorists and practitioners argue about such things as the relative merits of demographic dimensions versus psychological segmentation, there is general agreement that markets are segmented. The trick is to use the right combination of dimensions in the right way. The "right combination" will vary from situation to situation. The art is to have a market segment whose customers are as homogeneous as possible in regard to needs, preferences, and anticipated response patterns to the proposed marketing mix. Real differences in consumer behavior should exist from one segment to another. We see attempts, of varying degrees of success, to segment markets that were once thought to be mass markets. For example, we have a cavity-fighter toothpaste for young children, a brightener type for teens, one with baking soda for another segment, and still another that has a nonabrasive base for those who don't want to wear their teeth down from brushing too much. Practically every generic product category has been segmented along several dimensions which do have significance for both consumers and marketers. One packaged goods marketer uses the boutique idea to show that segments are made, not born:

> The notion of new contexts is an underexploited opportunity area for packaged goods. Fashion merchandisers have led the way in practical segment formation by creating the "boutique" concept. A boutique is the formation of context. Products take on the meaning of the boutique theme. New meanings are created and new clusters of customers are formed. There are lots of packaged-goods boutiques waiting out there to be created through new marketing strategy techniques which begin long before we get to store promotion.[6]

Markets may also be segmented according to the benefits which customers are seeking in consuming a particular product. Generalizations from benefit segmentation studies suggest that it is easier to take advantage of existing market segments than create new ones, no brand can appeal to all consumers, products should be designed to fit exactly the needs of a segment, and a competitive edge can result from a benefit segmentation strategy.[7]

Before putting our concept of market segmentation to work by seeking out target markets for SB, let's remember that we are dealing with an art, not a science. However, the SBM can become skilled at this art. Target marketing is something like playing poker:

> The world's best poker player loses more pots than he wins. He is the best in the world because he wins most of the big ones, and he minimizes his lost hands. And this seems very important to me.[8]

TARGET MARKETS FOR SB

Many market segments are targets for both BB and SB. Sometimes BB and SB are directly competing for the same market segment. At other times they are cooperating

[6]William T. Moran, "Segments Are Made, Not Born," *Marketing Strategies,* ed. Earl L. Bailey (New York: The Conference Board, Inc., 1974), p. 16.

[7]Russell I. Haley, "Benefit Segmentation: A Decision-oriented Research Tool," *Journal of Marketing,* 32 (July 1968), 34.

[8]S. C. Schuppe, "Some Common Mistakes," *Marketing Strategies,* ed. Earl L. Bailey (New York: The Conference Board, Inc., 1974), p. 45.

members of a channel of distribution geared toward a specific segment. Thus we find both competition and cooperation between BB and SB in serving market segments. There are some market segments and conditions under which various market segments are more or less attractive to both BB and/or SB. In this section we'll take a look at those market segments which tend to be more attractive to the SBM. We might say, "Other things being equal. . . ." However, other things are never equal. Also, the universality of our list, as always, is subject to question. The thesis upon which this listing is based is that market segments characterized by internal homogeneity within each segment can be defined according to the satisfaction of consumer needs. These segments so defined are heterogeneous among themselves and possess different inherent market characteristics among themselves. SB marketers and BB marketers also possess different inherent advantages and disadvantages specifically in regard to reaching and serving different market segments. (See Chapter 1). These advantages and disadvantages are apparent in both the marketing mix variable and in the environmental (uncontrollable) variables of the marketer. Therefore, the matching of inherent *market* segment characteristics with inherent SB *marketer* advantages should point out market segments which would be especially attractive target markets for the SBM.

The above reasoning can be extended. In addition to *inherent* market characteristics which tend to favor the SBM, two other points of view may provide insights into market segments which represent special opportunities for the SBM. First, the nature of the SB marketing mix may be constructed and directed in such a way that certain market segments are made more attractive than these segments otherwise would be. That is, the SBM himself can control his product, price, place, promotion, and people in a way that makes certain market segments more attractive to him. For example, the SBM would probably be very unsuccessful if he tried to duplicate the marketing program of Procter and Gamble for shampoo. It is immediately apparent that the SBM wouldn't have the advertising dollars. However, by stressing very selective distribution and a promotional mix with heavy emphasis on personal selling, at least one SBM has been fairly successful in serving a small, but well-defined market segment with shampoo. Second, environmental conditions (uncontrollable variables) and changes in these environmental conditions affect the relative attractiveness of market segments as good target markets for SB. Environmental changes work in both directions and sometimes in both directions at once. The net result may be more attractive or less attractive targets for the SBM. For example, within the economic environment, the inflationary recession may work hardships on both BB and SB. However, it may open up a market segment previously unavailable to SB if BB feels the need to cut costs by narrowing its product line. *Business Week* recently reported these mixed blessings:

> To be sure, economic calamity is not universal among small businessmen. Many continue to thrive, and some even see strategic advantages in their size during a recession. "We can be more flexible, can move more quickly, and concentrate on smaller segments of markets," notes David Bigelow, president of R. C. Bigelow Co., a Norwalk (Conn.)-based specialty foods outfit that grosses about $10–million.
>
> Bigelow's most successful product is a spiced tea, Constant Comment. General Foods had a competitive brand that was abandoned. Now Bigelow is battling GF again in spiced- and fruit- flavored instant coffees. This time, Bigelow concedes, General Foods has "flattened us out a bit."
>
> Nevertheless, Bigelow is bullish about the future of small business. "I feel the large corporations are failing in this country, leaving opportunities for small specialty companies," he says. "Big manufacturers are making such bad products. The big, discount-type retail operators run stores where no one gives a damn about the

customer. So there are opportunities for small businessmen. But it takes a strong individual to handle them."[9]

Briefly described on the following pages is a listing of market segments that are especially attractive target markets for SB. Please remember, when going over these market segments, that most marketers are small. Also, following the generalizations listed here is certainly no guarantee of success. It may help to improve the odds over head-on competition with large firms. Many of the items listed below also apply equally well to the industrial market; however, our main interest here is with the consumer market.

Market segments representing especially attractive target markets for the SBM are arbitrarily grouped under (1) market-related targets, including (a) market characteristics and (b) consumer behavior; (2) the marketing mix variables (i.e., the 5 P's); and (3) the environmental variables. Some of the suggested SB targets are better than others. Likewise, our listings and examples are not by any means complete.

Market-Related Targets: According to Market Characteristics

1. Market segments based upon needs that BB cannot afford to fulfill, due to characteristics of the market which limit the availability of economies of scale, offer target market opportunities for SB. Such market characteristics are customizing, short delivery time, numerous product variations, and limitations on market size due to geographic isolation or other factors. Examples of these market characteristics are numerous. Small retailers may thrive, almost without local competition, in small, isolated communities. Customized printing shops compete very favorably on small jobs requiring quick delivery time. Although the list is almost endless, BB is constantly seeking ways to serve such market segments by changes in technology and/or marketing techniques. For example, how many small "printing" jobs are now handled internally by copy equipment marketed by some of our largest companies?

2. Market segments may vary in their attractiveness to SB depending on the consistency of demand. On the one hand, those segments which experience great fluctuations in demand (such as on a seasonal basis) may present target opportunities for SB. This is often true, particularly since BB does not possess the required flexibility to deal with more than the stable portion of the fluctuating demand. On the other hand, markets which have stable demand are usually considered more desirable by both BB and SB. Stable demand does not necessarily imply that the products used to satisfy that demand are not changing. Examples of SB in seasonably fluctuating industries are numerous. Among them are the packing of agricultural products, holiday marketing, tourism, and sports-related marketing. Although some BB is also involved in these endeavors, these large firms often cooperate with SB in order to serve such temporary markets.

3. Market segments of such a size and character that SB can act as a dominant force within such segment(s) are attractive to SB. This idea is expanded later in this chapter under the "principle of market dominance." In economic terms, we are saying here that target markets do exist where the optimum scale is small, especially from a marketing point of view and not merely from a production point of view. In fact, the diversity in optimum scales of operations between production and marketing accounts for most of the channel of distribution systems in existence today.

[9]"Small Business: The Maddening Struggle to Survive," *Business Week,* No. 2387 (June 30, 1975), p. 97.

4. Market segments where large lump sum capital is not required for rapid growth (or, at least not required for obtaining a reasonable share of the market segment) tend to favor SB. If growth is possible in small increments on a pay-as-you-go basis or on a borrow-as-you-go basis, rather than on a heavy lump sum basis, SB can more advantageously serve such segments. In short, capital intensive industries are often BB rather than SB and growth is easier in the less capital intensive areas.

Market-Related Targets:
According to Consumer Behavior

1. Market segments where high customer loyalty (brand or store) is possible are good targets for SB. For example, segments where customers can be retained over the years, and where new customers can be obtained through word-of-mouth advertising, are usually favorable markets for SB.

2. Market segments whose customers have a more favorable than average attitude toward SB in general tend to be good targets for SB. An example of this is the SBM who, in his role as a consumer, patronizes small businesses rather than large chains or discount stores whenever possible.

3. Market segments with strong group identity may tend to favor SB—especially if the SBM is a member of the group. One example of this would be members of a subculture (whether based on race, religion, national origin, or so on) patronizing the SBM of the same subculture. Another example is the citizen with strong community identity patronizing the local SB merchant. BB finds it difficult to achieve the same strong degree of group identity.

4. Market segments whose buying habits and/or patterns are not in compliance with the methods and procedures of BB represent target opportunities for SB. This deviation in buying habits and/or patterns from the norm of BB may take any of several forms. For example, a segment may require extra locational or time convenience. This is illustrated by the success of "quick" food stores, which compete profitably for a market segment although massive supermarkets offer more variety at lower prices. Another example, in the opposite direction, is the "heavy user" market. Although such a market is attractive to most marketers, the "heavy user" segment can be of special interest to the SBM if he can more advantageously reach this target than the BB competition. Flexibility in the SB marketing mix in all the five P's have made this work. An excellent but vanishing example is the local brewery. Incidentally, successful local breweries have also used some of the above-mentioned segmentation strategies, such as group identity.

5. Market segments placing high value on the expertise of a specialist are often good targets for SB. For example, a sporting goods manufacturer dealing only in quality products associated with one sport tends to gain the prestige-oriented market segment. The BB full-line sporting goods manufacturers may have the major portion of the overall market, but the prestige market will be most difficult for them to penetrate.

Targets According
To Marketing Mix Variables

1. *Product.* Market segments being served by a product (i.e., a goods-services combination) with a high proportion of services and a low proportion of goods provide good targets for SB. Thus in both the consumer and industrial markets, we see an

abundance of SB firms in the so-called service industries. Technical service and personal service are both difficult to mass produce and mass market.

2. *Product.* Market segments requiring unique services, such as special customer services, are often targets for SB. If such unique services are of the skilled personal nature, the presence of SB is very likely. A variation of this market segment is where a very important part of the "product" is an intangible known as atmosphere. Examples are bars and fine restaurants. Another variation is the market for specialty products.

3. *Product.* Market segments which require new product development are often good target markets for SB, but only when the development time is short, since costs and risks are usually directly related to time. Also, in the area of new product development, SB targets may be created as voids due to the new product development of BB. For example, IBM product development of computers creates a void for software packages.

4. *Product.* Market segments which can be satisfied with a narrow but distinctive line of products favor SB. Broad product lines require heavier investments for both production and marketing.

5. *Product.* Market segments in which the products are extremely perishable (either from a physical or fashion point of view) are often good targets for SB. For example, by using modern preservatives, one of the world's largest firms can mass-market bread. However, that segment requiring a non-preservative product will patronize the local bakery. High fashion in women's apparel provides other examples. The stage of, as well as the speed of, the product life-cycle also affects the attractiveness of certain market segments for SB.

6. *Place.* Market segments are attractive to SB if they are ones in which big customers cannot take advantage of the SBM. Such big customers who might take advantage would not very often be ultimate consumers. They would be large intermediaries such as giant wholesalers or retail chains. For example, the SBM who thinks he would "have it made" if he could get A&P to handle his product is probably being naive. Markets served by open channel systems usually favor SB. Likewise, when BB tries to integrate its own channels vertically, this may create market voids which SB can fill. For example, if a large manufacturer decides to integrate vertically by servicing retailers directly through manufacturer-owned sales branches, the eliminated wholesalers may become more interested in better representing their remaining (small) suppliers.

7. *Place.* Market segments where channels of distribution are in the process of rapid change may represent unusual market opportunities for SB. This would be so particularly if the SBM is not well entrenched in the traditional channels of distribution. He would therefore have less to lose and more to gain by taking advantage of change.

8. *Price.* Market segments—and there are some—which SB can serve at a lower price are obviously attractive to SB. There is such a thing as diseconomies of large scale. SB does at times have a cost advantage over BB. To the extent that this cost advantage is reflected in pricing policies, SB will have lower selling prices. At a somewhat opposite extreme, SB may choose to serve markets where direct price comparisons are either unimportant or very difficult to achieve.

9. *Promotion.* Market segments which can be promoted effectively with a heavy proportion of personal selling and a light proportion of mass selling (advertising) in the promotional mix are often targets for SB. However, we are not suggesting here that all SB firms use such proportions in any or all market segments. The conditions must be appropriate. An example of success is the SB cosmetics firms which have experienced rapid sales increases based upon personal selling. Much of this personal selling expense has been of the variable cost type due to commission forms of sales compensation.

10. *People.* Market segments for which the people (in the firm) variable is very important are often very good targets for SB. Personal treatment received by customers and the personalities of employees can usually be more easily managed and controlled by SB than by BB. Examples of the SB advantage in close customer contact are taverns, ice cream parlors, and franchise arrangements where the SBM (franchisee) combines with BB (franchisor) to get the "best of both worlds."

Targets According To Environmental Variables

1. Market segments are often good opportunities for SB if great resources are not required in order to compete. SB may wish to compete by using a low ratio of fixed costs to variable costs in both production and marketing. Or, SB may compete favorably when the time period from market investment to market payoff is short. SB flexibility and short-term responsiveness to the market are important from a competitive viewpoint.

2. Market segments can be either more or less desirable for SB due to changing economic conditions and how such changes affect demand. For example, inflationary times may open new segments in the "do-it-yourself" market. The marketing of a kit may be a real opportunity for the SBM during such a period. Likewise, the switch from a sellers' market to a buyers' market may tend to favor SB more than BB.

3. Market segments are sometimes limited in size and number (for a single firm) by legal restrictions. An example is the liquor retailing business. Hence, SB is favored by legislation.

4. Market segments using products which (due to the state of technology) have short production runs are often good target markets for SB. The longer the production run, the more vulnerable the SBM is to competition from BB.

TARGET MARKET STRATEGY FOR SB

The determination of which market segments are the best or most appropriate target markets for a particular SBM is a subjective process. The generalizations of the previous sections can be of assistance; but in the end the SBM must say to himself, "This is the appropriate method by which to segment the market, and segments X, Y, and Z are the appropriate target markets for my company." Hindsight will judge the wisdom of the decision but will offer little help in the strategic decision-making process. In this section, we discuss two broad principles of selecting market strategy, along with some steps for locating the target market. Keep in mind that there is no single best way to locate the target market. The method presented below is not sophisticated.

Two Principles of Selecting Market Strategy

The first of our two "principles" we'll call the principle of *market simplification for SB.* Simply stated, this principle tells us not to make the problem of market selection any more complex than necessary. The SBM, in an attempt to prove his sophistication, is sometimes tempted to emulate BB. To do so in selecting market strategy would be a severe mistake. Keep the problem as simple as possible! To get caught up in techniques which may be meaningful to BB but meaningless to SB is a counter-productive activity for the SBM.

However, this principle does not tell the SBM to be myopic in defining market segments and targets. It tells him to strip away the fancy trimmings in order to clearly identify the targets themselves. The methods of BB are often not appropriate for SB.

Our second "principle," which ties in with the first, we will call the principle of *market dominance for SB*. Basically, this principle states that within any given market segment which the SBM has selected for a target market, he should be able to command enough sales (share of market segment) to exercise some degree of market dominance over that segment of the total market. This principle should hold true for primary targets, but need not be present to the same degree in secondary markets. Let's back up to our principle of market simplification for a moment before discussing market dominance further. The two principles do relate to each other. They both say, "Do your own thing: Don't be a copycat of BB."

Our first principle may suggest that the SBM should define the total market differently than the BB would; or, at least, that the SB should be much less concerned with the total market than the BB. What is most important to the SBM is not how large the total market is, but how large the particular market segments are at which he is targeting his marketing. The SBM should be very concerned with these segments and what share of the market *within* these segments he is getting. There are certainly enough big businesses around to compete for and be concerned with the remaining market segments. The real concern the SBM should have regarding the total market for a generic product is: How are the market segments I have selected as target markets doing in comparison to the total market? Are they above average or below average, and what is the trend over time? Thus, the relationship between selected segments and the total market is of some importance; but what the SBM is doing within the selected segments should be of primary importance. To illustrate, using the geographic dimension, a supermarket operator in a rural Illinois town should be most concerned with what is going on in that particular rural Illinois town (his selected target market). How much of the town's business is he getting? Is overall business in the town expanding? This Illinois supermarket operator may find it interesting to note what is happening to A&P's share of the market on the East coast, but this should simply be "interesting" and not necessarily meaningful in rural Illinois. The general trend of supermarket sales across the nation is of secondary importance to what is going on in the rural Illinois target market. Such items of secondary importance may, however, have long-term implications; but in any event, the SBM should define markets to suit his own purposes. Share of the market segment is probably a more meaningful measure for the SBM than is share of the total market for a generic product.

The principle of market dominance poses the question of how large a share of a particular market segment the SBM should strive to attain. In other words, what is the optimum share of market in any given market segment? The principle states that the SBM should have enough sales to exercise at least some degree of market dominance. What if such a share is not obtainable in a given market segment? In such a case, the SBM should probably not be marketing to that segment. Under such circumstances, marketing cost per unit will be high, obtaining distribution will be difficult, inventory turnover will be slow, and so forth. In short, marketing will be inefficient.

Before attempting to answer the question of how large a share of a market segment is necessary to achieve some degree of market dominance, let's refer to Figure 4–1. This figure has the total hypothetical market divided equally into twenty market segments (labeled A through T), each containing 5% of the total market for the generic product class. Since there are twenty equal rectangles, each represents 5% of its "total" market for the generic product class. In reality, segments are not of equal size and markets are multi-dimensional.

Here are two market selection strategies which illustrate extremes which the SBM might consider:

1. Attempt to obtain 2% of the total market by obtaining approximately 2% in each of the twenty market segments.
2. Attempt to obtain 2% of the total market by obtaining 40% of one specific market segment, such as rectangle "J."

Clearly, if the dimensions of market segmentation are meaningful, strategy #2 appears to be superior in terms of marketing efficiency. Strategy #1 amounts to little more than mass marketing by the SBM. The 40% share of segment "J" would usually be considered a fairly good amount of market dominance. While providing for marketing efficiencies for the SBM, it should be remembered that the principle of market dominance seldom if ever affords the SBM the market power of a monopolist. In most cases, competition from both large and small firms is ever present.

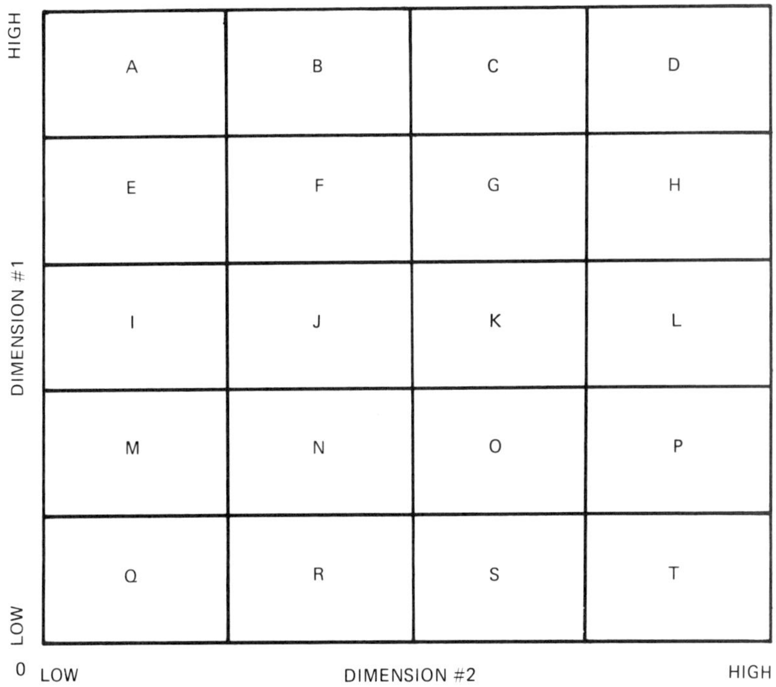

*Since There Are Twenty Equal Rectangles, Each Represents 5% Of The "Total" Market For The Generic Product Class. In Reality, Segments Are Not Of Equal Size And Markets Are Multi-Dimensional.

Figure 4–1   The Total Market Divided into Market Segments According to Two Dimensions

What is the optimum market share of a market segment for the SBM? Like the answer to most questions—it all depends. Clearly, 2% of a segment is usually much less than optimum. Over 90% would probably be too large a share in many cases because the law of diminishing returns would set in. That is, after passing a certain point, the SBM would be spending too much marketing effort to serve a greater share of the market. After the optimum has been reached in a particular market segment, the SBM should look to other market segments or to completely different markets for alternate marketing opportunities. The point, and perhaps the only one that can be made, is a general one. The SBM should have the idea in mind that an optimum share does exist. He should remember that this is an *optimum,* not a *maximum* share. And he should attempt to define that optimum or ideal share for each of the market segments in which he operates. For BB, the optimum and points beyond may be defined by fear of antitrust action. For SB, such is not the case. Market segmentation does permit the SBM to be a *big fish* in a small pond. Keep in mind that as the size of the pond increases, the *big fish* doesn't seem so big!

Steps for Locating the Target Market

Many methods are available for locating the target market. The five steps outlined below give just a brief idea of one approach which is a compromise between mere intuition and hiring an expert to do the job. This approach "involves attempting to solve the problem one's self, utilizing basically free outside resources such as those of a university bureau of business research, the Small Business Administration, or some other organization of similar type."[10] The five steps which are explained in detail by Strickland and Parrish are:

1. Define the "typical" customer or client in terms of basic characteristics (e.g., white males, females 30 to 50 years old, etc.).
2. Select one characteristic and using census or other demographic data, locate and plot those areas under consideration which have relatively high densities of individuals possessing that characteristic.
3. Using the next characteristic, repeat step two. Continue the procedure until all characteristics have been plotted.
4. Locate the overlap areas which contain the highest densities of all characteristics. These constitute the target market.
5. In the event that all high density areas (i.e., those having the highest income, the largest number of young males, etc.) do not neatly coincide, subjectively weigh each characteristic according to its relative importance. For example, a high income might be considered twice as important as the proper age.[11]

Of course, as its authors note, the above procedure does not guarantee absolute accuracy, but it does provide a workable approximation. Other good sources for applying market segmentation to target marketing appear under the concept of market gridding as defined by McCarthy and by Boone and Kurtz.[12]

[10]A. J. Strickland, III and R. D. Parrish, "Locating An Organization's Target Market Using The New Computer Based Census Data," *Journal of Small Business Management*, 12, No. 3 (July 1974), 27.

[11]Strickland and Parrish, p. 28.

[12]See E. Jerome McCarthy, *Basic Marketing: A Managerial Approach* (Homewood, Illinois: Richard D. Irwin, Inc., 1975) or Louis E. Boone and David L. Kurtz, *Contemporary Marketing* (Hinsdale, Illinois: The Dryden Press, 1974).

CHANGING MARKETS

Although it sounds much like a well-worn axiom, we'll say it anyway: *Change* is one thing the SBM can count on. In regard to markets, their size, and the share obtained by any SBM, the combinations of change are numerous. For planning market strategy, it is important that the SBM be aware of changes taking place. Consider the following combinations of change which may face the SBM:

1. The sales of the SBM are increasing at a rate faster than the sales of the market, resulting in the SBM acquiring a larger share of a larger market.
2. The sales of the SBM are increasing at the same rate as the sales of the market, resulting in the SBM maintaining his share of a larger market.
3. The sales of the SBM are increasing at a rate slower than the sales of the market, resulting in the SBM acquiring a smaller share of a larger market.
4. The sales of the SBM stay the same while the sales of the market increase, resulting in the SBM acquiring a smaller share of a larger market.
5. The sales of the SBM stay the same while the sales of the market stay the same, resulting in the SBM maintaining his share of an unchanged market.
6. The sales of the SBM stay the same while the sales of the market decrease, resulting in the SBM acquiring a larger share of a smaller market.
7. The sales of the SBM are decreasing at a rate faster than the sales of the market, resulting in the SBM acquiring a smaller share of a smaller market.
8. The sales of the SBM are decreasing at the same rate as the sales of the market, resulting in the SBM maintaining his share of a smaller market.
9. The sales of the SBM are decreasing at a rate slower than the sales of the market, resulting in the SBM acquiring a larger share of a smaller market.

The above list looks only at the directions and magnitudes of sales. As we know from the previous discussion, markets are multi-dimensional. Therefore, change can be taking place in many directions at the same time. People are constantly entering and exiting from markets. The importance of different market dimensions changes and sometimes results in regrouping the market into different market segments. The important subject of measuring and/or estimating market size and share is beyond the scope of the present chapter; but information for helping the SBM to do this for himself is available. For example, the Small Business Administration has a *Small Marketer Aid* of four pages which covers this topic for the small retailer. Its summary states:

> Knowing what his market share is can help the small retailer to see whether his firm is progressing or falling behind. Is the store getting its fair part of the sales made in its area? Or is it missing sales because the owner-manager is not aware of the potential?
>
> To determine his share of a competitive market, such as the used car market or the furniture market, the small retailer needs facts about: (1) the geographical area in which he does business, (2) his competitors and (3) total sales for his merchandise lines in his area. The *Aid* also gives examples of sources of readily available information.[13]

[13]Arthur W. Cornwell, "Sales Potential and Market Shares," *Small Marketers Aids,* No. 112 (Washington: Small Business Administration, 1965).

Finally, it might be suggested to the SBM that the concept of market share is more relevant to the competitive marketer than to the innovative marketer. Under competition, the SBM fights for a share of what already exists, whereas under innovation, the SBM creates new markets. Change brings about new market opportunities for SB. Environmentalism is but one example:

New Opportunities for Small Business. Fortunately, the picture for small business is not totally negative by any means. In fact, as always in the case of change, a number of opportunities will be created by the environmental control measures for small enterprise to prosper. As an example, the increased regulation of automobile emissions provides increased business for auto service and repair shops, which are frequently small proprietorships. In addition, a wide range of technical services could be provided by small entrepreneurs in the maintenance and installation of certain types of industrial equipment of anti-pollution requirements. Small manufacturers and suppliers of control equipment may be a possibility.[14]

BIBLIOGRAPHY

Books

BOONE, LOUIS E., AND Kurtz, David L. *Contemporary Marketing.* Hinsdale, Illinois: The Dryden Press, 1974.

McCARTHY, E. JEROME. *Basic Marketing: A Managerial Approach.* Homewood, Illinois: Richard D. Irwin, Inc., 1975.

Articles and Periodicals

ARTHUR, JAMES C. "Every Marketing Target Has a Bull's-Eye," *The Conference Board Record,* 11, No. 9 (September 1974), 58–61.

CORNWELL, ARTHUR W. "Sales Potential and Market Shares," *Small Marketers Aids,* No. 112 Washington: Small Business Administration, 1965, pp. 1–4.

HALEY, RUSSELL I. "Benefit Segmentation: A Decision-oriented Research Tool," *Journal of Marketing,* 32 (July 1968), 30–35.

LEATHERS, CHARLES G. "Environmentalism and Small Business," *Journal of Small Business Management,* 10 (October 1972), 16–20.

LINDEN, FABIAN. "The Consumer Market in 1980: An Overview," *The Conference Board Record,* 9, No. 6 (June 1972), 30–33.

MORAN, WILLIAM T. "Segments Are Made, Not Born," in Earl L. Bailey, ed., *Marketing Strategies.* New York: The Conference Board, Inc., 1974, pp. 15–20.

PETERSON, JAMES R. "Market Fragmentation Reconsidered," in Earl L. Bailey, ed., *Marketing Strategies.* New York: The Conference Board, Inc., 1974, pp. 3–6.

SCHUPPE, S. C. "Some Common Mistakes," in Earl L. Bailey, ed., *Marketing Strategies.* New York: The Conference Board, Inc. 1974, pp. 45–48.

SISSORS, JACK Z. "What Is a Market?" *Journal of Marketing,* 30 (July 1966), 17–21.

"Small Business: The Maddening Struggle to Survive," *Business Week,* No. 2387 (June 30, 1975), pp. 96–101 and p. 104.

SMITH, WENDELL R. "Product Differentiation and Market Segmentation as Alternative Marketing Strategies," *Journal of Marketing* 20 (July 1956), 3–8.

STRICKLAND, A. J., III, AND PARRISH, R. D. "Locating An Organization's Target Market Using The New Computer Based Census Data," *Journal of Small Business Management,* 12, No. 3 (July 1974), 27–34.

[14]Charles G. Leathers, "Environmentalism and Small Business," *Journal of Small Business Management,* 10 (October 1972), 19.

5

Intermediate Markets For SB

Our coverage of the intermediate (or industrial) markets will be somewhat less comprehensive in scope than that traditionally given in many general marketing texts. We will focus on specific problems of the SBM relative to the intermediate markets. Specifically, we will briefly describe the nature and characteristics of industrial markets. Secondly, organizational buyer behavior will be examined. Third, our attention will turn to the segmentation question: How, and by what practical means, can the SBM segment industrial markets? Market target strategy for the SBM in the industrial market is our fourth topic. Finally, we will direct our attention toward the SBM selling to government. Here, the emphasis is on selling to the federal government.

Some marketers strongly suggest that the stage of development of the marketing literature in the industrial area lags considerably behind that in the consumer area. For example, a 1974 article in the *Journal of Marketing* stated:

> The investigation of this question has still further significance for the student of industrial marketing. Many studies of industrial buying motivation have sought to investigate the industrial buying process through inferences drawn as a result of analyzing the content of industrial advertisements. These studies are still widely quoted and, through assimilation into the general literature, form much of the available empirical evidence about the industrial buying process. McCarthy, as recently as 1968, said: "The motives we will discuss are not new but are the classical ones presented by Copeland in 1924. More recent work has merely expanded the list or provided other organization schemes." Modern industrial marketing literature is still liberally sprinkled with terms such as "classical buying motives," "traditional buying motives," and the like, which were derived from the pioneering efforts of Copeland and others.[1]

[1]Gordon McAleer, "Do Industrial Advertisers Understand What Influences Their Markets?" Reprinted from *Journal of Marketing* published by the American Marketing Association, 38 (January 1974), 15–16.

The aim of this chapter is *not* to examine these "traditional buying motives." Our intent is to briefly review the present state of the art from the practical perspective of the SBM. In doing so, we'll try to be more in tune with 1974 (and beyond) than with 1924. Because the industrial market is composed of many and varied subunits, the individual SBM should use this chapter only as a framework around which to build his own industrial marketing program.

NATURE AND CHARACTERISTICS OF INDUSTRIAL MARKETS

Introduction

In the previous chapter, it was stated that a market is composed of (1) *people* with (2) *money* and (3) a *willingness* to spend that money for satisfactions. We also stated that, in the industrial market, what we mean when we talk of *people* is a business firm, a governmental unit, or a private institution such as a school or church. More specialized industrial markets such as the farm market will not be specifically discussed here.

The industrial market is also known as the intermediate market. Its purchases are not for personal gratification but are for resale in one form or another. Such resales may be to other members of the industrial market and/or eventually to the consumer market. Thus, by industrial market, we mean the market for industrial goods and services. The *purpose* for which the goods or services are to be used is the determining criterion. For example, a ball-point pen to be used in an office would be considered an industrial good sold to the industrial market, while an identical ball-point pen sold to an elementary school child through a discount store would be considered a consumer good sold to the ultimate consumer market. Thus the manufacturer and marketer of ball-point pens (if he is selling to both markets) should consider himself to be a marketer both of consumer goods and of industrial goods. Such is the case even though his consumer markets are reached indirectly through intermediate sales to wholesalers and retailers. Our present chapter focuses on the industrial market from the perspective of the SBM. It should also be mentioned that this SBM could be, but need not necessarily be, a manufacturer or processor. He may be a distributor.

An Example Of Differences: Industrial vs. Consumer Markets

For the purposes of developing target market strategies, the segments of the industrial market are quite dissimilar from those found in the consumer market. Although no single customer is of great importance to many consumer goods marketers, consider the following:

At the other extreme, however, one industrial customer might have enough purchasing potential to comprise a market segment into itself. Take, for example, fiber glass insulation. United States Steel Corporation's 64-story office building in Pittsburgh required carloads of insulation. So did the World Trade Center in downtown New York. In such cases, each building can represent a market segment, but with a very definite time relationship—a segment opportunity that exists only once. (Once the insulation has been installed, that market segment ceases to exist, of course, as an outlet for the product.)

An added difference between consumer and industrial market segmentation is the complexity of the former. . . .[2]

Nature of Demand In Industrial Markets

The above example is illustrative of some of the differences existing in industrial markets. The major demand characteristics are inelastic demand, derived demand, and fluctuating demand.

By saying that demand in industrial markets is *inelastic,* we mean that total demand (for the industry) for a product will be affected very little by changes in price. However, the inelastic nature of demand is not so simple. (Neither is the whole concept of elasticity, which we will leave to the economists.) What we are saying here is that industrial markets tend to be less price sensitive in the quantities they demand. The individual industrial marketer who lowers his price may have very short-run gains in business until his competitors can retaliate. In the end, however, the industrial customers can only use so much. Why? Because their demand is derived ultimately from the consumer market. The relative inelasticity of an industrial product also depends on how large a percentage factor that product represents in a customer's cost structure. Generally, the less the cost of an industrial product as a percent of an industrial customer's finished goods, the more inelastic the demand for this industrial product will be. For example, an item making up only one percent of an industrial customer's cost structure would tend to be relatively inelastic in the eyes of that industrial customer.

Derived demand, as hinted above, is closely related to inelasticity of demand. It simply means that much of the demand of the industrial market is derived from the demand of the ultimate consumer market. Different types of industrial goods and services are affected somewhat differently due to the derived nature of demand. For example, the demand for component parts may be affected almost proportionately and immediately by changes in demand in the consumer markets. Installations are often long-range decisions based on long-range projections of demand in consumer markets. An apparently good marketing mix will not work well in the absence of demand. And the industrial marketer serving intermediate customers (derived demand) ultimately depends on the demand which those customers face. For this reason, large industrial marketers will sometimes attempt to stimulate consumer demand. However, such a strategy is probably not feasible for the SBM in the industrial field.

Fluctuating demand, that is, more widely fluctuating than in consumer markets, is characteristic of industrial markets. This follows from derived demand. The classic example is that of shoes (a consumer good) and shoe-making machinery (an industrial good). If the demand for shoes goes down a little (say 10%), the demand for machinery goes down very much, as shoe manufacturers see no need to replace machinery since they currently have excess capacity. Of course, this example is grossly oversimplified, but it does illustrate the point. Other reasons for wide fluctuations in demand are inventory adjustment of middlemen in anticipation of price changes, poor demand forecasting, bottlenecks, shortages, and poor economic forecasting.

[2]P. Dudley Kaley, "Market Segmentation Considerations," *Marketing Strategies,* ed. Earl L. Bailey (New York: The Conference Board, Inc., 1974), p. 57.

Classification of Industrial Products

The categories of industrial products (goods and services) traditionally used include, in McCarthy's terminology, (a) installations, (b) accessory equipment, (c) raw materials, (d) component parts and materials, (e) supplies, and (f) services.[3] Other authors have similar lists with similar definitions. The classification of consumer goods into such categories as convenience, shopping, specialty, and so forth is based largely upon the subjective buying behavior of individual consumers. This is not so in the case of industrial goods. For industrial markets, the classification of products is based largely on how the products are to be used. Thus industrial buyer behavior follows from anticipated use in a very direct sense. We would therefore expect industrial buyer behavior (discussed below) to differ among industrial product categories based upon anticipated use.

Classification of Industrial Markets

The total industrial market may be classified into subunits according to various purposes. As indicated above, our divisions will be business, government, and private institutions. Also, we have arbitrarily excluded the farm market as a separate category, although the farm market is certainly part of the industrial market.

The business sector will be described further using Standard Industrial Classification (SIC) codes. Special emphasis is also given later in this chapter to the topic of how SB can sell to government. Obviously, all these categories can be further subdivided in order to identify internally homogeneous and much more meaningful market segments.

Concentration Of Industrial Markets

In terms of both geography and size, industrial markets do tend to be concentrated. In manufacturing, the northeastern portion of the United States dominates. However, this is a macro approach and includes only total manufacturing as measured by value added or by number of employees. For a particular firm, SB or BB, the interest is not in the macro approach to geographic concentration. The individual firm wants to know only of the geographic location of its potential markets. Therefore, while total manufacturing data may indicate a geographic concentration closely paralleling the delegation voting strength at a national political convention, such a concentration may or may not be of interest to a specific industrial marketer. In any event, the industrial marketer is interested in geographic market patterns and trends for his specific targets.

Concentration by size of company also exists. Size concentration varies from industry to industry, as shown by the data in Table 5–1.

Size concentration does have marketing implications for the SBM. Such implications also hold in the government and institutional sectors of the industrial market. Regarding size concentration, a *Business Week* article stated:

But even before the recession hit, the apparent calm on the concentration front concealed the fact that the situation differs markedly between producer goods and consumer goods industries. Over the 1947–70 period, concentration in producer

[3]E. Jerome McCarthy, *Basic Marketing: A Managerial Approach* (Homewood, Illinois: Richard D. Irwin, Inc., 1975), p. 284.

Table 5–1 Percentage of Shipments by Large Manufacturing Companies in Selected Industries, 1972*

	Percentage of Total, Ranked by Company Size			
	4 Largest	*8 Largest*	*20 Largest*	*50 Largest*
Motor vehicles and car bodies	93**	99	99+	99+
Motor vehicle parts and accessories	61	69	78	86
Aircraft	66	86	99	99+
Photographic equipment and supplies	74	85	92	95
Electronic computing equipment	51	63	78	90
Tires and inner tubes	73	90	89	99+
Automotive stampings	69	72	79	87
Organic fibers, noncellulosic	74	91	99+	100
Soap and other detergents	62	74	85	92
Malt beverages	52	70	91	99
Aircraft engines and engine parts	77	87	94	97
Metal cans	66	79	92	99

*Source: U.S. Bureau of the Census, *Statistical Abstract of the United States: 1975* (96th edition; Washington, D.C., 1975), pp. 737–740.
**For example, this means that the 4 largest companies accounted for 93% of the shipments, that the 8 largest companies accounted for 99% of the shipments, and so forth.

goods actually declined, while rising substantially in many consumer-oriented industries. The reason, argues Mueller, is product differentiation—the use of advertising and other promotional methods to build up brand-name loyalty and generate higher profit margins.[4]

BUYER BEHAVIOR

Buyer behavior in the consumer market has been intensively studied by marketers, especially over the last decade. This topic, as it relates to the SBM, is the subject of the following chapter. Organizational buyer behavior (also called industrial buyer behavior) has not been as thoroughly investigated. Our purpose in this section is to give the SBM a limited exposure and a basis for developing his own framework for understanding organizational buying behavior. The SBM who is operating constantly in the industrial market should find it very beneficial to read the entire book, *Organizational Buying Behavior* by Webster and Wind.[5] These authors describe in detail a general model for understanding organizational buying behavior. In order for the SBM to market effectively to BB (and

[4]"Small Business: The Maddening Struggle to Survive," *Business Week*, No. 2387 (June 30, 1975), p. 99.
[5]Frederick E. Webster, Jr. and Yoram Wind, *Organizational Buying Behavior* (Englewood Cliffs, New Jersey: Prentice-Hall, Inc., 1972).

to other large organizations such as government and private institutions), it is imperative that the SBM understand buying behavior within the organizational setting. The same imperative applies when the SBM is selling to small and medium-sized organizational units. Organizational buying behavior probably differs by size of organization, but research in this area is rather meager.

Webster and Wind list the following characteristics of organizational buyer behavior:

First, and perhaps most important, organizational buying decisions are much more complex by the fact that more people usually are involved in them and different people are likely to play different buying roles. . . .

Second, organizational buying decisions often involve major technical complexities relating to the product or service being purchased. . . .

Third, organizational buying decisions typically take longer to make than consumer (individual) buying decisions. . . .

Fourth, the greater time required for organizational buying decisions means that there are significant lags between the application of marketing effort and obtaining a buying response. . . .

Fifth, each buying organization is likely to be significantly different from every other buying organization in the potential market in ways that may require viewing each organization as a separate market segment. . . .

Finally, the organizational members participating in the buying function are neither purely "economic men" nor are their motives purely emotional and irrational.[6]

Organizational buying is viewed by Webster and Wind as "a decision-making process carried out by individuals, in interaction with other people in the context of a formal organization."[7] They go on to say:

. . . Thus, the four classes of variables determining organizational buying behavior are *individual, social, organizational,* and *environmental.* Within each class, there are two broad categories of variables: Those directly related to the buying problem, called *task* variables; and those that extend beyond the buying problem, called *nontask* variables.[8]

To obtain a comprehensive understanding of organizational buying behavior is difficult even after reading many books and articles and after much practical experience. To expect a deep understanding from our brief treatment of the subject here would certainly be unrealistic. One more quote from Webster and Wind may add some more light. In their book, they state:

The organizational buying model presents a framework for analyzing and understanding organizational buying behavior. This provides the marketing personnel of firms whose customers are organizational buyers with guidelines for collecting and analyzing the required marketing information. This information ideally should cover four major aspects of organizational buying:

[6]Webster and Wind, pp. 6–7.
[7]Frederick E. Webster, Jr. and Yoram Wind, "A General Model for Understanding Organizational Buying Behavior," *Journal of Marketing,* 36 (April 1972), 13.
[8]Webster and Wind, "A General Model," p. 13.

1. The identity of the buying center;
2. The nature of the buying decision process;
3. The buying situation (new task versus modified rebuy versus straight rebuy);
4. The nature of the factors affecting the buying decisions—the environmental, organizational, interpersonal, and individual characteristics.

Knowing this information provides the marketing strategist with the necessary inputs to answer the following marketing questions:

1. Which market segment(s) should the firm pursue?
2. What should be the firm's marketing strategy concerning products, price, promotion (both personal and non-personal), and distribution?
3. How should the marketing function be managed? That is, how should marketing operations be organized, planned, implemented and controlled?
4. What should be the marketing research activities of the firm?[9]

The above discussion of organizational buying behavior takes the point of view of a general model. Others have researched some limited areas of buying behavior. A few will be cited for illustrative purposes. One controversial study dealt with attribute importance for different industrial products. Regardless of the tenability of this study's results, it is interesting to note the seventeen attributes rated by purchasing agents. They are:

1. Overall reputation of the supplier
2. Financing terms
3. Supplier's flexibility in adjusting to your company's needs
4. Experience with the supplier in analogous situations
5. Technical service offered
6. Confidence in the salesmen
7. Convenience of placing the order
8. Data on reliability of the product
9. Price
10. Technical specifications
11. Ease of operation or use
12. Preferences of principal user of the product
13. Training offered by the supplier
14. Training time required
15. Reliability of delivery date promised
16. Ease of maintenance
17. Sales service expected after date of purchase[10]

Another study selected four industrial market segments: consulting engineers, architects, electrical contractors, and nonresidential building contractors. After checking 48 advertising appeals, the study concluded "that advertisers to each of these market

---

[9]Frederick E. Webster, Jr. and Yoram Wind, *Organizational Buying Behavior* (Englewood Cliffs, New Jersey: Prentice-Hall, Inc., 1972), p. 110.

[10]Donald R. Lehmann and John O'Shaughnessy, "Difference in Attribute Importance for Different Industrial Products," *Journal of Marketing,* 38 (April 1974), 38.

segments *did not* correctly perceive the influence of advertising appeals upon the respective market segments concerned."[11] The advertising appeals compared were:[12]

1. Claims about the product itself (in general)
2. Dependability
3. Quality
4. Uniformity
5. Durability in use
6. Made to specifications
7. Made to standards
8. Ease of installation
9. Costs less to install
10. Economy in operation
11. Low maintenance cost or effort
12. Time saving in operation
13. Labor saving in operation
14. Cost saving in operation
15. Efficiency in operation
16. Ease of handling
17. Automatic operation
18. Increasing output
19. Increasing profits
20. Protection from irreparable loss in operation
21. Safety
22. Adaptability—the product is capable of being modified in order to make it fit a new use or situation
23. Flexibility—can meet new uses or situations by using the existing controls without modification
24. Portability—product can be physically transported easily
25. Simplicity in operation
26. Easy to repair
27. Educational information, such as how to select, use, store, maintain, evaluate, or install the product
28. Price
29. Newness of the product
30. Physical characteristics of product, such as weight, strength, appearance, and so forth
31. Physical features of the product, such as moisture resistance, corrosion resistance, and so forth
32. Product performance, such as more speed, power, quiet, and so forth
33. Claims about the seller of the product (in general)
34. Reliability of the seller
35. Research and development reputation of the seller
36. Ability to keep delivery promises

[11]McAleer, p. 22.
[12]McAleer, p. 18.

37. Ability to deliver product promptly
38. Complete line of products
39. Complete stocks are maintained
40. Engineering and design services are available
41. Dependable repair service is available
42. Claims about the market acceptance of the product (in general)
43. It is widely bought or used
44. It is widely specified
45. A testimonial by a buyer of the product
46. A testimonial by a specifier of the product
47. An announcement of a new installation
48. Claims about the container of the product

A third study, done on the nursing home industry, found similarity between consumer and industrial markets in regard to the subject of opinion leadership.

> Specifically, institutional opinion leaders were found to have significantly greater interpersonal interaction with administrative personnel of other nursing homes, and to be more likely to seek the advice of others, than nonleaders. It is reasonable to assume, then, that their social contacts serve as an arena for the two-way flow of communication—they both "supply and demand" information and advice. In addition to such informal communication encounters, the evidence indicates that opinion leaders judge their institutions as quicker to accept new products and services.
>
> For these reasons, the identification of those administrators who are opinion leaders might offer a dual payoff. First, if the institution is indeed more responsive to new products and services, then the probability is greater that it will be among the first purchasers of a new item that is perceived as worthwhile. Second, when the opinion leader meets with colleagues from other institutions he might stimulate interest and similar action on the part of those with whom he is in contact.[13]

Remember, that the studies cited above are partial studies and should be regarded as such. At the present state of the art, the individual SBM selling to the industrial market should (a) formulate his own general model of organizational buyer behavior; and then (b) fill in his general model, where possible, with research and experience bearing on the specific industrial target markets he wishes to serve.

HOW TO SEGMENT INDUSTRIAL MARKETS

Segmentation strategy for industrial markets is analogous to that of consumer markets (See Chapter 4). It is also true for industrial marketers that the most basic and most important strategic marketing problem facing the SBM is the proper definition and selection of each of his target markets. Segmentation can facilitate the solution of this problem.

[13]Leon G. Schiffman and Vincent Gaccione, "Opinion Leaders in Institutional Markets," *Journal of Marketing*, 38 (April 1974), 53.

Bases Of Segmentation

A comprehensive book entitled *Market Segmentation* states, "Recent texts and articles on industrial marketing (Alexander, Cross & Hill, 1967; Rowe & Alexander, 1968; Wilson, 1968; Dodge, 1970) . . . include at best no more than brief mention of market segmentation. Yet, since the concept of segmentation is a logical outgrowth of the marketing concept and of economic theory, it is at least as applicable. . . ."[14] The only real differences between using segmentation in industrial versus consumer markets are the bases or dimensions upon which market segments are based. Industrial customers who respond in homogeneous fashion to the mix of the industrial marketer are aggregated to form a market segment.

Two sets of bases are advocated by Frank et al. when segmenting industrial markets. These two sets are used in combination. The two sets are called (a) general organizational characteristics and (b) situation-specific organizational characteristics. Bases from both the general set and the situation-specific set would be used together in the process of defining any market segment. Although we are oversimplifying here, let's adopt these two sets of bases. Within the first base, that is, the *general* set, we have two subsets: (1) demographics; and (2) task, structure, and technology. Demographics includes such bases as size, SIC code, end use of product, geography, and so forth. The task, structure, and technology subset (which is often used by industrial salesmen, but not by segmentation strategists) includes segmenting according to variables in (a) the buying task, (b) the buying structure, and (c) the buying technology. Thus, from the general set, we most often use demographics such as SIC codes and geography. Among the *situation-specific* set, our second base, we find the following possible bases of segmentation directed towards various suppliers: product usage, degree of source loyalty, nature of the buying center, the buying situation (e.g. new task, straight rebuy, or modified rebuy), buying center attitudes, and so on.[15]

From the above listing and sublisting of bases (or dimensions) for segmenting industrial markets, it appears that no shortage exists. As with consumer market segmentation, the real art is to choose the significant bases and then to gather appropriate marketing information in order to make such segments operational as target markets. Because of its extreme popularity as a part of most segmentation strategies, we'll now take a brief look at the SIC code as one base of industrial market segmentation.

The SIC Code

The Bureau of the Budget of the federal government has classified the industrial market into ten (A through J) Divisions which have been further subdivided into Major Groups (two-digit classifications), and then again subdivided into three- and/or four-digit classifications. The ten Divisions are:[16]

---

[14]Ronald E. Frank, William F. Massy, and Yoram Wind, *Market Segmentation* (Englewood Cliffs, New Jersey: Prentice-Hall, Inc., 1972), p. 91.

[15]Frank, Massy, and Wind, pp. 91–102.

[16]For complete details, see the *Standard Industrial Classification Manual,* most recent edition, printed by the U. S. Government Printing Office, Washington, D.C.

A. Agriculture, Forestry, and Fisheries
B. Mining
C. Contract Construction
D. Manufacturing
E. Transportation, Communications, Electric, Gas, and Sanitary Services
F. Wholesale and Retail Trade
G. Finance, Insurance, and Real Estate
H. Services
I. Government
J. Nonclassifiable Establishments

The SIC code is classified by establishment, not by the entire company. The basis of classification and assignment to an industry code for each establishment is its *major* activity, that is, products produced or handled, or services rendered. An example of SIC codes in the "Services" industry is:

Two digit   — 70 Hotels, Rooming Houses, Camps, and Other Lodging Places
Three digit   — 708 Trailer Parks and Camps
Four digit   — 7081 Trailer Parks
                      7082 Sporting and Recreational Camps

SIC codes may be used along with much government data (arranged according to SIC codes) to define market segments and estimate market potential. The use of SIC codes among industrial marketers is not new. For example, in 1954 Hummel described the use of SIC codes to estimate market potentials in the machine tool industry.[17]

Although SIC codes are probably one of the most frequently used bases of industrial market segmentation, they are most often used in combination with other bases such as geographic units. From that point, the situation-specific bases of segmentation might be employed to meet individual needs. Keeping good marketing records in terms of the SIC code does have other advantages in terms of marketing research, sales analysis, and other activity areas of marketing.

Prospecting

Presented here are brief ideas for identifying new business and recapturing business from present or past accounts. These simple, unsophisticated ideas can be used by even the smallest SBM in the industrial market. Hummel, mentioned above, states:

Once the composition of the industrial market is determined—that is, the industries having use for the product, the number of plants in each industry, and the relative market values of each industry—marketing research can utilize this information to pinpoint those industrial concerns that have a use for the product or that afford the greatest probability of becoming a new account. These prospects must be defined by names and addresses of companies—not merely percentage or dollar figure by areas—so that field salesmen can call for specific follow-up.

[17]Francis E. Hummel, "Market Potentials In The Machine Tool Industry—A Case Study," *Journal of Marketing,* 19 (July 1954), 34–41.

There are four major areas where marketing research can determine industrial concerns that have a high probability of becoming new industrial prospects—by use of (1) industrial directories, (2) surveys, (3) trade-show attendance lists, and (4) advertising and promotional inquiries.[18]

Our second prospecting idea comes from an *SBA Management Aid*.[19] Here, the author shows how to develop a simple customer profile for each account based upon the following information:

1. An industrial indentification, preferably an SIC number.
2. Number of employees.
3. Customer's name.
4. Sales for the current year.
5. Sales in dollars for each of the previous years.
6. The difference between sales in the current year and those in the poorest of the previous years.
7. The difference between sales in the current year and those in the best of the previous years.

Of course, the exact information needs may vary from one SBM to another. The *Management Aid* then presents key questions and methods of simple analysis which the SBM can perform with the above data. These are presented under such topics as reviewing your present market, looking for hidden sales trends, magnifying the source of gains, penetrating your present market, and so forth.

TARGET MARKET STRATEGY FOR SB IN THE INDUSTRIAL MARKET

Much of what was said in Chapter 4 concerning target market strategy (in the consumer market) is also applicable for the industrial market. The principles of market simplification for SB and market dominance for SB certainly apply to the industrial market. The SB industrial marketer is also interested in the optimum market share of each market segment in which he operates. The application of some of these basics will differ slightly in the industrial market. For example, if a single industrial customer is viewed as a complete market segment, the optimum share question may be rephrased: What percentage of this customer's total requirements for product X should we attempt to supply? Or, an alternate question may arise in order to avoid the captive supplier problem: What percentage of our total output of product X should be sold to any single customer?

The steps in locating a target market are also somewhat different in application in the industrial market. However, by comparing the SIC example of this chapter with the five-step process quoted in Chapter 4 on the consumer market, one notes many similarities in the general process.

---

[18]Francis E. Hummel, "Pinpointing Prospects For Industrial Sales," *Readings In Basic Marketing,* eds. E. Jerome McCarthy, John F. Grashof, and Andrew A. Brogowicz (Homewood, Illinois: Richard D. Irwin, Inc., 1975), p. 128.

[19]James E. Gulick, "Profile Your Customers To Expand Industrial Sales," *Management Aids,* No. 192 (Washington: Small Business Administration, 1968).

The extensive discussion of target markets for SB in Chapter 4 is certainly applicable for industrial marketing. Some industrial market segments do exist which are more attractive than others to SB. In the industrial field, it is also true that SB marketers and BB marketers possess different inherent advantages and disadvantages in regard to reaching and serving different market segments. Therefore, some industrial market segments are more attractive to SB than to BB. In Chapter 4, "attractive" market segments were listed under the following classifications: (1) market-related targets according to market characteristics, (2) market-related targets according to consumer behavior, (3) targets according to the marketing mix variables, and (4) targets according to environmental variables. With the exception of #2 above, where the words *organizational buyer behavior* would be substituted for *consumer behavior,* the listings on Chapter 4 can be very applicable to the industrial market.

A review of Chapter 4 in its entirety is strongly suggested for the reader who is interested in determining target market strategy for the SBM in the industrial market. As has been stated more than once above, the proper identification and definition of each of his target markets is probably the most *important* and most *basic* strategic marketing problem facing the SBM. It is amazing to find so many SB firms (perhaps not SB marketers) which have failed to recognize the problem, let alone attempt to solve it. On the other hand, most successful firms (marketers) have based sound marketing strategies on well-defined markets. This is true for both SB and BB in both the consumer and industrial markets.

In addition to SB manufacturers selling to the industrial market, there are various middlemen (many of whom are small) selling to the industrial market. An excellent example is the industrial distributor. Why do industrial customers purchase from industrial distributors? Alexander et al. give the following reasons:

1. The distributor is usually able to deliver goods quicker than the manufacturer.
2. The distributor may reduce the buyer's purchasing costs and paperwork.
3. In some instances, the distributor can deliver goods at lower prices than if the industrial buyer purchases direct.
4. Adjustments can be made more easily with the distributor.
5. A savings on incoming freight costs may result from using the distributor.
6. The distributor may sometimes serve as a quick source of general product information.
7. To the small buyer, the distributor may represent a reasonably liberal source of credit.
8. Geographic proximity of the distributor and his salesmen, and frequent customer visits results in a type of service which cannot be duplicated by many manufacturers.[20]

The same authors list the following general circumstances in which the industrial distributor is likely to command the patronage of the industrial buyer:

1. The small plant is compelled to purchase many items from the distributor. . . .
2. The large industrial plant is likely to depend on the distributor as a source of supply for emergency items. . . .

[20]Ralph S. Alexander, James S. Cross, and Richard M. Hill, *Industrial Marketing* (Homewood, Illinois: Richard D. Irwin, Inc., 1967), pp. 223–226.

3. The buyer for a large plant may look to the industrial distributor as a source from which to obtain articles he must purchase in amounts so small that he cannot hope to enjoy quantity discounts in their purchase. . . .

4. Even the large firms must buy from the distributor some articles it purchases in substantial quantities. . . .

5. In procuring some articles, the large industrial buyer can save more through buying from distributors who can give quick delivery, thereby keeping his inventories at a minimum, than by purchasing in large lots at quantity discounts direct from the manufacturer.[21]

Up to this point, we have considered target market strategy for the SBM in the industrial market in respect to competitive markets. It should also be mentioned that the innovative SBM is welcome to create new market opportunities in the industrial field. One marketer suggests looking at the "sleepers" or "nonmarkets" such as the market for left-handed shears and other tools. *The Wall Street Journal* featured an article on a woman who became a consultant as a "neatness expert" to help "messy" business people better organize themselves.[22]

SB SELLS TO GOVERNMENT

Introduction

A large and increasing portion of the gross national product (GNP) of this country is the result of government rather than private spending. Although, collectively, government may be viewed as the largest consumer of goods and services, there are many government buying and consuming units. Within each of the levels of government (federal, state, local, and international) distinct market segments do exist. Our brief remarks here will concentrate on the U.S. federal government. As part of the industrial (or intermediate) market, government is similar in many respects to the remainder of the industrial market. However, the SB industrial marketer who wishes to sell to government should not overlook the unique buying rigidities of governmental units.

The SBM should regard each governmental purchaser as a separate target market for which a separate marketing mix is developed. Marketing help is available from government publications and trade associations for the SBM interested in government as a market. As with any target market, the SBM should regard the government target markets as markets with specific needs and competitive alternatives for filling these needs. In other words, government is the customer. The marketer, and not the customer, will have to adapt. The marketer must say to government customers, just as Burger King says to its customers, "Have it your way. . . ."

In this section, our purpose is to describe the U.S. "qualified products lists" briefly, to examine the extent to which SB has participated in selling to the U.S. government, and to examine some unique market opportunities for SB to sell to the U.S. government.

---

[21]Alexander, Cross, and Hill, p. 227.

[22]Roger Ricklefs, "A 'Neatness Expert' Tidies Up After All The Rest of Us Slobs," *Wall Street Journal,* March 3, 1975, p. 1.

The Qualified Products Lists

Many SB marketers undoubtedly avoid selling to government because they feel it simply isn't worth the bother. Government segments do take some investment of time, money, and effort for market development. An example of this is the qualified products list. Such qualification is *not* a routine requirement for government specifications. In fact, such pretesting before bidding exists in only a small percentage of the cases. For example, the life expectancy of a storage battery can be easily pretested in order to avoid delays later on. For such products, qualification is often used as part of the purchasing procedure. To assist the SBM in getting his product on the lists, the SBA has prepared a *Management Aid,* the summary of which states:

> Most items which the Federal Government buys are purchased on the basis of standard specifications. Some of these items have to pass tests before the Government can undertake any action and award a contract. When such items have passed the test, they are put on a qualified products list.
>
> This *Aid* discusses what is involved in getting a product on a federal agency's *qualified products list.* This *Aid* does not set rules which must be followed. Rather, its purpose is to give owner-managers of small plants an idea of what might be expected of them.
>
> The requirements for each individual item may vary. Before a small manufacturer invests his time and money into qualifying a product, he should check with the Government agency or activity responsible for qualification.[23]

The *Aid* has anticipated and answered most of the questions the SBM (manufacturer or distributor) will face in getting his products on the list. Such questions are: which products must be qualified, what the lists mean, when lists are open, what the lists contain, steps in getting on lists, laboratory testing, and removal from lists. The SBA will also provide other forms of assistance to the SBM wishing to sell to government.

Extent of SB Participation
In The Government Market

Here again, our concern is with the federal government. "Uncle Sam" wanted small business as a supplier primarily out of necessity due to war. Recent government–SB relations prior to the creation of the SBA have been described as follows:

> In 1942, during World War II, the Smaller War Plants Corporation was established to mobilize the production capacity of small business firms and to determine the means by which such firms could be most efficiently organized for war production. In 1946 the SWPC lending authority was transferred to the Reconstruction Finance Corporation, an agency created in 1932 to help pull the nation out of the depression.
>
> Then, in 1951, a second, temporary small business agency was created—the Small Defense Plants Administration—to assist in the participation of small firms in

---

[23]"Getting Your Product On Qualified Products Lists," *Management Aids,* No. 42 (Washington: Small Business Administration, 1970).

defense production for the Korean War. However, its lending authority was limited to recommending firms to the RFC. When the SDPA started phasing out, Congress was reluctant to let die the idea of assistance to small business.

Several bills were introduced providing for federal machinery to enable small business to make a full contribution to the American economy.

The outcome was legislation, signed into effect by President Eisenhower on July 30, 1953, creating the present day Small Business Administration.[24]

Two major areas of government procurement are defense and space. In these areas, the total amount of business available to SB is influenced by the ability and willingness of large prime contractors to subcontract to SB. Evidence indicates that large prime contractors, as well as government agencies, are making more than a token effort to buy from SB.

SBA has plenty of help in its goals. Major government purchasers from the aerospace industry, such as the Department of Defense and the National Aeronautics and Space Administration, have established specialized staff offices throughout their commands and centers for the purpose of enhancing the small business share of government procurement.

Harvard W. Powell, Director of the Defense Department's Small Business and Economic Utilization Policy Office, states: "The Defense Department remains firmly dedicated to assuring that the small business community receives a fair share of its (DOD) procurement awards. During Fiscal Year 1974, the Defense Department spent $34.5 billion with U.S. business firms of which small business received $7 billion. . . .

Robert Anderson, President and Chief Executive Officer of Rockwell International, a major prime aerospace contractor, reports:

"In the past two years, an average of 33 percent of our purchase dollars under all government contracts was awarded to small business firms. This amounted to $154 million in 1974." This record is not unlike those found throughout the aerospace industry.

Regarding minority enterprises, Anderson said: "Last year our purchases from minority-owned business climbed to $9 million—a 300 percent increase in just three years. Looking ahead, we have projected that more than $50 million will be placed with minority businesses over the next five years." He added that prime contractor support of small and minority businesses makes sense because it helps maintain the broadly diversified industrial capacity needed by our government and industry.[25]

Obviously, the material in the preceeding paragraphs is of great interest to certain types of SB firms and of practically no interest to others. SB firms are many and varied in size and interests. The very small firm is considered SB along with some SB firms of fairly substantial size, according to the latest official definitions of SB by the SBA.

Some interesting insights into the government market for SB were gained by the author while supervising a research project for one of his graduate students. These insights are shared in the remainder of this chapter in a generalized and undocumented format.[26]

[24]"A Salute to Small Business: 'The Gateway To Opportunity'," *Aerospace Perspectives*, 4, No. 2, published by the Aerospace Industries Association (May 1975).
[25]"A Salute to Small Business."
[26]The author wishes to thank his former MBA student, Mark Benton, for his contribution to this material in the form of an unpublished research paper.

Where determined to be competent by the federal government, SB may bid against BB for government business. In addition, certain business is "set aside" for SB. The SBA has also acted as a prime contractor in subcontracting "Section 8a" business to minority business persons. The effectiveness of those programs and various other government procurement programs has varied.

In some cases, when invited to do so, SB did not bid. In the Department of Defense (DOD), such was the case for approximately six percent of the total defense expenditure. What were the reasons for this apparent lack of interest? SBA officials conjectured that SB sometimes became discouraged by bid requirements, unavailability of specifications and other information, and so forth. On the contrary, government contracting officers felt that the major reason for not bidding was lack of interest in the particular procurement. They felt that size and technology limitations, along with restrictive covenants of government contracts (minimum wages, OSHA, etc.), diminished interest in bidding.

In other cases, SB did bid but was not the low bid. As a percentage of total DOD awards to all firms, this condition existed for about six to eight percent of total dollars spent.

SB has in fact won much business from DOD. Over the years, SB has won about twelve to seventeen percent of DOD total dollar awards to all firms. SB has also won about five percent of DOD total dollar awards to all firms, on the basis of SB "set-asides." In total, then, SB has won about seventeen to twenty-two percent of DOD business. These figures are, of course, totals. They do not reveal that much of the success of SB has been in the areas of supplies and services.

"Set-asides" are those federal government procurements which may be set aside for SB and on which BB will be excluded from bidding. In effect, then, SB competes only with SB for these contracts. As mentioned above, SB has won about five percent of DOD total dollar awards to all firms, on the basis of "set-asides." An underlying assumption of set-asides is that SB firms operating under such contracts will (a) also seek government contracts not reserved under the set-aside program and (b) compete in the private market segment. This does not always happen. Often, the reason it doesn't happen is because the SB firms are so satisfied with the one contract that long-range growth objectives are ignored. Another reason may be that the one contract is so unique in its requirements that carry-over to other contracts or to the private sector is difficult.

Minority business is another interest of government procurement. Under what is referred to as "Section 8a subcontracting," the SBA, acting as the prime contractor, can enter into contracts with federal agencies for supplies and services. These contracts are then awarded to minority firms for performance. The program has not been without publicity and controversy. In contrast to the "set-aside" program, the "8a" program removes some procurement from the competitive process to the point that nonminority SB firms cannot bid. This has had an adverse effect on some SB firms. In some cases, the SBA has approached minority employees and has attempted to establish them as "8a" contractors for the same work for which their former employers had been competitively bidding. A natural resentment on the part of these SB firms resulted. Another criticism of "8a" is that some SB minority firms chose the more protected "8a" program when they could have qualified for competitive forms of government contracts. In other words, incentive to improve was lacking. As in many "crash" programs, implementation of the program was taking place, by necessity, before all the ramifications of the program could be seen.

In conclusion, there are many possible target markets for SB in the government market. This is true at all levels of government. The individual SBM must determine which of these possible targets represent good opportunities for him in this uniquely competitive part of the industrial market.

BIBLIOGRAPHY

Books

ALEXANDER, RALPH S., CROSS, JAMES S., and HILL, RICHARD M. *Industrial Marketing.* Homewood, Illinois: Richard D. Irwin, Inc., 1967.

FRANK, RONALD E., MASSY, WILLIAM F., and WIND, YORAM. *Market Segmentation.* Englewood Cliffs, New Jersey: Prentice-Hall, Inc., 1972.

McCARTHY, E. JEROME. *Basic Marketing: A Managerial Approach.* Homewood, Illinois: Richard D. Irwin, Inc., 1975.

U. S. Bureau of the Budget. *Standard Industrial Classification.* Washington: U. S. Government Printing Office, 1967.

WEBSTER, FREDERICK E., JR., AND WIND, YORAM. *Organizational Buying Behavior.* Englewood Cliffs, New Jersey: Prentice-Hall, Inc., 1972.

Articles and Periodicals

"Getting Your Product On Qualified Products Lists," *Management Aids,* No. 42 Washington: Small Business Administration, 1970, pp. 1–4.

GULICK, JAMES E. "Profile Your Customers To Expand Industrial Sales," *Management Aids,* No. 192 Washington: Small Business Administration, 1968, pp. 1–8.

HUMMEL, FRANCIS E. "Market Potentials In The Machine Tool Industry—A Case Study," *Journal of Marketing,* 19 (July 1954), pp. 34–41.

HUMMEL, FRANCIS E. "Pinpointing Prospects For Industrial Sales," in E. Jerome McCarthy, John F. Grashof, and Andrew A. Brogowicz, eds., *Readings In Basis Marketing.* Homewood, Illinois: Richard D. Irwin, Inc., 1975, pp. 125–133.

KALEY, P. DUDLEY. "Market Segmentation Considerations," in Earl L. Bailey, ed., *Marketing Strategies.* New York: The Conference Board, Inc., 1974, pp. 56–59.

LEHMANN, DONALD R., and O'SHAUGHNESSY, JOHN. "Difference in Attribute Importance for Different Industrial Products," *Journal of Marketing,* 38 (April 1974), 36–42.

McALEER, GORDON. "Do Industrial Advertisers Understand What Influences Their Markets?" *Journal of Marketing,* 38 (January 1974), 15–23.

RICKLEFS, ROGER. "A 'Neatness Expert' Tidies Up After All The Rest of Us Slobs," *Wall Street Journal,* March 3, 1975, p. 1.

"A Salute to Small Business: 'The Gateway To Opportunity'," *Aerospace Perspectives,* 4, No. 2 (May 1975).

SCHIFFMAN, LEON G., AND GACCIONE, VINCENT. "Opinion Leaders in Institutional Markets," *Journal of Marketing,* 38 (April 1974), 49–53.

"Small Business: The Maddening Struggle to Survive," *Business Week,* No. 2387 (June 30, 1975), pp. 96–101 and p. 104.

WEBSTER, FREDERICK E., JR., and WIND, YORAM. "A General Model for Understanding Organizational Buying Behavior," *Journal of Marketing,* 36 (April 1972), 12–19.

6

Consumer Behavior Affects SB

IMPORTANCE OF UNDERSTANDING CONSUMER BEHAVIOR

The successful SBM is truly an advanced student of buyer behavior. More specifically, if he sells to the consumer market, he is a student of consumer behavior. Success, in the absence of understanding the consumer, is not likely. The expertise of the successful SBM in the consumer behavior portion of human behavior would no doubt rival the expertise of many psychologists and sociologists. However, the most successful SBM would probably be among the first to admit a deficiency in his understanding of the consumer.

A real danger can exist among SB marketers if they neglect a methodical study of the consumer. This danger may be especially prone to haunt the "very small" of the SB marketers because they say to themselves with false confidence, "I know my customers." "Knowing your customers" is certainly an advantage enjoyed by many SB firms, but it is not the same thing as understanding consumer behavior. In addition to knowing *who* the market is, the SBM will want to answer such questions as *when, what, where, how,* and last but not least *why.* Can the SBM who thinks he "knows his customers" really give satisfactory answers to these questions? Can he answer the questions for potential customers? Customers and consumers are not the same. Is he aware of this? And, very important to success, if the SBM can answer the above questions, does he have an adequate framework within which he can use this information in an orderly fashion to aid in developing successful marketing strategies for those target markets he wishes to serve?

In this chapter, we will briefly study consumer behavior by using a framework which fits very well into our SBMM model presented in Chapter 3. This consumer behavior framework fits the center "C" pentagon of our SBMM model. It deals with the consumer market. Industrial market behavior was discussed in Chapter 5. Our coverage is

87

necessarily brief and incomplete. The reader should therefore approach the chapter with two basic objectives: (1) to gain exposure to some of the fundamental ideas concerning consumer behavior, and (2) to develop his own practical and more comprehensive framework for understanding consumer behavior with special reference to his specific target market interests.

A FRAMEWORK FOR CONSUMER BEHAVIOR

The consumers patronizing BB and SB are often the same people. Even when they are not the exact same people, their *basic* human behavior (and consumer behavior) does not differ much from BB to SB. Thus, even though some nonbasic differences may exist, the framework for understanding consumer behavior is equally applicable to both BB and SB. On a per customer basis, the understanding of consumer behavior may be more important to SB than to BB (because the SBM has fewer customers, each of which makes up a greater proportion of his total market), but the topic is equally vital to marketers of all sizes serving consumer markets.

The model (or framework) of consumer behavior presented here is adapted from Walters (1974 edition) as developed in the 1970 edition by Walters and Paul.[1] The static representation of this model has been adapted to fit the SBMM model and is reproduced as Figure 6–1, below. Most readers would find it worthwhile to read a consumer behavior book from cover to cover. Recent years have produced several good books on the subject of consumer behavior.

As can be seen from Figure 6–1, the consumer behavior model is composed of (1) a purchase strategy, immediately surrounded by (2) individual influences, and then bounded by (3) environmental influences. This model is similar in many ways to our SBMM model in Chapter 3; however, we promise not to conceptualize to the point we did in Chapter 3. In our view, the consumer, like the SBM, is a strategist. How does the consumer formulate, execute, and control purchase strategy? The SBM wants to know (not so he can oppose the consumer) in order to help the consumer to achieve his or her goals while at the same time enabling the SBM to serve that target market at a profit. Thus, understanding consumer behavior is putting the marketing concept into practice.

In distinguishing among terms such as *consumer, purchaser, influencer, customer,* and *user* our main purpose is to avoid confusion. This may be impossible, because the meanings do overlap. Our most comprehensive term is *consumer.* The consumer is the *purchaser,* that is, the purchase decision maker if not also the actual purchasing agent. If the consumer is an actual rather than merely a potential consumer, and if he patronizes a product or a firm, he is a *customer* for that product or firm. If the consumer or someone else physically or otherwise consumes the product or service, he is the *user.* A consumer may or may not be a user. One who influences a consumer (and this role is important in much consumer decision-making) is an *influencer.* Some persons play multiple roles. For example, the *user* who physically or otherwise consumes the product or service may also act as an *influencer* on the *consumer.* Try some concrete examples to further add to the confusion. What are the

---

[1]The original model presented in C. Glenn Walters and Gordon W. Paul, *Consumer Behavior: An Integrated Framework* (Homewood, Illinois: Richard D. Irwin, 1970), p. 16 has been modified somewhat in later writings by Walters. For ease of understanding, our adaptation is based on the 1970 model, although insight was also gained from C. Glenn Walters, *Consumer Behavior: Theory and Practice* (Homewood, Illinois: Richard D. Irwin, 1974) and numerous other sources.

roles of the (1) baby who refuses to eat the baby food purchased at the supermarket by the (2) father from a list prepared by the (3) mother?

As part of human behavior, consumer behavior is a very complex subject. Our model, adapted from Walters and Paul, is necessarily an oversimplification of reality. From a dynamic decision process point of view, as implied by the use of the term *behavior,* Walters and Paul state:

> The process begins when the consumer is made aware of some deficiency in his assortment of goods.
>
> The stimulus causes the basic determinants to go into action, and the thought process begins. The consumer perceives his needs and becomes aware of a motive for acting. Attitudes structure his thoughts about what should be done about the problem. Thus, the consumer begins to develop his purchase strategy based on his internal determinants. These basic determinants have already been influenced by the environment, but as the individual develops strategy, he may seek further advice and guidance from the environment. He may, for example, ask for a family's opinion, and at some point he will probably obtain the opinion of a salesman. Once a course of action has been decided upon, the consumer takes action on his decision.
>
> The process ends when the problem created by the stimulus is resolved and the assortment is back in equilibrium. If the consumer is dissatisfied, feedback causes the person to begin searching for another solution. The result, whether satisfaction or dissatisfaction, becomes a part of the consumer's future decisions as experience. In a real sense, the process never ends, because most consumers are always in some state of disequilibrium. Communications is the vital link that ties the basic determinants to the environment.[2]

The paragraphs quoted directly above summarize the dynamic process of consumer behavior. They should probably be reread for additional insights after reading the rest of this chapter. These brief paragraphs, along with Figure 6–1, are the framework of consumer behavior which will be discussed and expanded upon in the rest of this Chapter.

CONSUMER PURCHASE STRATEGY

Our view of the consumer is one which recognizes that although he is often influenced by emotions, the consumer is a normal and rational decision maker. This normal consumer faced with unlimited wants, limited time and money, and inadequate information and training is rarely operating under ideal circumstances. In a manner similar to that of the SBM, the consumer resorts to a strategy in order to make the best of the situation. The consumer purchase strategy consists of two major types of decisions: (1) the determination of a target assortment and (2) market-related decisions concerning specific actions to provide the assortment.[3] Target assortment decisions involve both short and long run decisions made in determining the product(s) desired by the consumer. The target assortment is that ever-changing combination of products and services necessary to satisfy the consumer. While decision making is a continuous process and takes place wherever the consumer happens to be, assortment decisions are more likely to be home-

---

[2]C. Glenn Walters and Gordon W. Paul, *Consumer Behavior* (Homewood, Illinois: Richard D. Irwin, Inc., 1970), p. 18.

[3]See Walters, Chapters 24–29 for a complete discussion.

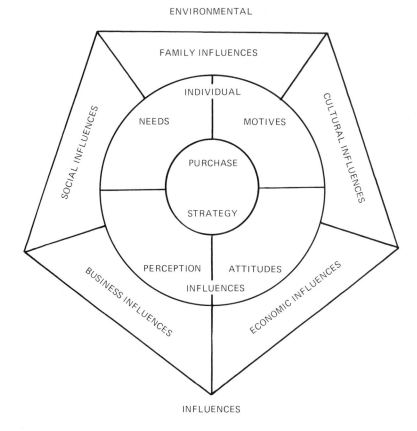

Figure 6–1   A Model of Consumer Behavior.

Source: Adapted from Walters and Paul, p. 16. Used with permission.

related and specific action decisions tend to be market-related. Market-related decisions (or purchase tactics) involve how the consumer will relate to the market in order to obtain the goods and services desired.

Determining Target Assortment

The six steps in assortment planning are: (1) Make an inventory of personal product requirements; (2) evaluate assortment deficiencies; (3) determine individual product preferences; (4) negotiate assortment preferences among family members; (5) order family preferences; and (6) determine purchase responsibility.[4] These six steps are somewhat of an ideal model. In actual practice, the consumer may perform this goal-setting mental activity by changing the sequence of steps, or in some cases, by completely eliminating certain steps. Also, the degree of formality in various steps may vary. For example, some

[4]Walters and Paul, p. 160.

assortment deficiencies will appear on a written shopping list; others will not. Another example of variation would be the differences in family negotiation depending on such factors as family structure, size, compatibility, and so on. Likewise, the determination of purchase responsibility will vary according to such factors as type of product, family organization, and purchase competence.

Development of Market-Related Purchase Tactics

The consumer is now ready to enter the marketplace to fill the assortment needs. Remember, our logical sequencing may vary in practice. The numerous market-related decisions for which consumers develop purchase tactics involve what, when, where, and how to buy. A logical series of steps for the market-related portion of the consumer purchase strategy is: (1) problem recognition, (2) search for information, (3) evaluation of information, (4) purchase decision, and (5) postpurchase evaluation.[5]

The problem recognition step ties together assortment decisions and market-related decisions. Whereas assortment decisions involve general categories of consumer needs and the ordering of priorities, the problem recognition step gets down to specifics. Problem recognition involves purchasing decisions dealing with specific brands, prices, and retail outlets. Problem recognition takes place anytime the consumer is undecided as to how to proceed regarding a market situation. Problems are not always recognized. Once the problem is recognized, the consumer can proceed.

Information search is both the mental and physical activity involved in obtaining market-related data. Information may come from past experiences, stored in the mind of the consumer. External information sources include nonbusiness sources such as reference groups and business sources such as store visits and observation, personal salesmen, and advertising. The amount and type of search behavior will vary.

For step 3, in Walters's words:

> *Information evaluation* is a group of consumer activities undertaken to determine and compare alternative solutions to market-related problems. The problems considered may include selecting product or brands, stores, services, methods of search, or purchase timing, to name a few. Evaluation takes the consumer right up to the point of making a decision on a course of action. The decision itself is not a part of evaluation.
>
> The definition of evaluation suggests that there are four steps necessary in evaluation: (1) systematize information, (2) establish decision criteria, (3) determine type alternatives, and (4) compare alternatives.[6]

The purchase decision is the making of a selection from the available alternatives. Such a selection, which is usually not easy, involves the areas of product decisions, store decisions, and method of purchase decisions. Product decisions include brand decisions, such as whether to use a private label or a nationally advertised brand; price and deal decisions, such as whether or not to use a coupon; and impulse decisions. Store decisions include the choice of store, such as a large or a small store; display and shelf decisions, such as buying the product displayed at eye level; and store layout decisions. Method of purchase decisions include such factors as telephone purchasing, consumer attitudes

---

[5]C. Glenn Walters, *Consumer Behavior* (Homewood, Illinois: Richard D. Irwin, Inc., 1974), p. 483.

[6]Walters, p. 546.

toward time and distance, and multiple purpose shopping trips. The complexity of the consumer purchase decision can be seen by reviewing the items listed in this paragraph and by noting the incompleteness and lack of detail in the breakdown.

Postpurchase evaluation is feedback. As such, it may be viewed as the final step in one market-related decision process and as the beginning of another as new problem recognition results. Whether formal or informal, the postpurchase evaluation may produce favorable, unfavorable, or mixed feedback. Experience gained from the purchase process is likely to result in some change in the consumer's behavior.

The above brief outline of consumer purchase strategy is a good general framework, but it is obviously an incomplete oversimplification. In order to make this framework more complete, but hopefully not much more complex, we now look to the individual influences which affect consumer behavior: needs, motives, perceptions, and attitudes. Later on, we will also consider the environmental influences on consumer behavior.

BASIC DETERMINANTS:
INDIVIDUAL INFLUENCES ON CONSUMER BEHAVIOR

The basic determinants of consumer behavior—needs, motives, perceptions, and attitudes—are those influences within each individual that affect human behavior. Although these influences have been intensively studied by psychologists and others, considerable disagreement does exist among the experts; and many of the research findings are more exploratory than conclusive. In spite of these shortcomings, we'll survey some of the more popular ideas concerning the individual influences.

Walters and Paul give the following definitions and examples of the basic determinants:[7]

1. A *need* is the lack of something useful, required, or desired. It is a condition requiring relief.
2. A *motive* is an impulse that causes one to do something or act in a certain way. By making us aware of our needs, motives give us a reason for action.
3. *Perception* is the particular awareness or observation one gives to objects or ideas through the senses.
4. *Attitude* means a broad group of innate human feelings or points of view that pattern human behavior. The relationship of these four basic determinants may be illustrated thus:

Basic Determinant and Example

Need: Clothing
Motives: Warmth and Style
Perception: See Ski Jacket
Attitude: Appears Warm & Stylish
Objective: Wear Ski Jacket

The individual consumer is the basic unit of consumer decision making. The basic determinants are tied together differently in each consumer according to his self-concept. Now let's briefly examine each of the four determinants.

[7]Walters and Paul, p.14.

Needs

The recognition of a felt need is the starting point in the decision process. Since the consumer is faced with several needs, it is necessary that he be given a reason to act on the need. The reason to act is called a motive. Needs have both physiological and psychological dimensions. The most widely used listing of needs identified the following types in a hierarchical ordering:

1. Physiological needs.
2. Safety needs.
3. Belongingness and love needs.
4. Esteem needs.
5. Need for self-actualization.[8]

The hierarchy of needs concept states that man fulfills a lower order need, then progresses to the next level only when all lower order needs are fulfilled, and so on up the hierarchy. Solid evidence does not exist to support the hierarchy. In fact, it may not be safe to assume more than a two-level hierarchy composed of existence and security needs at one level, and the higher order needs at another.[9]

Regardless of the hierarchy question, it is obvious to all that conflict among consumer needs does arise. When such need conflict arises, Walters suggests that "the individual can act in one of several ways: (1) he can assign a priority to his needs and attempt to satisfy the most dominant; (2) he can attempt to find one solution for several needs; (3) he can partially satisfy several needs; or (4) he can take no action."[10]

Motives

Motives are internal states of consumers that direct customers toward some goal-satisfying activity in order to reduce the state of tension so that the consumer can return to an equilibrium state. Motives are the reasons *why*, the reasons that motivate us to act. They are derived from needs and may be classified in somewhat similar ways. Motives may be symptomatic of needs and are sometimes paid more attention by both consumers and marketers than are needs. For example, a consumer may satisfy his thirst (motive) by drinking enormous quantities of his favorite beer rather than considering his actual physical body requirements (needs) for liquid and nourishment. Both consumers (marketing students not excluded) and marketers are well aware of the emphasis on motives.

Perceptions

Among marketers, the saying is: "Consumers act as they perceive." To perceive is to see, hear, touch, taste, or smell something. Perception is becoming aware through the senses as well as fitting this awareness into the individual's framework. Perception is more

[8]Abraham H. Maslow, *Motivation And Personality* (New York: Harper & Row, 1970), pp. 38 ff.
[9]E. E. Lawler and J. L. Suttle, "A Causal Correlational Test of The Need Hierarchy Concept," *Organizational Behavior and Human Performance*, 7 (1972), 265–287.
[10]Walters, p. 253.

than mere sensation in that it includes the experience of the perceiving individual. As any witness to an auto accident knows, people perceive what they see differently. Perception is subjective in that we see what we want to see. Perception is also selective, as is evidenced by the number of products or advertisements that actually register with a consumer in a supermarket or via the advertising media. And perception is of short-lived time duration. Also, consumers tend to sum up perceptions received from various stimuli via various senses into a meaningful total. Thus, consumers will add together TV advertising, packaging, product texture, product smell, and so forth to form perceptions.

Attitudes

Attitudes are formulated as a result of learning from experience. Consumers have attitudes about such things as products, companies, stores, shopping centers, and advertisements. Consumers are not born with attitudes. Through learning, consumers form a strong attitude toward this or a negative attitude toward that. The learning often takes place over a long period of time. Both attitude formation and attitude change are rather slow processes. This fact works both for and against the marketer. He should not expect consumer attitudes to change much overnight, but change is a part of our way of life, and consumer attitudes do change.

Six causes of consumer attitude change listed in Walters are: (1) a change in the product, (2) perceptual change, (3) change in attitude strength, (4) change in the store of information, (5) change in product importance, and (6) change in communications.[11] One of the simplest and easiest ways to change consumer attitudes is to change the product (or store) and let consumers know about the change. Perceptual change is an attempt to change consumer attitudes without actually making the physical change, but rather by communicating new information to consumers so that they will perceive the product differently. Weak attitudes, whether positive or negative, are more easily changed than strong attitudes. Thus a marketer may wish to strengthen attitudes favorable to him and to attempt to weaken attitudes which are unfavorable toward him. A change (usually an increase) in the store of information will change attitudes. Consumers with a limited store of information, such as children or less educated adults, are more susceptible than others to contradictory information. Consumer attitudes toward products that are very important to the consumer are less likely to change than are attitudes toward products of lesser importance. A change in communications can be used to change consumer attitudes by using effective communications (mass or personal) with one or more of the above causes of attitude change.

The understanding of consumer behavior through studying the individual influences (basic determinants) can also be enhanced by investigating learning theory and personality theory. For our purposes, these will simply be mentioned as items closely related to attitudes. Now, let's look to the interpersonal, or environmental, variables.

ENVIRONMENTAL INFLUENCES ON CONSUMER BEHAVIOR

As can be seen in Figure 6–1, the environmental influences on consumer behavior are family, social, cultural, business, and economic. Much of what was discussed in the previous section regarding basic determinants was based upon the discipline of psychol-

[11]Walters, pp. 172–177.

ogy. In like manner, the following material on environmental influences relies heavily upon the social sciences, such as sociology. However, our emphasis is from the point of view of the marketer. For example, many seemingly superficial changes, looked at from the point of view of sociology, may be very significant changes when seen from the point of view of the marketer. Even more significance may result for some individual marketers. The degree of significance is illustrated by a change in dress code for American men which has gradually replaced such items as the white shirt and necktie with the less formal turtle neck and male neck jewelry. We are attempting to combine the findings of social sciences with marketing in order to better understand consumer behavior.

Family Influences

The family is the basic social unit in most societies. It is also a most important consumption unit. Like other institutions, the family does change. Regarding family dynamics, Walters states:

Because of their effect on consumption, it is useful to have an awareness of the changes taking place in American families. Some of the more important of these changes are summarized below:
1. The role of the husband as family leader is decreasing in importance over time.
2. There is less emphasis on providing for the necessities of life.
3. There is a lessening of family unity.
4. Women and children are becoming increasingly independent.
5. Family members have greater mobility outside the home.
6. There is an increase in leisure activities.
7. More leisure is family oriented.
8. Husbands are participating more in family recreation.[12]

Family formation and stage in family life-cycle affect consumer behavior. Most persons in our society are at one time or another members of two families: the one into which they are born and the one which they help to form through marriage. Changes from one stage of family life-cycle to another create marketing opportunities. Examples of such changes are marriage, the birth of a first child, the time when the last child enters school, the time when all the children have grown up and are possibly no longer living at home, a surviving partner, and so forth. The pattern is, of course, varied by such factors as early death, divorce, family versus career orientation, and so forth. Other factors whose interactions influence family purchase behavior are family life styles, consumer roles of individual family members, and other roles played by family members, for example: The consumer role of the working wife (and her husband) is affected by the demands of the work role. Television advertising for microwave ovens and canned soup has emphasized a change in traditional husband-wife roles.

Social Influences

Consumers hold membership in, and their consumer behavior is affected by, various formal and informal social groups. *Reference groups* and *social classes* are two of the most important group concepts for understanding consumer behavior. Reference groups are

[12]Walters, pp. 240–241.

simply those groups of people who have some influence or who serve as a point of reference to an individual consumer. He identifies, at least in his aspirations, with the reference group whether or not he is actually a member of the group. The values of the reference group serve as a guide to the individual in such actions as purchasing. Thus we have the great American pastime of "keeping up with the Joneses."

Status-seeking behavior can also be viewed from a framework of social class. The author feels very fortunate to have been a former graduate student of W. Lloyd Warner. Warner's classification of social classes is based upon occupation, source of income, house type, and dwelling area. Note that social class is not the same thing as income class. Thus, while a certain income level (or wealth) may facilitate membership in a certain social class, *source* of income rather than amount is used as a criterion. Thus, a truck driver may have more income than a college professor, but their social classes may be in reverse order. Consumer behavior does vary among the different social classes. That is the main reason for our interest in social class. Although consumers of different social classes do purchase some of the same products at some of the same retail outlets, they do so for different

Social Class	Membership	Population Percentage
Upper-upper	Locally prominent families, third- or fourth-generation wealth. Merchants, financiers, or higher professionals. Wealth is inherited. Do a great amount of traveling.	1.5
Lower-upper	Newly arrived in upper class, "nouveau riche." Not accepted by upper class. Executive elite, founders of large businesses, doctors, lawyers.	1.5
Upper-middle	Moderately successful professionals, owners of medium-sized businesses, and middle management. Status conscious. Child- and home-centered.	10.0
Lower-middle	Top of the average-man world. Nonmanagerial office workers, small-business owners, and blue-collar families. Described as "striving and respectable." Conservative.	33.0
Upper-lower	Ordinary working class. Semi-skilled workers. Income often as high as the next two classes above. Enjoy life. Live from day to day.	38.0
Lower-lower	Unskilled, unemployed, and unassimilated ethnic groups. Fatalistic. Apathetic.	16.0
Total		100.0

reasons. They view these products and purchases differently. Perceptions and attitudes regarding self, others, products, and so forth do vary by social class. Warner's[13] social classes are shown in the table on page 96.

Although many changes have taken place in our society since Warner and his colleagues conducted their research, most marketers are aware of the importance of recognizing social class differences in their marketing strategies.

Cultural Influences

From his culture, the consumer learns the expected norms of behavior such as laws, mores, and customs. He also learns of the accompanying rewards and sanctions for enforcing these norms. Successful marketers are also aware of these cultural values and use them in their marketing. For example, gift-giving is a cultural universal found in all cultures, but the unique manner and conditions of appropriateness are specifically defined in our culture, especially with regard to certain holidays. Examples of the core culture of the U.S. are friendly rather than authoritarian parent-child relationships, casual style of dress, easily prepared foods, enlightened attitudes toward women, and so forth.[14]

The U.S. culture has also included what may be called the "small business ethic."[15] The SBM himself may hold certain values regarding the virtues of SB. More important to consumer behavior is whether or not, and to what extent, consumers also regard SB differently (and perhaps as being more virtuous) from BB.

Subcultures, that is, groups within a larger culture, often tend to help define market segments. Such subcultures may be based upon ethnic background, age, or some other dimension. The SBM should attempt to recognize the existence of such subcultures as potential target markets that may in many cases be better served by SB than by BB.

Business Influences

Business intends to, and does, very greatly affect consumer behavior. Marketers are active agents of change in consumer behavior. Advertising, for example, is intended to persuade as well as to inform consumers. Since the announced purpose of business influence is quite often to sell products and services to consumers, and since consumers are most often aware of this purpose, a natural skepticism may result. In order to influence consumers effectively, this skepticism must be overcome by continually proving to the consumer that the business is influencing him in the right direction. This continual proof results in branding, heavy advertising, use of slogans, and image-building for company, brand, and store.

Economic Influences

The amount of money that consumers have to spend definitely influences their behavior. For most consumers, spending depends on income. For a few consumers, wealth,

---

[13]Social classes are from *Social Class In America* by W. Lloyd Warner, Marchia Meeker, and Kenneth Eells, (New York: Harper & Row, 1960). The particular list here has appeared in many places, including *Consumer Behavior* by Walters and *Contemporary Marketing* by Boone and Kurtz.

[14]For a more extensive listing see Louis E. Boone and David L. Kurtz, *Contemporary Marketing* (Hinsdale, Illinois: The Dryden Press, 1977), p. 160.

[15]Ross M. Robertson, "The Small Business Ethic in America," *The Vital Majority*, ed. Deane Carson (Washington: U.S. Government Printing Office, 1973), pp. 25–36.

in addition to income, is also a factor. The income levels of different market segments can be cross-classified with other demographic dimensions such as age, sex, occupation, educational level, and so forth. In addition to the amount of income, consumer behavior may vary according to such factors as income stability and income expectations.

Communications

The above five environmental influences interact with one another to influence consumer behavior. This interaction process is basically a communications process. In some cases, communications may be direct. In others, a two-step flow of communications through opinion leaders may take place. The receptiveness of individuals to new ideas and change is known as the adoption process. Rogers classifies consumers as innovators, early adopters, early majority, late majority, and laggards.[16]

Thus far in the chapter we have very briefly described one model of consumer behavior. With our apologies to Walters and Paul for injustices caused by such brevity, let us now move on. We next digress for a moment to view the effects of consumerism on SB. We will then consider consumer research within the resources of most SB marketers. Finally, we'll look at some ways the SBM can use his knowledge of consumer behavior.

CONSUMERISM AND THE SBM

Since its creation about a decade ago, consumerism has certainly received its share of headlines. Consumerism differs from its predecessor, the consumer movement, in that consumerism is much more organized and has more political and legal involvement. Consumerism is an outgrowth of the failure of marketers to satisfy consumers adequately. As such, it serves as evidence of the lack of implementation or of poor implementation of the marketing concept. Just as the marketing concept was originally developed as a BB concept, so also consumerism gained most of its momentum as an anti-BB force. However, SB should take little comfort in this fact. BB probably simply served as an easier and more economical target for consumer advocates. SB may or may not have been doing a better job than BB in satisfying consumer needs. In any event, SB has felt, and will continue to feel, the impact of consumerism.

Simply because the SBM finds himself involved in a fierce competitive struggle to sell his products or services does not mean that consumers are necessarily overjoyed with the results of that competition. Certainly, the SBM must be competitive, but that competition serves a purpose only if it serves consumers. The consumer has rights and has recently been willing to exercise these rights. Former President Kennedy's Consumer Advisory Council outlined the consumers' rights as (1) the right to safety, (2) the right to be informed, (3) the right to choose, and (4) the right to be heard.

An article in the *Journal of Small Business Management* describes the following areas of questionable practices after stating:

> One problem with the consumer movement has been a tendency to generalize concerning business behavior in general on the basis of isolated examples of questionable practices. Nevertheless, some businessmen do fail to recognize sufficiently that in the long run only a satisfied customer is a profitable customer, and that the success of a firm is based not upon a single purchase but rather upon repeat

[16]Everett M. Rogers, *Diffusion of Innovations* (New York: Free Press, 1962), pp. 168–171.

purchases. A sound customer-business relationship which produces repeat purchases never relies upon a policy of caveat emptor—let the buyer beware. Such a dishonest and short-sighted approach serves only to increase the uncertainty and mistrust of the consumer.[17]

The areas of questionable practices are partial disclosure, initial contact deception, bait and switch, free gift promotion, unordered substituted merchandise, lo-balling, pyramid sales, and work-at-home schemes. In addition to these specific practices which may be both illegal and unethical, consumerism involves other issues. Among these issues are false or misleading advertising, "truth in lending," "truth in packaging," warranties, service, product liability, and discrimination in marketing—such as allegedly takes place in the ghetto.

CONSUMER RESEARCH THE SBM CAN DO

Consumer research may be viewed as that portion of marketing research (See Chapter 7) which deals with the consumer. Actually, the entire study of the area of consumer behavior could be viewed as a form of research. This is so because the understanding of consumer behavior is simply a means to an end. Therefore, in broad terms, we might say that anything the SBM does to better understand his consumers is a form of consumer marketing research. But let's get specific. Can the SBM conduct meaningful consumer research? If so, what are some examples of specific projects that are feasible for even the smaller of the SB firms?

Buying habits represent repeated patterns of consumer purchase behavior. Consumer buying habits, from the point of view of the consumer, represent a great convenience. From the point of view of the SBM, buying habits represent an aid to the predictability of consumer actions. The analysis and understanding of buying habits is therefore important. Buskirk, in his popular principles book, offers the checklist on page 100 as a tool for analyzing consumer buying habits:[18]

Such a checklist as Buskirk's can be used with differing degrees of sophistication, depending on the amount and accuracy of the information made available. The SBM may wish to create his own checklist, using the one presented above as a reference. Informal as the checklist may be, it may prove to be very useful.

Image (of company, product, and/or store) is another area where the SBM can often do some fruitful consumer research. In a *Small Marketers Aid*, Blackwell suggests the following image research for small retailers:

Some small retailers can use formal marketing research as an aid in keeping their images sharp. They use local, or nearby, talent to conduct a study.

For example, a nearby college or university may be able to recommend a graduate student who could help measure your image as a part of his degree requirements. Or a business professor may be willing to use your store as a case example in one of his classes.

Another source of help in marketing research may be local advertising agencies and media. If you place considerable advertising with a newspaper, radio or television

[17]Lonnie L. Ostrom and John L. Schlacter, "Let The Seller Beware," *Journal of Small Business Management*, 12, No. 3 (July 1974), 35–38.
[18]Richard H. Buskirk, *Principles of Marketing* (Hinsdale, Illinois: The Dryden Press, 1975), p. 123.

Sample Check List For Making An Analysis Of
Consumer Buying Habits

WHO:

Who uses the product? _____
Who makes the buying decision? _____
Who influences the buying decision?_____
Who makes the actual purchase? _____

WHEN:

When during the year is the product bought?
_____

When in the life cycle of the decision maker is
the product bought? _____

Is the product purchased in connection with
any other purchase or event? _____

WHAT:

What is the need?_____
What is now used to meet the need?_____

What problems are being encountered with the
present solution?_____

What are the consumer's spending patterns? _

WHERE:

Where is the buying decision made? _____
Where is the actual purchase made? _____
Where do the retailers want to buy? _____

HOW:

How much does the buyer want to buy? _____
How is the product used?_____
How must the goods be delivered? _____
How is the transaction financed? _____
How does buyer go about acquiring product?
_____

How much effort will buyer make to acquire
product? _____
How often is product bought? _____
How much service does the buyer want? _____
How are negotiations concluded?_____

---

station, they may help you measure your image. Or they may already have studies which include your own store or which would apply to your type of business. You might also get marketing information from your trade association, trade papers, vendors, or a resident buying office, if you use one. [19]

From the above quote, we notice that two types of consumer research data are available. One, called primary data, is that which is gathered from the field by the SBM and his researchers. The other, referred to as secondary data, is existing data available

---

[19]Roger D. Blackwell, "Knowing Your Image," *Small Marketers Aids*, No. 124 (Washington: Small Business Administration, 1967), p. 7.

from other sources, such as libraries and trade associations. Secondary data is usually less expensive. It is available to the SBM for the effort of seeking it out and interpreting it to his own situation. Generally, secondary data should be thoroughly investigated before collecting primary data.

Another example of exploratory consumer research which can be useful to many small retailers is suggested by the following set of questions:

The following questions should be helpful in jotting down your conclusions about: (1) the kinds of people you are serving, or seeking to serve; (2) what they need, want, and will buy; and (3) how you can serve them best.

Talking with two types of customers can be helpful in working out answers to the questions listed below, especially to questions 1 through 6. One type is your best customers. The other is composed of persons whose income, business, social status, or location makes them logical customers even though they are not regular patrons of your firm.

1. When do my customers like to shop?
_____ a.m. to _____ p.m.

2. Do my customers like to shop during evening hours? If so, what nights of the week? _____ .
What hours? _____ a.m. to _____ p.m.

3. How do my customers like to pay?
_____ percent, cash
_____ percent, 30 days credit
_____ percent, revolving credit

4. What quality of merchandise do my customers usually buy?
_____ percent, top quality
_____ percent, moderate quality
_____ percent, low quality

5. What type of store has most appeal to my customers?
_____ percent, new and flashy
_____ percent, conventional, service type
_____ percent, discount type

6. How do my customers handle service on the mechanical products they have bought?
_____ do-it-themselves
_____ use service which is already available in the community
_____ use available service and would buy more if it were available

7. Who does most of the buying in the homes of my customers?
_____ percent, the man
_____ percent, the woman
_____ percent, they shop together

8. What is the income level of my average customer?
_____ above average
_____ average
_____ below average

9. What is the age level of my average customer?
_____ elderly
_____ middle aged
_____ young and recently married

10. What is the general attitude of my customer toward his community?
_____ proud and helping to develop
_____ settled and satisfied
_____ disturbed and moving out

11. How does my customer react to new and different merchandise or promotional activities?

_____ responds quickly

_____ responds slowly

_____ responds so slowly that I cannot afford to put great effort into it

12. What major changes has my customer made in the last 2 years?

_____ income increased steadily

_____ income declined

_____ changed shopping habits[20]

The consumer research suggested here has been very elementary. Its requirements in terms of time, talent, and money are well within the reach of nearly every SBM. More sophisticated and comprehensive consumer research, where feasible, is certainly advocated. Knowing the consumer and attempting to understand consumer behavior are very important to the SBM if he is going to develop a marketing mix which will be effectively "on target."

HOW SB CAN USE CONSUMER BEHAVIOR

If the SBM is going to spend time, talent, and other resources studying consumer behavior, he certainly wants to put the results to work. Rather than simply being able to say "that's interesting," the SBM wants to answer the question, "In what ways can I use this knowledge of consumer behavior in order to develop better marketing strategies and more effective specific marketing tactics?" Marketers have been using consumer behavior knowledge for centuries. Although the formal study of consumer behavior as a separate discipline is of very recent origin, one of the best and most widely quoted articles on using such types of information was published over two decades ago. The following twenty items are quoted from Britt, with accompanying comments relating the items to SB.[21] Portions directly quoted are italicized. These twenty principles of learning (with comments) are presented below.

1. *Unpleasant things may sometimes be learned as readily as pleasant things, but the most ineffective stimuli are those which arouse little or no emotional response.*

The application of this psychological principle for the SBM is in the selection of advertising appeals and their manner of presentation. Very neutral and nonemotional appeals and presentations are likely to be less effective than those employing either pleasant or unpleasant things. Thus, the SBM who does his own TV commercial (a practice not recommended for most) may be more effective, if his delivery is very pleasant or even if it is uniquely unpleasant but not too offensive, than if his delivery were rather neutral.

2. *The capacities of learners are important in determining what can be learned and how long it will take.*

The SBM should know his target market, particularly since bright people get complex messages, and in less time, that may go right over the heads of many other

[20]Dwayne Laws, "Pleasing Your Boss, The Customer," *Small Marketers Aids,* No. 114 (Washington: Small Business Administration, 1965), pp. 2–3.

[21]Steuart Henderson Britt, "How Advertising Can Use Psychology's Rules of Learning," *Printers' Ink,* 252 (September 1955), pp. 74, 77, & 80.

persons. Therefore, in advertising and in other communications, the SBM should expect to be very patient. Since market segments are not often based upon learning capacities, variation in capacities within the target markets of the SBM is likely. This may suggest that less complex advertising messages be employed or that when complex messages are used, additional time be given for such messages to be learned.

3. *Things that are learned and understood tend to be better retained than things learned by rote.*

While frequent repetition is important (and expensive) for remembering an advertising message, if the message is understood, it will be better retained. For example, if the SBM is using a slogan or jingle in his TV advertising, an explanation and elaboration will probably enhance its value.

4. *Practice distributed over several periods is more economical in learning than the same amount of practice concentrated into a single period.*

The marketing application is that an advertising campaign should usually extend over a long period of time. Patterns of concentration are sometimes in order. A gift shop concentrating on Christmas and Mother's Day does make sense. However, even in these cases, continuous communications at a reduced level are probably warranted.

5. *When teaching people to master mechanical skills, it is better to show the performance in the same way that the learner would see it if he were doing the job himself.*

Anyone who has tied a necktie on another person knows that the point of view or perspective in a TV demonstration or live demonstration by a salesman does make a difference when teaching mechanics to potential consumers.

6. *The order of presentation of materials to be learned is very important.*

Since points given at the beginning and end are better remembered than are points made in the middle of a message, the SBM, in his advertising, should, when giving several reasons to buy, place the most important at the beginning and end.

7. *If material to be learned is different, or unique, it will be better remembered.*

Although most advertisers strive to be unique in some way in their message, layout, media, and so on, real uniqueness is difficult to obtain, especially if the product or store advertised is itself not unique. However, in many cases the SBM may have some truly unique features in his product or store. If so, he possesses a real potential advantage. For example, a unique location may be either uniquely good or uniquely bad, depending on how the SBM advertises it. Nearly everyone in the Omaha, Nebraska area knows that Mangelsen's (a variety and hobby store) was located "JUST NORTH OF THAT AWFUL TUNNEL." With the closing of the "awful tunnel" in 1976, Mangelsen's changed their former copyrighted slogan to the new copyrighted slogan that says, "JUST NORTH OF THAT DELIGHTFUL DETOUR." Completion of the new underpass will require a new slogan.

8. *Showing errors in how to do something can lead to increases in learning.*

The application for the SBM is to show both what to do and what *not* to do. This can be done in media advertising as well as during in-store product demonstration. Improved consumer satisfaction will result from using the product correctly. For products requiring servicing, a service organization trained in conveying such *do* and *don't* information to present customers can make them repeat customers.

9. *Learning situations which are rewarded only occasionally can be more efficient than those whose constant reward is employed.*

For the SBM who uses deals, premiums, and other special offers, these promotions are likely to be more effective if used for short periods of time than if they are almost continuously in use. For short time periods, consumers regard them as a bonus; but after a lengthy period consumers come to expect them and may even feel cheated if they are discontinued. The SBM should therefore change deals from time to time, and have at least some time periods which establish what the basic offering is without such deals. For example, the dry cleaning firm that always has the same coupon deal in effect may find that this is a less effective promotional device as time goes by.

10. *It is easier to recognize something than it is to recall it.*

This learning principle suggests to the SBM that his product, package, brand name, and all other marketing communications should be easily recognized by the consumer. It also suggests that all of these should be used in combination to reinforce each other. For example, the package, or the store sign, should be shown in the visual advertising media.

11. *The rate of forgetting tends to be very rapid immediately after learning.*

This means that the SBM cannot expect infrequent advertising to pay off. Competition is helping consumers forget other advertising—assuming that they did once learn the advertising message. Much advertising, and other forms of promotion, is therefore necessary in order to keep consumers from immediately forgetting the message. In too many instances, the SBM is most guilty of violating this principle of learning, especially when he is communicating to several market segments because he has not accurately defined his appropriate target markets.

12. *Messages attributed to persons held in high esteem influence change in opinion more than messages from persons not so well known, but after several weeks both messages seem equally effective.*

This principle relates directly to the use of testimonials in advertising. For a long-range campaign to change opinions favorably toward his product or store, the SBM does not need a high-priced "hero"; but for a short campaign he may wish to use a "star."

13. *Repetition of identical materials is often as effective in getting things remembered as repeating the same story but with variations.*

From this principle, the SBM should gather that proven advertisements can be used over and over again and that many variations of the same basic theme may not be necessary.

14. *In a learning situation, a moderate fear appeal is more effective than a strong fear appeal.*

This principle states that if the SBM uses a fear appeal in his advertising message which is too strong, the consumer will reject the entire message.

15. *Knowledge of results leads to increases in learning.*

The SBM can use this principle by telling consumers specific benefits (results) from purchasing and using the advertised products and services.

16. *Learning is aided by active practice rather than passive reception.*

Here the SBM is told that consumers are more likely to remember his sales message if they can somehow participate in his marketing efforts. Means of accomplishing this are through easy-to-enter contests, coupon redemptions, sweepstakes, and other promotional ideas that require the consumer to do something.

17. *A message is more easily learned and accepted if it does not interfere with earlier habits.*

The SBM is advised here to tie his advertising message to that which is familiar and habitual to the consumer. Thus he would suggest that his product is an improved way of getting a familiar job done rather than a completely different method for performing some new function.

18. *The mere repetition of a situation does not necessarily lead to learning. Two things are necessary—"belongingness" and "satisfiers."*

The first refers to things fitting together somewhat logically and the second refers to the reward. The SBM can make his advertising more effective by using these two.

19. *When two ideas are of equal strength but of unequal age, new repetition increases the strength of the earlier idea more than that of the newer idea.*

The application for marketing is fairly obvious in the area of branding of products. An older brand may require less advertising than a newer brand in order to attain the same degree of brand association with a product category. This means that the SBM attempting to gain brand position against older established brands will have a difficult time. On the other hand, the SBM with an established brand may be able to protect his brand's position on a smaller advertising budget.

20. *Learning something new can interfere with the remembering of something learned earlier.*

The SBM whose TV advertisement was followed immediately by that of his competitor is well aware of the truth of this principle.

The above twenty principles of learning and the accompanying comments are not in most cases related to a specific business. They deal primarily with the consumer market but are probably equally applicable to the industrial market. They do give the SBM and his advertising helper an idea of how an understanding of consumer behavior can be of specific value to the SBM.

The above twenty principles concentrated heavily on promotional strategy and tactics. Consumer behavior also relates to the other elements of the marketing mix. This is true at both strategic and tactical levels. Consumer behavior also has implications for SB manufacturers, middlemen, and retailers. None is excluded simply because he does not deal directly with the consumer. The SBM should look at each of the "five P's" and at his target markets to see how his marketing program can be improved as a result of improved understanding of the consumer. The following brief examples may suggest areas of application to the SBM for his particular business.

From an understanding of the adoption process based upon the diffusion of innovation, a major household appliance dealer may formulate a more targeted approach to selling such new items as garbage compactors and microwave ovens. How does this SBM do this? Briefly, based upon past sales records (which are ideally available in usable form), he classifies all customers into one of the following groups: innovators, early adopters, early majority, late majority, and laggards. Neither his information nor his classification need be exact. He may base his classification on such factors as whether or not consumers own other appliances, such as dishwashers and color TV sets; how long these appliances have been owned; and so forth. The SBM is then immediately ready to target his major sales efforts in appropriate order to each of the classes of customers. To the extent that early adopters for one major appliance are also early adopters for another, his sales efforts will be more directed and more productive.

The influence of consumer behavior on people strategy is seen by contrasting the stores of two retailers in the same line but in different small communities. Retailer A practiced passive personnel policies, especially with the large number of part-time, high school age employees. Personnel problems such as high absenteeism and turnover naturally resulted. But more importantly, the image of the store suffered to the extent that besides no longer being an "in" place to work, it was no longer an "in" place to shop. On the other hand, store B had a positive approach toward the people variable, especially the part-time, high school age group. The results were that it enjoyed the service of the most popular and very talented young employees. More importantly, store B was able to use the high caliber of its people as an effective part of its marketing mix. Consumers of all ages tended to associate favorably with the resulting image.

Against such established firms as the local version of Yellow Cabs, how does a new and smaller taxicab firm use consumer behavior in order to compete? Anyone who has ever taken a cab can readily see the advantages of using only vehicles with the larger back seat, equipped with passenger-operated air conditioning and stereo FM. Then package that superior product with a name such as Happy Cab, and the firm's understanding of consumer behavior becomes even more apparent.

The understanding of images based upon consumer behavior can bring several marketing examples, both BB and SB, to mind. The children's store with the lollipop tree (or the sucker tree, if you prefer) is an example. This store is certainly aware of the roles played by different family members in the consumer purchase decision process. The savings and loan associations and the banks are careful in selecting the premiums they offer to savers. Their images are as much at stake with the premiums as with other services. Images are also conveyed to consumers by such items as specialty advertising: calendars, matches, balloons, and so forth. Restaurant operators catering to family dining are well aware that young children will let everyone enjoy the meal if they do. The concept of store image is applicable even to the very young.

Small manufacturers of consumer products will also benefit from understanding consumer behavior. One example is a small manufacturer who spent more for a unique package, even though this meant raising the price of his product. Knowing where certain types of consumers expect to purchase a product at retail affects the manufacturer's channel of distribution strategy, and in turn, all his other marketing mix strategies. Thus, buying habits are important in channel choice. This is illustrated by the small manufacturer of health and beauty aids who was unsuccessful in attempting to limit his product to a single type of outlet. Through an understanding of consumer behavior (parent and child), numerous toy manufacturers have prospered in competition with the giants of TV children's advertising. Many other examples at the manufacturer level could be cited by looking at the marketing mix of nearly any successful SBM who is a manufacturer.

In all phases of the marketing strategy planning, the SBM should constantly be considering consumer behavior. His understanding of consumer behavior should tell him: *yes,* do this; or *no,* don't do that because. . . .

BIBLIOGRAPHY

Books

BOONE, LOUIS E., AND KURTZ, DAVID L. *Contemporary Marketing.* Hinsdale, Illinois: The Dryden Press, 1977.

BUSKIRK, RICHARD H. *Principles of Marketing.* Hinsdale, Illinois: The Dryden Press, 1975.

MASLOW, ABRAHAM H. *Motivation and Personality.* New York: Harper & Row, 1970.

ROGERS, EVERETT M. *Diffusion of Innovations.* New York: Free Press, 1962.

WALTERS, C. GLENN *Consumer Behavior.* Homewood, Illinois: Richard D. Irwin, Inc., 1974.

WALTERS, C. GLENN, AND PAUL, GORDON W. *Consumer Behavior.* Homewood, Illinois: Richard D. Irwin, Inc., 1970.

WARNER, W. LLOYD, MEEKER, MARCHIA, AND EELLS, KENNETH. *Social Class In America.* New York: Harper Torchbooks, 1960.

Articles and Periodicals

BLACKWELL, ROGER D. "Knowing Your Image," *Small Marketers Aids,* No. 124. Washington: Small Business Administration, 1967, pp. 1–8.

BRITT, STEUART HENDERSON. "How Advertising Can Use Psychology's Rules of Learning," *Printers' Ink,* 252 (September 1955), pp. 74, 77, and 80.

LAWLER, E. E., AND SUTTLE, J. L. "A Causal Correlational Test of The Need Hierarchy Concept," *Organizational Behavior and Human Performance,* 7 (1972), 265–287.

LAWS, DWAYNE. "Pleasing Your Boss, The Customer," *Small Marketers Aids,* No 114 Washington: Small Business Administration, 1965, pp. 1–4.

OSTROM, LONNIE L., AND SCHLACTER, JOHN L. "Let The Seller Beware," *Journal of Small Business Management,* 12, No. 3 (July 1974), 35–38.

ROBERTSON, ROSS M. "The Small Business Ethic in America," *The Vital Majority,* ed. Deane Carson (Washington: U.S. Government Printing Office, 1973), pp. 25–36.

7

Marketing Information
For SBMM

THE ROLE OF MARKETING INFORMATION IN SB

In Chapter 2, marketing information was listed as one of the functions of marketing. What purpose does marketing information serve for SBMM? Marketing research and the somewhat broader concept of marketing information serve as the cornerstone of the marketing concept. (Although distinctions are sometimes made between *marketing research* and *marketing information*, we will use these terms somewhat interchangeably except when discussing the marketing information system, MIS.) If the SBM is to use the model proposed in this book in order to implement the marketing concept for his SB, he must receive marketing information. A customer orientation without marketing information is ridiculous. Marketing information, as such, is not one of the elements of the SB marketing mix, but it does aid the SBM in identifying problems and making decisions about the elements (5 P's) of the SB marketing mix. Marketing information is necessary for the strategic planning, execution, and control of both the overall SBMM model and for each of the "five P's." Good decision making in all these areas requires good marketing information. However, it does not necessarily follow that good decisions will always result from the presence of good information. Even the best information is old when the SBM is making decisions about the future.

Our approach to marketing research for the SBM will be a managerial and nontechnical approach. That is, we will not go into detail concerning the techniques of marketing research. Our reason is as follows: Although some simple and unsophisticated marketing research can and perhaps should be done by the SBM himself, the degree of complexity involved in most marketing research will require the direction (or at least the assistance) of a technically trained marketing researcher. Such technical specialists are available to SB and should be used. Our managerial approach, rather than considering "how to" do marketing research, will consider such questions as:

1. What marketing research should be done?
2. How much should be spent for marketing research?
3. To what extent should the SBM participate in specific steps of the research process?
4. What types of research are appropriate for the SBM in the absence of technical specialists?
5. What sources of marketing information are available to the SBM?
6. What are appropriate areas of application for the SBM to use marketing research information?
7. How should the SBM work with marketing research consultants and agencies?

The above questions are managerial ones that should be answered by the SBM. They can also be answered within the scope of our chapter since the answers rely on cooperation with technical specialists rather than on all attempts to make the SBM into such a specialist.

Does the role of marketing research vary by size of firm? The *Handbook of Marketing Research* states:

> Marketing research serves the same purposes in small firms as it does in large ones. However, for a small firm the costs of research, compared with the value of the information produced, are higher than for a large firm, thus limiting the frequency of its use. Consequently, research is more likely to be used for strategic entry decisions, such as what business to enter or where to locate a store, than for tactical surveillance of environmental change or resources allocation decisions. Since they cannot attain economies of scale in spreading research costs over many units of output, small businessmen must learn to do research for themselves or hire consultants to do it for them. Although outside consultants may take longer to learn the firm's problems, they bring a breadth of experience in solving problems that most small businessmen cannot duplicate.[1]

As we have discussed in previous chapters, decision making is different in SB. Marketing information requirements for decision making are also different. For example, the SBM may find that the cost of a "wrong" decision is less than the cost of additional marketing information. The SBM may find it advantageous to use trial and error to solve certain marketing problems, whereas such a course of action may at times not be feasible for BB. The optimum amount of information is probably less for the SB than the BB for making similar decisions. Specific research functions performed are often determined by the characteristics of a business. Since BB and SB often differ in their characteristics, one would expect the research function to vary by size of business. Also, even among SB firms, the marketing research needs will vary due to the characteristics of individual firms and their line of business.

After dividing companies into the following four sizes—(1) the billion dollar highly diversified company; (2) the $300 million multiproduct company, primarily in one field; (3) the ten to fifty million dollar "smaller" company; and (4) the one-customer or limited-market company—Myers and Mead recognize vast differences in the role of marketing research in companies of various sizes. They state:

> In the case of the "smaller" companies, a corporate planning function often does not exist. Planning, if it is done at all, is done by an Executive Committee or by an

---

[1]George Fisk, "The Functions of Marketing Research," from *Handbook of Marketing Research,* by Robert Ferber (ed.) Copyright ©1974 by McGraw-Hill Book Company, pp. 1–21. Used with permission of McGraw-Hill Book Company.

informal alliance of top management throughout the firm. The various functional areas of the firm are less closely interwoven, so that marketing gets its budget for the year and lays plans somewhat more independently. Each function tries to optimize its own operations, which often results in suboptimum effectiveness for the total company. Also, each function tends to have greater flexibility and autonomy. Marketing research often has a more direct role in major corporate decisions in small companies than in the giants.[2]

The above authors did not comment on the role of marketing research in the one-customer or limited-market company. However, they do state: "Thus the role of marketing research in most companies should be to *integrate, organize, and interpret the various data flows to provide marketing intelligence which will improve the quality of managerial decision making throughout the firm.*"[3] This statement brings to mind the American Marketing Association definition of marketing research as the ". . . systematic gathering, recording, and analyzing of data about problems relating to the marketing of goods and services."[4] At this point, we may conclude that (1) the role of marketing research in a specific SB is determined by both the size and the characteristics of the business and (2) that the function or purpose of marketing research is to act as a tool for marketing management in decision making.

THE SCOPE OF MARKETING INFORMATION IN SB

Now, let's turn our attention to the scope or extent of use of marketing research in SB. Two levels of questions may be asked. First, the *macro* question: To what extent has SB engaged in marketing research? Secondly, the *micro* question, which each SB firm must ask itself: How much marketing research should we do; or, how much should we spend for marketing research?

An AMA survey indicates that most SB firms have no individual specifically assigned to perform the marketing research function.[5] Another study indicates that less than five percent of all research and development expenditures are by small firms.[6] On the *macro* question, we must conclude that (a) SB does very little or no marketing research, (b) SB is informally organized in this area, and/or (c) SB tends to rely heavily on outside assistance.

A study of six categories of small business in the New Orleans area dealt with the various sources of information used to solve marketing and other problems.[7] Here, the question of *whether* or not SB sought marketing information was replaced by the question of *where* such information was sought. The six categories of SB in this study probably represent some very small firms. The six categories and the number of firms in each for this study were: restaurants (22), gasoline service stations (15), contractors (41), service firms (20), financial firms (29), and manufacturing firms (32). The information and advice

[2]James H. Myers and Richard R. Mead, *The Management of Marketing Research* (Scranton, Pennsylvania: International Textbook Company, 1969), p. 11.

[3]Myers and Mead, p. 11.

[4]Committee on Definitions, Reprinted from *Marketing Definitions: A Glossary of Marketing Terms* published by the American Marketing Association, Chicago, 1960, p. 16.

[5]Dik Warren Twedt (ed.), Reprinted from *1973 Survey of Marketing Research* published by the American Marketing Association. (Chicago, 1973), p. 41.

[6]Thomas Hogan and John Chirichiello, "The Role of Research and Development in Small Firms," *The Vital Majority: Small Business In The American Economy*, ed. Deane Carson (Washington: U. S. Government Printing Office, 1973), pp. 309–310.

[7]Daniel S. Juhn and Kenneth J. Lacho, "Getting Information: Where Do Small Businessmen Go?" *Louisiana Business Survey*, 6, No. 3 (July 1975), 11–13.

sources (not necessarily marketing research) cited by the small businessmen surveyed were as shown in Table 7–1.[8]

Now that some perspective of marketing research has been gained from attempting to answer the *macro* question, let's look at the *micro* question. Is marketing research one of those things the SBM can't afford but yet can't afford to be without? A more moderate approach suggests that the question is how much should the SBM spend for marketing research. The SBM is a risk taker and a decision maker. Risk can sometimes be reduced by obtaining additional information—at a cost. But all risk cannot be eliminated. Good marketing research costs money. It also costs time and talent. The SBM should seek assistance from research only when he thinks risk can be reduced substantially at a reasonable cost.

Theoretically, the SBM decides how much to spend for marketing research by balancing the cost of increasing units of information against the payoff of these additional units. In other words, is the payoff equal to or greater than the cost? The theory could, of course, be made more complex by considering such things as opportunity costs. Regardless of how complex the theory may be, the practice of actually determining how much to spend for research is most difficult. The following broad guidelines may be of slight assistance. First, the SBM should never spend any money for poor research or the "wrong" research just because the price seems to be "right." Marketing decisions will not be improved and may even be hampered by such research. Secondly, at the other extreme, the SBM should not buy better or more marketing research than he needs. For example, " . . . five really knowledgeable and sophisticated purchasing agents can be fifty times more valuable to an industrial researcher than 100 superficial, inexperienced, or lazy buyers."[9] In other words, the SBM should spend, but he should spend well. Third, the SBM should never spend dollars gathering data from primary sources—such as via surveys—until he has thoroughly checked the availability (or lack of) of such data in existing secondary sources. This is simply the principle of not paying for what you can get for free. Fourth, since the SBM cannot afford all the marketing research he might like, projects where the payoffs are greatest should be selected first. Finally, decision making is different in SB than in BB. The SBM often looks for satisfactory rather than optimum problem solutions. The SBM may therefore operate successfully with substantially less perfect information than that required by the bureaucracy of BB. Whether called *marketing research* or some other name, all marketers do perform some marketing research. Each SBM must decide how much.

A BRIEF DESCRIPTION OF THE RESEARCH PROCESS

The purpose of this section is not to present a condensed presentation of the research process in order that the SBM can do his own research on a condensed or "mini" basis. Our approach is managerial, not technical. As stated earlier, much of marketing research is technical. The purpose of this section, then, is to make the SBM more aware of the research process. He needs such an awareness in order to make the right managerial decisions and in order to work effectively with research specialists. Also, at times, the SBM will necessarily get quite involved in various steps of the research process. Although it may seem contrary to some of the statements made above, there are some instances when the

[8]Juhn and Lacho, p. 12.
[9]Richard C. Christian, "It May Pay To Think Small," *Journal of Marketing*, 27 (July 1963), 80.

Table 7-1 Information and Advice Sources for Small Businessmen in the New Orleans Area*

	Total Number of Choices**		Number of First Choices	
Accountant/Consultant	86	(20%)	31	(24%)
Other Owners	76	(17%)	40	(31%)
Banker	48	(11%)	11	(9%)
Attorney	48	(11%)	10	(8%)
Trade Association	42	(10%)	12	(9%)
Friend or Relative	39	(9%)	10	(8%)
Supplier	36	(8%)	5	(4%)
Reading Material (Specify)	28	(6%)	2	(2%)
Local College or University	18	(4%)	6	(5%)
Public Library	12	(3%)	2	(2%)
Other	7	(2%)	0	(0%)
	440	(100%)	129	(100%)

*Defined as the following parishes: New Orleans, Jefferson, and St. Bernard.

**Response to the following question: "Where are the best places to get advice or information when you have managerial problems? Check 1 by the best source, 2 for the next best, and 3 for third choice."

Source: Daniel S. Juhn and Kenneth J. Lacho, "Getting Information: Where Do Small Businessmen Go?" *Louisiana Business Survey*, 6, No. 3 (July 1975), 11–13.

SBM himself will actually perform most, if not all, of a particular marketing research project. These instances are generally limited to simple projects or to projects that are determined to be complete after the early exploratory stages. In these instances, the SBM needs to know his own limitations and know when to rely on the experts. Our purpose here is to make the SBM aware of the research process in marketing.

Marketing research is a process of discovering and solving marketing problems. There are many kinds of problems and many kinds of research to deal with them. For example, the purpose of marketing research could be for exploratory information, for specific information, or for continuous feedback. The purpose is going to affect both the extent and emphasis of the research process. Our discussion here is perhaps most directed toward specific information, but our process is general enough to encompass all kinds of marketing research.

The research process in marketing is more than simply making up a questionnaire and doing a survey. Research is based on the scientific method. Variations of the so-called scientific method are familiar to us all. Likewise, the marketing research process may be divided into a number of steps. The specific number, of course, will vary from author to author. The list we have selected contains thirteen steps. Although these steps are distinct, it should be remembered that the researcher is likely to be involved with more than a single step at any given point in time, even though earlier steps will be completed before succeeding steps are completed. The steps of the research process are:

1. Recognizing and defining the problem within its environment.
2. Making an exploratory investigation of its major aspects.
3. Formulating the appropriate research design.

4. Determining the adequacy of available, or secondary, data.
5. Specifying sources and methods of gathering needed primary data.
6. Designing questionnaires or other forms of securing the data.
7. Sampling the data from the entire defined population.
8. Conducting the field investigation, when primary data are to be obtained.
9. Planning the interpretation of the data in terms of the decision model and the research design.
10. Editing the returned forms and tabulating the results.
11. Making statistical analyses of the results.
12. Interpreting the meaning of the processed and analyzed data in terms of the problem and the decisions necessary for its solution.
13. Presenting the findings to those who will reach the decision.[10]

Step 1: Recognizing and defining the problem, within its environment.   Problem definition is the initial stage at which the information needs of the SBM as a decision maker and the problem solving talents of the marketing researcher come into contact. It is a most important stage since a poorly or improperly defined problem will result in poor research, or even worse, the wrong research—however good or poor it may be. Symptoms are not problems, but as in the case of a medical illness, symptoms may be indicative of problems, and symptoms may aid in identifying problems. Problems may be overt or covert. They may also be positive or negative. For example, a positive marketing problem could be the need to recognize a new marketing opportunity even though present sales were extremely good. We might also suggest that Step 1 is a two-part step composed of (1) recognizing or identifying and (2) defining. Both parts are necessary. Step 1 also implies a knowledge of the environment in which the problem exists. The SBM may have such a knowledge from his day-to-day contact with the business. The cooperating researcher will need to conduct some background study in order to acquire such knowledge. The need for background information makes it especially critical that the SBM take a very active role in Step 1 of any marketing research project.

Step 2: Making an exploratory investigation of its major aspects.   The purpose of the exploratory investigation is to search out possible solutions to the problem. It is a search for hypotheses which relate directly to the problem. The marketing researcher plays the major role in this step. He should conduct the exploratory investigation personally. The methodology is informal. Sources of information may include consumers, middlemen, suppliers, service departments, company departments and executives, noncompeting firms, and virtually any other source which might have some information in the problem area. Informal unstructured interviewing by the researcher himself is often the data gathering device. From written reports based upon notes from each interview, the researcher does his analysis. Based upon the informal investigation to this point, a decision may be made (by the SBM and the researcher) (1) to terminate the research and make the marketing decision on the basis of what has been learned so far, or (2) to proceed to a formal research design.

Step 3: Formulating the appropriate research design.   Here the technical expertise of the marketing researcher really comes into play. The SBM usually does not have the time or

[10]David J. Luck, Hugh G. Wales, and Donald A. Taylor, *Marketing Research* (3rd ed.; Englewood Cliffs, New Jersey: Prentice-Hall, Inc., 1970), p. 22.

the background (even if he has the inclination) to go beyond this point without experts. The following eighteen steps used in planning research design tell us the story (See Table 7-2). Notice that many of these items appear later, since this list is for *planning* research design.[11]

Step 4: Determining the adequacy of available, or secondary, data. Secondary data are data that have been previously compiled by someone other than the researcher. Many marketing decisions rely entirely upon secondary data since such decisions do not warrant the costs associated with gathering primary data. Sources of secondary data can be either internal (within the firm) or external. Internal sources include sales records, credit records, stock records, and so forth. External sources are library materials, trade associations, government publications, and so on. Once secondary data have been obtained via a systematic search rather than through a limited casual browsing, such data must be evaluated. A later section of this chapter covers secondary data in more detail.

Step 5: Specifying sources and methods of gathering needed primary data. This step is necessary before questionnaires or observation forms can be designed. In this step, the researcher is asking: From whom are we going to seek the primary data and what combination of data gathering methods are we going to use? Obviously, telephone interviews among male consumers will have different requirements than personal observation and interview among female shoppers in supermarkets.

Step 6: Designing questionnaires or other forms for securing the data. This task is obviously one for the research expert. Any SBM who has tried to construct his own questionnaire is well aware of this fact. Even the experienced marketing researcher has difficulty in attempting to eliminate bias while securing the desired information in usable form.

Step 7: Sampling the data from the entire defined population. While every "nth" name from a customer list or a telephone directory may be a sufficient sampling procedure for some purposes, such a sample will often prove to be inadequate, inefficient, and even misleading. Even a truly random sample is often less efficient than judgment or quota sample designs. Estimation and elimination of some sampling error are part of the job of the marketing research specialist.

Step 8: Conducting the field investigation when primary data are to be obtained. The actual collection of primary data in the field is often "farmed out" to firms that maintain field staffs throughout certain geographic areas. Such staffs are trained in interviewing and observation techniques. This practice is followed by both BB and SB. However, for some types of field work, college students under good supervision may prove to be excellent temporary field workers.

Step 9: Planning the interpretation of the data in terms of the decision model and the research design. This is another planning step. As such, initial phases of this step would have begun several steps ago and would culminate here. Interpretation includes both logical and statistical aspects. Planned interpretation must be somewhat flexible in order to allow for unanticipated happenings. The degree of flexibility is determined directly by the formal structure of the research design.

[11]David J. Luck, Hugh G. Wales, and Donald A. Taylor, *Marketing Research* (4th ed.; Englewood Cliffs, New Jersey: Prentice-Hall, Inc., 1974), p. 96.

Table 7–2   Eighteen Steps For Planning Research Design

Questions Faced	*Steps to Take or Choices*
1. Have we correctly determined the data needed to measure the outcome of the alternative solutions?	1. Anticipate data analysis and processing.
2. What approach shall be used?	2. Select either experimental, historical, indirect inferential, or descriptive approach.
3. What specific data are needed for that approach?	3. Write exact statements of data to be sought.
4. From whom are such data available?	4. Search and examine relevant secondary data.

5. How should primary data be obtained?
  a. What are the types of data?
  b. What general collection methods shall be used?
  c. How the sources should be contacted?
  d. How may the data be secured from the sources?
  e. Shall there be a complete count of the population or a sample drawn from it? How chosen?
  f. How will the field work be conducted?
	5. Determine remaining data gaps.

	6. Define the population from which primary data may be sought.
	7. Determine the various needed facts, opinions, and motives.
	8. Plan for obtaining data by survey, observational or mechanical methods.
	9. If using a survey, decide whether to contact respondents by telephone, by mail or in person.
	10. Consider the questions and forms needed to elicit and record the data.

	11. Decide on the coverage of the population:
	  a. Choose between a complete enumeration or sampling.
	  b. If sampling, decide whether to select from the whole population or restricted portions of it.
	  c. Decide how to select sample members.

Table 7–2   (Cont'd.)

Questions Faced	*Steps to Take or Choices*
	12. Map and schedule the field work.
	13. Plan the personnel requirements of the field study.
6. How will the data be interpreted and presented?	14. Consider editing and tabulating requirements.
	15. Anticipate possible interpretation of the data.
7. Can the study be afforded, and is it approved?	16. Consider the way the findings may be presented.
	17. Determine and budget costs and submit research proposal.
8. Is the design really workable and well directed toward the problem solution?	18. Pretest the design.

Source: David J. Luck, Hugh G. Wales, and Donald A. Taylor, *Marketing Research* (4th ed.; Englewood Cliffs, New Jersey: Prentice-Hall, Inc., 1974), p. 96. Used with permission.

Step 10: Editing the returned forms and tabulating the results.   This step consists of such information processing tasks as editing returns, determining classifications, coding, and actual tabulation by hand or by machine.

Step 11: Making statistical analyses of the results.   In addition to the logical interpretation, as mentioned above, statistical analysis, using various statistical tests of the data, is usually performed. Knowing which statistical tests to use and how to perform them is within the area of the marketing researcher. If machine tabulation is used, computer programs are available to perform (but not interpret) most of the statistical analysis.

Step 12: Interpreting the meaning of the processed and analyzed data in terms of the problem and the decisions necessary for its solution.   The use of statistical inference and judgment of the experienced researcher are combined in this step in order to answer the question: What do the data mean, or what can we conclude from the data, in terms of the marketing problem for which the research was conducted?

Step 13: Presenting the findings to those who will reach the decision.   Such presentations may take a variety of forms, depending upon the specific needs of the information users. Both written and "in person" reports are common. The purpose of reporting should be to present the information in such a way that it can and will be used in making the appropriate decision(s).

Of the thirteen steps described very briefly above, it should be noted that the SBM is (or should be) most heavily involved in only the very early and very late stages. Although the SBM must rely very heavily on the technical expertise for the intermediate steps, good research practice suggests maximum involvement of the marketing researcher in all steps. The SBM can do some research for himself; but, for complex projects, the above series of steps should point out the need to hire the expert.

SOURCES OF SECONDARY
MARKETING RESEARCH INFORMATION FOR SB

As indicated earlier, the securing of secondary marketing research data serves two purposes: (1) It provides sufficient information by itself for the making of decisions regarding marketing problems; and (2) it aids in the formal research design by uncovering problem areas and enabling the researcher to do a better job in collecting and using primary data. Although secondary data is inexpensive in both dollar and time costs, it does have some disadvantages. Secondary data may be out of date, inaccurate, too general, too specific, and so on. Among the things to consider when evaluating secondary data are:

1. The character of the organization supplying the data should be considered.
2. The organization's experience, personnel, finances for research, freedom from bias or personal interest, and standards should be considered.
3. The authority under which the data were gathered and the predetermined standards set for collection of the information are important considerations.
4. The units in which the data are expressed must be sufficiently defined. Such sample concepts as "house," "consumer," and "automobile" are subject to varying definitions. Composite units are particularly troublesome when comparing different sources.
5. In every case, a check should be made to determine if more recent data are available from the same or other sources. Figures, sometimes even historical data, are revised as more information is gathered.[12]

Secondary data may be either internal or external to the SB firm. Internal data may exist in any part of the SB firm and may or may not be in the exact desired form. For example, accounting records on sales expenses may need to be reclassified for a particular marketing problem. Examples of internal secondary data are customer complaint records, shipping and billing records, price lists, expense ratios, operating statements, inventory records, guarantee records, service records, and so forth. Ideally, good advanced planning has provided that such records be kept, and that they be kept in accessible and usable form. However, planning cannot anticipate all the possible uses of data and the economies of keeping too many records must be considered. Therefore, internal secondary data must sometimes be derived by reworking and reorganizing existing records.

External secondary data for marketing is available from many sources. The specific sources of interest will depend upon the type of business and the type of marketing problem being researched. Some sources are available which are specifically directed toward the interests of SB firms. In the present chapter, we will briefly discuss some basic sources selected to aid the SBM in beginning his search for secondary data. It should be mentioned here that nearly every textbook on marketing research contains an extensive discussion and listing of external secondary data sources.

One good starting point would be an article that is probably, even today, more classical than outdated. "Where to Find Marketing Facts" begins by saying:

Keep this article. Some day it can save you many hours of important time. It should also provide you with useful information that otherwise you might miss.

The material in this article is for reference purposes of marketing management

---

[12]Steuart Henderson Britt and Irwin A. Shapiro, "Where To Find Marketing Facts," *Harvard Business Review,* 40, No. 5 (September–October, 1962), 178.

people, both senior and junior. If you are responsible for having other people provide you with marketing data, the references given will tell you what sources they should use. If you are responsible for providing marketing data for other people, the references will tell you where to look. And if you are a teacher or student of marketing, you can save yourself many hours of time by using these references.[13]

After discussing some general sources such as periodicals, indexing services, trade sources, and government, the same article goes on to discuss 46 basic sources of marketing facts and figures under five categories: (1) Guides to reference sources, (2) Selected marketing bibliographies (topical and current), (3) Directories (of business organizations, of associations, of marketing and advertising organizations, and of media); (4) Geographical market and population data (from government and nongovernment sources); and (5) Business and economic statistics.[14]

The above materials will lead to other sources via footnotes and other references. Most libraries also have trained staff members who can and will aid the marketing researcher, especially if he has indicated through his own initial efforts that he is relying on the expertise of the librarian rather than simply using the librarian to compensate for his own laziness.

Another beginning point in searching for secondary data might be the *Statistical Abstract of the United States*. This source is especially useful when searching for statistical data. Concerning the *Statistical Abstract*, McCarthy states:

> The most useful of summaries, the *Statistical Abstract of the United States*, is similar to an almanac. It is issued each year and lists more than 1,000 summary tables from work being published by the federal government as well as other groups. References to world markets are included. Detailed footnotes can guide one to more specific detail on a topic. Each issue contains a "Bibliography of Sources and Statistics," about 40 pages in length, that lists all *Abstract* sources, classified by type of subject.[15]

A third starting point for the SBM in his search for secondary data might be the Small Business Administration (SBA). In addition to listing SBA publications, the SBA publishes extensive bibliographies relating to many SB marketing topics. These bibliographies cite both governmental and nongovernmental sources. Booklets (for sale at a very nominal cost) of the SBA include those in the Small Business Management Series and those in the Small Business Research Series. Free Management Assistance Publications of the SBA include: (1) Management Aids, (2) Small Marketer Aids, and (3) Small Business Bibliographies. A reasonably complete listing of SBA publications dealing with SB marketing is currently available from the SBA. SBA publications may be obtained at SBA field offices in most major cities. The above, and other, SBA publications may also be obtained from the Washington offices of the SBA (if free) or the Governmental Printing Office (if a charge is made). The addresses are:

Small Business Administration
Washington, D.C. 20416

Superintendent of Documents
U.S. Government Printing Office
Washington, D.C. 20402

[13]Britt and Shapiro, p. 44.
[14]Britt and Shapiro, p. 44.
[15]E. Jerome McCarthy, *Basic Marketing: A Managerial Approach*, (5th ed.; Homewood, Illinois: Richard D. Irwin, Inc., 1975), p. 557.

SB APPLICATIONS OF MARKETING RESEARCH

The purpose of this section is to show, by example, that the areas of application of marketing research in SB are varied and numerous. These examples of actual cases will serve to demonstrate the manner in which marketing research (based upon both secondary and primary data) has been applied to aid marketing decision making in SB. The examples may also suggest new applications for the SBM who relates these applications to his own business.

As a background for the SB examples, the marketing research activity areas noted in the American Marketing Association *1973 Survey of Marketing Research* are shown in Table 7–3.[16] These figures are for all responding companies, large and small.

Table 7–3   Research Activities of 1,322 Respondent Companies

	% Doing	Done By Mkt. Res. Dept.	Done By Another Dept.	Done By Outside Firm
Advertising Research				
A. Motivation Research	33	18	2	16
B. Copy Research	37	17	6	18
C. Media Research	44	16	10	21
D. Studies of Ad Effectiveness	49	26	7	21
E. Other	7	5	—	2
Business Economics and Corporate Research				
A. Short-Range Forecasting (Up to 1 Year)	63	43	23	1
B. Long-Range Forecasting (Over 1 Year)	61	42	22	2
C. Studies of Business Trends	61	46	16	3
D. Pricing Studies	56	33	25	2
E. Plant and Warehouse Location Studies	47	18	28	3
F. Product Mix Studies	51	36	16	2
G. Acquisition Studies	53	25	30	3
H. Export and International Studies	41	19	22	3
I. Internal Company Employees Studies (Attitudes, Communication, Etc.)	45	13	29	6
J. Other	4	3	1	—

[16]Twedt, p. 41.

Table 7-3 (Cont'd.)

	% Doing	Done By Mkt. Res. Dept.	Done By Another Dept.	Done By Outside Firm
Corporate Responsibility *Research*				
A. Consumers' "Right to Know" Studies	18	9	7	4
B. Ecological Impact Studies	27	8	16	5
C. Studies of Legal Constraints on Advertising and Promotion	38	7	28	5
D. Social Values and Policies Studies	25	11	12	4
E. Other	2	1	1	—
Product Research				
A. New Product Acceptance and Potential	63	51	9	8
B. Competitive Product Studies	64	52	11	6
C. Testing of Existing Products	57	35	20	7
D. Packaging Research: Design or Physical Characteristics	44	23	17	9
E. Other	3	2	1	1
Sales and Market Research				
A. Measurement of Market Potentials	68	60	8	6
B. Market Share Analysis	67	58	9	5
C. Determination of Market Characteristics	68	61	6	6
D. Sales Analyses	65	46	23	2
E. Establishment of Sales Quotas, Territories	57	23	35	1
F. Distribution Channel Studies	48	30	19	3
G. Test Markets, Store Audits	38	28	6	9
H. Consumer Panel Operations	33	21	3	12
I. Sales Compensation Studies	45	11	33	2
J. Promotional Studies of Premiums, Coupons, Sampling, Deals, Etc.	39	25	13	6
K. Other	2	2	—	—

Source: Dik Warren Twedt (ed.), Reprinted from *1973 Survey of Marketing Research* published by the American Marketing Association. (Chicago, 1973), p. 41. Used with permission.

Additional background into activity areas is given by a quote from the same AMA study. This quote is based upon a further breakdown of the data; however, the breakdown is not presented here. The AMA study notes:

> Marketing research is undertaken on a broad variety of subjects, which are grouped in this report under five major headings, with 36 subheadings. For all respondent companies as a group, the most common activities were determination of market characteristics, measurement of market potentials, market share analysis, and sales analyses.
>
> Differences in the research activities of industrial and consumer companies are most marked for consumer panel operations; studies of premiums, coupons, and deals; test markets and store audits; copy research; packaging research; and advertising effectiveness studies. Understandably, consumer companies were more likely to undertake studies in these areas than were industrial companies. The interesting point to note here is that in 25 out of 36 research categories, there were reasonably close parallels in the percentages of industrial and consumer companies engaging in these activities. [17]

The examples cited below tend to illustrate applications of marketing research in rather small firms. Some research, such as performance analysis, is possible by even the "very small" firm. Thus, although we are not always advocating the use of unsophisticated research designs, we are making a deliberate attempt in the following examples to show that even the "very small" SBM, by himself or with limited assistance, can obtain and apply useful marketing information. The SB which is not quite so small will be able to afford both more total marketing information and more sophisticated techniques. For all SB and BB firms, the range of application for marketing research is only as limited as the entire scope of the total field of marketing. Further examples of marketing research application can be found in most marketing research books, marketing books, and in other chapters of this book.

Example 1: Defining a market area.   Many young marketing professors, and their students, have at one time or another defined a market area for a proposed business. Most of these professors will agree that the businessman received excellent research at bargain prices. Hopefully, they are correct. Such studies may also entail projections of estimated sales and evaluation of alternative retail sites. One variation of this example concerns the legal requirements of certain businesses. Banks and savings and loan associations are often required by law to show the need for new facilities. Using marketing research findings for legal purposes differs somewhat from the usual business purposes. [18]

Example 2: General impression of a store's offering.   This application, quoted from a retailing book, is good if the retailer doesn't read too much into it. The information obtained is likely to be general rather than specific. An inexpensive sample method is:

> . . . the simple distribution of questionnaires which customers are asked either to drop in a box in the store or mail back. (The latter, of course, involves higher costs.) Such questionnaires are particularly good for the ongoing business that seeks to

[17]Twedt, p. 40.
[18]William H. Brannen and J. L. Carrica, "A Brief, Practical Primer For The Expert Witness," *Arizona Business Bulletin,* 18, No. 9 (November, 1971), pp. 10–15.

obtain a general customer reaction to the store's present assortment of products and services and to identify areas for improvement in the product and service mix being offered.[19]

Example 3: Layout and display effectiveness.

Another method of information collection is the *observation method.* Here no attempt is made to ascertain consumer reactions *per se.* Rather, unobtrusive observation of traffic patterns as consumers move through the establishment, or spend time at one display versus another, can provide the retailer with low-cost data on *display effectiveness* or on typical behavior patterns. This information can then be used as guidance in plans to change layouts or place merchandise to insure that it is seen by more customers.[20]

Example 4: Measuring advertising effectiveness through experimentation. Although it is almost impossible to measure advertising effectiveness, both large and small advertisers continue their efforts to do so. Reasonable success in measuring the comparative effectiveness of various components of the advertising mix does seem possible. For the retailer who has defined his advertising objectives:

> The success of such experimentation relates largely to *keeping records* and accumulating data which are related directly to the operation of the business of the specific firm itself. Comparison of the drawing power of one particular advertisement versus another similar one run at a later date, together with data on the resulting sales, provides the retailer with valuable information on the cost and profitability of such promotions. When these data are accumulated from a large number of ads placed in various media for different products, the merchant can identify quite clearly which products can be advertised in which media and at which particular times in his yearly sales cycle.[21]

Example 5: Adding new sales territories.

The experience of a small manufacturer of automobile dashboard accessories provides an example of using Census figures as an aid in adding new sales territories. "Where are the high concentrations of automobiles?" was his first question.

When he had the answer, he then looked to see which of the geographical areas under consideration had concentrations of auto supply stores and variety stores— the kinds of retail outlets that did the best job with his products in his established areas. He was able to find this information in the *Census of Business.*[22]

Example 6: To widen a market.

Another example of relating Census data to an individual company's problem is the market research done by a manufacturer of paneling and room accessories. His company had franchise arrangements with local contractors who used the materials to convert basements into finished rooms.

To widen his market, he first had to find an answer to: What areas will be best for franchises? The Census statistics on housing helped him to learn: (1) the type of homes that predominated in a particular area, and (2) whether they were built on concrete slabs or with a full basement.

He quickly ruled out the areas where the houses had no basements.

---

[19]Charles A. Bearchell, *Retailing: A Professional Approach* (New York: Harcourt Brace Jovanovich, Inc., 1975), p. 66.

[20]Bearchell, p. 66.

[21]Bearchell, p. 67.

[22]Solomon Dutka, "Using Census Data In Small Plant Marketing," *Management Aids,* No. 187 (Washington: Small Business Administration, 1973), p. 5.

His next question was: Can people in the particular area afford to finish off their basement? He examined data on family income and the number of children. Then he examined the statistics on car ownership. He looked for families that owned more than one car—an indication that they had discretionary income which might be spent for home improvement. As a result of his study of Census data, he was able to grant franchises in areas which had a good market potential. [23]

Example 7: Discovering future markets.

Census data can be useful also for keeping a company in step with its customers. One apparel manufacturer, for example, studies Census statistics for possible trends that might affect his business. When the figures showed that the population in the areas where he was selling had a high concentration of teenagers and young adults, he added new styles directed at these groups. [24]

Example 8: Selecting advertising media.   The use of Census data to create audience profiles around such demographics as buying power, age, sex, and so forth can be used for media selection. Such Census data can be updated and made more useful by using such secondary sources as the buying power index presented in *Sales Management* magazine's *Annual Survey.* Lower priced consumer nondurable products are especially appropriate for such indexes. Cosmetics is such a product category, as noted below:

> An example is seen in the experience of a cosmetics company which markets its products in several sections of the country. Its owner-manager uses Census data to keep track of the age groupings of the female population. From the Census figures, he learns what groups are prospects for certain of his products and where these groups are located. He then places his advertising in media which are used by members of the groups. He also sees that sales outlets are stocked with the advertised products. [25]

Example 9: Source of new product ideas.   The data from the Census and other secondary sources may suggest opportunities the SBM has not previously considered.

> The experience of a small meat packing plant provides an example of using Census data in new product development. Its owner-manager learned that the statistics for his sales area showed an impressive number of home freezers. In these, he saw a new market—cuts of meat sold in bulk lots for storage in home freezers. [26]

Example 10: Allocating salesmen's time.   From an analysis of sales records, the following typical example resulted.

> This company distributes supplies to the industrial market. The owner-manager formerly operated on the assumption that every industrial plant was a good prospect. But when he analyzed his sales records, he found that this was not true. Only a few customers—2 percent—accounted for half the total sales. And the same 2 percent accounted for more than half the gross profits. More than 90 percent of the customers were small ones—they accounted for less than 10 percent of the sales.
>
> The salesmen's call reports were then analyzed. They showed that salesmen were spending most of their time on the small accounts—those that offered little hope for

[23]Dutka, p. 5.
[24]Dutka, p. 5.
[25]Dutka, p. 6.
[26]Dutka, p. 6.

sales volume or profits. As a result, many big accounts with good sales and profit potential were being neglected.

On the basis of this information, the owner and his sales manager decided on a new program. They instructed the salesmen to use their selling time on accounts with volume potential.

Here are some of the kinds of information you may find by analyzing your sales records:

Which products should be pushed, which should be carried even though the profit margin is small, and which should be dropped.

Which territories are overstaffed and which are undermanned.

Which customers (individual or by category) are profitable and which are not.[27]

Example 11: Determining market potential for a new product. The use of salesmen as marketing researchers is not often advocated. However, under some circumstances, the use is not only feasible, it is desirable. Note the following example:

A salesman's main job is selling plus service, but don't overlook the opportunity to have your salesmen make little surveys during their regular sales calls. Here's how one small company used its salesmen in developing market plans for a new product, an item used by the steel industry.

The owner-manager needed to estimate the new product's total market potential so that he could determine his working-capital needs. It so happened that a steel plant's use of the new product would be proportional to the amount of water used by the plant for cooling purposes. "How much water do you use?" was the question the salesmen asked during regular calls on a number of steel plants.

The owner-manager then compared these water-use figures with each plant's known capacity for producing steel, pig iron, and coke. He worked out a ratio between production capacity and water use.

He then used statistics from the American Iron and Steel Institute to calculate the total amount of cooling water used by the steel industry. In this way, he arrived at an estimate of his potential market that was accurate enough to be used for forecasting purposes.

As a byproduct of this estimate, the owner-manager found himself with a list of water-use figures for every steel, iron, and coke plant in the country. With it, his salesmen were able to determine which plants had the best sales potential.[28]

Example 12: Selecting a store site. The SBA has provided a step-by-step recipe for using Census data in order to select a store site.[29] Examples of maps and Census data illustrate the procedures to follow. Another approach to retail site selection is the use of a traffic study. Such a study may be of automobile and/or pedestrian traffic. In addition to the SBA *Small Marketers Aid* on this subject, many case studies can be found.[30] For example, an

---

[27]Warren R. Dix, "Getting Facts For Better Sales Decisions," *Management Aids For Small Manufacturers: Annual No. 12*, ed. Jean B. MacArthur (Washington: Small Business Administration, 1966), pp. 24–25.

[28]Dix, p. 25.

[29]Louis H. Vorzimer, "Using Census Data To Select A Store Site," *Small Marketers Aid*, No. 154 (Washington: Small Business Administration, 1974).

[30]See, for example, James R. Lowry, "Using A Traffic Study To Select A Retail Site," *Small Marketers Aid*, No. 152 (Washington: Small Business Administration, 1973).

excellent article on pedestrian traffic counts appeared in the *Journal of Small Business Management.*[31]

Example 13: Measuring customer satisfaction. A simple postcard questionnaire can be used to improve customer relations, while at the same time gathering marketing information. This example illustrates:

> One way to keep up with what customers expect is by asking them. Some stores do it by making an opinion poll of their services.
>
> Suiter's, a department store, provides an example. The owner polls his customers and gets their opinions about the store's personnel, merchandise, services, and policies.
>
> He makes this survey by mailing a postage-paid card to all customers who secured cash refunds. The card, which the customers are urged to return, says: "In an effort to serve you more efficiently in the future, we would greatly appreciate your taking time to answer several brief questions."
>
> The questions are:
>
> "Was the refund given promptly?"
>
> "Were you served courteously?"
>
> "Were you approached without undue delay?"
>
> This question card serves Suiter's in several ways. For one thing, the owner is able to pinpoint discourtesy or indifference on the part of store personnel. It also provides a check on employee honesty to determine if the refund was legitimate.
>
> The card makes the customer feel that the store owner is interested in her opinion of the services which the store offers. It is an excellent means of creating customer loyalty.[32]

Example 14: Results of marketing promotion experiments. This example and the following one both deal with simple marketing experiments. The experimental method is probably greatly underutilized by both BB and SB. Our current example is little more than trial and error backed up with record keeping. Experience is practically synonomous with the uncontrolled experiment. Our marketing activity for the experiment could be practically any marketing activity. One often used by SB retailers is the result of a promotion. Of course, it should be noted that elaborate experimental designs, such as "Latin squares," could be set up. However, for many marketing research projects, such designs are often too expensive. This is especially true for SB. Results from simple designs are often satisfactory for SB. Our "pre-post" design is as shown in Table 7–4.

The SBM uses this simple design very often. He does not always keep good records of such "experiments." In fact, sometimes he doesn't even recognize that he is doing an experiment. He can even use the design after the fact. It can be used to measure the results of a promotion, such as in the example below, whether the promotion was a special display, cents-off deal, coupon, or whatever. The format is shown in Table 7–5.

From this example we see that the special display of brand X resulted in a sales increase of $150 or 50%. But our approach is admittedly very crude. If we assumed that the purpose of the special display was to sell the displayed item (and such is not always the

---

[31]Saul Sands, "Improved Pedestrian Traffic Counts For Better Retail Site Location," *Journal of Small Business Management,* 10 (January 1972), 27–31.

[32]Stuart G. Levy, Jr., "Building Repeat Retail Business," *Small Marketers Aids,* No. 108 (Washington: Small Business Administration, 1972), p. 3.

Table 7–4 Pre-Post Design

	Experimental Group		
	Symbol	$	%
1. Pre-measurement	A	—	—
2. Experimental variables introduced	Yes		
3. Post-measurement	B	—	—
Effect of experimental variable = B − A			

case), many questions still remain. From a research point of view, a major question is the lack of a control or control group. Was the same item advertised by our competitor? How was the weather? Were complementary or competing items also displayed? The list could go on and on. Also, in our example, we are certainly less than complete in our approach to the research process—we didn't even define the problem. But before leaving our examples of activity areas of marketing research application, let's show one more experimental design.

Example 15: Results of marketing promotion experiments (with control group). Here, our previous experimental design is expanded to include a control group as well as the experimental group. The two groups are, for all practical purposes, identical. For example, the SB retailer could have two nearly identical (in size, area, sales, etc.) retail stores. The experimental variable (e.g., the special display) is introduced into the experimental group but not into the control group. This design, if in fact the two stores are identical in all important aspects, attempts to net out the uncontrollable variables. In other words, changes taking place in the experimental group are the result of (1) the introduction of the experimental variable and (2) the uncontrollable variables. Changes taking place in the control group (into which the experimental variable is *not* introduced) are the result only of the uncontrollable variables. Thus the *post–pre* results of the control group are subtracted from the *post–pre* results of the experimental group to net out so that the remainder is the result of the experimental variable. The format for this design is shown in Table 7-6.

Table 7–5 Example of Pre-Post Design

	Experimental Group (Brand X)		
	Symbol	$	%
1. Pre-measurement (e.g., last week's sales or average week's sales)	A	$300	100%
2. Experimental variable introduced (e.g., build special display of brand X)	Yes		
3. Post-measurement (e.g., test week sales for brand X)	B	$450	150%
B − A = $450 − $300 = $150 or = 150% − 100% = 50%			

Table 7–6   Pre-post Design with Control Group

	Experimental Group (Brand X in Store #1)			Control Group (Brand X in Store #2)		
	Symbol	$	%	Symbol	$	%
1. Pre-measurement (e.g., last week's sales or average week's sales for brand X)	A	$300	100%	C	$290	100%
2. Experimental variable introduced (e.g., special display of brand X)	Yes in Store #1			No in Store #2		
3. Post-measurement (e.g., test week sales for brand X)	B	$450	150%	D	$310	107%

Effect of the experimental variable = [(B − A) − (D − C)]

in $ = [($450 − $300) − ($310 − $290)]   in % = [(150% − 100%) − (107% − 100%)]
    = $150 − $20   = 50% − 7%
    = $130   = 43%*

*Discrepancies may result if A and C are not identical.

Note that even though we have added a control group to our design, the design is relatively simple and as such is still subject to many criticisms. However, such a design, if used intelligently by an inquisitive SBM, can be helpful in getting better decisions for a broad variety of marketing problems.

The examples given here are but a brief sampling of the potential applications of marketing research by the SBM. Look for other examples wherever you find SB marketing problems—in other words, in any and all of the "five P's" of the SB marketing mix as well as in the SB market.

HOW SB WORKS WITH MARKETING RESEARCH AGENCIES AND MARKETING CONSULTANTS

One thing in common between BB and SB is that they both hire outside assistance when it comes to marketing information. Lawrence Gibson of General Mills stated:

Most marketing research departments use outside contractors to develop the bulk of their data. The company researcher concentrates on assisting marketing in problem definition before projects are undertaken and in data analysis at project completion. Although project management may be controlled by the client, most operating details are handled by the supplier.[33]

The major reasons for hiring outside marketing researchers and consultants are: (1) specialized skills, knowledge, and resources; (2) manpower and cost savings; (3) objectivity

[33]Lawrence D. Gibson, "Use of Marketing Research Contracters," from *Handbook of Marketing Research* by Robert Ferber (ed.) Copyright 1974 by McGraw-Hill Book Company, p. 1–128. Used with permission of McGraw-Hill Book Company.

and a fresh viewpoint; (4) anonymity of the company in securing information; (5) speed in completing a project; (6) management acceptance of the results; (7) exposure to outsiders' ideas; and (8) better contacts available to the outsider.[34]

Thus far, in this section, the comments made here are taken largely from studies dealing primarily with large businesses. Does the SBM also work with outside marketing consultants and research agencies? Yes, or at least he probably should in many cases. The problem of selecting marketing research services is discussed in a *Small Marketer Aid,* #17, by Gordon and reproduced elsewhere. He introduces the subject by asking the questions the SBM might ask himself:

> Suppose your business has a marketing problem. It may be that a solution can best be achieved with the help of an independent marketing research organization or consultant. How would you go about choosing this type of professional service? What factors would govern the selection; and which are the most important? How could you be reasonably sure that you had picked the right service? What would these services cost? These are just a few of the perplexing questions that confront the executive of a small business when he begins the search for professional marketing research assistance.[35]

Marketing research and consulting services tend to specialize. Such specialization may be by the type of industry served, but it occurs often on the basis of services provided. The following categories are often listed.[36]

1. Statistical services and sources
   Government agencies and publications
   Local business sources
   Trade associations
   Advertising media
2. Market planning, consultation, and surveys
   General management consultants
   Marketing consultants
   Marketing research firms
   Advertising agencies
3. Specialized research organizations
   Field interviewing services
   Statistical tabulating services
   Consumer panel services
   Product testing services
   Packaging and industrial design services
   Psychological services

Different combinations of the above types may be found. Directories are available from the American Marketing Association as well as from other sources. The SBM needs

---

[34]*Using Marketing Consultants and Research Agencies* (New York: National Industrial Conference Board, Inc, 1966), p. i.

[35]William C. Gordon, Jr., "Selecting Marketing Research Services," *Readings In The Marketing Research Process,* ed. Keith K. Cox and Ben M. Enis (Pacific Palisades, California: Goodyear Publishing Company, Inc., 1973), p. 150.

[36]Gordon, p. 150.

to know (a) which marketing research services he really needs and (b) which marketing researcher or consultant he should hire. The answer to the first question will be determined by the kinds of marketing problems with which the SBM is dealing. Gordon sheds some light on the second question by suggesting eight steps for choosing marketing research services. In abbreviated form, these steps are:[37]

1. If you have had previous experience (satisfaction) with a marketing research or consulting firm, discuss present needs with them in order to gain the benefit of their previous knowledge of your business.
2. A researcher or consultant located in your immediate city or area can result in cost and time savings.
3. If you have had little or no experience in selecting outside marketing research services, but have your own marketing research staff, consult with them.
4. Talk to business friends and acquaintances, such as bankers, newspapers, trade associations, professional associations, and college faculty members.
5. Narrow your list of prospects to a reasonable limit; then investigate these further through their published literature and by personal visits.
6. Check background and performance with the research service's previous and present clients.
7. Ask no more than two or three of your top choices to submit proposals, along with time and cost estimates based on uniform specifications.
8. You are now ready to make whatever formal arrangements are necessary.

Relationships between the SB and the marketing researcher or marketing consultant are often quite informal. Although a contract has the advantages of having more details down on paper, a "letter of understanding" is often the extent of the formality. Such is sometimes also the case with BB as well. In order to avoid misunderstandings, it is important to have a complete prior agreement on who is to do what, when it is to be done, and so forth. Since researchers often are more limited in their involvement with the client's business than are consultants, a different set of relationships is likely to develop between the SB client and the marketing researcher than those between the SB client and the marketing consultant. However, the research and consulting functions are sometimes performed together. In any case, the final decision making on the marketing problem and the follow-up—to see that the research and/or consulting are properly used in the making of a better marketing decision—are the responsibility of the SBM and his marketing management.

IS MIS FOR SB?

MIS (management information systems, or in the case of marketing, marketing information systems) has, in recent years, been the most up-to-date approach to handling marketing information in very large firms. MIS is not yet a universal approach, even among very large firms. However, this does not exclude the MIS approach from being applicable to at least some small businesses. Mini-computers and mini-information systems are changing the cost and attitude perspectives of some SB firms.[38] Systems are

---

[37]Gordon, p. 150.
[38]Wagdy Sharkas, "The Mini Information System—An Aid To Small Business Survival," *Journal of Small Business Management*, 12 (July 1974), 39.

being custom designed to meet the needs of very small firms.[39] Other SB firms are "plugging into" the systems of suppliers, trade associations, and other suprafirm organizations. Perhaps, the question in the near future will be *which* MIS the SBM should use.

BIBLIOGRAPHY

Books

BEARCHELL, CHARLES A. *Retailing: A Professional Approach.* New York: Harcourt Brace Jovanovich, Inc., 1975.

FISK, GEORGE. "The Functions of Marketing Research," in Robert Ferber, ed. *Handbook of Marketing Research.* New York: McGraw-Hill Book Company, 1974, pp. 1–16 to 1–30.

GIBSON, LAWRENCE D. "Use of Marketing Research Contractors," in Robert Ferber, ed. *Handbook of Marketing Research.* New York: McGraw-Hill Book Company, 1974, pp. 1–128 to 1–141.

HOGAN, THOMAS AND CHIRICHIELLO, JOHN. "The Role of Research and Development in Small Firms," in Deane Carson, ed. *The Vital Majority: Small Business In The American Economy.* Washington: U.S. Government Printing Office, 1973, pp. 305–323.

LUCK, DAVID J., WALES, HUGH G., AND TAYLOR, DONALD A. *Marketing Research.* 3rd ed. Englewood Cliffs, New Jersey: Prentice-Hall, Inc., 1970.

LUCK, DAVID J., WALES, HUGH G., AND TAYLOR, DONALD A. *Marketing Research.* 4th ed. Englewood Cliffs, New Jersey: Prentice-Hall, Inc., 1974.

MCCARTHY, E. JEROME. *Basic Marketing: A Managerial Approach.* Homewood, Illinois: Richard D. Irwin, Inc., 1975.

MYERS, JAMES H. AND MEAD, RICHARD R. *The Management of Marketing Research.* Scranton, Pennsylvania: International Textbook Company, 1969.

TWEDT, DIK WARREN (ED.). *1973 Survey of Marketing Research.* Chicago: American Marketing Association, 1973.

Using Marketing Consultants and Research Agencies. New York: National Industrial Conference Board, Inc., 1966.

Articles and Periodicals

"Basic/Four Corp. Used Ad, Sales, PR, and Education Methods To Show Small Businesses How To Increase Their Productivity With Its Computers," *Marketing News,* April 11, 1975, p. 7.

BRANNEN, WILLIAM H. AND CARRICA, J. L. "A Brief, Practical Primer For The Expert Witness," *Arizona Business Bulletin,* 18 (November 1971), 10–15.

BRITT, STEUART HENDERSON AND SHAPIRO, IRWIN A. "Where To Find Marketing Facts," *Harvard Business Review,* 40, No. 5 (September–October, 1962) 44–50, 171–78.

CHRISTIAN, RICHARD C. "It May Pay To Think Small," *Journal of Small Business Management,* 27, No. 3 (July 1963), 80–81.

DIX, WARREN R. "Getting Facts for Better Sales Decisions," in Jean B. MacArthur, ed. *Management Aids For Small Manufacturers: Annual No. 12.* Washington: Small Business Administration, 1966, pp. 23–29.

DUTKA, SOLOMON. "Using Census Data In Small Plant Marketing," *Management Aids,* No 12. Washington: Small Business Administration, 1973, pp. 1–7.

GORDON, WILLIAM D., JR. "Selecting Marketing Research Services," in Keith K. Cox and Ben M. Enis, eds., *Readings In The Marketing Research Process.* Pacific Palisades, California: Goodyear Publishing Company, Inc., 1973, pp. 150–162.

JUHN, DANIEL S. AND LACHO, KENNETH J. "Getting Information: Where Do Small Businessmen Go?" *Louisiana Business Survey,* 6, No. 3 (July 1975) 11–13.

LEVY, STUART G., JR. "Building Repeat Retail Business," *Small Marketers Aids,* No. 108. Washington: Small Business Administration, 1972, pp. 1–4.

[39]"Basic/Four Corp. Used Ad, Sales, PR, And Education Methods To Show Small Business How To Increase Their Productivity With Its Computers," Reprinted from *Marketing News,* published by the American Marketing Association, April 11, 1975, p. 7.

LOWRY, JAMES R. "Using A Traffic Study To Select A Retail Site," *Small Marketers Aid,* No. 152. Washington: Small Business Administration, 1973, pp. 1–12.

SANDS, SAUL. "Improved Pedestrian Traffic Counts For Better Retail Site Location," *Journal of Small Business Management,* 10 (January 1972), 27–31.

SHARKAS, WAGDY. "The Mini Information System—An Aid To Small Business Survival," *Journal of Small Business Management,* 12 (July 1974), 39–41.

VORZIMER, LOUIS H. "Using Census Data To Select A Store Site," *Small Marketers Aid,* No. 154. Washington: Small Business Administration, 1974, pp. 1–12.

Reports

Committee on Definitions. *Marketing Definitions: A Glossary of Marketing Terms.* American Marketing Association. Chicago, 1960.

III

THE
SBMM
ENVIRONMENT

All business firms, large and small, operate in an environment over which these firms have very little control, at least in the short run. The environment of the SBM may be viewed from points of view representing five major categories of variables which affect SB. These five are economic, competitive, political and legal, societal and cultural, and scientific and technical variables. The interrelationship of the five environmental variables with the SBMM model was shown conceptually in Chapter 3. In the present part of the book consisting of Chapter 8, the specific effects of each of these environmental variables is shown in detail. We will then be ready to study the five "P's" of the SB marketing mix.

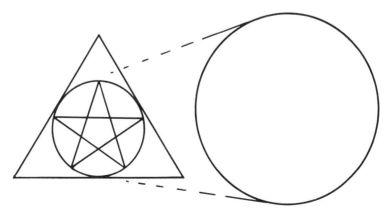

PART III: THE SBMM ENVIRONMENT

8

Environmental (Uncontrollable) Variables For SBMM

THE SBMM ENVIRONMENT

The SBM can select his target markets. He can also combine the five "P's" as he desires in order to formulate a distinctive marketing mix. However, the SBM cannot control the environment in which he operates. He must anticipate the environment and adapt to it in formulating and executing his marketing strategy. The manner in which the environmental variables fit into the SBMM model and into the management of marketing strategy was discussed in detail in Chapter 3. In the present chapter, we will build on the conceptualization of Chapter 3 by showing the practical implications of the environment for the SBM. The environmental variables which the SBM must take into account, both by anticipating and by adapting for them, may be grouped as follows:

1. The economic environment.
2. The competitive environment.
3. The political and legal environment.
4. The societal and cultural environment.
5. The scientific and technological environment.

Each of the above will be considered in detail, but first some general statements concerning the relationships of the environmental variables to SBMM are in order. A brief review of Chapter 3 reminds us that:

1. These items are variables, that is, the environment of SBMM is constantly changing.
2. At least in the short run (and in the case of SB, perhaps even in the long run), the environmental variables are beyond the control of the SBM.

133

3. Although the labels for categorizing the environment into five variables may be the same when speaking about both BB and SB, differences exist in the ways in which BB and SB relate to the environment.
4. SB is affected by its environment and can also (at least by collective action) affect its environment.
5. The customers comprising the target markets of the SBM are also influenced by the environment.

Although history may repeat itself, the SBM should not take much comfort from this. He is faced today with more nonrecurring or new exogenous variables than ever before. The environment appears less stable to the SBM than to his BB counterpart. This is probably a correct perception, since the SBM is not viewing the environment from the security of a large, diversified corporation. However, the SBM does possess more flexibility to deal with the greater instability of the environment. Our investigation in this chapter will reveal the SBMM environment within which the SBM can successfully formulate his marketing strategy. Marketing strategy formulation itself begins in the next chapter with a discussion of product strategy.

THE ECONOMIC ENVIRONMENT FOR SBMM

The economic environment of the markets in which the SB is operating affects the responsiveness of potential customers to the SB marketing mix. Since SB markets are sometimes more specialized and localized than BB markets, the SBM is often most interested in economic conditions by industry or by locality. Such industry or local conditions may lead or lag the country's economy as a whole. In any event, they are connected to national economic conditions. Among the economic conditions that may affect markets are recession, depression, recovery, and prosperity. These conditions are further influenced by such factors as interest rates, availability of money (for both business and consumers), willingness to buy, future expectations, buying intentions, employment levels, and so forth. A continuously unfavorable economic environment such as the lengthy recession of the early to mid 1970s is unfavorable for most SB firms.

What can the SBM do about the economic environment? It is beyond his control. He must therefore try to anticipate it and adapt to it. To anticipate what the economic changes will be, the SBM needs simply to read what the so-called experts predict. However, this may often prove confusing, especially since expert economists are often in disagreement. It has been said (probably by an economist) that about the only thing you can get two economists to agree upon is the general direction of the GNP. Even here we may have difficulty in reaching agreement. Each SBM will certainly want to watch the economic trends in the trade press for his industry. If the SBM is local, he may also wish to note the local predictions, such as those made by university bureaus of business and economic research. A third source of information on economic conditions is what other SB firms think about the economy. Such information is reported four times a year by the National Federation of Independent Business (150 West Twentieth Avenue, San Mateo, California 94403 or 490 L'Enfant Plaza East, S.W./Suite 3206, Washington, D.C. 20024). A recent copy of this quarterly report stated:

This report is the eighth in a continuing series focusing on the behavior of the small business community in the U.S. economy. Findings are based on a representative sample of the membership of the National Federation of Independent Business surveyed during July 1975. The number of firms surveyed was 5,485, of which 2,033 responded, for a response rate of 37%. Descriptive information characterizing the respondents in terms of annual sales volume, industry classification, number of employees, geographical location, form of business organization, and community size is contained in the Appendix.

The topics in this survey cover a wide range of issues including the following:

Most Important Problem Facing Business Today

Price Trends and Expected Price Changes

Earnings Trends

Dollar Sales Volume

Real Sales Expectations

Inventory Levels and Expected Inventory Changes

Employment

Expected Capital Expenditures

Capacity

Credit Conditions

Expectations Regarding Expansion

Expected General Business Conditions[1]

The information contained in the *NFIB Quarterly Report* is presented (with charts and tables) in a very understandable form. It is accompanied by a necessary minimum of economic analysis that can be easily interpreted by the individual SBM to his particular firm. Perhaps the only major criticism of the *Report* might be that the data is somewhat dated by the time of publication. The following excerpt from the "highlights" is typical:

1. Data provided by small business respondents to the NFIB Eighth Quarterly Economic Survey, conducted in July 1975, lead to conclusions similar to those nationally reported elsewhere:

a. An economic recovery is under way.

b. That recovery is something less than spectacular.

c. There appears to be a flatness in the performance of some economic indicators which introduces considerable uncertainty about the strength of the economy in the next three to six months.

d. There are a number of distinctly disturbing signs that point to continuing difficulties in sustaining the recovery.[2]

The "highlights" and the findings of the report identify five economic factors that seemed to be maintaining a relatively steady pattern from last quarter. These five are (a) inflation as the most important problem of small business, (b) prices and price increases, (c) satisfaction with inventory levels, (d) steady or lower interest rates and availability of credit, and (e) attitudes of SB toward expansion and general business conditions. This same report also commented on four items that point to possible problems that may make continued economic recovery difficult. These are (a) expected price increases, (b) excess capacity, (c) changes in size of labor force, and (d) plans to (or not to) make expenditures for equipment or physical facilities.[3] These conclusions are based on 1975 data.

[1]*NFIB Quarterly Economic Report For Small Business* (San Mateo, California: National Federation of Independent Business, October 1975), p. 2.
[2]*NFIB Report*, p. 1.
[3]*NFIB Report*, p. 1.

Once the SBM has anticipated what economic conditions (i.e., the economic environment) will be, it is up to him to adapt his marketing strategies to the anticipated conditions. An example of how he might do this is given by going along with, rather than against, the economic trends. For example, if the federal government gives a tax "rebate" to all U.S. income tax payers, the SBM should find some way to go along with this trend in his marketing mix. The SB retailer might offer his own "rebate." Or he might offer a special price for merchandise paid for with the tax rebate check. Numerous other rebate promotions have been used. Examples of creative recession marketing mixes are especially numerous among the do-it-yourself market. Promotions involving honest attempts to help consumers fight inflation have also been very popular in recent years.

THE COMPETITIVE ENVIRONMENT FOR SBMM

Competition is as much a part of the American way of doing business as apple pie is a part of the American diet. Both competition and apple pie are not equally well liked by all. The competitive structure of an industry does affect the marketing strategy of the SBMM. Examples of such were given in Chapter 4, where we noted that certain markets and markets calling for unique marketing mixes tended to be more favorable for SB than BB.

Competition does not always mean price competition. In fact, price is only one of the five "P's." We may find other forms of competition such as product, place, promotion, and people. The SBM is using tools in all these five "P's" to *compete* with other large and small firms who are also using some combination of similar tools. The competitive environment is composed of all those other firms which are actually, or at least potentially, serving the target markets of the SBM. To be somewhat redundant, the competitive environment is composed of all forms of competition from all competitors. This environment, like others, is in a continual state of change. Also, the SBM must anticipate and adapt to the competitive environment.

The SBM anticipates and adapts to the competitive environment (a) in selecting target markets to serve and (b) in the strategies and tactics he employs to serve these target markets. In selecting target markets, the SBM evaluates the attractiveness of market segments to various competitors and also evaluates the relative attractiveness of competitive offerings to these target markets. The SBM then selects those target markets in which he will have a good chance of achieving the desired sales and profits. Once the desired target markets are known to the SBM, he competes by anticipating the marketing strategies and tactics of all firms competing for such target markets. He adapts his own marketing strategies and tactics in the light of what competitors are doing or might do. For example, the SBM who anticipates that a very large competitor is going to offer a reduced price may counter by keeping his own price the same or only slightly lower, but also changing some other variables in his own marketing mix. Thus, he may offer a slight price reduction along with a slight product change, and use heavy promotion for a short period of time.

Strange as it may seem, the SBM may at times play the role of the competitive leader rather than becoming a follower. This is especially true in limited and specialized markets. For example, the recreational vehicle (RV) industry has only recently been invaded by such giants as General Motors. This example demonstrates that the competitive environment is market determined, that is, the structure and the amount of competition faced by SB are determined to a large degree by the structure and size of the markets being served. Markets also have life-cycles. As the RV market matures, the competitive structure of the industry is changing. Any SBM in the RV industry will want to take these changes into account in (a) selecting target markets and (b) employing marketing strategies and tactics.

A complete listing of factors which, taken together, make up the competitive environment would certainly include most of the following:

1. *Ease of entry and exit.* The ease with which competitive firms may enter and exit the industry of the SBM is a two-edged sword. On the one hand, easy entry due to such factors as low capital and skill requirements may have made it easy for the SBM to get into this market, but it may also make it easy for many other (perhaps too many) small firms to overcrowd the market. On the other hand, difficulty of entry has often been viewed by economists as a sign of lack of competition within an industry. If entry is too difficult, all SB firms may be excluded. In any event, the ease of entry and exit will affect the ways in which industry members compete.

2. *Industry structure.* The concentration, or lack thereof, of an industry has been categorized by such terms as perfect competition, pure competition, imperfect competition, monopolistic competition, oligopoly, monopoly, and so forth. The present and anticipated industry structure do influence the SBM and his marketing strategy.

3. *Direct and indirect competition.* Direct competition refers to products and services that are similar in nature, while indirect competition comes from substitute products and services. In today's affluent society, substitutability seems to increase as discretionary spending power increases.

4. *Industry economics.* The economics of the industry (along with those of the individual firm and those of the nation) affect competition. Such items as cost and profit structures, total industry demand, raw materials supplies, and so forth are involved.

5. *Effects of other environments.* The environmental variables interact among themselves. An example of the interrelationships may be seen when one questions how a legal change could bring about change in the competitive environment. Wendell O. Metcalf, president of the National Council for Small Business Management Development (NCSBMD) recently asked, "For example, will the Administration be successful in scrapping the Robinson-Patman Act, the law purportedly enacted to shield smalls from predatory pricing practices? If the law is scrapped, how seriously will it affect small business?"[4]

THE POLITICAL AND LEGAL ENVIRONMENT FOR SBMM

This environment has more than its share of the action. In the article cited above, Metcalf says, "Government regulation will, in some cases, limit small business activity and add expense. In other cases, special benefits and advantages will be provided for small business. In either case the managers who are aware of the rules of the game and take proper action will fare better than those who do not."[5]

[4]Wendell O. Metcalf, "President's Corner," *Newsletter: National Council For Small Business Management Development,* 15, No. 2 (December 1975), 5.
[5]Metcalf, p. 5.

Historical Perspective

The assumption of competition among numerous small firms was the American ideal which embraced the free enterprise concept. Many changes have taken place since the passage of the Sherman Act in 1890. We will *not* review the chronology of major marketing legislation to the present time. Such a review can be found in many basic marketing books. SB now faces a political and legal environment based on bigness: big government, big labor, and big business. The situation may be summarized thus:

> Legislative thinking in the United States has traditionally been based on the idea that competition among many small firms, or free enterprise, is the desirable norm. Any efforts to fix prices, limit markets, or control or restrain business were held to be not only undesirable but impossible to enforce. But as industry grew larger and more powerful and *combinations* of firms developed in restraint of competition and monopolistic groupings, this "laissez-faire" approach lost support. Starting in 1890 a series of laws evolved to curb monopolies and protect competition. Many of these laws affect decisions concerning the marketing mix.[6]

The SBM has a tremendous task today in keeping up with what is going on in the political and legal environment. Outside legal assistance is almost imperative. Heavy as this burden may be, the back of the SB camel is not yet broken.

Primary and Secondary Effects

The marketing mix of the SBM may, in some cases, be the direct or primary target of legislation or regulatory agency action. The SB marketing mix is probably affected even more often in an indirect or secondary manner due to changes in the legal environment directed elsewhere, such as (a) other parts of the firm or the overall firm, for example, pension plans and (b) big business, for example, suppliers or customers of the SBM. Some legislation has both primary and secondary effects on the SB marketing mix. What, for example, are the primary and secondary effects of the following items:

1. The fact that promotional allowances must be offered to all sellers on an equally proportionate basis?
2. The illegality of exclusive dealings arrangements?
3. The illegality of phoney brokerage allowances?
4. FTC proposals imposing new rules and regulations on franchising?
5. EPA regulations make it economically unfeasible to expand although market demand cannot be met with current capacity?

Little imagination or experience is required to cite both primary and secondary implications from the above in regard to the SB marketing mix. It should be noted that both primary and secondary effects can be either advantageous and/or disadvantageous for the SBM. Even legislation whose primary intent is supposedly procompetition may sometimes have the opposite effects in practice.

[6]William T. Ryan, *Self Review in Principles of Marketing* (Homewood, Illinois: Learning Systems Company, 1971), p. 115.

The diversity of potential problems in the legal environment does, however, challenge the imagination. As an example of this diversity, consider the listing in Table 8–1, which deals only with the potential legal problems in the selling process of small retailers.[7]

Can the SBM successfully compete in this environment of federal, state, and local legislation and regulation? What are the choices? In the short run, at least, the political and legal environment is a given. This means that, in order to formulate a successful

Table 8–1   Potential Legal Problems in the Selling Process

Selling Stages:	*Activities:*	*Potential Legal Problems:*
Pre-Sale	Media Advertising	Deceptive Advertising
		Non-disclosure of Material Facts
		Unfair Advertising
		Deceptive Pricing
	Credit Practices	Unfair Credit Practices
		Deceptive Credit Representations
Point-of-Sale	Selling Practices	Deceptive Packaging, Labeling
		Non-Availability of Advertised Items
		Oral Misrepresentations regarding Product/Service
		Unfair or Deceptive Games and Contests
	Contracts	Unfair Contract Terms
		Unclear Contracts
		Deceptive Contract Terms
		Unfair or Deceptive Lease Contracts
Post-Sale	Product Performance	Unreasonable Consumer Safety Hazard
		Unsatisfactory Performance/ Quality of Product
	Service Adequacy	Failure to Perform Delivery
		Failure to Perform Refund/ Exchange
		Repair Problems (guarantees/ warranties)
	Credit Practices	Unfair or Incorrect Billing
		Unfair Creditors Remedies
		Unfair Methods of Debt Collection

Source: James E. Stafford and William A. Staples, "Legal Guidelines For The Marketing Activities of Small Retailers," *Journal of Small Business Management,* 13, No. 2 (April 1975), 16.

[7]James E. Stafford and William A. Staples, "Legal Guidelines For The Marketing Activities Of Small Retailers," *Journal of Small Business Management,* 13, No. 2 (April 1975), 16.

marketing mix, the SBM must adapt to the environment. It is the only political and legal environment around at the present time. The environment cannot be separated from the market. There are some things the SBM must take as givens. Let's now examine some of the monetary and other costs to SB for maintaining this political and legal environment. Then we'll look at some of the ways in which government assists SB.

Costs to SB
From the Political and Legal Environment

Several editorials have recently appeared in *The Wall Street Journal* concerning SB. One article described the small businessman as the "new forgotten man" and noted the contribution of SB to our society:

> But small business is even more important politically than economically. It is integral to that diffusion of power and wealth, and to the economic and social mobility, which are the hallmarks of a liberal society. It is the small businessman who builds up those large fortunes which then sustain the not-for-profit sector—the universities, foundations, philanthropies—which is so important a buffer between the public and private sectors.[8]

The costs to SB are of two major varieties: taxes and paperwork. Of course, managerial time and legal advice are also very costly. In an article reporting the comments of Senator Gaylord Nelson (head of the Senate Small Business Committee), this observation is made:

> Tax rates discriminate against small business. The largest corporations pay only about 25 percent of their income in federal taxes because of loopholes, while many medium-sized firms pay more than 50 percent. Thus a small firm attempting to accumulate capital to grow may be paying twice as much as a giant competitor.[9]

The incidence of business taxes on SB may be summarized as follows:

> In conclusion, it appears that small enterprises tend to experience stronger competitive constraints against shifting their taxes either forward or backward than do large corporations. The same conditions make it easier for large firms supplying small firms to shift taxes to the latter, thereby increasing the total tax burdens absorbed by small enterprise. In addition to the incidence of these taxes, many small firms also bear the extra burden of compliance costs of sales taxes and the personal income taxes of employees. Relatively elastic demand causes total profits to fall when prices are raised due to taxes, which is a real burden of the tax on the firm.

> In the final analysis, the level of government at which a tax is levied is perhaps the most crucial factor affecting the incidence of taxes on small enterprises. Federal taxes affect virtually all business firms in the same market, whereas state and local taxes affect only those firms operating in the respective taxing jurisdiction. Since the

[8]Irving Kristol, "The New Forgotten Man," *The Wall Street Journal*, November 13, 1975, p. 18. Reprinted with permission from *The Wall Street Journal*, © Dow Jones & Company, Inc. 1975. All Rights Reserved.
[9]Reprinted from *Marketing News*, published by the American Marketing Association, November 7, 1975, p. 1.

latter normally will not encompass the entire market, the result may be discriminatory tax burdens, causing differences in costs that tend to affect the profits of the affected firms. Municipal taxes are, of course, the most likely to fall heavily upon the taxed firm. One aspect of local taxation that might be noted is that larger firms may possess sufficient political influence, if only indirectly through the importance of their local payrolls, to obtain more favorable tax breaks. Smaller business firms, especially those in large metropolitan areas, tend to have no such influence unless they realize their common vulnerability and resort to organized defensive tactics, i.e., support tax ordinance proposals that are broader-based and less burdensome on local enterprise.[10]

The paperwork battle is something else. Cutting through all the government red tape can be both expensive and time-consuming. The government, all the way up to (and including) the president of the United States, admits that government is smothering SB in excessive paperwork. However, a solution to this problem has not yet been implemented. Some SB firms who have not revealed their identities have attempted their own solution: disregarding (or filing in the circular file) much of the nonmandatory government paperwork. It should be pointed out that such a solution may be risky, since it is often difficult to determine what reporting is and what is not mandatory.

The cost of dealing effectively with the political and legal environment will probably continue to rise. Such costs cannot be avoided, but by careful control they can be kept in line. Suggested ways of reducing the cost of the legal environment include: (a) using insurance in order to reduce the risk of litigation and settlement, (b) preventing litigation by more effective legal planning, and (c) complying with the laws. From these three general prescriptions flow the following specific suggestions for the SB firm: Collect accounts receivable yourself; use a CPA rather than an attorney for tax work; determine if incorporation is necessary; consider putting an attorney on the payroll; consider using paralegal help; avoid litigation; review insurance; use firm personnel (not attorneys) for routine data gathering; monitor legal changes; know local legal fee rates; deal directly with counsel; and use all sources available in order to stay current.[11]

Government Assistance to the SBM

The beginning and ending paragraphs from a brief article in *Business Week* report:

It is the official national policy that small business deserves a thumb on the scale to help balance the greater financial muscle and managerial sophistication of the big corporations. But with just over 4,000 employees, a fiscal 1976 budget of $119-million, and a rather hazily defined constituency, the Small Business Administration, which is charged with carrying out that policy, has little hope of being an aid to more than a handful of the close to 10-million small businesses in the country. It generally gets good marks for what it does, but a lot of heated criticism for not doing a lot of other things. . . .

Such cases are not uncommon. When Milton Stewart, president of the National Small Business Assn., is asked how government can help small business, he answers,

---

[10]Charles G. Leathers, "Incidence Of Business Taxes On Small Firms," *Journal of Small Business Management*, 10 (April 1972), 15–16.

[11]William L. Call and Allan H. Savage, "Can Small Business Afford To Defend Itself?" *Journal of Small Business Management*, 13, No. 2 (April 1975), 1–4.

"To start with, get off our backs." Bureaucrat Tom Kleppe's goal is to make sure that other bureaucrats do just that.[12]

In addition to the SBA, other agencies of the federal, state, and local governments do provide assistance to SB. The management assistance programs of the SBA also involve retired executives, college students, paid technical experts, and many other volunteers. Thus, the political and legal environment does provide benefits to the SBM, both directly and indirectly through others. More could be done, but it must be remembered that regardless of how much assistance the SBM receives, he must be his own marketing strategist.

THE SOCIETAL AND CULTURAL ENVIRONMENT FOR SBMM

The societal and cultural environment affects the SBM most directly through customer (consumer behavior and industrial buyer behavior) behavior toward the firm. These topics were discussed in Chapters 6 and 5 respectively. Another way in which the SBM is affected by this environment is through public attitudes toward business in general, and toward SB in particular. Here, we will take a closer look at the relationship of business (especially SB) and society. This relationship does influence the role of SB and the success of the marketing mix of the SBM. How has this relationship changed and what changes might be expected in the future?

Many of the ideas presented in the following paragraphs are speculation about the future. It is hoped that the SBM, whether he be student or practitioner, will form his own framework concerning the social implications and responsibilities of SB marketing. In formulating such a framework, the SBM should remember that our culture does endorse change. The *status quo* is not the way of the future. Will the new marketing concept for SB be the societal marketing concept in which social outputs of the SB firm are measured in social terms as well as economic terms? To what extent will the SBM satisfy the newly defined consumer-citizen?

The American Management Association recently surveyed presidents of large, medium, and small companies from the manufacturing and service industries on the subject of social responsibilities.[13] What do the presidents say?

> Business executives expect that during the next five years social responsibility pressures on them will increase in several identifiable areas. Expectation of decreasing pressures is almost nil. Many of the respondents expect the following social pressures to increase significantly:
>
> Needed response to changing aspirations of minority groups and female employees.
>
> Improvement of physical working environments (regulations by the Occupational Safety and Health Administration, etc.).
>
> Job enrichment programs.
>
> Better consumer relations.

---

[12]"A Box Score On The Controversial SBA," *Business Week*, No. 2387 (June 30, 1975), pp. 100–101.

[13]Reprinted by permission of the publisher from John L. Paluszek, *Business and Society: 1976–2000,* An AMA Survey Report, © 1976 by AMACOM, a division of American Management Associations. pp. 1–46.

Two other social pressures scored especially high among executives of firms in which the issues are relevant: reduction of damaging environment effects (of manufacturing processes or products) and product safety improvement.[14]

The small companies (1 to 500 employees) in the AMA survey expressed more variation in their opinions than did medium and large companies. Among the small company presidents were such opinions as this one:

There is a real need for the development of new instruments to better understand public expectations. . . .

Smaller companies, with their flexibility, may be the hope of American Business in the future as it tries to adapt to new public demands.

Greater accountability is virtually assured.

Consumer groups will continue to grow in influence and a new government social audit arm—the Internal Social Responsibility Service?—is a distinct possibility.

More staff people—and therefore higher overhead costs—will be needed to handle the increasing demands of the federal government.

The corporation will continue its evolutionary course, but perhaps more as a mutant than as a "straight-line" descendant of its ancestors.[15]

The AMA study gives some direct quotations from presidents of small companies concerning what they foresee for the relationship between American business and society for the year 2000. Two such representative quotations follow:

With present attitudes in many government areas I seriously question whether free enterprise as we have known it can change swiftly enough to survive to 2000. (president, age 50–59, 100 to 499 employees, merchandising: wholesale/retail company). . . .

The biggest problem facing American corporations in the next 25 years will be the systematic destruction of our ability to make profits by both federal and state governments and the dissemination of misinformation to the young people of America by the teaching profession, whose knowledge of corporate workings is so erroneous as to border on lunacy. . . . Unless we can do something about this, and soon, the word 'corporation' will be studied in Latin class along with the "buggy whip." (president, age 30–39, 100–499 employees, manufacturer of industrial goods).[16]

In view of the opinions of SB presidents, as expressed in the AMA survey, is it realistic for the SBM to ask himself whether his social responsibility is limited to what is specifically required by the law? Should the SBM look beyond what is most profitable in the short run? The SBM does need to be realistic as well as idealistic. While SB cannot afford the luxury of doing nothing, SB must be able to afford what it does in the area of social responsibility. An example of a practical approach in adapting to the societal and cultural environment is given below. This example deals specifically with ecology, one of today's major challenges in the SB marketing environment. In dealing with ecology, the SBM may consider doing and avoiding the following:

[14]Paluszek, pp. 1–2.
[15]Paluszek, pp. 12–15.
[16]Paluszek, pp. 12–13.

DO:

+ Develop a genuine interest in environmental cleanup.
+ Adopt ecology as a long-term motif.
+ Find out how your customers and prospects feel about your environmental theme.
+ Be alert to business opportunities from ecological dislocations.
+ Investigate local problems and propose to fill continuing needs.
+ Confine your efforts to activities that fit into the scope of your operations.
+ Identify specific buyers or segments who are willing and able to pay for your depollution offerings.
+ Ask your suppliers for written explanations of the ecological effects of their products.
+ Check out vendors' claims.
+ Feature valid, documented contributions to better quality of life.
+ Tie in with governmental and other legitimate antipollution programs related to your business.
+ Sponsor occasional contests or activities for ecological improvements of direct benefit to your customers.
+ Launch antipollution activities that bring customers to your store, generate leads for your products, etc.
+ Set specific operational objectives (like 25 inquiries for a new product) on each short-term effort and keep a record of results.
+ Experiment with price specials, various advertising messages and media, contests, and so on, for promotion of ecology-related goods and services.
+ Enlist the local newspaper editor in planning a series of events which will result in published stories about your business.
+ Offer free advice on where to get information about ecology.
+ Involve potential buyers in environmental activities (as in prizes for suggestions, judged by a panel of customers) or form a council.
+ Gain the enthusiastic support of your employees for your ecological policy.
+ Support your association's efforts for equitable regulations concerning environmental standards for equipment, marketing practices, and allocation of depollution sub-contracts.
+ Time your moves when effective demand and economic conditions are favorable.
+ Assess the likely courses, benefits, and risks of new laws, new inventions, new public attitudes.
+ Study reports of ecological problems and commercial solutions.

DON'T:

— Exploit people's fear about health and survival.
— Look for immediate payoff from long-term campaigns.
— Try to convince customers of the seriousness of ecological maladjustments.
— Offend or embarrass anybody indifferent to environmental blight.
— Dabble in everything ecological; instead specialize on a viable product or market basis.
— Pretend that commercial efforts which benefit the environment are motivated solely by zeal for civic improvement.

— Commit your firm to current opinions which new scientific evidence may refute.

— Depend on continuing government support if at all avoidable.

— Subvert cleanup programs for short-term gain (like producing bottles for "deposit" collectors).

— Let rhetoric stampede you into commercially unsound projects.[17]

THE SCIENTIFIC AND TECHNOLOGICAL ENVIRONMENT FOR SBMM

Science and technology are major environmental influences on marketers because our culture (consumers) places a high value on technological change. Marketing both influences, and is influenced by, this environment. Changes in marketing technology which have been influenced by the technological environment are primarily in the methods of marketing. Examples are self-service, discount houses, planned shopping centers, vending machines, new credit plans, automatic check-out and inventory systems, communications systems, and so forth. Marketing has marketed technology in the form of many new products and services to the consuming public. All this change has been possible because our society is not tradition-bound to the point of being unreceptive to new ideas. Indeed, our society has probably been more open to change than any other in history. High technology has supported, and has been supported by, this open society. The interrelationship between society and technology may bring about a somewhat changed perspective on the technological environment in the future. Social marketers are not the only persons commenting on this. For example, the following insight is found in an introductory management text:

Next to the social environment, the technological environment is probably most important to contingency management. One could reason that technology is even more important than the social environment because it has a more direct, pragmatic impact. However, technology has been a devastating force for enough years for management to finally begin to successfully cope with it. Alvin Toffler's 1970 book *Future Shock* was primarily concerned with the technological impact on society and its organizations. He described future shock as "the shattering stress and disorientation that we induce in individuals by subjecting them to too much change in too short a time." As a reaction to this future shock, society has reached a point where people are not asking what technology can do but instead what technology should do.

Technology is no longer given free rein. Society is now more interested in checking and evaluating technology to make sure that it is contributing to the betterment of humanity. The rejection of the supersonic transport airplane, the cutback in the space program, and the general public outcry against genetic engineering, all technologically feasible, are but representative examples of the new outlook toward technology. Technology is no longer an end in itself for society or, more importantly, for management.[18]

[17]Harold W. Fox, "Ecology: A Marketing Challenge For Small Business," *Journal of Small Business Management*, 10 (October 1972), 15.

[18]Fred Luthans, *Introduction to Management: A Contingency Approach* (New York: McGraw-Hill Book Company, 1976), p. 62.

How does SB interact (affect and be affected by) with the scientific and technological environment? The individual SBM interacts here, as he does in other environments, by anticipating and adapting. In order to anticipate the technological environment and the opportunities it will present, the SBM must try to fully understand the logic of present marketing techniques. He must be especially aware of efficiency and effectiveness in both his own marketing methods and in the methods of the customers he is serving. Examples of SB success in creating new market opportunities through innovation based upon successful adaptation to technology are the following:

> Economically, small business plays a critical role in the process of innovation. When one surveys the new products and new processes of the past 25 years, it is extraordinary how many of them were introduced by aggressive entrepreneurs or smaller business firms. The Xerox copier, the Polaroid camera, the mini-computer, high-fidelity recordings, frozen foods, wash-and-dry clothing, etc.—the list is long and impressive. Nor is it only product innovation that small business is so good at. It also rates high marks for conceptual innovation, for coming up with a new way of organizing older services. Containerization; the discount store; the motel; franchising the sale of hamburgers, fried chicken, and other food products—these, among others, were ideas in the head of an individual that proved fruitful and beneficial because our economic system permitted them to compete with existing ideas as to how things should be done. Obviously, not all the innovations of entrepreneurs succeed; indeed, most of them fail, as they are bound to, in a high-payoff situation. But this brash willingness to risk failure is itself one of the major merits of a system of "free enterprise."[19]

HOW SHOULD THE SBM DEAL
WITH THE ENVIRONMENTAL VARIABLES?

Now that each of the five environmental variables affecting the SBM has been described, we ask: How should the SBM deal with the environmental variables? They are variables, that is, they do change. They are uncontrollable, at least in the short run. And they do affect the marketing mix of the SBM and the responses potential customers make to that marketing mix. In the short run, the SBM must anticipate change and adapt to it. In the long run the SBM can, individually and collectively, influence the environmental variables.

Thus, in the short run, the effectiveness of the SBM in dealing with the environment may be limited to his ability to predict the effects, force, and direction of change. He must also have a good sense of timing. The inherent flexibility of SB will then permit the SBM to quickly adapt his marketing strategies and tactics. Perhaps SB has an advantage in this flexibility. However, it should be remembered that the flexibility only *permits* the adaptation; it does not guarantee it. The SBM must actively adapt to change. Also, the flexibility of SB is counter-balanced by disadvantages, such as the lack of resources necessary to adapt and the severity with which the environment can sometimes deal with a small localized marketer.

In the long run, the individual actions for dealing with environmental variables also include the two tools of *anticipate* and *adapt*. Here, of course, the adaptations are those involving the planning, execution, and control of entirely new overall marketing strategies.

[19]Kristol, p. 18.

Examples of adaptation are: relocation of a retail store, adding or dropping certain customer services in conjunction with changes in pricing policy, product line expansion or contraction, realignment of the sales force, changes in channels of distribution, and so forth.

In addition to adapting to the environment in the long run, the SBM, acting collectively with others, may actively influence the environment. Among the most important means of collective action are trade associations and national business associations. Examples are the Institute of Life Insurance, the National Association of Manufacturers, the U.S. Chamber of Commerce, the National Federation of Independent Business, and the National Council for Small Business Management Development. These last two organizations are SB oriented.

The National Federation of Independent Business (NFIB) boasts a membership of more than 400,000 firms. It claims the "largest individual membership of any business organization in the United States." Its *Quarterly Economic Report for Small Business* was quoted earlier in this chapter. It is an active force in Washington. The NFIB also surveys and reports to its large membership on a wide range of current issues of interest to the SB firm. Through its newsletter, called *Mandate,* the NFIB collects and passes along SB opinion on such matters as improvement of rail service, grain export control, Small Business Administration cabinet status, minimum wages, and so on. Affiliation with the NFIB will not only lend great moral support to the SBM but will also be of great practical value to the SBM in dealing with the environmental variables. The address is 150 West Twentieth Avenue, San Mateo, California 94403.

The National Council for Small Business Management Development (NCSBMD) has, for the past two decades, been serving the needs of SB. (The name of this organization was recently changed to International Council for Small Business.) For thirteen years it has published the *Journal of Small Business Management,* the widely accepted standard in its field. The orientation of the NCSBMD is education. Its *Newsletter* conveys information about SB management training films, tape cassettes, a new SB bibliography, and other items of interest to SB. Other worthwhile organizations, too numerous to mention, are available to serve the SBM in dealing with the environment. Every trade has at least one such association. Many lines of business are served by more than one association. The SBM should actively participate in those groups which are of most benefit to him.

Trade associations perform many functions for their members. Some of the more important services performed by trade associations for SB companies are:

1. Promoting better accounting and record-keeping methods.
2. Sponsoring industry-wide meetings and developing leadership within the industry.
3. Operating a liaison service between Federal agencies, the Congress, the industry, and its individual members. Some trade associations also provide liaison service for their members with State and local governments.
4. Providing publicity and public relations programs for the industry.
5. Fostering industry-wide technical research.
6. Maintaining a labor relations service within the industry designed to prevent work stoppages and promote industrial harmony.
7. Issuing special information bulletins to their members. These bulletins report on current affairs affecting the industry, on Government orders and legislation, and other, similar matters.
8. Gathering statistics for the industry.
9. Publishing specialized data concerning their industries. Many of these relate to such

activities as promoting sales, educating the public to possible uses of the industry's products, or attracting qualified individuals into employment within the industry.

10. Offering training courses to employees of member companies.

11. Supplying other services to the industry such as credit reporting services, savings on the purchase of insurance, and varied economic studies.

12. Furnishing the industry with specialized technical advice that few small members, individually, would be able to afford.[20]

The existing trade associations (with few exceptions) represent businesses of all sizes. SB and BB do have many common interests in dealing with the environment. There are times, however, when the interests of SB and BB are not the same. Their interests may even be in conflict. One writer suggests that the lack of organization among SB is critical:

> If small business is going to survive in this country, it is going to have to organize itself more effectively so that its interests are respected. Just why it has so far failed to do this, I do not know. But I do know that unless it does, it will perish from neglect. And much that is precious to the American way of life will perish with it.[21]

BIBLIOGRAPHY

Books

LUTHANS, FRED. *Introduction to Management: A Contingency Approach.* New York: McGraw-Hill Book Company, 1976.

RYAN, WILLIAM T. *Self Review in Principles of Marketing.* Homewood, Illinois: Learning Systems Company, 1971.

Articles and Periodicals

"A Box Score On The Controversial SBA," *Business Week,* No. 2387 (June 30, 1975), pp. 100–101.

CALL, WILLIAM L. AND SAVAGE, ALLAN H. "Can Small Business Afford To Defend Itself?" *Journal of Small Business Management,* 13, No. 2 (April 1975), 1–4.

ELTON, REUEL W. "How Trade Associations Help Small Business," *Management Aids For Small Manufacturers,* No. 32 (Washington: Small Business Administration, 1971), pp. 1–3.

FOX, HAROLD W. "Ecology: A Marketing Challenge For Small Business," *Journal of Small Business Management,* 10 (October 1972), 11–15.

KRISTOL, IRVING. "The New Forgotten Man," *The Wall Street Journal,* November 13, 1975, p. 18.

LEATHERS, CHARLES G. "Incidence of Business Taxes On Small Firms," *Journal of Small Business Management,* 10 (April 1972), 12–16.

Marketing News, November 7, 1975, p. 1.

METCALF, WENDELL O. "President's Corner," *Newsletter: National Council For Small Business Management Development,* 15, No. 2 (December 1975), 5.

STAFFORD, JAMES E. AND STAPLES, WILLIAM A. "Legal Guidelines For The Marketing Activities Of Small Retailers," *Journal of Small Business Management,* 14, No. 2 (April 1975), 15–20.

Reports

NFIB Quarterly Economic Report For Small Business. San Mateo, California: National Federation of Independent Business, October 1975.

PALUSZEK, JOHN L. *Business and Society: 1976–2000.* An AMA Survey Report. New York: AMACOM, 1976.

[20]Reuel W. Elton, "How Trade Associations Help Small Business," *Management Aids For Small Manufacturers,* No. 32 (Washington: Small Business Administration, 1971), p. 1.
[21]Kristol, p. 18.

THE
MARKETING MIX
OF THE SBMM

This part of the book is the payoff portion—in the sense that the SBM has control over the "five P's" of the marketing mix. The material in previous chapters built the necessary foundation for a better understanding of the total SBMM model. We should know the relationships of the parts of our model: the market, the environment of uncontrollable variables, and the marketing mix of controllable variables. It is these controllable variables of product, place, price, promotion, and people that will capture our attention in the next few chapters.

After having determined a target market, the SBM organizes and controls the five P variables. He also recognizes the influence of the uncontrollable environment on his alternative marketing strategies. The controllable P variables are evaluated singularly and as an integrated whole in the quest for successful marketing programs. The marketing mix of the SBM (a) should be directed explicitly toward the needs of a particular market segment; (b) may (up to a point) substitute one variable or subvariable for another; (c) should employ every variable to the ideal level; and (d) should rely on marketing research as well as sound judgment to determine this optimum or ideal mix.

SB marketing strategy is built from a combination of top-down and bottom-up strategic planning. From the top-down approach, we have already examined the general framework of marketing strategy flowing from the differential advantage of the firm. We continue this top-down analysis into each of the five P's, but at the same time we begin to use the bottom-up approach in order to formulate a product strategy, a place strategy, a price strategy, a promotion strategy, and a people strategy. The resulting marketing strategy is the integrated combination of all five.

Product strategy is naturally considered first because, in its broad meaning, product is the total offering through which the SB firm most directly interfaces with the market. Product strategy develops around such questions as product development over time, product line, and product features such as packaging, branding, guarantees, and so forth. *Place* involves channels of distribution and physical distribution. Channel systems such as suprafirm organizations are especially germane to the who, when, and where questions of the SBM. *Price* is sometimes underutilized as a strategic variable by both SB and BB marketers. *Promotion* is the communication variable by which the SBM persuades the target customer. It may be divided into advertising, personal selling, and sales promotion. *People* is the controllable variable of the marketing mix which is probably unique to SB. The absence of the bureaucratic hierarchy in SB makes it possible to employ people effectively as a part of the marketing strategy. The right people are every bit as much a part of a successful marketing mix as right product, place, price, and promotion.

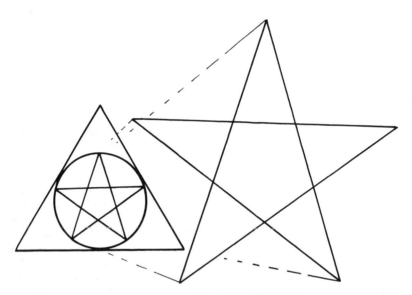

PART IV: THE MARKETING MIX OF THE SBM

9

Product Strategy
For SBMM

Even if the foods were exactly the same, breakfast at Brennan's famous restaurant in the French Quarter of New Orleans would not be the same product as breakfast at the equally famous, legendary Old Home Cafe. Of course, the foods are not exactly the same. Every marketer, small or large, can offer a unique product that encompasses more than a physical thing. In this chapter, we examine product strategy for the SBM and we mean *product* in the broad sense of the term.

Product strategy is a marketing strategy question, but it is also an overall company strategy question. The first concern of any businessman is: What business should our company be in? Another way to state this same question would be: What target markets should we attempt to serve and what product offerings should be employed in order to accomplish this? Thus, basic product strategy flows from the basic goals and objectives of the firm. Among the major goals of the SB firm may be growth of the firm. This is, however, not a goal of many SB firms. In fact, many SB firms have goals that specifically exclude growth. Other SB firms have specific growth goals and still other SB firms may have only vaguely defined goals. Whatever the situation may be, the product strategy, or lack of a product strategy, follows very closely from overall company goals.

The resources of the SB firm are related to firm goals. Whether a firm is new or has been in existence for quite some time, the firm has a somewhat unique set of resources. Some of these resources are marketing resources, while others lie outside the area of marketing but may be used to complement the marketing program. An analysis of firm resources can yield the strengths and weaknesses of the firm and point to the differential advantage of the firm around which the firm's marketing strategy can be built. The analysis of resources may be facilitated by using an inventory checklist such as the one shown in Table 9–1.[1]

[1]Charles H. Kline, "The Strategy of Product Policy," *Harvard Business Review*, 33, No. 4 (July–August, 1955), p. 92. Copyright © 1955 by the President and Fellows of Harvard College; all rights reserved.

151

Table 9–1   Inventory of Company Resources

Financial strength	Money available or obtained for financing research and development, plant construction, inventory, receivables, working capital, and operating losses in the early stages of commercial operation.
Raw material reserves	Ownership of, or preferential access to, natural resources such as minerals and ores, brine deposits, natural gas, forests.
Physical plant	Manufacturing plant, research and testing facilities, warehouses, branch offices, trucks, tankers, etc.
Location	Situation of plant or other physical facilities with relation to markets, raw materials, or utilities.
Patents	Ownership or control of a technical monopoly through patents.
Public acceptance	Brand preference, market contracts, and other public support built up by successful performance in the past.
Specialized experience	Unique or uncommon knowledge of manufacturing, distribution, scientific fields, or managerial techniques.
Personnel	Payroll of skilled labor, salesmen, engineers, or other workers with definite specialized abilities.
Management	Professional skill, experience, ambition, and will for growth of the company's leadership.

Source: Charles H. Kline, "The Strategy of Product Policy," *Harvard Business Review,* 33, No. 4 (July–August, 1955), 92. Used with permission.

Firm resources are not fixed in the long run. Our approach to produce strategy can therefore be dynamic. Present strengths and weaknesses can be changed. But that is the long run. For the short run (usually of more interest to the SBM), resources are relatively fixed and the differential advantage of the firm changes very little. The differential advantage derived from the above resources analysis is the cornerstone of the firm's marketing strategy and consequently of the firm's product strategy. The differential advantage may be described as follows:

Most firms desire an advantage over their competition. Usually the advantage is most desirable if it occurs in the marketing sector of the firm's activities. Within the marketing sector the advantages sought are in the form of observable differences in the product or the marketing functions of the firm. If these differences are of sufficient character and quality to give the firm a preferred position in the consumer's acquisition of product and services, then the difference can be called a *differential advantage.*[2]

Nearly every SBM should be able to find a differential advantage for his firm. His differential advantage, based upon his resources, may be in such things as technical

[2]David J. Luck and Arthur E. Prell, *Market Strategy* (New York: Appleton-Century-Crofts, 1968), p. 36.

knowledge, exclusive product features, established market contacts, a strong consumer franchise, superior location, superior personnel, personalized service, and so forth. The differential advantage is anything that meaningfully and favorably differentiates the SBM from his competitors. The more important the differential advantage is to the market, the more significant it can be to the SBM. For example, if an exclusive product feature were perceived by customers to be very desirable and important, this could represent a great differential advantage for the SBM. However, such a differential advantage may prove to be temporary if the product features are copied by competitors.

The search for the differential advantage can be aided by using the principle of market simplification and the principle of market dominance discussed in detail in Chapter 4. A differential advantage should always exist in order for the SBM to be successful. At the very worst, the SBM would not want to compete in market segments where he possessed no advantages and several disadvantages. Through creative marketing strategy, the SBM can sometimes create a differential advantage where none previously existed.

The SBM should usually be a target marketer rather than a mass marketer. Market segmentation and product differentiation were discussed as alternative marketing strategies in Chapters 4 and 5. Here, we'll expand on these concepts somewhat. Our purpose is to determine the most basic of our strategy decisions: How do we match the product with the market? The product-market matching strategy alternatives are as follows:

1. *Undifferentiated marketing*—the firm puts out only one product and tries to market it to all buyers with one marketing program.
2. *Differentiated marketing*—the firm designs separate products and/or marketing programs for each market segment.
3. *Concentrated marketing*—the firm concentrates all its efforts in one or in a few lucrative market segments.[3]

In our terminology of previous chapters, undifferentiated marketing (#1 above) is similar to so-called product differentiation, but the term *undifferentiated marketing* may be more descriptive and less confusing. Differentiated marketing and concentrated marketing (#2 and #3 above) are two forms of market segmentation. An extreme form of market segmentation not mentioned above would be customized marketing. Since the SBM is usually a target marketer, his product-market matching strategy should normally be #2, differentiated marketing, or #3, concentrated marketing. A limited number of SB firms will be customized marketers. SB firms will probably find it most difficult to successfully employ a #1 undifferentiated marketing strategy for matching products and markets. Under a market segmentation strategy for determining the product-market match, the SBM will actually have several marketing strategies (one for each target market), and each of these will have a product strategy component.

We consider product strategy before other marketing mix areas because product is so important as an interface with the market. The SBM may also find it naturally convenient to first consider product strategy. However, this does not necessarily mean that actual product strategy decisions will always chronologically precede strategy decisions for place, price, promotion, and/or people. Good products are extremely important. The

---

[3]Philip Kotler, *Marketing Management: Analysis, Planning, And Control* (2nd ed.; Englewood Cliffs, New Jersey: Prentice-Hall, Inc., 1972), p. 182.

SBM with good products that meet the needs of the specific target markets is likely to be fairly successful in spite of other shortcomings in the marketing mix. For example, a firm may have practically no marketing research, inefficient distribution, and poor advertising; but it may receive consumer patronage because of the superiority of its product. A firm with a bad product will find even limited success to be beyond its grasp. Ideally, the SBM will combine a good product strategy with the other elements of the SB marketing mix.

THE MEANING OF PRODUCT

Under the marketing concept, it makes sense to use a customer orientation when defining terms such as *product. Product* is:

1. *All* that is transferred from the firm to the customer when a purchase takes place.
2. The capacity to obtain satisfaction and utilities (or perhaps profit, in the case of an intermediate customer) for the buyer.
3. *Not* simply a physical or tangible article or product, as a very narrow definition might suggest.
4. *Not* simply a single intangible service.
5. A component part of a customer's larger symbol or total life style rather than an isolated item.
6. Composed of a complex of features and attributes which are both tangible and intangible.
7. A goods/services combination.
8. Dynamic—in the sense that it changes over time.

By combining the above elements into a more compact definition, we may state that: *Product* is the total dynamic goods/services combination of features and attributes offered by the firm and purchased by the customer to provide for or enhance the capacity for satisfaction, use, or profit.

A brief explanation of this rather lengthy definition seems in order. First, product is the total offering. Secondly, the dynamic nature of product means that the offering of the firm is changing in response to the needs of the market. The ratio of goods to services may be changing and the combination of features and attributes included as parts of the product may be changing. The concept of the product life-cycle details the dynamic nature of product.

Third, product is a goods/services combination. We use the term "goods" here to mean the same thing as "product" in the narrow sense. Many marketing writers use "product" for both the narrow and broad meanings of the term. Thus, in the following quote describing the goods/services combination, we might substitute the word "goods" in place of "physical products":

> The outputs of an enterprise that have value to other units in the economy are usually described as physical products (tangible outputs) and services (intangible outputs). Some types of economic activity, such as manufacturing, result primarily in physical products; others, such as banking and retailing, result primarily in services. However, most product-producing enterprises also generate a stream of

associated services (sales calls, repairs, financing, etc.), and most service-producing enterprises jointly provide some physical products along with their service output. In retailing, for example, the connection between physical products and the services of display, storage, selling, and financing is obvious and essential.[4]

The goods/services combination may be pictured as a continuum, with goods at one end and services at the other, such as in Table 9–2 below. However, a product is seldom 100% goods or 100% services. Varying the proportions of goods and services in the combination is one method by which the SBM may offer a unique product strategy. In fact, this is very often the basis of product strategy for many small retailers who offer extensive customer services.

Fourth, product is composed of features and attributes. Remember that these attributes can be physical or nonphysical as they relate to goods and/or services. Examples of features and attributes are packaging, branding, warranty service, installation, credit, delivery, attachments and accessories, repair service, parts availability, and the entire range of possible physical features and customer services.

Fifth, by stating "offered by the firm and purchased by the customer," we are including all types of firms and customers. Since we are using the term *product* in a broad sense, manufacturers, wholesalers, retailers, and service firms all have products. For example, a small garage which services the delivery vans of a dry cleaning firm is offering a product to an industrial customer. Even though this product may be mostly a service, the SB garage operator should have a product strategy. By customers, we mean customers in both the industrial market and the consumer market.

Sixth, the purpose of the product is to provide for or enhance the customer's capacity for satisfaction, utility, or profit. Capacity for profit applies only to the industrial market. Capacity for satisfaction is usually associated with the consumer market but may also apply to the industrial market. In effect, the customer is not buying a physical item. He is buying what that item can do for him. The same is true if he is buying a service. The driver is not interested in buying gasoline to fill the tank of his automobile. He is buying the continued capacity of the auto to perform as desired—moving from place to place, with good acceleration, while providing air-conditioned comfort to the occupants of the auto.

In formulating product strategy, we are using the term *product* in the broad sense. Everyday usage which limits *product* to a physical object or article is too restrictive and tends to give us the false sense of security that *product* is a simple, tangible concept. Such is not the case. The truth is that the customer does not view product in the narrow sense in the customer purchase strategy; and the SBM should not view product in the narrow sense in formulating product strategy.

Table 9–2 The Goods/Services Continuum

Goods	100%	90%	80%	70%	60%	50%	40%	30%	20%	10%	0%
Services	0%	10%	20%	30%	40%	50%	60%	70%	80%	90%	100%

Product = Goods & Services at any point on the continuum.

[4]Lee E. Preston, *Markets and Marketing: An Orientation* (Glenview, Illinois: Scott, Foresman and Company, 1970), p. 171.

SOME PRODUCT STRATEGY GENERALIZATIONS:
WITH SPECIAL REFERENCE TO SB

In our discussion of target markets in Chapter 4, we identified several types of market segments which make attractive target markets for SB. In relation to the "product" variable of the marketing mix, we noted (a) products with a high proportion of services to goods, (b) unique services, (c) new products when development time is short, (d) a narrow and distinctive line of products, and (e) perishable products. This list, of course, is only a partial one; but it does remind us that product strategy for SB flows directly from the identification of market targets. The following list of generalizations from the American Management Association suggests product strategy direction for the SBM who is considering some innovation in his existing product strategy:

Every commercial enterprise, whatever its size, exists for the purpose of spending money to create value in excess of the money spent.

A small company makes its living by filling needs the big company cannot afford to fill (by producing products or services in response to variables inimical to large-scale production, such as short delivery time or custom features).

The small company does best in a market that is stable for its products (a small business that must continually move into new markets has picked wrong products).

The small company is favored by products that have short production runs; the longer its production runs, the more vulnerable to competition from larger companies a small company is.

Great variability of demand, seasonally or volumetrically, favors small company operations.

Small companies should look for products that are required in high quality; high-volume methods which favor large companies are often deficient in the quality of the article or service produced.

Increasing product variation and complexity create new opportunities that favor exploitation by small companies.

Companies that serve markets highly sensitive to product features must take pains to avoid getting trapped into product stasis. (Market *stability* at times results from design *mobility*.)

Small companies should strive for recognized degrees of exclusivity for their products or services; because the investment capacity of small companies limits their investments in production facilities and expertise, they benefit less from freezing product designs than large companies.

Small firms are favored when their products or services cannot easily be combined with other products or services, either in production or sales.

Small companies should resist having a full product line when it diminishes having a distinctive line; the small company competes most effectively when its items appeal to customers because they are distinctive rather than because of graduations among them.

Small companies that risk large portions of their resources in projects which do not offer the possibility of learning early whether the innovations will be successful engage in unjustifiable and, possibly, deadly risks. (Seven out of eight hours of time devoted to product development in this country are spent on projects that do not achieve commercial success.)

Small companies should avoid products that require long investment of time; risks rise in direct proportion to the stretching of time between the first investment and the earliest possibility of payoff.

Opportunities for small business relate to the stage of maturity of the industry or product involved. Small businesses tend to be important producers or suppliers of components, of products in early stages of development, while large firms tend to dominate the markets for older, established products.[5]

The above general guidelines to SB product strategy can be easily related to the target market strategy of SB and the general advantages of SB. For the individual SBM, such a list should be modified and expanded to reflect the goals and the specific differential advantage of that SBM.

Product strategy generalizations for SB may also be suggested by comparing the product requirements in two hypothetical firms (manufacturers of synthetic organic chemicals) which differ only in size. As the example shows in Table 9–3, the size difference results in product strategies that differ at nearly every point.

Table 9–3   Example of Product Strategy in Large and Small Companies

Product requirements	Company A Net worth $500,000,000	Company B Net worth $500,000
Capital investment	High	Low
Sales volume	Large volume	Small volume
	Mass markets	Specialized markets
	Many applications	Many to few applications
	National distribution	Local or specialized distribution
Similarity to present distribution channels	High to moderate	High
Effect on going products	Good to fair	Good
Competition	Relatively few companies	Few to many companies
	Sound pricing	Sound pricing
	Good possibility of securing a large percentage of the market	Desirable market position variable
Cyclical stability	High	High
Technical opportunity	Great	Moderate to small
Patent protection	Great	Great to none
Raw materials	Basic materials	Intermediate or basic materials
	Many suppliers	Many to few suppliers
Manufacturing load	Standard products	Standard or custom products
	Mass production	Specialized production
	Few grades and sizes	Few to many grades or sizes
Value added	High	High to moderate

Source: Charles H. Kline, "The Strategy of Product Policy," *Harvard Business Review*, 33, No. 4 (July–August, 1955), 98. Used with permission.

[5]Reprinted by permission of the publisher from Theodore Cohn and Roy A. Lindberg, *How Management Is Different in Small Companies,* An AMA Management Briefing, © 1972 by American Management Association, Inc., p. 26.

The product strategy generalizations given thus far seem to be most applicable to the SBM who is a manufacturer. What about the SBM who is a wholesaler, retailer, or service firm? These firms must also have product strategies. In some instances, such as the franchisee, product strategy may be determined by the franchisor. SB retailers and wholesalers tend to favor nationally advertised brands over private-label merchandise. SB wholesalers sometimes specialize in narrow product lines or in the limited functions they perform. SB service firms, that is, those SB firms whose product involves mostly service and very little goods, also differ from BB service firms in product strategies. For example, SB services are often less mechanized, call for smaller investment, are aimed at limited markets, and are more labor intensive. Specific product strategies for SB, derived from the above and from other generalizations, are cited later in the chapter. Product tactics may also vary in effectiveness according to the size of the firm.

One special area of product strategy difference betwen BB and SB is the strategy for new product development. Although product development may be a rather routine and continuous activity in many large firms, it is often a periodic activity at best among many SB firms. Whether the SB firm is new or has been in existence for quite some time, new product development may require outside expertise in both the strategy formulation and the process itself. The new SB enterprise faces both unique opportunities and problems in this area. For example, a new SB firm may find it advantageous to subcontract the production activity initially to an existing experienced manufacturer in order to obtain such advantages as a firm cost of goods, lower total investment, experience, product availability at an earlier date, and the freedom to concentrate its own activities on the marketing problems. SB firms generally tend to avoid products and businesses requiring much development. SB firms do operate in high technology fields, but their roles tend to be highly specialized.

THE "HOW TO" OF PRODUCT STRATEGY PLANNING FOR SB

Within the entire field of product strategy, there is one strategy area that is a core strategy. All other product strategy areas are supporting strategies. The core strategy area is the one which we have already discussed: the product-market matching strategy. To review briefly, we stated that the product-market matching strategy of the SBM would almost always be one of target marketing. Target marketing can result from differentiated marketing (also called market segmentation), from concentrated marketing, or, in the extreme case, from customized marketing. Target marketing, in conjunction with the SB principles of market simplification and market dominance, is the core marketing strategy which we call the product-market matching strategy. The specific nature of this strategy for an individual SBM will depend on company goals and objectives, specific target markets selected, the marketing environment, and the differential advantage of the firm.

Let us now look at a step-by-step method for planning the SB product strategy. These steps apply to our broad definition of product and are equally applicable to all SB marketers whether they are manufacturers, wholesalers, retailers, or service firms. The eight steps are:

1. Record the current product strategy.
2. Identify strategic product problems.

3. Divide current strategic product problems into core strategy areas and supporting strategy areas.
4. Formulate alternative product strategies at both core and support levels.
5. Evaluate these alternatives in various combinations.
6. Choose the new product strategy.
7. Plan the details of implementation of the new product strategy.
8. Set performance standards and monitor feedback.

The above list should look somewhat familiar. It is essentially the same process used in Chapter 3 to formulate overall marketing strategy for SB. Here, the eight-step method is adapted to product strategy formulation. What goes on in each of the eight steps will therefore be quite different, even though the process is very similar. Using this eight-step outline for product strategy formulation will require the SBM to work hard and to fill in the outline methodically. The required tools are a note pad, a conference room, good leadership, and a good marketing management team.

Step 1—Record the current product strategy. This first step in our conference method of product strategy formulation is the first opportunity to do it right (or wrong). Remember, although we are also concerned with product in the narrow physical sense, our main concern is with recording product strategy in the broad sense of the term. What exactly do we record? First, we should state in very specific terms the core product strategy, that is, the product-market matching strategy for our SB firm. This should be done for each of the target markets we serve, as should each of the eight steps in our process. Thus, although product strategy may be somewhat similar from target market to target market, we should have a separate strategy and we should record that separate strategy for each target market served. Remember that in Chapter 3 we had an overall marketing strategy for each target market served. These were then combined into the overall marketing program for the entire SB firm. Whether or not it is advisable to combine the several product strategies of the SB firm's several target markets into an overall product program may be debated. This author feels that while some overlap may exist, an overall product program for the SBM may be a misleading way of looking at things, since it may tend to shift the emphasis from the target market(s) to the product(s).

What does the SBM record in addition to the product-market matching strategy? The obvious answer is: everything else that describes his current product strategy. He should record the answers to such questions as are given in Table 9–4 below. The SBM should be honest and as complete as possible in describing the current product strategy. Once this has been accomplished, we have an information base for moving on to the next step.

Step 2—Identify strategic product problems. If the current product strategy is not perfect, some product problems (or opportunities) exist. Some of these problems may have been indicated in Step 1 when answering the questions suggested in Table 9–4 on page 160. The strategic problems must now be specifically identified and defined in operational terms. These strategic product problems may exist in either the core (the product-market matching strategy) or in any of the supporting product strategies. Remember also that we are looking at strategic rather than tactical product problems. These product problems will usually relate in some way to place, price, promotion, and/or people since product strategy is not formulated in a vacuum.

Problems are not the same thing as symptoms of problems. The SBM must make sure that what he is identifying is the real problem rather than simply a surface symptom that a product problem does exist. The broad definition of product must be used if problems are to be correctly identified. For example, ignoring the relevant customer services area may mean ignoring the product problem entirely, if this is the area in which an important product problem exists. The SBM is attempting, in this step, to identify all important product problems. Many strategic product problems that exist today could not have been anticipated the last time product strategy was reviewed, perhaps a year earlier.

Table 9–4 Some Questions The SBM May Ask About Product Strategy

1. *Core strategy.* Is our product-market matching strategy of target marketing one which best relates product strategy to (a) the overall marketing strategy of the firm, (b) to other marketing mix (price, place, promotion, and people) strategies, and to substrategy areas of product? Should we be serving this target market? If so, should we be using this product to do so? In what ways, such as greater penetration within the same market, could we better serve the present target market? What other target markets, if any, should we consider serving with the present product offering or with a new product offering? Is product strategy compatible with our goals and differential advantage?

2. *Product line strategy.* How many products (goods/services combinations) are we offering this target market? What is the assortment in terms of width and depth choices? What is the proportion of goods to services in our offering? How does this compare to competition? Is our present offering well positioned with respect to the target market and the competition? Should the product be repositioned by employing a strategy of trading-up or trading-down due to existing market conditions? Has product-line expansion, modification, or deletion been tried? What does sales analysis by product line show?

3. *Product life-cycle.* At what stage in the product life-cycle is our product? At what pace or speed is the product moving through the product life-cycle? Should we attempt to influence the stage by recycling the product through such means as product innovations? Is the target market we are serving considering the product to be in the same stage of the product life-cycle as are other market segments? How do we adjust all our marketing mix strategies (product, place, price, promotion, and people) as the product moves through the life-cycle? When is our timing (a) before, (b) the same as, or (c) after that of our competition?

4. *Product identification and feature strategy.* Do we use individual or family brands? Do we stress reseller (private labels) brands or manufacturer (nationally advertised) brands? What is the actual degree of brand familiarity of our brands among our target market customers? How important, and for what purposes, is branding important for our product offering? In what ways are packaging and labeling positive attributes of our product? Is the warranty a silent or speaking part of our product? What is our protection strategy (patents, license, and other legal means) for our product? Does our customer services strategy fit the needs of our target market? How do repair and maintenance services fit into our product strategy? What physical product features, such as style, quality, design, and so forth, are unique to our product and our strategy? Is physical size (such as units of purchase) a part of our strategy? How much and what do we know with reasonable certainty about our product image? Is this image consistent with our product strategy and our other strategies?

5. *New product development.* Are we in the new product development business for the present target market or for other target markets? What is the relationship of new product development to present products? At what stage(s) of new product development are we actively involved?

6. *Finally.* Does our product strategy satisfy both the requirements of our target markets and the objectives of our firm? In what ways are we exceeding or falling short?

If our investigation results in no serious product problems being identified, we should immediately shift to an even more positive frame of mind by asking ourselves what unrealized opportunities exist that could be realized by changes in our product strategy. Of course, such changes should not adversely affect our present sound product strategy.

Step 3—Divide current strategic product problems into the core strategy area and supporting strategy areas. This should not be difficult. We have already stated that the single core strategy area of product strategy is the product-market matching strategy. In other words, what product(s) we market and to whom we market them is determined coincidentally with the adoption of a strategy of differentiated marketing (or target marketing). This target marketing could also take the form of concentrated marketing or customized marketing, as previously discussed. However, markets do change. Our core strategy must therefore change. This change in core strategy will probably not be a shift from our basic target marketing approach; rather, it will be a shift of emphasis on how we apply our target marketing. For example, if the size and shape of our traditional target market changes (and it usually will), we may wish to shift our product strategy emphasis. This shift may be accomplished in a number of ways, such as: (a) moving from concentrated marketing to differentiated marketing by redefining what was one target market to two or more target markets; (b) redefining the dimensions of markets and the subsequent needs along which product and market are matched; and (c) calling for different levels of support from the supporting strategies. Problems in the core product strategy probably occur much less frequently than those in the supporting areas, but when they do occur their impact may be very great.

Most product strategy problems are in the supporting strategy areas. In Table 9–4 we note that potential problems in the supporting strategy area might be classified under such headings as product line strategy, the product life cycle, product identification and feature strategy, and new product development. The number of strategic product problems possible in the supporting area is almost unlimited. The SBM has presumably identified those that are really important in Step #2 above. If this was done, this part of Step #3 is somewhat clerical. However, supporting product strategies should not be neglected by the SBM, because they always spell the measure of success of the core strategy. And some supporting product strategies are sometimes more important than others.

Now that the SBM (i.e., you) has (a) recorded the current product strategy, (b) identified strategic product problems, and (c) determined which of these problems are core area and which are supporting area, we are ready to plan for the future. Where can we go from here? What are the options? Where do we want to go?

Step 4—Formulate alternative product strategies at both core and support levels. The SBM now begins the innovative process of creating new alternative product strategies. This does not necessarily mean new products in the narrow sense of the term, although, in the broad sense, the product offering may be new. The formulation of new strategies may take place at both the core and support levels even though problems were identified in only one level. At this stage, we are attempting to keep from limiting our thinking. Product strategies work in combination with each other; in combination with the overall marketing strategy; and in combination with place, price, promotion, and people. In the next step, alternative product strategies will be evaluated. In the present step, we are seeking to find the alternatives.

Alternative product strategies are found by looking for then. Where does the SBM look? In order to stimulate thinking, the SBM and his marketing team may wish to look at a ready-made repertoire of strategies. One such repertoire does exist in the appendix of *Market Strategy*. In its introduction, the authors state:

> The typing and classifying of strategies provide merely one basic element needed for strategic thinking. The user of a repertoire obviously must possess a clear and comprehensive definition of his organization's objectives and policies and an ample description of the situation before he can use the repertoire intelligently. Then, he must apply the all-important creative and artistic abilities to transform a general, brief description of a type of strategy into a full and specific statement of what is to be done—and how, and when. A substantial conception of a full-blown strategic plan must be in mind before expected results of alternative schemes can be projected and the best one chosen for elaboration and detailed planning.[6]

The above source goes on to list some of the more frequently used alternative strategies, several of which are:

1. Expanding product's rate of purchase by present buyers by (a) making existing designs obsolete, (b) obtaining sharper brand differentiation, (c) making the product more widely or conveniently available, and (d) increasing the unit of purchase.
2. Induce new uses of the product by (a) adding features or qualities serving new uses, (b) buyer education regarding new uses, (c) product proliferation, and so forth.

The above partial listing is merely suggestive. However, it should be noted that many of these strategy alternatives involve more than simply product. They involve the integration of product with other parts of the marketing strategy. Other sources of ideas for alternative product strategies can often be obtained from the trade journals. Successful strategy ideas travel very quickly. In the next step, the SBM evaluates the attractiveness of all alternatives for his particular SB.

Step 5—Evaluate these alternatives in various combinations. The product strategy alternatives generated in the previous step are now evaluated by the SBM. However, we are merely evaluating the alternatives. We are not yet *selecting* an alternative. Each alternative and each meaningful combinations of alternatives should be evaluated in terms of our firm goals and resources. The SBM should consider the potential sales and profits of each, the competitive reactions which might be expected, the effectiveness of alternative product strategies in solving current marketing problems identified in Step #2 above, the effect upon other areas of the marketing mix, and so forth.

Each member of the marketing team may have his own criteria for evaluating product strategy alternatives. In order to get maximum input and benefit, the SBM should make up a master list of criteria before the actual evaluation discussion begins. The weighting of individual criteria by individual marketing team members need not be standardized, but some general understanding of the relative importance of each criterion is helpful. If core strategies are discussed first, and then followed by a discussion of alternative supporting product strategies, these discussions should be continued by a consideration of various combinations of core and supporting product strategies.

Step 6—Choose the new product strategy. The SBM, probably with the advice of other

[6]Luck and Prell, pp. 175–176.

members of his management team, should now be ready to make a choice. This product strategy choice is one that he plans to live with for some time, possibly for a year or longer. The new product strategy will be a combination of a core (perhaps the same old core) strategy and its supporting strategies. Very likely, at least some of the supporting product strategies will be new. The implementation of the new product strategy may require tactical adjustment on a frequent basis.

The chosen product strategy will be that combination which the SBM decides is best for his firm at the present time. It need not necessarily be similar to that of his competitors. The strategy probably will not, however, be a radical departure from the old product strategy in most cases. In those instances where a radical departure is involved, such a departure should be based upon sound information concerning the target market and/or the firm's goals and differential advantage. For example, a former slow-growth firm may decide to make growth much more important in its goals because of a recent technical advantage it gained in the product area. In such a case, a rather radical change in product strategy would be expected. A back-up product strategy may also be chosen by the SBM; however, the SBM should not plan to go to the back-up unless the primary product strategy is found to be unworkable even when aided by tactical product adjustments.

Step 7—Plan the details of implementation of the new product strategy. When we use the word "new" here, we are referring to the new strategy, not the new product. However, a new strategy does usually result in a new product—in the broad meaning of the product. That is, the total offering will usually be new and different.

In this step, the SBM spells out the details of exactly how the revised product strategy is to be implemented. How, when, where, and by whom are certain things going to be done? Any details of implementation which the SBM does not specify in this stage will probably not get done. Or, if such items are accomplished, they may be performed inefficiently or ineffectively due to the lack of planning. What we are saying is that if the SBM wants the product strategy to be what he has decided it to be, the details of implementation must be specified. In the absence of such details, subordinate operating personnel will make up their own rules as they go along.

Step 8—Set performance standards and monitor feedback. This step is a planning step rather than the actual control process itself. In both qualitative and quantitative terms, the SBM is asking for the criteria to use in later determining in what ways and to what extent the specific objectives of product strategy have been accomplished. The actual application of these criteria will come later during the control phase of management. In this step, then, we are defining what our criteria for measuring success will be.

The second portion of this final step is to plan for constant feedback from the market concerning our product strategy. With such feedback, the SBM will make the product strategy more effective. The form and sophistication of the feedback will vary, but even the smallest firm should provide for it.

The above eight-step outline is a format by which the SBM can plan his product strategy. The execution and control of that strategy follow. Filling in this outline involves much hard work. The SBM may be tempted to say: "We know what our product and product strategy are—let's get on with it." Such a lack of planning will probably result in a "me too" firm limited by a narrow definition of product. Now, let's illustrate each of the above steps with a hypothetical SB retailer. Our illustration will necessarily be less complete than the real thing.

AN ILLUSTRATION OF SB PRODUCT STRATEGY PLANNING

For purposes of illustration, we will assume that we are presently operating a small convenience food store. Our store is located in a suburb near apartments and single-family dwellings, and near a shopping center containing two major supermarket chains. For our illustration, other assumptions must be made from time to time, which, in a real case, could be fact rather than assumption.

Our SBM is a retailer. His product is therefore probably heavily oriented in the direction of the customer services provided rather than toward the mere physical goods offered for sale. The SBM is also quite small. As a single store operator, his management team is probably one person: himself. However, he may receive advice from outsiders, such as his voluntary group wholesaler, trade association, other retailers, and so forth.

For our example, we'll take the following as given:

1. *Goals*—sales and profit growth at the present location with very little additional investment. A 15% sales growth this year is estimated to produce a 20% to 30% profit growth. We want to stay in the same business serving the same target market.

2. *Target market*—the residents within walking distance and short-time driving distance to our store. Special emphasis is taken to *not* serve the exact same needs as supermarkets. Store hours, convenience, personal service, and so forth are used in order to segment the market.

3. *The marketing environment* is economically very favorable in this locale with high discretionary income. Culturally and socially, the market area is favorable in social class values, family structure, age composition, and leisure time activities. Other environmental factors will be assumed to be about average.

4. *The differential advantage* of the firm is experienced management, time and place convenience, excellent modern physical facilities, and a prime location.

Our SBM is now ready to begin the eight-step process. We are, of course, assuming the existence of a current overall marketing strategy and a strategy in the areas of price, place, promotion, and people.

Step 1—Record the current product strategy.   Core strategy for matching product and market is to target market toward immediate geographic area and some passerby traffic, with emphasis on filling convenience needs rather than weekly grocery needs—and to offer convenience and service at slightly higher prices. Our target customers are willing to pay for the convenience of not having to enter a shopping center and large supermarket for a few items. They do demand quality, but will accept some substitute products. Some of the passerby portion of our target market is different, but this portion of our business is too small to call for a separate marketing strategy. We really don't know how well (or how large a share) we are serving the present target market. Perhaps better feedback is needed. We are the only convenience food store in the area, although we obviously compete with many other types of retailers.

Supporting strategies are in the areas of product lines carried, customer services offered, business and neighborhood (rather than product life-cycle) life-cycles, store identification and image, and so forth. (Assume here that we have listed all categories of merchandise carried and all customer services offered.) The stage in the life-cycle of our store and neighborhood is fairly young. The store is three years old and the neighborhood is about the same age. However, convenience type food stores have existed in other parts of this community and in other communities for many years. Store identification and image are thought to be good, whatever that means. Perhaps more attention should be paid to this item. New products are added from time to time and old items are dropped. The method used is trial and error, according to what should sell. Is this sound in the overall sense?

Step 2—Identify strategic product problems.   Some strategic product problems may exist in the following areas:

1. Product-market matching (core) strategy: Do we know the extent to which we are satisfying our target market?
2. What goods/services combinations could be offered that we are not now offering?
3. In what ways is the composition of our neighborhood target market changing, and how does this affect product?
4. Are we properly identified in terms of awareness and image among our target market?
5. What should our policy be on accepting or rejecting new products, deleting old ones, and determining customer services?

From the above types of probing questions, the SBM can look at the situation in order to determine where the real strategic product problems lie and to define these problems specifically in operational terms. Thus, he may see a need to set turnover and markup criteria on new product decisions on a category-by-category basis. He may note that some products do not fit the quality standards of the store's stated product strategy. He may identify a series of symptoms that leads him to believe that a problem such as store image does exist, or at least that his perception versus customer perception versus noncustomer perception of store image is not the same. Once all the product problems (opportunities) have been specifically identified, our SBM should take one more look at them, or perhaps he should have a friend in the same line of business take a look at the problems. This will give additional assurance that the real problems have been properly identified.

Step 3—Divide current strategic product problems into the core strategy and supporting strategy areas.   In the core area, our SBM lacks information on the extent to which he is satisfying the needs of the market by his current product offering. Thus, he should formulate plans to get the needed information. Only then can he determine whether or not a serious strategic product problem exists in the core. The SBM is probably going to find that some market changes do require some change in emphasis. On a periodic basis, this examination of the core product strategy can serve to prevent the rise of any serious problems.

Most of the problems identified will be supporting strategies. Thus, from Step #2 above the SBM should classify those items actually determined to be problems at this point. He should also give a brief reasoning for the logic of each supporting strategy problem. For example, he might reason that the new product evaluation problem is a problem not because proper evaluation criteria did not exist but because they were not used. The reason the criteria were not often used was because of the persuasive introductory deals of supplier salesmen. Such analysis of current problems in this step will be a big help in the next step.

Step 4—Formulate alternative product strategies at both core and support levels.   For purposes of illustration, let's deal only at the support level here, and let's deal specifically with the problem our SBM faces regarding new products. What are some alternative product strategies he might consider for this problem? Here are a few:

1. Establish new criteria and operating rules for new product additions. Some ideas to consider would be the following: (a) add only new products which replace discontinued products; (b) check every potential addition against a checklist; (c) restrict new products to certain categories; (d) add new products but not new suppliers; and so forth.

2. Handle the problem on a periodic basis by balancing additions and deletions within a given period.

3. Install follow-up measures to evaluate new products at given points in time after adding them to see if they should be continued.

4. Add only products that are really new rather than those which are merely substitutes for products currently carried.

5. Buy new products on a guaranteed sale basis, such as on consignment.

6. Consider expanding space available for new products by interior store remodeling, incorporating increased shelf capacity.

7. Add new products only after customer requests.

A listing of alternatives such as the one above is certainly not exhaustive. The SBM could probably list 50 or 100 alternatives, but he should keep to those that have reasonable feasibility of implementation. The same is true for all of the other problems identified above.

Step 5—Evaluate these alternatives in various combinations.   Here again we'll restrict ourselves to the new product problem area. Our SBM is looking at all the alternatives for this problem area and for other strategy areas of the store that may be affected by the decision here. Thumbing through a few trade journal articles could be a big help in this step. Such articles would give our SBM the benefit of alternative evaluation by other store operators. Of course, each situation is unique and our SBM must adapt the evaluation to his own goals, target market, market mix, and environment. In this step, our SBM is sorting out the good and bad points of each alternative new product strategy—and its effectiveness in combination with other firm strategies.

Step 6—Choose the new product strategy.   After the SBM has gone through the above steps for all problem areas, he is ready to make the choices that, taken together, comprise the new product strategy. He may not make changes in some areas even though he feels changes are in order. He may simply not have the time or other resources to change everything at once.

This step is a good time for our SBM to record in outline form the new product strategy. For example, he might fill in some of the following:

1. New core strategy for product matching with market is target marketing. The market is immediate geographic area defined as —, with some additional passerby traffic. Characteristics of target customers are —. Convenience in the forms of time such as extended store hours, access—, and so forth—are a major part of our product. Market share at current time is to be determined by —.

2. Supporting product strategies are product lines and customer services listed here —, a business and neighborhood life cycle defined as follows —, and a store identifica-

tion (awareness) and store image to be specifically defined by research currently in progress. Our new product policy is operationally stated in the following checklist —.

Step 7—Plan the details of implementation of the new product strategy.   Here the details are spelled out. The two information needs (on market and on store identification) will be planned as research projects to be done formally by a marketing researcher or informally by the SBM. The new product system will be completely spelled out. Before it can be put into full operation, a time lapse of a few weeks may be necessary in order to clear out some present merchandise. Such details will be planned. For example, the SBM may simply impose a four week moratorium on all new products. The details of implementation are a necessary part of the plan even though our SBM is the only manager in this SB.

Step 8—Set performance standards and monitor feedback.   Here our SBM sets up a list of criteria for measuring performance of the product strategy plan and for getting feedback. The convenience store operator may have sales and markup objectives by each product category. For example, if film processing pickup service is added, what will be the expected sales in units, dollars, number of customers, and so on? What total dollar markup should this service produce? What level of service in terms of return time, make-good on goofs, lost orders, and so forth will be demanded for our customers from the film processor? How will we follow up on a routine basis in order to insure this?

Performance standards and feedback monitoring must be planned for all areas of the product strategy. The SBM will then be ready for execution and control of the product variable.

Our discussion of product continues in the following chapter.

BIBLIOGRAPHY

Books

KOTLER, PHILIP. *Marketing Management: Analysis, Planning, And Control.* 2nd ed. Englewood Cliffs, New Jersey: Prentice-Hall, Inc., 1972.

LUCK, DAVID J. AND PRELL, ARTHUR E. *Market Strategy.* New York: Appleton-Century-Crofts, 1968.

PRESTON, LEE E. *Markets and Marketing: An Orientation.* Glenview, Illinois: Scott, Foresman and Company, 1970.

Articles and Periodicals

KLINE, CHARLES H. "The Strategy of Product Policy." *Harvard Business Review,* 33, No. 4 (July–August, 1955), 91–98.

Reports

COHN, THEODORE AND LINDBERG, ROY A. *How Management Is Different in Small Companies.* An AMA Management Briefing. 1972.

10

More Product Strategy
For SBMM

In the last chapter we introduced SB product strategy, defined *product* in a broad sense, examined some product strategy generalizations for SB, and considered the "how to" of product strategy planning for SB. In the present chapter we will examine in more detail some of the important product strategy areas for SB. These areas are: (a) product line and mix, (b) the customer services mix, (c) product identification and feature strategy, and (d) new product strategy for SB. In the appendix to this chapter, the product life cycle (PLC) is examined. The PLC has direct implications for marketing strategy formulation in place, price, promotion, and people as well as in product.

PRODUCT LINE AND MIX STRATEGY FOR SB

In the previous chapter, we defined *product* in the broad sense to be more than a physical entity. But whether we use a broad or a narrow definition, a single product firm does not represent reality. Even among the smallest of SB firms, multiproduct marketing is the rule. For convenience in structuring and describing this multiproduct reality, some marketers have adopted the terms *product line* and *product mix*. According to the American Marketing Association, these are defined as follows:

> PRODUCT LINE—A group of products that are closely related either because they satisfy a class of need, are used together, are sold to the same customer groups, are marketed through the same type of outlets or fall within given price ranges. Example, carpenters' tools. *Comment* Sub-lines of products may be distinguished, such as hammers or saws, within a Product Line. . . .
> PRODUCT MIX—The composite of products offered for sale by a firm or a business unit. *Comment* Tooth paste is a product. The 50 cent tube of Whosis

ammoniated tooth paste is an item. Tooth pastes and powders, mouth washes, and other allied items comprise an oral hygiene product line. Soaps, cosmetics, dentifrices, drug items, cake mixes, shortenings and other items may comprise a product mix if marketed by the same company.[1]

The above AMA definitions seem to focus more attention on *product* in the narrow or physical sense. Our perspective need not be that limited. Product line and mix are also concepts applicable to the broad definition of product. The SBM may wish to consider both the narrow and broad perspectives. One author suggests that while the above terminology of line and mix "may have merit for some purposes; . . . it may also obscure the essential point: all product collections in the marketing system are based upon some underlying independent relationship either with respect to costs or with respect to demand."[2] For marketing purposes, collections of products based upon demand seem to be more relevant. However, production and cost limitations should not always be ignored. We should also note that our above terminology is equally applicable for manufacturers, wholesalers, retailers, and service firms. Each type of firm will interpret the terminology in a slightly different manner.

For BB and for growth-oriented SB, the entire core strategy of market segmentation may imply the creation and marketing of additional product lines (as opposed to a market redirection of the existing product line(s)). In fact, the objective of market segmentation may sometimes be to determine the limits to which product lines can be expanded. For many SB firms, this is not the case. The SBM with stability or a slow-pace growth objective will look to product line analysis as a continuous management task, but his new product development efforts will tend to be on an intermittent basis.

On a continuous basis, the SBM will wish to evaluate the product mix in terms of width, depth, and consistency. These three dimensions of product assortment are described as follows:

> The width of the product mix refers to *how many different product lines are found within the company*. . . .
> The *depth* of the product mix refers to the *average number of items offered by the company within each product line*. . . .
> The *consistency* of the product mix refers to *how closely related the various product lines are in end use, production requirements, distribution channels, or in some other way*.[3]

In summary, then, we have the firm's product mix made up of a series of product lines, which in turn are made up of individual products or items. Width is how many product lines are offered; and depth is the number of items within each line. Consistency is how closely related the product lines are. The SBM makes product strategy decisions in all these areas. For example, the decision of a single-store retail druggist to adopt a strategy of scrambled merchandising by adding a limited depth of such widely inconsistent lines as automotive supplies, glassware, toys, and diet foods illustrates one variation of such a strategy at the retail level.

[1]Committee on Definitions, Reprinted from *Marketing Definitions: A Glossary of Marketing Terms* published by the American Marketing Association, Chicago, 1960, p. 16.
[2]Lee E. Preston, *Markets and Marketing: An Orientation* (Glenview, Illinois: Scott, Foresman and Company, 1970), p. 180.
[3]Philip Kotler, *Marketing Management: Analysis, Planning, And Control* (2nd ed.; Englewood Cliffs, New Jersey: Prentice-Hall, Inc., 1972), p. 439.

With the above definitions and structures in mind, let's now examine some of the areas of product line and mix strategy as they apply to the SBM. With different markets in mind, we would expect SB to differ from BB in product strategy. In effect, the consideration of product line and mix by the SBM is asking the basic question: What are the products (goods/services combinations) we should be offering to our target markets? Substrategy areas of product line and mix include width, depth, and consistency questions over the product life-cycles of the firm's *overall* product offerings. Here, we discuss both increases and decreases in the product offering. Other substrategy questions arise at the level of each *individual* product offering. Some of these are positioning (and repositioning) of the product, product modification, and new product development for SB. These individual product substrategy questions are treated later in the chapter. Some strategy options for overall product offering are suggested in Table 10–1.

Expanding the Product Offering

Whether the SBM is a manufacturer, wholesaler, retailer, or service firm, expansion of the product offering may be considered as a means of increasing sales and/or profits. The SBM should exercise caution when expanding the product offering. As a target marketer, the SBM cannot hope to be all things to all people. He usually specializes by purposely limiting the product line(s). Nevertheless, the SBM may at times need to expand his product offering in order to better satisfy his target market(s). For example, if the salesforce is spending much time and effort overcoming buyers' objections that our product offering is not complete by itself and that these buyers must go to our competitors to purchase a complete line (or to complete our line), the course of action seems clear. We can better serve our buyers, and increase sales at the same time by expanding the product offering. In this situation, we may be able to better utilize the time and effort of our salesforce (by no longer having to overcome this objection) so that salesforce costs are not increased by the added product offering. In addition, we are no longer sending our potential customers to our competitors.

In any contemplated expansion of the product offering, the SBM should make sure that the expansion will not in any way impair the firm's differential advantage. Growing in

Table 10–1   Some Product Line and Mix Options for the SBM

A. For the SB product mix:
   1. Increase width by offering new product lines.
   2. Change width by offering different product lines.
   3. Decrease width by offering fewer product lines.
B. For each of the SB product lines (or for as many as all the SB product lines):
   1. Increase depth by offering more items within a line.
   2. Change depth by offering different items within a line.
   3. Decrease depth by offering fewer items within a line.
C. For product mix consistency:
   1. Increase consistency by offering more similar product lines.
   2. Change consistency by offering product lines with different forms (but the same degree) of consistency.
   3. Decrease consistency by offering less similar product lines.
D. Combine above options in order to achieve product line and mix objectives for the SB.

too many directions at once or at too rapid a rate can be very dangerous for SB. An expanded product offering often requires an expanded resource base in most other areas of business. A more complete product offering (such as a full line rather than a limited line) may offer such advantages as increased product identity, increased dealer support, the spreading of promotional costs, and stronger products being able to help carry weaker ones. However, disadvantages are also possible for the SBM who attempts to market a full line. The major disadvantage is that the SBM, because of his size in comparison to other full-line marketers, is spread so thin that he is unable to make a real impact on the target market with any of his products. If this is so, the above advantages are mere illusions. Thus, the product offering of the SBM can be either too broad or too narrow. If the SBM is going to err in this regard, he is usually probably safer to err on the side of having a product offering that is too narrow. An error in this direction may be somewhat restrictive on his rate of growth; but it will leave him much less vulnerable to head-on competition from BB.

Relationships of products within the lines of the product mix and the relationships of some product lines to other lines are important to the SBM. The basic question is: Are such relationships of products and lines ones of substitutes or ones of complements? Substitutes will tend to spread the existing market of the SBM over a greater number of products or lines. This will probably be less profitable, but substitute products and lines may sometimes seem necessary due to competitive actions. Complementary products and lines will tend to enhance the sale of existing products and lines. Complementary relationships may strengthen the marketing impact of the SBM in his selected target markets.

Methods of expanding the product offering employed by BB are sometimes beyond the means of many SB firms. Mergers and acquisitions to accomplish vertical (backward or forward), horizontal, or conglomerate integration have often been used by BB. Product and marketing innovations are available to SB. Sometimes such innovations are available on a licensing or franchise basis. We discuss increased variety within a line later in the chapter.

Contracting (Decreasing) the Product Offering

There is much less pressure on the SBM to decrease the product offering than there is to increase the product offering. In fact, there may quite often be pressure from suppliers, customers, and the firm's own management to continue the marketing of weak or "sick" products and product lines. Product elimination tends to be neglected in companies of all size ranges. Reasons for avoiding the issue are both real and, sometimes, psychological. For example, if we eliminate product line XYZ, do we eliminate those employees now producing it? Or: Are we going to eliminate the product line on which the company was founded thirty years ago?

The costs of continuing to carry sick products are also very real. Some of these costs are excessive management time, excessive marketing effort by promotion and the salesforce, and the projection of an undesirable image. Lost opportunity costs to the SBM are probably even greater. That is, timely elimination of sick products could allow marketing effort to be focused on "healthy" products and increase the desires of management to find new replacement products. Carrying of sick products or product lines is more serious for SB than for BB, in the sense that SB usually has more limited resources. The SBM should therefore have a periodic review of all products and lines in order to determine the desirability of each in the product mix.

One method for reviewing products and product lines is to examine those with less than average performance. Performance can be measured in terms of sales, profits, and so forth. Trends are important. Distribution cost analysis by product and by product line can be used. However, such analysis should always be used from the marketing systems perspective in order to avoid dropping products that are critical to the total marketing effort.

Some alternate product elimination strategies dealing with the product lines and individual products within a line are listed below. The SBM may wish to consider the merits of each of the following courses of action once a decision to eliminate has been made.[4]

1. Prune the product line by selectively eliminating products from the line. This can be made more acceptable to customers if the SBM can show customers that these reductions can give the customer such advantages as fewer items to order and inventory.
2. Phase out by announcing the product's ultimate elimination and by giving customers the opportunity to purchase in limited quantities until the actual date of expiration.
3. The run-out or limited offering may be used to remove active marketing support from the product while continuing to permit customers to purchase it. Sometimes marketing support is merely reduced substantially rather than removed.
4. Manufacture and/or market on a contract basis only.
5. Abandonment by selling or licensing the product to someone else or simply by dropping the product due to no other acceptable alternative.

Whatever the elimination strategy turns out to be, it is certain that it won't please everyone. The SBM must make such decisions according to his own situation. Rules of thumb such as sales per square foot or lineal foot, minimum turnover, or percent of sales for a given product category may be helpful to the SBM in implementing his strategy on a day-to-day and on a periodic review basis. The important thing for the SBM is to have a product elimination policy that reflects his overall product strategy. The overall picture is important. The rule of thumb or, "decision rule fails, at least in its simple forms, when it is applied to large product groups in the aggregate or to individual items that have a special role in determining the character of the marketing agency."[5]

Additional Comment on Expansion And Contraction

The so-called 80–20 principle or 80–20 rule is a type of thinking that can be useful to the SBM when considering both product expansion and contraction. In a later chapter, we'll see other uses of the 80–20 principle. As applied to product, the principle states: 80% of the products (or product lines) account for only 20% of the sales; or conversely, 20% of the products account for 80% of the sales. This 80–20 distribution seems to be true too often in marketing. Of course, in order to use the 80–20 principle effectively, the SBM must have a pretty good idea of what an ideal product mix is for his firm. If 70–30 (30–70)

[4]See George S. Dominguez, *Product Management* (American Management Association, Inc., 1971), pp. 145–147 and David T. Kollat, Roger D. Blackwell, and James F. Robeson, *Strategic Marketing* (New York: Holt, Rinehart and Winston, Inc., 1972), pp. 223–226.
[5]Preston, p. 183.

is closer to the ideal, the SBM would seek to add products with sales promise to those 20% that now account for 80% of sales. The intended result would be that 30% of the products would now account for 70% of sales. Likewise, by dropping products from those 80% that now account for 20% of sales, the intended result would be that the former 80% of products would now be 70% of products, accounting for 30% (rather than only 20%) of sales. A word of caution is in order for this two-pronged attack. We have been dealing here in the abstract. The SBM must also pay attention to the realities of implementing such a program. The SBM must serve the needs of his target markets. In fact, sometimes his target market is those customers "left over" from the distribution cost analysis or 80–20 principle used by a BB competitor. The target market always comes first; decisions based on distribution cost analysis come second.

THE CUSTOMER SERVICES MIX FOR SB

Because of the importance of the customer services mix as a submix of the overall product offering of the SBM, it warrants separate attention. By customer services, we mean those accompanying services that go along with the physical product or principal service to comprise the total product offering. For example, delivery service by a dry cleaning firm (a so-called service firm) or by a department store (a merchandise retailer) is still delivery service. And in either case, it should be considered a customer service. Customer services are offered by manufacturers, wholesalers, retailers, and service firms. Customer services may be offered to intermediate customers and to final customers. For example, an appliance manufacturer may offer in-warranty repair service or handling of consumer complaints through a service contractor or a manufacturer's service center, even though the concerned housewife purchased the appliance from a local furniture store or a national discount chain. From the point of view of the housewife, the customer service source is less important than her satisfaction with the total product offering she thought she purchased. Our emphasis will be on customer services at the retail-to-consumer level; however, it should be emphasized that other members of the channel of distribution have a real stake in customer services mixes both at this level and at other levels of distribution. A sampling of popular customer services at the retail-to-customer level is given in Table 10-2 on page 174.

Importance of Customer Services to the SBM

In addition to the prices that customers pay for products, customers also incur other costs of engaging in purchasing activity. Such costs may be classified as: (a) monetary costs, such as transportation and parking fees; (b) time and effort costs, such as waiting in a checkout line; and (c) psychological costs, such as those associated with encountering an unfriendly sales person. Examples could also be cited at other levels of distribution besides retailing. Customer services may be viewed as a positive step on the part of the SBM to reduce in some way, or to compensate for in some way, the costs incurred by the customer. Thus, customer services is a major tool of differentiation available to the SBM. A cartridge of Kodak film is not the same product when purchased at a photo shop rather than at a discount drug store. The major reason is that the customer services mix is different.

Strategy questions concerning the customer services mix are very similar to those questions already posed concerning the product mix. The SBM desires a mix of customer

Table 10–2   A Sampling Of Customer Services Offered By Retailers

Adjustments	Layout and appearance
Advertising	Lessons
Air-conditioning	Lighting
Alterations	Location convenience
Auditorium	Lockers and checkrooms
Baby strollers	Merchandise information
Bottle returns	Message service
Bridal registry	Money orders and traveler's checks
Bulletin boards	Music
Carry out to car	Notary public
Check cashing	Paging service
Cleanliness	Parking
C.O.D. orders	Party counseling
Cooking schools	Personal shopping service
Coupon redemption	Play rooms
Craft classes	Postal services
Credit	Returns and allowances
Customer complaints	Rest rooms and lounges
Delivery	Shopping carts
Display	Special orders
Door man or automatic door	Telephone calls out free
Express checkout lanes	Telephone ordering
Fashion shows	Testing before buying
Gift certificates	Trade-ins
Guarantees	Trading stamps
Hours	Unit pricing
Installation	Utility bill payment agency
Interior decorating service	Wrapping
Layaways	

services composed of complementary services which, internally, have a high degree of consistency and which, externally, are consistent with the overall marketing strategy.

The importance of customer services generally, and of specific customer services in particular, will vary according to such factors as target markets served, product types, location, competition, fads, and so forth. For example, free piercing of ears (or even offering the service at a charge) may be a desirable customer service for a jewelry store if fashion trends so dictate for the clientele served by the store.

Just as the physical portion of the product offering may be viewed by the SBM as a form of nonprice competition by using features to differentiate it, so also with customer services. As with price competition, the level of intensity of customer services competition and other forms of nonprice competition tends to vary considerably. The SBM is faced with many alternative customer service strategies from which to make a selection. For example, he may choose to be a follower by offering only those customer services offered by his direct competitors. Or he may be quite distinctive by creating a customer services mix which is very well suited to his own business but which would be very difficult for a competitor to imitate effectively. The SBM may have a strategy of offering essentially the same services but of performing these services to a higher standard. Or the SBM may, in fact, have a rather limited customer services offering but he may project an effective image by actively promoting the services that are offered.

Customer Services Competition

The competitive intensity of a market may not be easy to determine by observing the level and similarity of customer services. Critics sometimes charge that customer services are forced upon the consuming public. Additional customer services are usually accompanied by somewhat higher prices. Equity questions and questions of marketing strategy effectiveness do pose themselves to the SBM who is offering "free" customer services. By "free" we mean that the cost is hidden in the price of the product.

PRODUCT IDENTIFICATION AND FEATURES

The strategies for identifying the products of the SBM, and for determining what physical and functional features such products should have, are too often neglected by SB. Copying the branding practices of BB, using the least expensive package available, and providing features for too broad a market can limit the success of the SB product strategy. Product identification includes packaging, branding, and related legal protection. Regarding features, the SBM may modify quality, style, positioning, image, and other physical features such as size and color. SB marketers at all levels of distribution face strategic product decisions in the above areas.

Packaging and SB

Packaging and labeling have increased in importance in the marketing mixes of firms of all sizes. Self-service in the retailing of many consumer products has been a major factor. The importance of packaging is perhaps somewhat overstressed by some members of the packaging industry. They would suggest that packaging be a major component of the marketing mix as a "sixth P" along with product, place, price, promotion, and people. Effective use of packaging certainly can increase the impact of all areas of the marketing mix. For example, an outstanding package may have more promotional value than media advertising. A new package may make the product a new product which appeals to market segments not previously available to the SBM. A package which significantly improves the product may become the differential advantage upon which to base an entirely new overall marketing strategy. Packaging is important! What would L'eggs, for example, be without it?

Among the functions performed by packaging are physical containment and protection of the product in storage and use. Some packages also have a re-use value. Packaging is a part of the product. Promotional functions of packaging are acting as a convenient means of product identification, communicating a product image via advertising media such as television and newspapers, and acting as a forceful but subtle silent salesman at the point of sale. Packaging affects price on both the cost and selling price sides. Packaging affects place by raising or lowering transportation and warehousing costs, according to the characteristics of the packaging employed. Place is also affected in that different middlemen in the channels of distribution are appropriate according to types of packaging. For example, nails were once purchased by the pound at the local hardware store, which packaged them in a brown paper bag. Today, the channels of distribution for prepackaged nails are much broader, including, at the retail level, discount stores, self-service hardware and lumber stores, supermarkets, drug stores, and variety stores. Packaging also affects the people variable of the marketing mix, especially through the implementation of self-selection and self-service.

For the SBM, packaging may play an even more important role in the marketing mix than it does for BB. Why? Because the SBM may not be able to afford an expensive mass media advertising campaign or a high-powered sales force. Minimal packaging for performing the physical packaging functions mentioned above is necessary for most marketers. The added cost to the SBM of using packaging as an effective marketing device to promote and communicate are often small. In other words, getting the package to work much harder by paying a little more for it makes good marketing sense for the SBM. He cannot afford to pass up such a bargain.

Outside assistance for packaging is the rule rather than the exception for firms of all sizes. Packaging suppliers are prepared to examine the individual needs of each marketer. Some contract packagers will even perform the entire packaging operation on a fee basis. The rapid rate of change in the packaging industry, the degree of specialization involved, and the importance of packaging from both the marketing and legal requirements points of view make it almost essential for the SBM to use outside expertise.

An example of effective packaging is provided by Saunders Archery Company, which utilized the packaging expertise of Cheskin Associates. An evaluation of the colors and design layouts of the packaging needs resulted in recommendations for using two new colors and for a similarity of design on all Saunders packages. The colors chosen had high visibility and association with sunshine, nature, and the great outdoors. Design similarity was used in order to create brand identification for the entire Saunders line. This quality manufacturer was able to maintain an image for its family of related products through packaging.

For intermediate markets purchasing industrial goods, the importance of packaging may not be the same as with some consumer products, such as so-called impulse items. However, in the industrial market also, packaging can be a positive part of product strategy. *Business Week* cites the following examples:

> A West Coast design company is promoting four-color and silk-screen packaging to its industrial manufacturing clients—maintaining that "every box should be a billboard." Melvin Small, president of Los Angeles-based United Container & Display Co., says that the small industrial manufacturer, whose advertising and promotions budgets are restricted, must exploit every possibility to stay competitive with the big companies. Thus far, apparently, Small's message is getting through in that 25% of his 135 industrial clients are going for packaging that closely resembles that found in consumer goods. Rodac Corp., of Carson, Calif., and one of United Container Co.'s clients, is quick to agree. Harvey Rodstein, president of Rodac, is now placing the company's heavy-duty polishers and ratchets in red, white, and black boxes with a silk-screen halftone that shows a muscular arm holding a representation of the product. "We're trying to establish an identity," comments Rodstein. "We're a small company fighting a lot of bigger companies." Auto Trend Products, also in Los Angeles, recently switched from packaging products in a drab box that cost 21¢ to putting them in a multicolored one that costs 87¢. "Sales went up 20%," comments Vice-President Charles Haggard.[6]

[6]"Marketing Observer," *Business Week*, March 3, 1975, p. 38.

Branding and SB

Brand is the inclusive generic term which may be defined as a "name, term, sign, symbol, or design, or a combination of them which is intended to identify the goods or services of one seller or group of sellers to differentiate them from those of competitors."[7] A *trademark* is a brand that has been given legal protection. A *brand name* is that part of a brand that can be vocalized.

For most marketers, the question is not whether branded or unbranded products should be sold. Most products are branded. The important brand strategy questions are: (a) *who* should do the branding, (b) *what* specific brands should be used, and (c) *how important* a role can and should branding play in the product mix? Answers to these questions will vary from BB to SB and from one SB to the next. The answers will also tend to parallel packaging strategy, since packaging and branding are very closely related.

From its basic function of product identification, branding provides benefits to both consumers and marketers. For the consumer, branding permits repeat purchases of satisfactory products and some assurance that quality will remain fairly uniform over time. Rigid product inspection is therefore not necessary. For some products, branding also helps fill the status needs of consumers: take, for example, the name "Cadillac," For the marketer, the basic objective of branding is to gain some measure of market control. Good will can be built by providing satisfactory products over time and by advertising the brand. The amount of market control necessary to make a brand somewhat protected from substitute products will depend on such factors as product distinctiveness, importance of product to customers, product knowledge, and continued promotion for reinforcement. In addition to encouraging repeat sales, branding may also make new product introduction easier by using the same brand, may help to stabilize prices and to segment target markets, and may be used in developing channels of distribution.

Who should do the branding? The options for the SBM are given here for manufacturers and retailers. The SB manufacturer may:

1. Sell exclusively under his own brand. This would be a manufacturer brand(s) and is sometimes also known as a national brand, or perhaps, in the case of many SB firms, a regional brand.
2. Sell exclusively under the brands of others: dealers and distributors. This is sometimes called a private label.
3. Combine manufacturer branding and private branding in a proportion that meets both market needs and company goals.

The SB retailer has essentially the same options, but he is looking at branding from a different level of the channel of distribution. The SB retailer may:

1. Sell exclusively under his own brand, that is, a private label.
2. Sell manufacturer brands exclusively, that is, "national" or "nationally advertised" brands.
3. Combine manufacturer and private brands in a desired proportion.

[7]Committee on Definitions, Reprinted from *Marketing Definitions: A Glossary of Marketing Terms* published by the American Marketing Association, Chicago, 1960, p. 9.

With the above options in mind, what should the SBM do? Exceptions can be found and opinions differ. In the opinion of this author, as a manufacturer the SBM should usually follow alternatives #1 or #3 above. That is, he should either sell under his own brand exclusively; or, if he is going to produce some product for private labels, he should (in advance) determine the optimum proportions of manufacturer brand and private brand. Alternative #2 above changes the SB firm from a SBM to a SB manufacturer, perhaps even to a captive manufacturer. The SBM (manufacturer), using the principle of market dominance, can effectively use his own brand for the selected target market(s).

For the SB retailer, the situation is somewhat different. In the author's opinion, the SB retailer is usually not in a position to market his own private brands advantageously. Exceptions can be found. For example, a specialty tobacco shop may do an excellent job with its own special blend (carrying its own brand) of pipe tobacco. In addition, the SB retailer often needs the consumer confidence that is afforded by carrying branded products of well-known manufacturers. SB retailers have been able to enjoy some of the advantages of private brands which are owned by such suprafirm organizations as voluntary group wholesalers, cooperative wholesalers, and other middlemen's organizations. Such private brand advantages to SB retailers include the nonavailability of such brands to competitors and the resulting inability of consumers to make direct price comparisons, higher markup percentages, and prices below those of nationally advertised products.

A marketing tactic which may bolster the image of the product sold under the name of the SBM is to use quality packaging. Another idea may be to add a certification mark, such as the Good Housekeeping Seal of Approval. Warranty strategy may also parallel and reinforce brand strategy for the SBM who wishes to sell under his own label.

What specific brands should be used? Here, we will attempt to answer only that part of the question that deals with whether or not the SBM should use family or individual brands. The other part of this question deals with how to select a good brand. Our only comment is that the SBM can probably find a brand that has much greater marketing value than his own personal name. (For an excellent discussion on selecting a brand or trademark, see Otto Kleppner, *Advertising Procedure,* Englewood Cliffs, New Jersey: Prentice-Hall, Inc., 1973, pp. 159–168). Now, let's get back to the family versus the individual brand question. This is often a less serious problem for the SBM than for BB because SB product lines tend to be much more narrow. The general guidelines suggest that family brands (using the same brand name, such as Heinz or Dairy Queen, for a number of related products) are beneficial in getting more mileage from promotional dollars. Products using the same family brand should be similar in quality and fairly closely related in product category. On the other hand, individual brands may be created which better fit the promotional needs of a specific product. This is especially true for products which are significant innovations. The number of products in many SB firms is usually so small that the SBM is not interested in a string of individual brands to promote intracompany brand competition, such as Procter & Gamble does with detergents. However, the SBM may wish to use different brands for different market segments in a somewhat limited manner. For example, the SBM may use different brands for the industrial and consumer markets. Such brands would accompany different strategies in such areas as package size, price, and so forth.

How important a role can, and should, branding play in to product strategy of the SBM? This depends primarily on the importance of branding to the customer. If brand is, or can be made, important to the customer, then the SBM should act accordingly. For reasons of status, repeat purchase convenience, trade-in or resale value, and so on, branding is more or less important for different product types. The SBM should not underestimate the value consumers place on brands. For example, is brand at least part of the reason why a consumer will pay twice as much for a Scott's lawn spreader as an unknown brand? Brand familiarity or acceptance may be described in terms of three degrees: brand recognition, brand preference, and brand insistence. One author also has a negative or zero category called nonrecognition.[8] While brand insistence may be the ultimate goal, the SBM should be patient. For many products, the costs of achieving brand insistence may outweigh the benefits. The degree of brand familiarity or acceptance can also vary according to types and intensity of the middlemen used and the nature of the target markets served.

Legal Protection for Products

Product liability is an area of risk for which the SBM must be insured, both for his own protection and in order to sell to knowledgeable wholesalers, retailers, and industrial and ultimate consumers. Enough said![9] Other areas of legal product protection are patents, copyrights, trademarks, and licensing. Legal assistance should be sought by the SBM in these areas. A basic understanding of these protections and their marketing implications may be obtained by the SBM from many sources. (For example, see H. Ross Workman and Melvin J. Stanford, "Patent And Copyright Protection" in *Journal Of Small Business Management,* October, 1974, pp. 47–51; or see Bernard J. McNamee, "A Primer On Patent, Trademark and Know-How Licensing" in *MSU Business Topics,* Summer, 1970, pp. 11–20.)

Product Modification— Positioning and Repositioning

Product features may be used to position (and reposition) the products of the SBM. Such positioning can be with respect to other products in the line, with respect to other lines, with respect to competitors' products, and with respect to market segments. Position is the product space the product occupies. It is influenced by tangible product features and attributes as well as by the image of the product as it is perceived by the target customers. The SBM will want to know the present position of his product(s) and what the implications of certain product modifications would be for repositioning his product(s). Since the SBM often markets to a very select and narrowly defined target market, modification decisions are necessary from time to time in order to match the needs of that small target as exactly as possible.

Positioning the product—and repositioning it—can be radical steps, such as changing Marlboro from a female to a male cigarette or making Right Guard a deodorant for the entire family. Many repositionings, however, are either trading up or trading down. Such strategic changes are made by middlemen as well as by manufacturers, but not necessarily always at the same times. Trading up is an attempt to market a product of

[8]E. Jerome McCarthy, *Basic Marketing: A Managerial Approach* (Homewood, Illinois: Richard D. Irwin, Inc., 1975), p. 253.

[9]See Lonnie L. Ostrom and John L. Schlacter, "Product Liability: An Awakening Giant," *Journal of Small Business Management,* 13, No. 2 (April 1975), pp. 9–14.

higher quality (supposedly, at least) at a higher price. Trading down is an attempt to market a product of lower quality at a lower price. Neither move (up or down) is easy for the SBM to make successfully. Reducing risk and increasing the chances for success when trading up or down can be aided by several tactical approaches. Success is more likely if at least several of the following conditions are present:

1. A distinctly different form accompanies the introduction of the new product and differentiates it from the older one.
2. Easily observable (for the purchaser) value differences exist between the higher- and lower-priced lines.
3. Different marketing channels, in whole or in part, are used for the sale of the new lines.
4. Brand identification clearly differentiates the products.
5. Promotional orientation accompanying the sale of the new product is distinctly different from that of previous lines.[10]

An advertising agency executive, speaking on how local regional companies can compete with national organizations, illustrates how advertising can be more effective if the product of a service firm is properly positioned:

> We determined that the company positioning should center around a better alternative for personal loans," he said. "This was accomplished by positioning City Loan as a loan and savings institution. As a loan and savings institution, the company is perceived as a more credible, stable, and reliable organization—the type most people want to deal with.[11]

In addition to quality modification, the SBM may wish to modify features, style, or intangibles, such as the product warranty. Although we will consider only these three, many other forms of product modification are possible.

Features are physical things that may enhance the value of the product. Such features may be either standard or optional at extra cost. Features may also provide extra revenue for the SBM. Unique features are often available to the SBM at little or no cost. Using unique features is an excellent product strategy for SB: However, the SBM should take care to insure that the unique features are meaningful to his target customers. Although highly successful unique features tend to be copied by competitors, BB may be less flexible than SB in quickly changing to successful product features.

Style modification may help to create product obsolescence. The merits and demerits of planned obsolescence will not be argued here. It is well known that people like changes in style. But the uniqueness of a style that makes it so fashionable one day also makes it unfashionable the next day. Fashions (and fads) have life-cycles. The SBM usually has little influence over the fashion life-cycle; but he can (a) determine from the market at what stage of the fashion life-cycle any particular style is, (b) estimate the pace of the fashion life-cycle, and (c) attempt to match his product offerings to the style interests of his target market. Although style may often be associated with clothing and

---

[10]Thomas A. Staudt, Donald A. Taylor, and Donald J. Bowersox, *A Managerial Introduction To Marketing*, (3rd ed.; Englewood Cliffs, New Jersey: Prentice-Hall, Inc., 1976), p. 216.

[11]Reprinted from *Marketing News* published by the American Marketing Association, February 27, 1976, p. 9.

automobiles, the SBM should be aware that most products, especially consumer durables, are affected directly—or at least indirectly—by style.

Intangible modifications are those which deal with changes in the intangible part of product. Many of these intangibles were discussed in the previous section on customer services. One intangible which was not mentioned was warranty. Warranty can apply to goods and/or services portions of the product. For the SBM, warranty can represent an area of extreme importance in the total product strategy. It is the contention of this author that SB should strongly consider offering and fulfilling a better and more comprehensive product warranty than does BB. The SBM needs to emphasize the warranty more because his brand may be less well known. The consumer product warranties law which recently went into effect provides for two basic classes of warranties: "limited" and "full." Although consumers may not yet be aware of legal changes, the SBM who provides for a "full" warranty and who promotes this fact aggressively may gain a significant differential advantage. Warranty may be especially important to consumers for products whose purchase requires a great deal of installation. Examples would be a replacement roof, a central heating and air conditioning system, or a water heater. From the consumers' viewpoint, both the product and its proper installation must be covered. The warranty is only as strong as its weakest link. This has channel of distribution implications because the warranty is part of the product.

NEW PRODUCTS FOR SB

New products are important for both BB and SB. The new product planning and developing processes are pretty much the same for both BB and SB; at least this is true in the sequence of necessary steps for a successful new product program. However, implementation of individual steps may vary considerably by company size. New product strategy will also vary by company size. We will, therefore, confine ourselves to a discussion of new product implementation and strategy which emphasizes those aspects unique to SB. Complete discussions of new product planning and development may be found elsewhere.[12]

New product strategy for SB was first mentioned in this book in Chapter 1, where we quoted an American Management Association study. Two conclusions of that study were:

22. Because the risks of failure of original products are great and can cause more serious losses for small companies than for large companies, small firms should lean more toward evolution than invention in product development.

23. When small firms must risk their future on new products (not externally available), they should aim at radical development; many of the greatest product innovations have come from small firms.[13]

[12]For example, see James A. R. Stauff, *How to Plan and Develop New Products That Sell* (Chicago: The Dartnell Corporation, 1974); John T. Gerlach and Charles Anthony Wainwright, *Successful Management of New Products* (New York: Hastings House, Publishers, 1968); or Peter Hilton, *New Product Introduction: For Small Business Owners* (Washington: Small Business Administration, 1961).

[13]Reprinted by permission of the publisher from Theodore Cohn and Roy A. Lindberg, *How Management Is Different in Small Companies,* An AMA Management Briefing, © 1972 by American Management Association, Inc., p. 3.

The above study tended to emphasize new products from the technical side and from the point of view of the SB manufacturer. Technology is certainly important; however, our brief examination must recognize technology simply as a part of the SBMM environment. We should also state that the new product question is of importance to nonmanufacturing SB firms such as wholesalers, retailers, and service firms. The manufacturers' perspective is traditionally discussed for purposes of convenience.

A second perspective on product strategy in general, and on new product strategy in particular, is that appropriate strategy changes over time. One author, after stating that "New product marketing is the ultimate test of marketing skill and daring," goes on to show how a new business environment and a new consumer have changed the rules of product strategy.[14] After citing recurring recession, shortages, high prices, inflation, capital shortages, static or declining real disposable income, uncertain consumer expectations, and so forth, product strategy changes as shown in Table 10–3 were suggested.[15]

Does the SBM have a real choice insofar as product innovation is concerned? Perhaps in the short run the answer can be *yes*. And the SBM is usually most involved with short run rather than with long run strategy planning and decision making. In fact, short run profits may be enhanced or even maximized by the decision not to offer new products. In the long run, however, mere survival—or a perhaps more desirable state of survival with growth—proves the worth of the axiom "innovate or die."

What are some of the new product strategy issues unique to SB? Regardless of the actual new product planning and development process used (and the process may have any number of steps according to the author selected), the following suggestions should help the SBM toward successful new products.[16]

1. The path for successful introduction of a new product should be shorter for SB because fewer people are involved and the channels of communication among these people are shorter. However, such direct communication is not automatic.

2. If and when a new product development is undertaken by SB, the element of risk is proportionately greater than for BB since the necessary amount of committed capital and other resources is proportionately greater for SB. The SBM should therefore attempt to minimize such risks to the extent possible.

3. The SBM should be sure to *plan* before getting into *development*. Don't skip planning.

Table 10–3 Product Strategies

1965–1973	*1974 → ?*
Push value-added products	Push basic products
Push full line	Push high-profit products
Try to sustain troubled products	Milk declining or obsolescent products
Add new sizes, forms, varieties	Prune marginal items

[14]Paul C. Harper, Jr., "New Product Marketing: The Cutting Edge of Corporate Policy," *Journal of Marketing*, 40, No. 2 (April 1976), 78.

[15]Harper, p. 78.

[16]See Stauff, *How to Plan and Develop New Products that Sell.*

4. As a new product planning device, budgeting is among the most important tools available to the SBM.

5. A commitment by the people of the SB firm to participate in the new product program is essential for success. This may include people from all parts of the firm. A single individual, reporting to a major executive, should be given full-time responsibility for the new product program. An unassigned task is seldom accomplished.

6. The SB firm should avoid the trap of developing techologically sound new products which it cannot possibly market due to lack of marketing resources.

7. The SBM who is currently enjoying success with present products is in a better position to plan for new products than he may be in the future. He should not sit back and count his money. For example, the SBM with a single product or a very limited line of products may want to expand his line in order to avoid loss of dealers to full-line competitors who "force" dealers to carry their full line or not carry their products at all.

8. Coordinating the new product development program is not necessarily less difficult for SB than for BB. The "one-man show" or "part-time committee" will not get the job done. An entrepreneur type who can eagerly devote his full time to the new product program should be appointed to coordinate the people and resources of the SB firm.

9. If the SBM is to use test marketing, it should be done in a scientific rather than a haphazard manner.

10. The SBM should never attempt to market a new product that does not have proper and sufficient marketing support behind it. In other words, when crossing the desert, don't take only enough water to get part of the way to the next oasis.

11. In the actual market introduction, the SBM should usually strive for almost instantaneous distribution in each market he enters. In addition to losing potential sales and giving competition time to retaliate, delays may drain the limited capital and other resources of the SB firm.

12. The second new product development program (and all succeeding ones) of the SBM will be easier than the first.

BIBLIOGRAPHY

Books

DOMINGUEZ, GEORGE S. *Product Management.* American Marketing Association, Inc., 1971.

GERLACH, JOHN T. AND WAINWRIGHT, CHARLES ANTHONY. *Successful Management of New Products.* New York: Hastings House Publishers, 1968.

HILTON, PETER. *New Product Introduction: For Small Business Owners.* Washington: Small Business Administration, 1961.

KOLLAT, DAVID T., BLACKWELL, ROGER D., AND ROBESON, JAMES F. *Strategic Marketing.* New York: Holt, Rinehart and Winston, Inc., 1972.

KOTLER, PHILIP. *Marketing Management: Analysis, Planning, And Control.* 2nd ed. Englewood Cliffs, New Jersey: Prentice-Hall, Inc., 1972.

MCCARTHY, E. JEROME. *Basic Marketing: A Managerial Approach.* Homewood, Illinois: Richard D. Irwin, Inc., 1975.

PRESTON, LEE E. *Markets and Marketing: An Orientation.* Glenview, Illinois: Scott, Foresman and Company, 1970.

STAUDT, THOMAS A., TAYLOR, DONALD A., AND BOWERSOX, DONALD J. *A Managerial Introduction To Marketing.* 3rd ed. Englewood Cliffs, New Jersey: Prentice-Hall, Inc., 1976.

STAUFF, JAMES A. R. *How to Plan and Develop New Products That Sell.* Chicago: The Dartnell Corporation, 1974.

Articles and Periodicals

HARPER, PAUL C., JR. "New Product Marketing: The Cutting Edge of Corporate Policy," *Journal of Marketing,* 40, No. 2 (April 1976), 76–79.

Marketing News, February 27, 1976, p. 9.

"Marketing Observer," *Business Week,* March 3, 1975, p. 38.

McNAMEE, BERNARD J. "A Primer on Patent, Trademark, And Know-How Licensing," *MSU Business Topics,* 18, No. 3 (Summer 1970), 11–20.

OSTROM, LONNIE L. AND SCHLACTER, JOHN L. "Product Liability: An Awakening Giant," *Journal of Small Business Management,* 13, No. 2 (April 1975), 9–14.

WORKMAN, H. ROSS AND STANFORD, MELVIN J. "Patent And Copyright Protection," *Journal of Small Business Management,* 12, No. 4 (October 1974), 47–51.

Reports

COHN, THEODORE AND LINDBERG, ROY A. *How Management Is Different in Small Companies.* An AMA Management Briefing. 1972.

Committee on Definitions. *Marketing Definitions: A Glossary of Marketing Terms.* American Marketing Association. Chicago, 1960.

APPENDIX FOR CHAPTER 10—
THE PRODUCT LIFE CYCLE

Products and people both have life-cycles. The concept of the product life-cycle (PLC) is a framework for marketing strategy. The PLC concept has been applied to various kinds of products and product groupings. For example, we could examine the PLC of calculators, pocket calculators, or Brand X pocket calculators, and so forth. Our analysis would vary according to our definition of product. The rationale for PLC is supported somewhat by the diffusion of innovation and the adoption process as described in consumer behavior. Some empirical research has been conducted which supports the PLC; and marketing educators, students, and practitioners generally ascribe to the concept. However, as with most areas in marketing, application of the concept will continue to lack scientific precision. Our purpose here is to present PLC very briefly as a marketing concept which can act as a framework for marketing strategy planning. The perspective of the SBM will be given at various points; however, PLC has traditionally been more closely associated with BB than with SB.

STAGES IN THE PLC

Although many other variations are offered by other authors and some of these other variations may depict a higher level of accuracy in describing the PLC, the four-stage PLC, including (a) introduction, (b) growth, (c) maturity, and (d) decline, is most common. Figure 10–A–1 shows such a PLC. In this figure, we note the following:

1. The horizontal axis is simply "time" and does not give units such as days, months, years, and so on. In fact, the proportion of time the product spends in each stage should vary from product to product; but our diagram does not clearly show this.

2. The vertical axis measures sales and profit. Again, the units of measure are not specified, but are likely to be dollars adjusted in some ways to insure comparability over time.

3. The top line shows sales of the product—for all sellers in the industry selling to target markets under concern.

4. The bottom line shows profits (losses) for the product for all sellers in the industry selling to the target markets under concern.

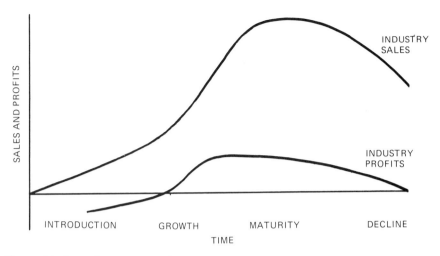

SALES AND PROFITS

INDUSTRY
SALES

INDUSTRY
PROFITS

INTRODUCTION   GROWTH   MATURITY   DECLINE

TIME

Figure 10–A–1   Product Life Cycle

5. The four stages of the PLC (introduction, growth, maturity, and decline) are shown in appropriate sequential order. However, for a particular seller, entry (or exit) is possible at any of the stages.

6. Since the width of each stage and the overall width of the PLC can vary considerably, the slopes of both the sales and profit lines can also vary considerably.

Additional meanings to the PLC shown in Figure 10–A–1 can be gained by viewing a summary diagram which depicts the life-cycle stages of various products. Figure 10–A–2 lists "termination" as a fifth stage and its vertical axis measures market saturation rather than sales and profits.[1]

Introduction is the first stage of the PLC. This is the demand creation or development stage. Due to high costs and relatively low sales, losses frequently occur in this stage. Promotional costs are especially heavy, due to the need for introducing the product to middlemen and consumers. The product may or may not be technically proven, competitors are likely to be few, and the length of this stage will depend on the nature of the market and the marketing strategies employed.

Growth is the stage in which sales rise quite rapidly and profitability improves very substantially. Additional competition is therefore attracted to the industry in order to serve the additional demand for the product. The pioneering objective of introductory promotion was to get customers to try the product, but the promotional objective has shifted, in this stage, to one of attempting to build brand preference. Technology is improved and economies of scale begin to be employed. Unit prices may decline and the overall level of marketing activity remains high.

Maturity is the stage during which industry sales continue their climb, peak out, and begin their decline. Due to intensive competition, the profit decline will probably come before the sales decline. Supply may now exceed demand. One competitor's sales increases may be at the expense of other competitors. Repeat sales are important for many products. Promotion may emphasize product features. The "profit squeeze" may be on.

Decline may be brought about by a competing innovation or a radical change in customer preferences. Sales decline and profits decline. In fact, losses may occur, as many competitors are reluctant to leave the industry. Production and/or marketing becomes concentrated among a few firms. Marketing activity is at a low level or is almost completely terminated.

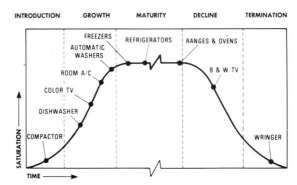

Figure 10–A–2   Life Cycle Stages of Various Products

Source: John E. Smallwood, "The Product-Life Cycle: A Key to Strategic Marketing Planning," MSU Business Topics, 20, No. 1 (Winter 1973) pp. 29–35. Reprinted by permission of the publisher, Division of Research, Graduate School of Business Administration, Michigan State University.

USES AND LIMITATIONS OF PLC

One author, who takes a comprehensive view of product, market, and profit life-cycles, states:

It is, hopefully, not redundant to list the principal uses of these concepts. These do not pretend to be either inclusive or exclusive; they merely indicate the major possibilities:

Determination of market entry.

Prediction of new product success.

Prediction of market needs.

Prediction of market trends and developments.

Analysis of performance—product, market, profit.

Isolation of problem areas.

Isolation of key products, markets, profit.

Assistance in planning.

Development of improvement programs.

Information source for decision making.

Product, profit, and market control and review.

Rapid assessment and continuous monitoring.[1]

Clearly, the PLC is a concept; and its use as an operational tool by the SBM may present some difficulties. Among the limitations to implementing the PLC concept are the following: (a) The stages of the PLC cannot always be easily identified, that is, both the shape of a particular PLC and where the product is at any given point in time; (b) not all products pass through all stages, and the time duration for each stage varies by product; and (c) the PLC itself is not a predetermined phenomenon, but is affected by the market forces. In spite of such limitations, the marketer can receive some conceptual assistance from the PLC in planning marketing strategy. For example, one author comments on the

[1]George S. Dominguez, *Product Management* (American Management Association, Inc., 1971), pp. 142–143.

usefulness of the PLC in sales forecasting, advertising, pricing and marketing planning.[2] In commenting on the use of PLC in product planning in the major household appliance industry, Smallwood states:

> Curiously enough, the very configuration of the product takes on a classical pattern of evolution as it advances through the PLC. At first, the new device is designed for function alone; the initial design is sometimes crude by standards that will be applied in the future. As the product maturation process continues, performance sophistication increases. Eventually the product develops to the point where competitors are hardpressed to make meaningful differences which are perceptible to consumers.
>
> As the product progresses through the product life-cycle, these modifications tend to describe a pattern of metamorphosis from "the ugly box" to a number of options. The adjustment cycle includes:
>
> Part of house: the built-in look and function. Light fixtures, cooking stoves, wall stoves, wall safes, and furnaces are examples.
>
> Furniture: a blending of the product into the home decor. This includes television, hi-fi consoles, radios, clocks, musical instruments, game tables, and so forth.
>
> Portability: a provision for increased *presence* of the product through provisions for easier movement (rollers or compactness), or multiple unit ownership (wall clocks, radios, even refrigerators) or miniaturization for portability. Portability and *personalization*, such as the pocket knife and the wristwatch, can occur.
>
> System: a combination of components into one unit with compatible uses and/or common parts for increased convenience, lower cost, or less space. Home entertainment centers including television, radio, hi-fi, refrigerator-freezers, combination clothes washer-dryers, clock radios, pocket knife-can-and-bottle openers are illustrative.[3]

Summaries of marketing strategy variations (i.e., different marketing mixes) can be found in several sources. The direct applicability of such suggested strategies is, of course, best judged by the individual SBM. Among the sources are:

1. In the article cited above, Smallwood presents a summary table of general characteristics of products and their markets.
2. A book which we have referred to several times, *Market Strategy* by David J. Luck and Arthur E. Prell, presents a repertoire of marketing strategies. One of these is organized according to the stages of the PLC.
3. Chester R. Wasson, in a book called *Product Management* (publisher: Challenge Books), presents, on pages 195 and 196, a "Summary Of The Changing Product Management Objectives Over The Market Life Cycle."
4. Wasson's thinking on the PLC concept is also given credit in *Marketing Strategy And Management* by Constantini, Evans, and Morris (publisher: Business Publications, Inc.) as they present, on page 249, "The Marketing Mix in Life Cycle Stages."

Having listed the above summaries and having given some implications of the PLC for product planning, let us now look briefly at recycling, or what Levitt refers to as "life extension" or "market stretching."[4]

As Levitt notes: "When a company develops a new product or service, it should try to plan at the very outset a series of actions to be employed at various subsequent stages in

---

[2]Smallwood, p. 32.
[3]Smallwood, pp. 34–35.
[4]Theodore Levitt, "Exploit The Product Life Cycle," *Harvard Business Review*, 43 (November–December 1965), 87.

the product's existence so that its sales and profit curves are constantly sustained rather than following the usual declining slope."[5] Although long-range advance planning may seem more ideal to some, short-range planning is more realistic, especially for SB. Such short-range planning may center around strategies for stretching out the more profitable stages of the PLC and/or shortening the less profitable or unprofitable stages. A programmed series of new product introductions and old product innovations (recycling) can help to level out sales and profits for a firm with a broad line of products. Such a plan will provide for more consistency in return on investment. Wide product lines, frequent new product developments, and consistency of return on investment are more characteristic of BB than SB. This does not mean that market stretching is not an appropriate strategy for SB; but it may be an appropriate strategy for slightly different reasons. Let us now briefly examine some other implications of PLC for SB.

IMPLICATIONS FOR SB

For both BB and SB, the PLC has implications for all areas of the marketing mix. Thus, for SB the PLC can be used to help formulate product, place, price, promotion, and people strategies as well as the overall marketing strategy of the firm. We will refer to PLC in later chapters to show the influence of PLC on marketing strategy formulation.

Some implications of the PLC concept which relate specifically to SB are:

1. SB is characterized by flexibility and more emphasis on short-term rather than long-term planning. The SBM should therefore be careful to evaluate as best he can whatever changes are taking place in the PLC. His attention should be directed specifically at the target markets he serves rather than at mass markets. In other words, the SBM should re-evaluate the stages of the PLC each time he considers any strategic marketing changes. In this way, several short runs add up to the long run.

2. The SBM may sometimes successfully compete in the general mass undifferentiated market in the growth stage, but it is very unlikely that the SBM can do so in the maturity stage. Therefore, if the SBM does not plan to exit the industry in the early portion of the maturity stage, he should be a target marketer.

3. Some SB firms may operate only in the decline stage by taking over existing products and markets that BB can no longer afford to retain. For example, Ipana toothpaste is a product which was sold by a BB firm to a SB firm in the declining stage of the PLC.[6]

4. In measuring the competitive value of market share for a product and how this value varies with the stage of the product in the PLC, SB should use different valuation criteria than BB. Quite often, the more appropriate criteria for SB deal with strength in a partinular segment of the market.[7]

5. The SBM can make profits in any stage of the PLC if he adapts his marketing strategy properly. However, due to the nature of competition (such as mass production in the maturity stage), the SBM may be wiser to exit early rather than late.

6. If the advance plan calls for the SB to lose money in an early stage of the PLC

---

[5]Levitt, p. 88.

[6]Philip Kotler, *Marketing Management: Analysis, Planning, And Control* (2nd ed.; Englewood Cliffs, New Jersey: Prentice-Hall, Inc., 1971), p. 437.

[7]For a discussion of market share strategy and PLC see Bernard Catry and Michel Chevalier, "Market Share Strategy and the Product Life Cycle," *Journal of Marketing,* 38 (October 1974), 29–34 as well as notes on the article in Robert Fides and Stephen Lofthouse, " 'Market Share Strategy and the Product Life Cycle': A Comment," *Journal of Marketing,* 39 (October 1975), 57–59 and in Bernard Catry and Michel Chevalier, "Market Share Strategy: The Concept and the Evidence," *Journal of Marketing,* 39 (October 1975), 59–60.

(e.g., the introduction stage), the financial resources of the SB firm become a major determinant of marketing strategy. A firm with small financial resources may be forced to exit before it can "cash-in" during the growth or maturity stage. Such firms should consider licensing, contract production, contract marketing, and so forth in order to best utilize available finances.

7. The SBM should consider appealing to entirely different target markets as the product passes through the stages of the PLC.

8. The SBM should remember that a target marketer (and the SBM is usually a target marketer) will often experience shorter but more profitable PLC than does a mass marketer.

9. The SBM should take great care to match his PLC strategy with the needs of his target market. For example, in fashion merchandising, the SBM who is ahead of his potential customers on the fashion can lose as much money as the SBM who is too late. The SBM should also be aware of the high cost of making a trend versus taking advantage of the trend. New York City's most popular "pop" radio station lets the other stations "make" the hits, then it plays only the top hits to the largest audience. The other stations are working for this station.

10. Finally, SB middlemen as well as SB manufacturers can utilize the PLC concept. SB middlemen make decisions about what products to carry; how many, when, and which to actively promote; when to drop products; when to lower prices; and so forth. An understanding of the PLC can aid in such decisions.

BIBLIOGRAPHY

Books

Dominguez, George S. *Product Management.* American Management Association, Inc., 1971.

Kotler, Philip. *Marketing Management: Analysis, Planning, And Control.* 2nd ed. Englewood Cliffs, New Jersey: Prentice-Hall, 1971.

Articles and Periodicals

Catry, Bernard and Chevalier, Michel. "Market Share Strategy and the Product Life Cycle," *Journal of Marketing,* 38 (October 1974), 29–34.

Catry, Bernard and Chevalier, Michel. "Market Share Strategy: The Concept and the Evidence," *Journal of Marketing,* 39 (October 1975), 59–60.

Fides, Robert and Lofthouse, Stephen. " 'Market Share Strategy and the Product Life Cycle': A Comment," *Journal of Marketing,* 39 (October 1975), 57–59.

Levitt, Theodore. "Exploit The Product Life Cycle," *Harvard Business Review,* 43 (November–December 1965), 81–94.

Smallwood, John E. "The Product Life Cycle: A Key to Strategic Marketing Planning," *MSU Business Topics,* 20, No. 1 (Winter 1973), 29–35.

11

Place Strategy for SBMM

Place is the controllable variable of the SB marketing mix dealing with channel of distribution decisions of where, when, and by whom products will be marketed. Physical distribution systems involving the transportation and storage functions are also a part of place strategy. This chapter focuses on channel of distribution strategy for SB. The following chapter covers some limited place strategy areas: location and site strategy for the SB retailer, retail store layout, and a brief look at some physical distribution questions from the SB perspective.

The importance of place strategy in the SB marketing mix is emphasized by (a) the impact of place on the other "P's" and (b) the long term nature of important place decisions. Although place strategy decisions do not necessarily come prior to decisions in other areas, their interdependence is almost obvious. For example, a manufacturer who has decided to utilize a certain channel of distribution must set his prices and discount structure accordingly. A retailer who has decided to affiliate with a voluntary group wholesaler such as Super Valu has at the same time made some decisions (or at least imposed some constraints) on such questions as what private label products to carry, what price policies to follow, what image to strive for in advertising and in personnel policies, and so forth. Not all place strategy decisions are long-term decisions; but the important ones, that is, the core strategy decisions, tend to be long-term decisions. For example, the decision of the above SB retailer to affiliate with Super Valu may establish a relationship that lasts longer than a generation. Long-term commitments are made on both sides. Another example is the selection of a new store site: It is hoped that a site will prove successful for a number of years. Relationships with both suppliers and customers tend to be long-term. SB firms tend to emphasize short-term planning more than long-term planning. Occasionally, however, such as in the case of core strategy decisions regarding place, the SBM is forced to think in terms of the long run.

The overall objective of place strategy is to organize and operate a system involving transportation, storage, and communications in order to make goods and services available to potential customers. The desires of customers and potential customers regarding the ideal place availability vary from market to market and from product to product. The task of the SBM is to match his place offering with the desires of his target market(s). In order to do this, place strategy must be a planned part of the SB marketing strategy. If he is a manufacturer, the SBM must choose the best "pipeline" for his products to reach the target market. If he is a wholesaler or retailer, the SBM must find suppliers that meet the needs of his target market. Decisions must be made regarding which firms, if any, other than the SBM will perform which marketing functions. Cost and efficiency considerations usually prohibit the marketer (BB or SB) from performing all marketing functions by marketing directly from producer to user. Channel of distribution decisions and other place decisions are not made in a vacuum, but are made in a constantly changing environment. For example, some recent changes in distributive institutions have been identified. They are:

1. Rapid growth of vertical marketing systems.
2. Intensification of intertype competion.
3. Increasing polarity of retail trade.
4. Acceleration of institutional life-cycles.
5. The emergence of the "free form corporation" as a major competitive reality in distribution.
6. The expansion of nonstore retailing.[1]

Adaptation to the above trends and to other trends yet to come will make the implementation of an ideal place strategy a real challenge for the SBM.

CHANNEL OF DISTRIBUTION STRATEGY

Let us now examine channels of distribution, a major portion of place strategy. As such, the purpose of channel strategy is to aid the SBM in attaining the ideal place objective. In addition to channel of distribution strategy, we will examine three additional strategy areas which are often of sufficient importance to the SBM to also be considered core strategies. These are location, layout, and physical distribution.

What Are Channels of Distribution?

The SBM is likely to concern himself with his immediate suppliers and customers instead of the entire channel of distribution. The implementation of the marketing concept demands the overall channel point of view. Place strategy in general, and channel of distribution strategy in particular, are similar to the other marketing variables over which the SBM has some control. They can be manipulated or controlled in order to enhance the SB marketing mix. What, then, is a channel of distribution? The American Marketing Association defines a channel of distribution as "the structure of intra-company organization units and extra-company agents and dealers, wholesale and retail,

[1]William R. Davidson, "Changes in Distributive Institutions," *Journal of Marketing,* 34, No. 1 (January, 1970), p. 7.

through which a commodity, product, or service is marketed."[2] The above definition was intentionally designed to be broad. Another acceptable definition of a channel of distribution, or trade channel, is: "an organized network of agencies and institutions which, in combination, perform all the activities required to link producers with users and users with producers in order to accomplish the marketing task."[3] The channel is usually thought of as including the producer and the user since they also perform marketing activities.

Some Underlying Principles

In both theory and practice, the channel of distribution concept is based upon functional specialization. Such specialization reduces the number of total transactions, provides for strategically located reserves, and provides for delaying (postponement) of product changes in form. Such postponement reduces inventory carrying costs that would result from higher value product forms. For example, it costs less to carry an inventory of wheat than an inventory of bread that would result from that amount of wheat. Thus, channels are involved with all the utilities: time, place, possession, and form. A somewhat similar approach is to view what happens in a channel not as one flow but as a group of several interrrelated flows. These are the physical flow of goods, the flow of ownership or control, the flow of information, and the flow of money.[4]

The underlying principles of the channel of distribution concept are very succinctly summarized from a functionalist point of view by Mallen:

> The basic message of all channel functionalists is as follows:
> 1. Marketing functions are the various types of job tasks which channel members undertake.
> 2. These functions can be allocated in different mixes to different channel members.
> 3. The functional mixes will be patterned in a way which provides the greatest profit either to the consumer (in the form of lower prices and/or more convenience) or to the channel members with the most power (which depends on market structure).
> 4. Should one or more channel members (or potential members) see an opportunity to change the functional mix of the channel in order to increase his profits, he will attempt to do so.
> 5. Should the attempt be successful, and if the functional mix change is big enough, it will (by definition) change the institutional arrangement in the channel, i.e., the channel structure.[5]

Some Misconceptions About Channels

In a classic article, McVey comments on some popular misconceptions concerning channels of distribution:

[2]Committee on Definitions, Reprinted from *Marketing Definitions: A Glossary of Marketing Terms* published by The American Marketing Association, Chicago, 1960, p. 10.

[3]Reavis Cox and Thomas F. Schutte, "A Look At Channel Management," *Modern Marketing Thought,* ed. J. Howard Westing and Gerald Albaum (New York: Macmillan Publishing Co., Inc., 1975), p. 267.

[4]Cox and Schutte, p. 273.

[5]Bruce Mallen, "Functional Spin-Off: A Key to Anticipating Change in Distribution Structure," *Journal of Marketing,* 37, No. 3 (July 1973), p. 19.

Further study of marketing textbooks may lead a reader to conclude that: (a) middlemen of many types are available to any manufacturer in any market to which he wishes to sell, and within each type there is an ample selection of individual firms; (b) the manufacturer habitually controls the selection and operation of individual firms in his channel; and (c) middlemen respond willingly as selling agents for the manufacturer rather than as purchasing agents for a coveted group of customers to whom the middlemen sell.

Yet none of these conclusions is entirely valid.[6]

Traditional Consumer Goods Channels

Alternative channels of distribution for consumer goods are shown in Figure 11–1. One or more of the alternatives may be employed at any given time. The first alternative from manufacturer (or producer) to consumer employs no middlemen and is known as direct distribution. The indirect channel alternatives in Figure 11–1 do not identify the specific subtypes of middlemen. Thus, the possible alternatives are far greater than those shown in the figure.

Industrial Goods Channels

Figure 11–2 shows six principal channels of distribution for industrial machinery, equipment, and supplies.[7] As with consumer goods channels, one or more of the

Figure 11.1   Consumer Goods Channel Alternatives

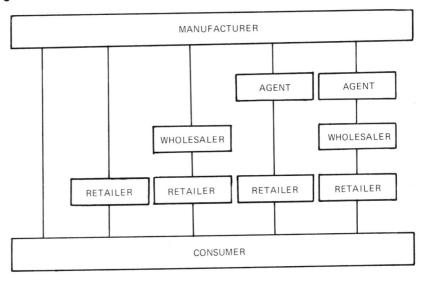

[6]Philip McVey, "Are Channels of Distribution What the Textbooks Say?" *Marketing Classics*, ed. Ben M. Enis and Keith K. Cox (2nd ed.; Boston: Allyn and Bacon, Inc., 1973), p. 298.

[7]William M. Diamond, *Distribution Channels for Industrial Goods* (Columbus: Bureau of Business Research, The Ohio State University, 1963), pp. 56–57.

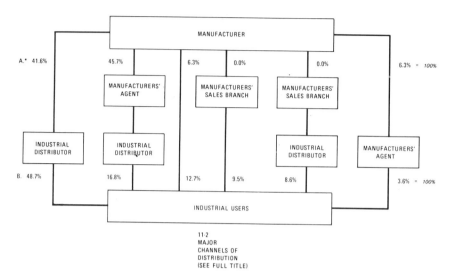

11·2
MAJOR
CHANNELS OF
DISTRIBUTION
(SEE FULL TITLE)

Figure 11.2   Major Channels of Distribution for Industrial Machinery, Equipment, and Supplies by Firms (or Producing Units) with Annual Sales under $1,000,000 and by Firms of All Sizes.

Source: William M. Diamon, *Distribution Channels for Industrial Goods* (Columbus: Bureau of Business Research, The Ohio State University, 1963, pp. 56–57. Used with permission.

alternatives may be employed at any given time. Both direct and indirect channels are shown. Also, subtypes and variations of the named middlemen do exist. Thus, the range of alternatives is actually greater than shown.

Industrial Channels for SB Manufacturers

The relative importance of alternate channels of distribution for industrial manufacturers does vary by size. This is shown in Figure 11–2. The survey upon which Figure 11–2 is based shows that channels involving manufacturers' sales branches are nonexistent for SB manufacturers, at least as the major or primary channel. Such channels are of only minor importance as secondary channels. Most small industrial manufacturers simply do not have sales branches.[8]

Other findings of the Diamond survey indicate the following tendencies:

1. SB manufacturers (under $1,000,000 annual sales) tended to make greater use of manufacturers' agents. This is a substitute for sales branches or a factory sales force selling to industrial distributors. This channel enables a small producer with limited financial resources to sell in wide geographic markets.

2. The agent is used primarily by the SB firm in selling to distributors who in turn sell to users.

3. Industrial distributors are extremely important to the SB manufacturers. By

[8]Diamond, pp. 57 and 75.

combining the 41.6% for the manufacturer to distributor to user channel with the 45.7% from the manufacturer to manufacturer's agent to distributor to user channel, we note that industrial distributors are involved in the sales of more than 87% of the primary channels of the SB firms.

    4. For BB manufacturers, on the other hand, manufacturers' agents were often secondary channels.

    5. Gross margins allowed tend to be inversely related to the sales volume size of the manufacturer. That is, higher gross margins are allowed by the SB firms. An explanation of this may be the attempts of SB firms to secure more aggressive promotion on the part of the distributor for products that are less well known in the trade. Also, the SB firm may require the distributor to perform additional functions.

    6. In general, BB manufacturers make greater use of direct distribution than do SB manufacturers.[9]

Types of Channel Systems

    Thus far we have been talking about, and thinking in terms of, the so-called traditional channels of distribution for both consumer and industrial markets. The reality of today tells us that channels are not composed of totally independent businesses at each stage of distribution. This is especially noticeable in consumer markets. Centrally coordinated and integrated channel systems seem to be the rule rather than the exception. What forms do these channel systems take? Today, channels of distribution may be classified as follows:[10]

    1. *Traditional* or *conventional* marketing channel systems, which are "those fragmented networks in which loosely aligned and relatively autonomous manufacturers, wholesalers, and retailers have customarily bargained aggressively with each other, established trade relationships on an individual transaction basis, severed business relationships arbitrarily with impunity, and otherwise behaved independently."[11]

    2. *Vertical marketing systems,* consisting of "horizontally coordinated and vertically aligned establishments which are managed as a system."[12] Types of vertical marketing systems (VMS) are *corporate systems, contractual systems,* and *administered systems.*

    Corporate systems are fairly synonymous with integrated chain store systems. The impetus for vertical integration may come from a retailer or manufacturer (e.g., Sears or Firestone). Corporate systems account for about 30% of all retailing.[13]

    Contractual systems are of three subtypes: wholesaler-sponsored *voluntary chains,* retailer *cooperatives,* and *franchising* organizations. Each involves a voluntary contractual integration of retail store (or service unit) with the supply unit at a prior level in the channel of distribution. It is estimated that from 35% to 40% of all retail trade is accounted for by contractual systems.[14] Franchising has been extremely popular in recent years. This relatively old form, used by auto manufacturers for retail dealers, and by soft-drink manufacturers for regional bottlers (wholesalers), has in recent years become very popular

---

[9]Diamond, pp. 54, 55, 57, 123, 159, 160.
[10]Davidson, p. 7.
[11]Davidson, p. 7.
[12]Davidson, p. 7.
[13]Davidson, p. 7.
[14]Davidson, p. 7.

in bringing complete management systems to retail and service firms in such areas as fast foods, car rentals, motels, and movie theaters.

The third type of VMS is known as an *administered* system. It refers to the vertical integration of a product line or a classification of merchandise rather than the integration of an entire store. The administered system is characterized by selective distribution involving comprehensive channel marketing programs that are usually developed and managed by the manufacturer.

Classifications of channels of distribution into other groupings, or along different dimensions than those given above, are certainly possible. In actual practice, the above "pure" types are actually found in various combinations. For example, the wholesaler who is the sponsor of a voluntary group may also operate a chain of corporate stores. The major point of the above discussion, and it is a very significant one for SB, is that vertical marketing systems of one form or another are a very important channel alternative. The SBM should certainly consider the advantages of being a part of a VMS.

CHANNEL STRATEGY FOR SB

Areas of channel strategy demanding the major attention of the SBM will be considered here. Important channel strategy questions for SB are:

1. What market coverage, in terms of selectivity and intensity, does the SBM desire in order to best serve his target market(s) at a profit?
2. Should the SBM market directly to the consumer or user, or should he market to them indirectly through the use of middlemen?
3. How many channel alternatives (dual or multiple distribution) and which types of middlemen should be employed?
4. What methods and criteria of selection should be employed in choosing specific channel members, that is, individual middlemen?
5. What should be the role of the SBM in the channel of distribution regarding such important issues as channel conflict and cooperation, channel control, leadership, and so forth?
6. Whether or not, and if so, when, should changes in channels of distribution strategy be made by the SBM?
7. Finally, special brief attention is addressed to the questions regarding channels of distribution for new SB firms or for new products of established SB firms.

Many of the above questions are asked from the point of view of the SB manufacturer. A manufacturer certainly does face different channel strategy alternatives than does the SB wholesaler, retailer, or service firm. However, a restatement of some of the above questions does make them very applicable to middlemen. For example, question #1 above for the retailer might be stated this way: In terms of the target markets I have selected, do the market coverage policies of supplier XYZ offer the appropriate degree of intensity or selectivity for me to serve my target market(s) profitably? Question #5 above is appropriate for all levels of distribution. An example of question #6 from a retailer's point of view may, in a specific situation, be: Should I become a member of ABC retail cooperative?

Market Coverage: Intensive Or Selective?

Intensity of distribution may sometimes refer to the geographic markets in which distribution is achieved. However, the term is usually used to refer to the *types* of outlets and the *number* of outlets employed. Our present perspective is that of the SB manufacturer. He may choose *intensive* distribution, *selective* distribution, or, in some cases, *exclusive* distribution. *Intensive distribution* involves attempting to sell through any and all outlets who are financially responsible and willing to sell the product. *Selective distribution* involves limiting the sale of the product in number and/or type of outlets to those middlemen who meet certain criteria deemed important to the successful sale of the product. *Exclusive distribution* is the extreme case of selectivity in which only one outlet (for a given level of distribution) is chosen to sell the product in a given geographic market. The three degrees of market coverage may be mixed at different levels of distribution. For example, the manufacturer may appoint an exclusive wholesaler in each of several geographic areas, who in turn may sell through either selective or intensive distribution to retailers. In any event, the logical starting point is the ultimate consumer or industrial user. Then the channel coverage policy works back toward the manufacturer. Characteristics of goods theory often influences the degree of market coverage. Convenience goods such as cigarettes and chewing gum have intensive distribution, while shopping and specialty goods often have selective or exclusive distribution.

The degree of market coverage (level of intensity of distribution) is shown as a continuum in Figure 11–3. At first, one might question why the SBM would be willing to give up market exposure. If the SBM has a choice, and does so on purpose, it may be for one of the following advantages: (a) to reduce cost; (b) to eliminate "undesirable" outlets; (c) to insure cooperation; (d) to gain initial distribution; (e) to eliminate the need for a level of distribution (e.g., wholesalers) by being able to deal directly with a limited number of retailers; and (f) to insure the adequate performance of functions, such as carrying inventories and providing service facilities.

From the perspective of the SB middleman, whether he is a wholesaler or retailer, the degree of market exposure policies of various manufacturers is also important. For example, the SB retailer selling better quality men's or women's clothing will wish to carry at least some lines on an exclusive basis. In fact, the exclusive franchise in many SB retail firms represents a major portion of the differential advantage for the SB retailer. Thus, SB retailers seeking to put forth an image involving a high degree of exclusivity must be

Figure 11.3 Continuum Showing Degree of Market Exposure

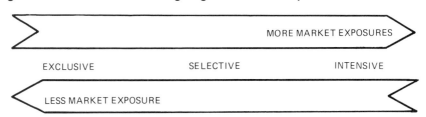

extremely careful in the selection of their suppliers. Retailers (and wholesalers) select manufacturers as suppliers every bit as much as they are chosen as outlets by these same manufacturers.

Direct vs. Indirect

Should the SBM market directly to consumers or users or should middlemen be employed; and if so, how many levels of middlemen should be used? This question really asks whether the SBM should perform all marketing functions himself or whether he should shift and share the marketing functions with others. Earlier in this chapter, we noted the great dependence SB manufacturers of industrial goods have upon middlemen. Most consumer goods (all but about 3%) pass through retail stores. Therefore, the SB manufacturer should examine the costs and alternatives very carefully before deciding to market directly, that is, without the use of middlemen. Avon, Fuller Brush, and a few other marketers have been extremely successful with door-to-door selling, a form of direct marketing. They are exceptions. Mail-order and other forms of direct marketing also pose limitations for many SB marketers. The degree of directness (or indirectness), however, need not be an all or nothing choice. For example, in the previous section we noted that exclusive (or, in some cases, selective) distribution may enable the SB manufacturer to effectively eliminate the wholesale level of distribution. The characteristics favorable to the use of direct distribution given by Cravens, Hills, and Woodruff are listed below in Table 11–1.[15] The SB manufacturer, especially if he has limited financial and other resources, should pay attention to these characteristics before deciding on direct distribution.

How Many and Which Types?

Most products are sold through more than one channel of distribution. The SB manufacturer must decide how many and which types of channels to employ. Likewise, the SB retailer must decide how many and which types of suppliers to employ. The SB wholesaler must answer both of the above sets of questions. Scrambled merchandising and the intensification of intertype competition in retailing have changed some long-standing channel structures for many products. Another factor which may lead to the use of additional channels is segmenting the market more finely into smaller targets. Such segmentation may ofter be a part of the marketing strategy of SB. The result is multiple channels of distribution, also known as dual distribution.

Dual distribution may be resented among competing types of middlemen. For example, the small independent drug store or hardware store probably felt they had plenty of competition before the time when many of their products became available at supermarkets, variety stores, and discount stores. For these SB retailers the dual distribution question is: Do we continue to carry and promote products which were once the sole property of our type of outlet but are now sold aggressively to and through other types of outlets? Some SB retailers may refuse to carry brands sold to other types of outlets. On the other hand, some manufacturers will create separate brands for different types of outlets. From either a manufacturer or middleman perspective, the dual distribution

---

[15]David W. Cravens, Gerald E. Hills, and Robert B. Woodruff, *Marketing Decision Making: Concepts and Strategy* (Homewood, Illinois: Richard D. Irwin, Inc., 1976), p. 532.

Table 11-1 Characteristics Favorable to Use of a Direct Distribution Approach

Type of Factor	*Illustrative Characteristics*
Market Targets	Relatively few customers comprise the market target.
	Size of purchase in terms of quantity or unit price is large.
	Customers tend to be concentrated geographically.
	Sufficient margin exists to support personal selling or mail contact efforts.
	Purchase decision represents a major, long-term commitment by the buyer.
Marketing Program	Personal selling is a major component of the marketing program.
	Intermediary functions are not needed (e.g., storage, local credit, inventory, packaging, etc.) or can be efficiently performed by the manufacturer.
	Marketing strategy favors a direct marketing approach (e.g., qualified intermediaries are not available).
Product/Service Characteristics	Product complexity requires use of manufacturer's personnel in selling and service (e.g., computer sales and service).
	Width of product line sufficient to support direct marketing approach (e.g., Avon Products, Fuller Brush).
	Product application assistance is required (e.g., steam turbines).
	Product technology changing rapidly.
Corporate Capabilities	Resources are available to support a direct marketing approach (e.g., establishment of a sales force).
	Firm has experience in marketing similar products to comparable market targets (e.g., direct channels exist).
	Sufficient time is available to develop needed direct marketing channels before potential competition becomes a threat (e.g., patent protection).

Source: David W. Cravens, Gerald E. Hills, and Robert B. Woodruff, *Marketing Decision Making: Concepts and Strategy* (Homewood, Illinois: Richard D. Irwin, Inc., 1976), p. 532. Used with permission.

question should be resolved by a consideration of the wants and needs of the target customers. An effective channel must provide the convenience and variety desired by the target customers, along with information flows and desired customer services.

Selecting Individual Channel Members

Once a decision has been made to employ a certain number of channels of the desired types of institutions, the SBM must then decide which specific firms within these types are to be selected. For the SB manufacturer, this means selecting specific wholesalers and retailers. For the SB retailers, this means selecting specific suppliers. For the SB wholesaler, the selection is again on both the buying and selling sides. What selection methods and criteria are available? And more importantly, will the selected channel members be available?

All potential channel members are not created equal. Some are very good and some are not so good. Securing a good wholesaler or other middlemen may be made somewhat easier by talking with the candidate's current suppliers and customers. An examination of the other lines carried by the prospect is also an indication of his suitability. In order to be prepared for the actual selection process, the SBM should have predetermined criteria against which to measure potential channel members. Suggestions to aid in selecting channel members are available. For example, the SBA has an *Aid* entitled, "How to Select a Resident Buying Office."[16] Trade associations and their trade shows represent an excellent opportunity for selecting channel members. The SBM *must* first know what he wants; then he must determine what is available to him at what cost.

The Role of SB In Channels of Distribution

What should be the role of SB and the SBM in the channel of distribution regarding such important issues as channel conflict and cooperation, channel control, leadership, and so forth? Generally, the SB does not play the role of channel leader or channel captain. This means that the SB firm is relegated to a follower role in most instances. But there are exceptions, as will be pointed out.

Channel leadership is based upon power and position within the channel. Professor Little explains why SB retailers and wholesalers are seldom channel leaders.

> In a complex, high mass consumption economy, small retailers and wholesalers have neither the position to lead nor the necessary economic power to do so. The key consideration in terms of position power is access to markets. Small retailers and wholesalers offer only a few customers to the channel system, and thus their bargaining position vis-a-vis large firms at any level in the channel is insignificant.[17]

A similar observation is made by McVey concerning middle-size and small companies:

> As to the many thousands of middle-size and small companies that truly character-ize American marketing, the power position is speculative, vacillating, and ephemeral. Strength in certain market areas, the temporary success of a product, ability to perform a certain needed type of financing or promotional effort—these and similar factors enable companies to assume power.
>
> On the other hand, financial reverses, an unfortunate sales campaign, or even the lack of accurate market news—these factors can shift power elsewhere, possibly to another link in the channel or to another firm in the same link. In any case, the opportunity of any firm is contingent upon the willingness of others to use it as a link in the channel.[18]

[16]Ernest A. Miller, "How To Select A Resident Buying Office," *Small Marketers Aids,* No. 116 (Washington: Small Business Administration, 1972).

[17]Robert W. Little, "The Marketing Channel: Who Should Lead This Extra-corporate Organization?" *Journal of Marketing,* 34, No. 1 (January 1970), p. 33.

[18]McVey, p. 300.

If the SB wholesalers and SB retailers are not potential channel captains, do they, when acting as members of vertical marketing systems, exert a marked influence on the leadership? Since "traditional" channels composed of small "independents" at the retail level have been replaced in many lines by vertical marketing systems with affiliated members, the power is concentrated by the combined wholesaler–retailer or retailer–wholesaler, depending on the emphasis. The vertical system also includes the manufacturer at times. The above combination type of institution is sometimes known as a multi-level merchandiser (MLM). Regarding the MLM, Little states:

> Most MLM organizations are large enough to have considerable economic power and, in addition, their position affords them access to large markets. They are also in a position to provide market information. Certainly, they can be considered as potential channel leaders.[19]

What about the SB at the manufacturer level? Can he be a channel leader? The SB manufacturer, although possibly hampered by the lack of economic power, is a potential channel leader *if* he has a good product. The differential advantage of a good product may, of course, not be permanent. A strong consumer franchise, however, if properly maintained, should enable the SB manufacturer to enjoy his leadership role into the market maturity stage of the PLC. In summary, regarding potential channel leadership, we may conclude that manufacturers (both BB and SB) and MLM organizations are potential leaders of marketing channels.[20]

An exception to the above guidelines is the household wooden furniture industry. The industry is competitive, with very low concentration at both the manufacturer and retailer levels. Channel control or leadership resides at the retail level because ". . . furniture retailers have gained the greatest influence over the final sale of the products of the industry."[21] The buying methods of retailers and the marketing practices of manufacturers illustrate the retailers' control. Examples of policies designed to cater to the retailers are: (a) the holding of manufacturers' exhibits at major market centers, which provide the retailers the opportunity to play one manufacturer against another at the same time on the same premises; (b) the use of store-order buying, which results in small retail inventories, large manufacturer inventories, and uneconomical lot size for shipments; (c) demand by retailers for exclusives; and (d) the desire for cumulative (rather than noncumulative) quantity discounts. Of perhaps more importance for channel control is the inability of the manufacturers to establish strong brand identity among ultimate consumers.[22]

For those many SB firms who are not channel leaders, and for whom the possibilities of channel leadership are not likely, is the concept of channel leadership and control a useful one? Yes! Even though channel leadership is not a part of the differential advantage of the typical SBM, good channel "followership" can be most important. The SBM should have and advantageously use available knowledge concerning the locus of economic and position strength within his industry. Little states:

[19]Little, p. 34.
[20]Little, p. 34.
[21]Louis W. Stern, "Channel Control and Inter-Organization Management," *Marketing Management Perspectives and Applications,* ed. Robert B. Woodruff, Gerald E. Hills, and David W. Cravens (Homewood, Illinois: Richard D. Irwin, Inc., 1976), p. 279.
[22]Stern, p. 279.

Small wholesalers, retailers, and manufacturers who are not leaders can also benefit from the knowledge of who holds a strategic position and economic power. The recognition of the source of leadership gives them the opportunity to seek out channels guided by those who appear to be best able to contribute to their own individual goals. Understanding the relationships between all members in the channel should also lead to acceptance of one's role within the channel(s) involved. Also, nonleader members should recognize the reality of competing channel systems.[23]

Two common strategy approaches used by manufacturers in order to secure channel cooperation are "push" and "pull" strategies. A push strategy employs personal selling and advertising to the channel members to gain their cooperation. A pull strategy circumvents the channel members by going to the final consumers through advertisers, coupons, samples, and so forth. In this way, the final consumers "pull" the product through the channel by forcing distribution at the retail store and subsequently at the wholesale level. A careful examination of many of the methods employed in both push and pull strategies strongly suggests that both may be regarded as methods of channel control as well as methods of channel cooperation. Consider the dual impact of such methods as cooperative advertising allowances, push money (PMs), dealer contests, display allowances, "free" goods, guaranteed sales, automatic order systems, training programs for store personnel, business gifts, free store fixtures, and so forth. Control and cooperation can be seen in each of these practices.

Changing Channels

Every so often it becomes apparent that changes have taken place which require changes in the channel of distribution. Probably the most frequent change is the adding or dropping of an individual channel member. However, for the very small SBM, such a change may be of such proportions as to, in effect, be considered a change in the distribution structure itself. Individual changes are part of the day-to-day management of channels. Structural changes are usually less frequent and may be classified according to dimensions:

> There are four dimensions of distribution structure in which change can be anticipated:
>
> 1. The number of channel levels
> 2. The number of channels or whether one, two (dual), or more (multi) channel types will be used
> 3. The types of middlemen that will evolve
> 4. The number of middlemen that will develop at each level[24]

Success, growth, and expansion of target markets may be reasons for the SBM to change marketing channels. Channels may now be available that were previously unavailable. Note the following example, based upon changes in customer location:

> Changes in location of customers are not confined to consumer markets. New firms that may be customers are being created all the time and old firms are constantly adding new locations. One industrial equipment manufacturer had to expand his

[23]Little, p. 37.
[24]Mallen, p. 19.

channels of distribution because of such changes in customer locations. Originally his salesmen sold only to customers in the northeast where his plant was located. On learning that there were potential customers in the far west, he decided to get that business by using a manufacturer's representative—a new type of channel for him.[25]

Another change which the SB manufacturer may overlook simply because it is "too close" to him is change within the SB firm itself. Using established channels for a new product may be less than optimum, as is illustrated by this example:

> For example, he may use his established channels without considering their suitability to a new product he is introducing. An industrial chemical company provides an example of this kind of problem. It tried to distribute a new line of farm and home fertilizers with the same channels that it used to distribute its industrial chemicals. When the expected sales volume did not materialize, the company rechanneled the new product so it would reach retail consumers.[26]

Finally, a caution should be given. Channel changes are often as final as "burning your bridges behind you." For example, the SB manufacturer that drops its agents all at once in order to install its own salesforce must be certain that such a salesforce is cost effective, has market contacts, and can immediately bring in the desired level of sales. The "drop" decision is not reversible.

New Channels

Channels of distribution for new firms and for new products, and new channels for old products must be developed. Such development takes time, talent, and money. A radically new product will present many channel problems to the SBM. When new channels are needed in order to reach new markets, the rapid acquisition of market and industry knowledge is vital for success. The following example illustrates:

> A small new enterprise developed a product that had to be distributed through floral supply wholesalers to retail florists. Its fortunes floundered for a year until it hired a sales manager who had thirty years' experience in selling to that industry. Within a week the product was carried by 300 floral supply wholesalers. He did it over the telephone. Such is the power of contacts. Knowing the people who must be contacted is of tremendous assistance. The new enterprise that has such a man in its organization has a definite advantage.[27]

FRANCHISING AND SUPRA-FIRM ORGANIZATIONS: A CLOSER LOOK AT CONTRACTUAL MARKETING SYSTEMS

In a previous section of this chapter we divided marketing channels into traditional channels and vertical marketing systems. The VMS was further subdivided into corporate systems, contractual systems, and administered systems. In turn, three subtypes of

---

[25]Leonard J. Konopa, "Are Your Products and Channels Producing Sales?" *Management Aids For Small Manufacturers,* No. 203 (Washington: Small Business Administration, 1969), p. 6.

[26]Konopa, p. 6.

[27]Richard H. Buskirk and Percy J. Vaughn, Jr., *Managing New Enterprises* (St. Paul: West Publishing Co, 1976), p. 285.

contractual systems were mentioned: wholesaler-sponsored voluntary chains, retailer cooperatives, and franchising organizations. In practice, some overlap of classifications may be found. Elements of franchising are very evident in voluntaries and retailer cooperatives.

The perspective for our present reclassification will be that of franchising systems. Our divisions of franchising systems will be:

1. Manufacturer–retailer systems, the most popular form.
2. Manufacturer–wholesaler franchises. Here we will also mention franchises in the industrial market.
3. Wholesaler–retailer franchises. Agency stores will be included here.
4. Service sponsor–retailer systems. These are the fastest growing and are also known as franchising company systems or as idea and service franchises.

Two principal ways in which the SBM may become involved in a supra-firm organization are as a franchisor or as a franchisee. The SBM who has a successful program that can be duplicated and operated successfully by others may decide to franchise his successful formula to others as a means of rapid growth with a limited amount of capital and other resources. However, the more common role of the SB firm is that of the franchisee. As a franchisee, the SBM has exchanged a degree of control over his marketing and other programs for what he hopes will be a proven successful program of the franchisor. We will consider only the marketing aspects of franchising. Under most franchising systems, the franchisee (the one who holds the franchise) gives up to the franchisor (the one who grants the franchise) at least some control over the "controllable five P's" of the SB marketing mix. The franchisor may also determine, to a large degree, the target market for the franchisee. How much control over product, place, price, and so on is given up by the franchisee, of course, depends on the terms of the agreement. Whether or not the SBM should give up such control by becoming a franchisee depends on such factors as how alike or different he wishes to be, his own management resources, firm goals, industry trends, advantages and disadvantages, and so forth. The limitation on marketing control for the SBM who has become a franchisee is shown below in Figure 11–4. Note that our hypothetical franchisee has given up all control of the product variable, and much control over location (place) and price. He retains a moderate degree of control over promotion, especially at the local level. He exercises considerable control over the people variable within a set of guidelines. The franchisor has most of the control in defining the target market.

A useful concept which has been used elsewhere in this book is the *supra-firm*. The supra-firm organization includes franchising in its broadest meaning, and it extends somewhat more broadly. The supra-firm is ". . . an organization outside the ownership-operation of the individual firm; some degree of goal commonality (mutual benefit) is recognized and shared with its small business members and a contractual (legal) relationship, beyond a simple buy-sell agreement, exists with individual firms."[28] Franchise organizations are supra-firms, but not all supra-firms are franchise organizations. The following classes of supra-firms may be identified:

1. Wholesaler voluntary chains
2. Retailer cooperative chains and warehouses

[28]Robert W. Little, "The Supra-Firm: Key To Small Retailer Survival," *Modern Marketing Thought,* ed. J. Howard Westing and Gerald Albaum (New York: Macmillan Publishing Co., Inc., 1975), p. 85.

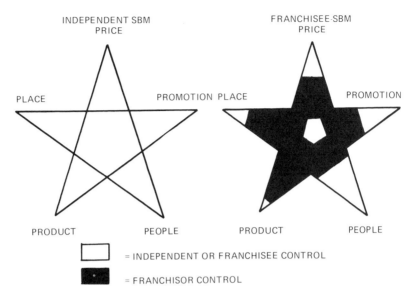

Figure 11.4   Control of Marketing Strategy for Independent SBM and Franchise SBM

3. Franchising
4. Shopping-center management
5. Shopping-center merchants' associations
6. Neighborhood associations
7. Stores with leased departments
8. Coordinated groups of voluntaries
9. Voluntary affiliates of corporate chains (associate stores)
10. Multi-use credit cards
11. Other supra-firms such as pooled buying groups and advertising agencies.[29]

The above list has special reference to the SB retailer or SB retail service firm. With such a variety of outside assistance for improving his operations, is the SBM going to "do it all himself" in order to maintain his "independence?" Except in the case of the SB specialist serving a very limited target market, SB involvement in supra-firm organization is very likely and is often a key to success. Bearing in mind the umbrella concept of the supra-firm, let us now examine the four types of franchising identified earlier in this section.

Manufacturer–Retailer Systems

Franchising of automobile and truck dealers and of gasoline service stations are among the oldest and the most popular in terms of sales activity. The importance of these two product groups as a portion of all franchise sales is shown in Table 11–2 below. About

29Little, "The Supra-Firm," pp. 85–89.

Table 11–2   Franchising In The Economy, 1974*

Kinds of Franchised Business	*Establishments (Number)* *Franchisees*	*Sales ($000)* *Franchisees*
TOTAL—ALL FRANCHISING	398,924	150,891,438
Automobile and Truck Dealers	32,652	89,465,000
Automobile Products and Services	43,918	3,577,050
Business Aids and Services	15,654	1,290,016
Accounting, Credit, Collection Agencies and General Business Systems	2,402	40,795
Employment Services	2,641	348,963
Printing and Copying Services	1,300	55,721
Tax Preparation Services	3,966	56,289
Miscellaneous Business Services	5,345	788,248
Construction, Home Improvements, Maintenance and Cleaning Services	13,216	807,659
Convenience Stores	5,177	1,293,000
Educational Products & Services	1,262	205,095
Fast Food Restaurants (All Types)	31,488	6,722,391
Gasoline Service Stations	168,800	29,458,000
Hotels and Motels	4,714	3,697,831
Campgrounds	1,495	72,981
Laundry and Drycleaning Services	3,822	240,692
Recreation, Entertainment and Travel	4,412	195,723
Rental Services (Auto-Truck-Aircraft-Boats)	7,460	390,500
Rental Services (Equipment)	1,126	88,480
Retailing (Non-Food)	46,593	6,114,768
Retailing (Food Other Than Convenience Stores)	12,042	702,044
Soft Drink Bottlers	2,520	6,381,000
Miscellaneous	2,573	189,208

Source: Adopted from *Franchising In the Economy, 1972–74,* U.S. Department of Commerce, p. 45.

30% of all retail sales in the United States are accounted for by franchising, according to one definition and estimate.[30] However, according to the same source, approximately 80% of those retail sales which are accounted for by franchising are due to two categories: automobile and truck dealers and gasoline service stations. This means that all other forms of franchising at retail (including auto products, convenience stores, fast foods, and other retailing) account for about 20% of franchise retail sales. In other words, retail franchising volume would be substantially less without autos and gasoline.

[30]U.S. Department of Commerce, *Franchising In The Economy 1972–74* (Washington: U.S. Government Printing Office, 1974), p. 5.

Manufacturer–Wholesaler Franchises

The soft drink industry, including such products as Coca-Cola and Pepsi, is the largest user of this form of franchise. The manufacturer ships syrup to the local bottler. The bottler is a wholesaler of soft drinks, even though much of his activity is also of a manufacturing or processing nature. Such franchises have traditionally been restricted in territory, that is, the bottler has sold to all retail outlets within a given territory. It is too early to tell the total effects of packaging changes upon this traditional channel of distribution.

Franchising in the industrial market is less common than in the consumer market. However, some industrial markets do employ franchising. Snap-on Tools is an example.

Wholesaler–Retailer Franchises

Voluntary groups and retail cooperatives are the major wholesaler–retailer franchise systems. In voluntary groups, ownership of the warehouse is by the wholesaler and ownership of the stores is by the various affiliated retailers. In the cooperative system, the member retailers cooperatively own the warehouse. Voluntary and cooperative chains are common in supermarketing, variety stores, hardware stores, home and auto parts stores, and more recently in the drug store area. Among the well-known names are Super Valu, I.G.A., Fleming, Red & White, Ben Franklin, Western Auto, Gamble's, Coast-To-Coast, Ace, True Value, and many others too numerous to mention. I.G.A. (Independent Grocers Alliance) is an alliance of retail member stores and several separate independently owned warehouses throughout the country. Some large corporate chains, such as Walgreen Drugs, act as voluntary wholesalers for affiliated stores, known as agency stores. These agency stores are similar in appearance to corporate stores but are owned by the several affiliated retailers. Sears and Montgomery Ward franchise agency stores in small towns. These operate primarily as catalog-order stores.

Service Sponsor–Retailer Systems

This fast growing area is also known as franchising company systems or as idea and service franchises. Service areas included are fast foods, campgrounds, recreation, entertainment, travel, hotels and motels, business and personal services, transportation leasing, educational services, and so forth. Many of the names are familiar to us all. Less well known, perhaps, are some of the corporate giants acting as franchisors. Here are some familiar names: Burger Chef (General Foods), Burger King (Pillsbury), Baskins Robbins (United Fruit), KOA, AAMCO, Hertz, Holiday Inns, Howard Johnson, Manpower, Putt-Putt, and Kopy Kat. The list reads like the signs on a main street in most of our cities. The key to service franchising is summarized as follows:

> Service establishments, traditionally burdened with high fixed costs and too often lacking in managerial know-how, are responding to new techniques under the franchising systems, and of carefully planned training methods—all help trim labor costs, enhance efficiency, and provide a more responsive customer service. The

achievements, in turn, benefit the new franchisee. In buying the know-how of a proven successful program he is eliminating the delay and cost of hiring and training technicians and salesmen and shopping for equipment.[31]

Advantages and Disadvantages of Franchising

Whether or not an individual SBM should become a franchisee is a matter to be determined on a case-by-case basis. Advantages and disadvantages of franchising exist for both the franchisor and the franchisee. From the point of view of the franchisor, the major advantage is an opportunity for rapid expansion by utilizing local capital and management talent and a motivated owner-operator distribution system. A major disadvantage is the necessary sharing of control over operations with the franchisee. From the point of view of the franchisee, the advantages are: (a) management training in proven methods of operations; (b) assistance in location, accounting, inventory control, and so forth; (c) possible lower risk of failure, since the franchise outlet is a new outlet of an established business rather than an entirely new business; (d) an established brand for the product or service supported by national advertising; (e) buying power; (f) financial assistance; and (g) a successful image which will be protected by both the franchisor and the franchisees. Among the disadvantages or limitations to the franchisee are: (a) the payment of a franchise fee, other fees, and a portion of the profits or sales; (b) less independence regarding products, territories, and other phases of the operations; (c) purchase restrictions; and (d) business continuity due to franchise terminations and buy-back options.

Socioeconomic Consequences Of Franchising

In the above section, we examined franchising from the *micro* or individual business point of view. Now we ask: What are the broader socioeconomic consequences of franchising? The following five purported favorable consequences are most often attributed to franchising:

1. Franchising greatly increases the opportunities for individuals to become independent businessmen. . . .
2. Franchised businesses have lower failure rates than other businesses. . . .
3. Franchising decreases economic concentration by providing a viable alternative to completely integrated vertical chains. . . .
4. Franchising provides opportunities for minority group members to own their own business. . . .
5. Franchising assists consumers by providing standardized products to an increasingly mobile public.[32]

The critics of franchising are quick to point out what are listed by Hunt as the purported unfavorable consequences of franchising:

[31]Franchising . . . , p. 3.
[32]Shelby D. Hunt, "The Socioeconomic Consequences of the Franchise System of Distribution," *Journal of Marketing*, 36, No. 3 (July 1972), pp. 33–35.

1. Franchising is an anticompetitive system of distribution. . . .
2. Franchise agreements are one-sided in favor of protecting the prerogatives of franchisors. . . .
3. Franchisors employ unethical techniques in selling franchises.[33]

You may draw your own conclusions regarding the above purported consequences. As a guide, a portion of Professor Hunt's summary is presented:

> Significant evidence exists that franchising has a net positive effect on the creation of new businesses. Franchising decreases economic concentration, but this positive advantage may be fleeting if the trend toward company-operated units continues. Similarly, although franchising provides standardized products for mobile consumers, corporate chains with company-operated units can often accomplish the same result. No "hard" evidence supports the assertion that franchised businesses have lower failure rates than other businesses. Although franchising may in the future bring significant numbers of minority group members into the mainstream of economic activity, present and past performance in this regard has been nominal.[34]

CHANNEL STRATEGY FORMULATION BY THE SBM

In this chapter, we have dealt mostly with the channel of distribution portion of place strategy. Channel of distribution strategy is a core area of place strategy. If we were to adapt our eight-step strategy formulation process to channel strategy formulation, in brief outline form we would have:

1. Record the current channel of distribution strategy.
2. Identify strategic channel problems.
3. Divide current strategic channel problems into core strategy areas and supporting strategy areas.
4. Formulate alternative channel strategies at both core and support levels.
5. Evaluate these alternatives in various combinations.
6. Choose the new channel strategy.
7. Plan the details of implementation of the new channel strategy.
8. Set performance standards and monitor feedback.

Successful use of the eight-step channel strategy formulation outline assumes that we have defined our target market(s), identified our differential advantage, and have some fairly good ideas as to our overall marketing strategy plans and those plans in other areas of the marketing mix. Company objectives, marketing objectives, place objectives, and channel of distribution objectives must also be firmly in mind. At this point, the SBM should be able to use the previous material of this chapter, along with the knowledge of his own business, to employ the above eight-step process in the formulation of a channel of distribution strategy plan.

---

[33]Hunt, pp. 35–37.
[34]Hunt, p. 38.

CREATING A NEW SECONDARY CHANNEL OF DISTRIBUTION: AN EXAMPLE OF SB INNOVATION[35]

Saunders Archery Company manufactures and markets a broad line of archery equipment, including nearly every archery product except bows and arrows. It also sells a complete line of sling-shots and targets. This well-established, successful SB firm has marketed under its own name and has produced some products under the private labels of other archery companies. The main channels of distribution for Saunders label merchandise have been:

1. Manufacturer to wholesaler (distributor) to retailer to consumer.
2. Manufacturer to retailer to consumer.
3. In some cases, other complementary archery manufacturers distribute Saunders' products through their channels.
4. In a few cases, manufacturer directly to consumer.

In order to supplement the above channel system, Saunders reviewed its present channel communications, consisting of catalog and other mailings, calling on key accounts, and meeting with distributors at trade shows. As an alternative to a major channel decision, such as hiring a small salesforce (which the company could not afford on a cost per call basis), Saunders Archery investigated Wide Area Telecommunications Service (WATS).[36] WATS was available on either and/or both an inbound or outbound basis. Saunders elected to begin with the inbound system (IWATS). Under IWATS, all incoming long-distance callers using the IWATS number could call the company without a separate charge for each call. The service was available for the state in which the company was located (intrastate) and for the rest of the continental United States on an increasing rate as the area expanded (interstate). Saunders elected not to buy the intrastate service due to the distribution patterns for its products. IWATS service was also available in varying quantities of time from ten hours per month (to meet the needs of many SB firms) to full-time service. Telephone company marketing representatives are trained to fit the service to the expected needs of their customers.

The ten-hour IWATS service selected by Saunders was a wholesale or bulk rate service rather than "free" long distance service. As such, the company took steps to insure the proper and effective use of this new marketing tool. Specifically, the following questions were asked:

Internal

1. Are the current marketing and office personnel suited for IWATS service?
2. Will a trained IWATS person always be available to answer the IWATS?
3. What communication channels does the company have to get information from the customer to the proper department?

[35]Materials in this section were related to the author by Tom Saunders. Tom is a son of Chuck Saunders, founder of the company.
[36]Frank K. Griesinger, " 'Save a WATS,' or Shortcuts to Good Use of A Long Distance Phone Service," *Administrative Management,* 34 (December 1973), pp. 26–28 and 91.

External

4. How can the IWATS number be made known? And to whom?

Answers to the first three questions vary widely from company to company and are basically the matching of good telephone selling technique with company operations and image. Question #4, for the SBM, is designed to determine who should have the IWATS number and how they should be encouraged to use it. For example, customers who have habitually called station-to-station collect must change long-standing habits. Telephone companies have pamphlets to help the SBM in advertising and using IWATS. Catalog distribution will determine whether or not the number should be in the catalog. If only middlemen are to use the IWATS, a special mailing can be used or the number can be prominently displayed on invoices, discount sheets, and in trade advertising.

What about results? Saunders installed an IWATS line primarily to make it easier for the middlemen to contact the company. The plan at the time was to build a sales base, using IWATS, which could eventually be switched to a more aggressive approach which also employed outbound service (OWATS). With an average order per dealer of about $350 list, the resources for maintaining a salesforce to cover the entire market could not be justified.

After installation and one month of using IWATS, a third quarter income check was made, adjusting the figures for the average archery industry growth of the period. The cost of IWATS was calculated to be 1.4% of the increase in sales. An added bonus was that the N.S.G.A. Sporting Goods Show in February became more profitable because new products that had been suggested over the telephone were in effect "pre-sold" to the trade in anticipation of the trade show. One product group showed an actual sales increase of 60%. It was felt by the company that a substantial portion of that increase was due to IWATS. The net effect of IWATS was to strengthen previous distribution for the company and to add new distribution via an economical and effective means of communication.

In summary, some underlying principles and misconceptions about channels of distribution have been examined. Channel systems for both consumer goods and industrial goods were discussed from the SB perspective. Types of channel systems were categorized according to the following outline:

1. Traditional
2. Vertical marketing systems
   A. Corporate systems
   B. Contractual systems
      1. Voluntary chains
      2. Retailer cooperatives
      3. Franchising organizations
         a. manufacturer—retailer systems
         b. manufacturer—wholesaler franchises
         c. wholesaler-retailer franchises
         d. service sponsor—retailer systems
   C. Administered systems.

Channel strategy questions for SB included intensive or selective market coverage, direct or indirect distribution, number and types of channels, the selection of individual channel members, the role of SB in the channel, and changes taking place to form new channels of distribution. Special emphasis was given to franchising and its impact upon channels of distribution for SB. Channel strategy formulation by the SBM was discussed briefly. Finally, an example was given to show how a small manufacturer established a new secondary channel of distribution.

BIBLIOGRAPHY

Books

BUSKIRK, RICHARD H., AND VAUGHN, PERCY J., JR. *Managing New Enterprises.* St. Paul: West Publishing Co., 1976.

CRAVENS, DAVID W., HILLS, GERALD E., AND WOODRUFF, ROBERT B. *Marketing Decision Making: Concepts and Strategy.* Homewood, Illinois: Richard D. Irwin, Inc., 1976.

DIAMOND, WILLIAM M. *Distribution Channels for Industrial Goods.* Columbus: The Ohio State University, 1963.

U. S. DEPARTMENT OF COMMERCE. *Franchising In The Economy 1972-74.* Washington: U. S. Government Printing Office, 1974.

Articles and Periodicals

ASPINWALL, LEO V. "Parallel Systems of Promotion and Distribution," in Ben M. Enis and Keith K. Cox, eds., *Marketing Classics.,* 2d ed. Boston: Allyn and Bacon, Inc., 1973, pp. 258–266.

COX, REAVIS, AND SCHUTTE, THOMAS F. "A Look At Channel Management," in J. Howard Westing and Gerald Albaum, eds. *Modern Marketing Thought.* New York: Macmillan Publishing Co., Inc, 1975, pp. 265–275.

DAVIDSON, WILLIAM R. "Changes in Distributive Institutions," *Journal of Marketing,* 34, No. 1 (January 1970), 7–10.

GRIESINGER, FRANK K. " 'Save a WATS,' or Shortcuts to Good Use of A Long Distance Phone Service," *Administrative Management,* 34 (December 1973), 26–28 and 91.

HUNT, SHELBY D. "The Socioeconomic Consequences of the Franchise System of Distribution," *Journal of Marketing,* 36, No. 3 (July 1972), 32–38.

KONOPA, LEONARD J. "Are Your Products and Channels Producing Sales?" *Management Aids For Small Manufacturers,* No. 203. Washington: Small Business Administration, 1969, pp. 1–8.

LITTLE, ROBERT W. "The Marketing Channel: Who Should Lead This Extra-corporate Organization?" *Journal of Marketing,* 34, No. 1 (January 1970), 31–38.

LITTLE, ROBERT W. "The Supra-Firm: Key To Small Retailer Survival," in J. Howard Westing and Gerald Albaum, eds., *Modern Marketing Thought.* New York: Macmillan Publishing Co., Inc., 1975, pp. 82–94.

MALLEN, BRUCE. "Functional Spin-Off: A Key to Anticipating Change in Distribution Structure," *Journal of Marketing,* 37, No. 3 (July 1973), 18–25.

McVEY, PHILIP. "Are Channels of Distribution What the Textbooks Say?" in Ben M. Enis and Keith K. Cox, eds., *Marketing Classics.* 2d ed. Boston: Allyn and Bacon, 1973, pp. 297–304.

MILLER, ERNEST A. "How To Select A Resident Buying Office," *Small Marketers Aids,* No. 116 Washington: Small Business Administration, 1972, pp. 1–4.

STERN, LOUIS W. "Channel Control and Inter-Organization Management," in Robert B. Woodruff, Gerald E. Hills, and David W. Cravens, eds., *Marketing Management Perspectives and Applications.* Homewood, Illinois: Richard D. Irwin, Inc., 1976, pp. 276–285.

Reports

Committee on Definitions. *Marketing Definitions: A Glossary of Marketing Terms.* American Marketing Association. Chicago, 1960.

12

More Place Strategy
For SBMM

The limited areas of place strategy covered in this chapter are:

1. Location and site selection strategy for the SB retailer. Here we will examine strategy questions rather than techniques for determining and evaluating retail locations and sites.
2. Retail store layout and space allocation strategy for the SB retailer. We will also note the importance of layout and space allocation from the perspective of the SB manufacturer whose products are sold in retail stores.
3. A very limited amount of attention will then be given to some important physical distribution questions.

Our reason for discussing the above strategy areas is to emphasize their importance for success in SB marketing. There is a big difference between having a retail location and having a strategy for retail location. The likelihood of securing the best retail location(s) is greater if the SBM has a good retail location strategy. The same form of reasoning applies to layout and space allocation and to the questions raised concerning physical distribution. All these are (or should be) strategic place decision areas rather than things that happen by chance.

LOCATION AND SITE SELECTION STRATEGY
FOR SB RETAILERS

What may be the most important decision the SB retailer makes is almost always made with an amazing lack of research, is often based solely on executive judgment, and all too often that judgment is made in the absence of a specified place strategy. We are speaking of location and site selection decisions for the SB retailer.

213

Meaning and Importance

Location decisions may be considered on three levels: (1) the selection of a market area, such as a town or city; (2) the selection of a type of location, such as downtown or in a planned regional shopping center; and (3) the selection of a specific unique site. The term *location* is sometimes used to refer to only the first level, to the first and second levels, and to all three levels. The term *site* is usually restricted to the third level. Thus, at the third level, the terms *site* and *location* are sometimes used interchangeably. Generally, in this chapter, the term *site* will be used to describe the third level.

Success in retailing is determined to such an extent by a good site and location that nearly every book and article surveyed by the author began the discussion of location by stressing its importance. Such comments as the following, are typical in expressing this importance:

1. Although a good location may be a major factor in the success of many retailers, it is almost impossible for even the best SB retailer to succeed in a bad location.
2. The advantages of a good location (levels 1 and 2) can be negated by a bad site (level 3).
3. Good site location decisions must be made continuously (or periodically) because the environment of a retail store does not remain static. It changes constantly by either getting better or worse.
4. Every time the retailer (even the successful one) renews a lease, he has made a location decision.
5. A good retail site is a major complement to but not a substitute for good merchandising strategy.
6. Because the store retailer operates from a fixed site location, he must be conveniently located for the customer to come to him.
7. Site selection is one of the most important factors in the success of SB retailers.

The importance of location (and site) in the marketing mix of the SB retailer can be further emphasized by examining the trade-offs between ideal location and other elements of the mix. To the extent that such trade-offs exist, they are not on a proportionate one-for-one basis. One prominent retailing book states:

> The location of a retail store determines to a large degree the sales made and the profits realized, thus playing a vital part in the store's success. Some retailers, such as those selling variety store merchandise and women's apparel, consider location so important that they prefer to pay a larger-than-usual rental to obtain desirable sites, even if this means other expenses must be restricted. Good locations frequently offset deficiencies in management, but poor locations seriously handicap even the most skillful merchandisers.[1]

High rental rates do not necessarily mean a good or ideal retail location. However, good locations usually do command high rents. Some retailers feel that, in terms of

[1]Delbert J. Duncan, Charles F. Phillips, and Stanley C. Hollander, *Modern Retailing Management: Basic Concepts and Practices* (Homewood, Illinois: Richard D. Irwin, Inc., 1972), p. 77.

drawing customers to a retail store, a degree of substitution can be exercised between expenses for rental of a good location and promotion expenses for such items as media advertising. In effect, a good location makes in-store advertising possible because of increased traffic flow. Other means of drawing traffic, such as price cuts or added services, could also be substituted. The contention of the present author is that the SBM should at least strive for the ideal mix, using substitutes only when necessary. As in football and other sports, the substitutes are seldom better than the first team. As any sports fan can tell you, however, occasionally an individual substitute really shines. Such exceptions can also be found in retailing. The inverse and disproportionate relationship between the quality of site location and the amount of promotion and advertising is suggested in Figure 12–1. For example, although an average location may call for an average promotional expense in order to achieve an effective retail marketing mix, a "worse" location may call for a "much more than average" promotional expense. In fact, Figure 12–1 may actually understate the handicap of the "worst" location. Perhaps the lines should be drawn in a curvilinear manner in order to indicate the compounding effect that takes place as the SB retailer deviates further and further from the ideal place strategy in his marketing mix.

How are these important site and location decisions made by SB and BB retailers? Many SB retailers simply seek an available site or find a vacant building. Many of these premises are vacant because the previous tenant (and perhaps several others before him) was not successful. In his haste to "get the front door open and start doing business," the SBM often underestimates the importance of a good site location. For example, most of the facilities recently vacated by A&P have become occupied. Strange as it may seem, many of the new occupants, using different marketing mixes, may be more successful than A&P was at these locations. With all this seemingly haphazard decision making going on concerning location, one might ask: Is there a developed scientific body of research to which the SBM can turn for the important site location decisions, or is the SBM left to executive judgment?

The location and site problems faced by the various kinds of retailers are not the same. For example, gasoline service stations, department stores, and supermarkets all have different site and locational requirements. Such variability makes research more difficult. Although most marketing students have at least heard of Reilly's Law of Retail Gravitation, or some modification of the original law, there seems to be some disagreement as to the recent progress in site and location research.[2] On the positive side, Applebaum states:

> The earliest attempts to employ "research" in evaluating and choosing store sites go back about a half a century ago. Since then, thanks largely to the interest of retail chain-store firms and shopping-center developers, this subject has been receiving increasing attention in the United States and abroad. A significant literature dealing with store-location research has already emerged.
>
> The retailing firms that employ store-location research in their expansion planning expect basically two things from the research:
>
> 1. An evaluation of specific sites as to their sales potential and the probability of a store's long-range success at the site.

---

[2]Basically, Reilly's original law says that two cities attract trade from an intermediate town in the vicinity of the breaking point approximately in direct proportion to the populations of the two cities and in inverse proportion to the squares of the distances from these two cities to the intermediate town.

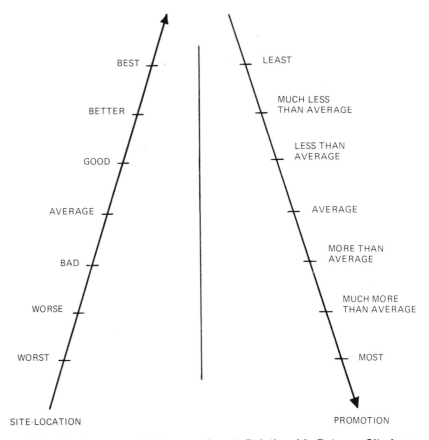

Figure 12.1   The Inverse and Disproportionate Relationship Between Site-Location Quality and Amount of Promotion Necessary

2. A store-location strategy plan or model that undertakes to select, from among the location alternatives in a given geographic area, those locations that will produce for the firm an optimum share of market potential, a minimum hazard for future sales erosion, and a maximum return on total investment over the lease period.[3]

The sophistication and comprehensiveness of such research is put into perspective by such quotes as the following:

Marketing contributions to the retail location decision revolve largely around a checklist of significant factors or gravitational models. While both the checklist and gravitational methodology can be useful in narrowing the range of the location decision, both methodologies rely heavily upon the subjective judgment of the researcher.[4]

[3]William Applebaum, "Guidelines for a Store-location Strategy Study," *Journal of Marketing*, 30, No. 4 (October 1966), p. 42.

[4]Bernard J. La Londe, "The Logistics of Retail Location," *Management Perspectives in Retailing*, ed. Ronald R. Gist (2d ed.; New York: John Wiley & Sons, Inc., 1971), p. 199.

Where does all this discussion leave the SB retailer? It strongly suggests that, like his BB counterpart, he should rely heavily on the judgment and advice of experienced experts. The typical SB retailer is not well versed in economic geography, location theory, and real estate. Thus it is suggested that the SB retailer should *not* (a) ignore or neglect the site-location problem, (b) perform superficial and largely useless retail site-location research, or (c) pay for in-depth retail site-location research which may be too costly. What he should do is formulate his own retail site-location strategy with the analysis and assistance of experienced experts. Such experts are available to SB retailers at a reasonable cost. Examples are real estate firms, voluntary group wholesalers, and franchisors. The franchisors are examined briefly in the following paragraph.

Most franchisors assign site selection responsibility to regional managers, who are assisted by staff specialists. Many franchisors acquire the site before looking for a franchisee. This tends to lessen the problem of land prices being bid up when word gets around that a franchise has been granted and that the franchisee is actively seeking a site. The role of the franchisee in the site selection process is very limited. He may be given a veto power over suggested sites or the right to suggest alternatives, but the final selection usually rests with the franchisor.[5]

The importance of the site-location decision may be expressed in costs such as higher overall costs with increased store size, high fixture costs, installation costs, high rents, and so forth. However, the real importance lies in the fact that every site is unique. Uniqueness can provide differential advantage to the SB retailer and this differential advantage cannot be duplicated. Two stores cannot occupy the same space at the same time. Because of this basic law of physics, we find such situations as a prosperous gasoline service station across the street from a marginal or abandoned station. Marketing strategy is built upon differential advantage. Serendipity may occasionally provide such a differential advantage. However, more often than not, the SBM must plan carefully. Note the following example:

> The location of a given retailer is unique. Once he has chosen the site, the space cannot be occupied by another. Through his desirable location, he thus achieves an advantage that is his alone. Merchandise may be duplicated, promotions can be imitated, and prices will be met; but a retailer's locational advantage is difficult to assail or neutralize.

> Spatial position as a differential advantage is illustrated by the following example. A druggist had a location adjacent to a college campus, but on a thoroughfare infrequently used. The residential area tapped by the converging roads consisted of a mere 200 families. Consequently, the druggist had an extremely precarious existence until the university built a 1,500-unit dormitory across the street from his store. He then enjoyed a brisk and profitable business from all the students living in the dormitory—not through his own foresight, of course, but because of his unique location.[6]

The Site-Location Strategy Questions

Since a unique site can represent such a potent differential advantage to the retailer, how can the SB retailer plan for such an advantage? This is strategic marketing planning

[5]E. Patrick McGuire, *Franchised Distribution* (New York: The Conference Board, Inc., 1971), pp. 71–73.

[6]John E. Mertes, "A Retail Structural Theory for Site Analysis," *Retailing: Concepts, Institutions, and Management,* ed. Rom J. Markin, Jr. (New York: The Macmillan Company, 1971), pp. 181–182.

and the strategic planning process (the eight-step process) can be adapted to formulate a place strategy for the SB retailer (See Chapter 3). The reader should be able to derive the eight-step process. This process must however, be applied to three levels: (1) market area or town, (2) type, and (3) specific site. These three levels represent the classes of alternatives or options available to the SB retailer. Important factors influencing each of the three levels will be discussed in the following sections.

A site-location strategy should be formulated *before* an analysis is made of any specific site. This strategy plan will show what site analysis should take place to fulfill the

Table 12-1   Factors To Consider When Analyzing Market Area, Type, And Site For SB Retailers

1. Market Area Factors
   A. *Market* factors such as population, size, purchasing power, and buying habits
   B *Environmental* factors such as economic, competitive, legal, and so forth
   C. *Other* factors
2. Type Alternatives And Factors
   A. *Type Alternatives**
      1. Free standing
         a. Neighborhood
         b. Highway
      2. Business associated
         a. Unplanned
            1. Downtown (or central business district)
            2. Edge of downtown
            3. Neighborhood business district
            4. Secondary business district
            5. Highway business string
         b. Planned shopping center
            1. Neighborhood shopping centers
            2. Community shopping centers
            3. Regional shopping centers
   B. *Type factors*
      1. Product-market factors such as target market size and classification of consumer goods
      2. Trade-off factors such as availability, rental rates, restrictions, and so forth
      3. Preferences of the SBM, that is, subjective factors of individual preference
3. Site Factors**
   A. Adequacy of present trading area potential
   B. Accessibility of site to trading area
   C. Growth potential
   D. Business interception
   E. Cumulative attraction
   F. Compatibility
   G. Minimizing of competitive hazard
   H. Site economics

*From RETAIL MANAGEMENT: SATISFACTION OF CONSUMER NEEDS by Raymond A. Marquardt, James C. Makens and Robert G. Roe. Copyright © 1975 by The Dryden Press, A Division of Holt, Rinehart and Winston. Reprinted by permission of Holt, Rinehart and Winston.

**Section 3 adapted from Richard L. Nelson, "Principles of Retail Location" in Ronald R. Gist, *Management Perspectives In Retailing* (2nd ed.), New York: John Wiley & Sons, Inc., 1971, pp. 204–208.

future plans of the SB firm. A basic difference between SB and BB arises at this point. SB may, in effect, skip level #1 entirely. That is, the SB retailer may select a market area (town or city) on such nonbusiness criteria as the present family residence of the SBM. This is a reality of SB marketing that is decided by each individual SBM. When considering different site-location alternatives, the SB retailer will find a strategy plan (preferably written) to be a good base. How could such questions as the following be adequately considered in the absence of a site-location strategy plan: find additional site(s), renew lease to remain at present site(s), increase the size of present site(s), remodel, move to a new site, terminate or abandon a site, place a site in a new type (e.g., shopping center) of location, place a site in a new market area, and some combinations of the above? Thus, our eight-step process of strategy formulation or some alternate approach[7] should be used to formulate a site-location strategy. Then, the analysis can take place at the three levels: (1) market area, (2) type, and (3) site. In outline form, this three-level analysis will consider the factors noted in Table 12–1.

Market Area

As stated above, the SBM often skips this level of consideration by limiting his market area to the town or city of his present residence. Limiting his market area in such a manner may, in fact, be a wise choice in some cases. It permits the SBM the opportunity to operate in familiar territory. On the other hand, it excludes many opportunities which may be more lucrative. What is suggested here is that even if the SB retailer has made a prior decision that his market area will be his "hometown," he should do some analysis of the important market area factors as they pertain to his type of retail business.

A survey of retailing books reveals different listings of factors to be considered when selecting a town or city for a retail business. In terms of our SBMM model, these factors can be listed under two headings; market factors and environmental factors. Examples of market factors are the population and population trends, size of town or trade area, purchasing power and its distribution, and buying habits. Examples of environmental factors are economic considerations, such as the character of industry and progressiveness, the nature and intensity of competition as measured by store saturation for the lines involved, state and local legislative factors, and other factors, such as special features of interest to a particular retailer or type of retailer. Such special features might be a college, a tourist attraction, an outdoor recreation facility, and so forth. Finally, the SB retailer may simply have a preference for living and doing business in a particular community or type of community. Small towns, for example, represent to many SB retailers a particularly attractive alternative.

Type Alternatives and Factors

The question we are dealing with in level #2 is: What types of customer traffic (mostly automobile and public, but in some cases also pedestrian) generation can be expected due to the location type selected? We are not dealing here with the specific site selected but with the type. For example, we are asking: What is the traffic expectation or trading area coverage if we locate our retail store in a regional shopping center rather than

---

[7]For an alternate approach see Applebaum, above citation.

in a neighborhood business district? Different location types offer different advantages and disadvantages to different retail store types. In the next subsection (dealing with site) we will ask such questions as: What factors should we consider in evaluating site X in regional shopping center Z; or what factors should be considered in evaluating site A in neighborhood shopping district B? In the present subsection we are focusing on the location or site *type* for our location strategy.

Retail type alternatives are usually classified according to structural or descriptive criteria. Such is the classification of type alternatives identified in Table 12–1.[8] Businesses may be located in isolated (or free standing) sites or located in association with other businesses. Neighborhood convenience stores such as grocery stores, barber shops, beauty shops, bars, and so forth have been located as free standing businesses. However, more and more of these former "neighborhood" businesses are being located in other location types. Highway (including interstate highways) locations for serving the food, lodging, and gasoline needs of travelers are often free standing locations. Such businesses are strategically located and in most cases naturally tend to be free-standing where traffic is less. However, where traffic is concentrated, as at major crossroads and interchanges, such businesses are clustered together. Market opportunity and needs determine the patterns. Generally, business-associated (rather than free-standing) location types tend to have a greater traffic generating power, due to the synergetic effect. However, this does not mean that business-associated locations are always better than isolated ones. Likewise, planned location types may or may not be better than unplanned ones.

Unplanned location types include downtown, the edge of downtown, neighborhood business districts, secondary business districts, and highway business strings. They are "unplanned" in the sense that no single plan was used for the overall shopping area, as would be the case in a "planned" shopping center. Hopefully, each individual business within an unplanned type location does have a site-location strategy plan. These individual plans should recognize the circular impact of store type on location type and of location type on store type. In effect, an effective "unplanned" shopping area is one which operates by decentralized planning rather than by centralized planning.

Market factors should be the determining ones in selecting a site-location type. The question is: Where (in terms of type) do the target market customers and potential customers of the SBM prefer to purchase? The location type selected is a limiting factor in determining the total size of the market area served by the SB retailer. For example, a small store located in a regional shopping center may draw customers from 30–40 miles away, while a store in a neighborhood business district may be largely limited to that neighborhood. However, this is not to say that one store will necessarily do more business or make more profit than the other.

Not all stores cater to the same target markets. This is true of stores selling similar goods and services. It is even true of different branch locations of chain and department stores. For example, the main downtown facility of a large bank may serve different market segments than the drive-in suburban branch at a shopping center or free-standing location. Supermarkets seek locations in both shopping centers and in free-standing locations. Automobile dealers seem to locate in both free-standing and business-associated (quite often with other auto dealers) locations. Success does not seem to be restricted to any single location type. However, target market selection and selection of location type do

[8]See Raymond A. Marquardt, James C. Makens, and Robert G. Roe, *Retail Management: Satisfaction of Consumer Needs* (Hinsdale, Illinois: The Dryden Press, 1975), pp. 116–119.

interact; and the marketing strategy of the SB retailer must take account of this interaction if success is to be the result.

Several other factors may influence the location type choice. Among these are rental rates, availability, restrictions, and the individual preferences of the SB retailer. Because of its increasing importance, let us consider some of these factors in conjunction with the question of whether or not the SB retailer should select the planned shopping center as a site-location type.

The SB retailer is treated differently from major chains and department stores by most shopping center developers and landlords. As such, he faces a distinct set of advantages and limitations as a shopping center tenant. One source comments:

> Customers like the shopping center's convenience. They drive in, park, and walk to their destination in relative safety and speed. Some shopping centers also provide weather protection and most provide an atmosphere created for shopping comfort. For the customer, the shopping center has great appeal.
>
> For the merchant making a decision whether to locate in a shopping center, these "plus" characteristics must be related to the limitations placed upon him as a tenant. In a shopping center, a tenant is part of a merchant team. As such, he must pay his pro rata share of the budget for the team effort. He must keep store hours, light his windows, and place his signs within established rules.[9]

Shopping center developers and owners look for successful retailers of all sizes. However, 60 to 70 percent of the floor space of many shopping centers is occupied by large chains and department stores. Thus, while a proven successful SB retailer may have a fair opportunity to secure a good shopping center site, the new (first-store) SB retailer is definitely at a distinct disadvantage. To some extent, this disadvantage is the result of being a poor credit risk due to the lack of a "track record." Lease guarantee insurance, available directly and indirectly through the Small Business Administration, is one way of overcoming this problem. Although not always desirable or feasible, SBA financing and other assistance is available for developing small business centers composed of SB retailers.[10]

Against the advantages of traffic, parking, image, balanced tenancy, and so on the SB retailer must weigh some real disadvantages. Among these is the high total occupancy cost when the SB retailer adds up the basic rent, plus the percentage of sales rent, plus maintenance costs for malls and parking lots, plus shared costs for utilities, plus tax increases, plus merchants' association and joint promotional costs, and so forth. Another disadvantage, or at least potential disadvantage, for the SB retailer is the difficulty of maintaining a distinct image or atmosphere in a large regional shopping center. It is not easy to keep from getting lost in the crowd. Finally, not all shopping centers are equally good. In some cases, shopping centers have been overbuilt. Population moves take place. Road changes occur. In effect, once the SB retailer has made a strategic decision to use the shopping center type of location, he is faced with the further question of deciding *which* shopping center(s) to use. In order to answer this question, he must carefully evaluate the

---

[9]J. Ross McKeever, "Factors In Considering A Shopping Center Location," *Small Marketers Aids*, No. 143 (Washington: Small Business Administration, 1970), p. 3.

[10]William N. Kinnard, Jr. and Stephen D. Messner, "Obtaining Competitive Locations For Small Retailers In Shopping Centers," *Journal of Small Business Management*, 10 (January 1972), pp. 25–26.

location studies of the developer. Such claims as "Serves a trading area of 100,000 persons within a five mile radius!" are usually quite meaningless when given for a neighborhood shopping center. The claim neglects to mention the competitive factors within the so-called trading area. Once having determined a specific shopping center (or centers) in which to locate, the SB retailer is now faced with the site problem of getting the ideal site within the center.

Site and Site Factors

The site question arises regardless of the site-location type selected. While a shopping center (especially a large one) type may involve the double question of (a) which center and (b) which site within the center, the choice of other site-location types does not answer the question of which specific site to select. Checklists, traffic counts, license plate checks, census data, and the advice of experts are available to aid in the actual selection process. However, before beginning the actual selection process, the SB retailer should know what he is looking for by formulating a strategy and by considering criteria for implementing that strategy. For example, if his site strategy calls for easy access and plenty of parking, many sites are automatically eliminated. As a basis for using such a strategy, let us briefly list and discuss Nelson's eight principles which should be used when applying selection criteria to a specific site:

1. *Adequacy of present trading area potential.* How much total volume of business of this type can be expected (by all sellers) based on the people, money, and willingness to buy within the trading area of the site?

2. *Accessibility of site to trading area.* Can potential business of three types—*generative* by the store itself, *shared* as the result of the generative powers of its neighbors, and/or *suscipient* (those in the area for nonshopping purposes)—be easily and conveniently served by the site?

3. *Growth potential.* Is the site in a trading area of growing population and income?

4. *Business interception.* Is the site on the major routes to potential destinations for shopping for the same product types?

5. *Cumulative attraction.* Does the site have greater customer attraction due to shared business with both competing and complementary stores?

6. *Compatibility.* Do other businesses adjacent to the site help each other by interchanging customers?

7. *Minimizing of competitive hazard.* Does the site take into consideration the location, character, size, and type of present and potential competitors; and does it minimize such competitive hazards?

8. *Site economics.* In terms of costs related to productivity, what is the efficiency of the specific site regarding such physical factors as size, shape, topography, facilities, and so forth?[11]

When the actual process of applying the strategy and principles takes place, some very practical questions will come up such as: Is the desired site available? Is it on the right (shady side and going home side are preferred by many retailers) side of the street? Are

[11]Richard Lawrence Nelson, "Principles of Retail Location," *Management Perspectives in Retailing*, ed. Ronald R. Gist, (2d ed.; New York: John Wiley & Sons, Inc., 1971), pp. 204–208.

there negative factors to consider, such as vacant stores or other dead spots? What has been the success-failure history of the site?

Service establishments, with some exceptions, are also concerned with the same site-location problems as other retailers. One book notes:

> An interesting characteristic of most service businesses is that a reputation for extra high quality of workmanship will attract customers in spite of a poor location to a far greater extent than is true of other kinds of business. However, since this is an exception, and since it comes about only after the reputation is earned, the beginner especially should seek the best location in which to build such a reputation.[12]

The selection of a site within a shopping center, especially a large regional shopping center, presents an additional challenge. Some of the factors to consider are location of shopping versus convenience goods stores, effect of center design on location, the importance of corner influence, the effect of non-retail facilities, and other considerations such as Sunday and late hours.[13] Convenience goods stores and shopping goods stores tend to be grouped separately. This works best because consumer purchasing patterns and parking needs vary for the two types of goods.

Shopping center designs are (a) the strip which may be modified as an "L" shape or a "U" shape, (b) the mall which may be open or covered, and (c) the hub or cluster design. As Berman notes, "Each type of formation has different characteristics with reference to parking facilities, nearness to the department store, nearness to complementary stores, visibility from the road, and existence of outlying shopping areas."[14]

Corner influence is the value added to a location because it is at the intersection of two streets. While this may be important in a business district, corner influence within a regional shopping center seems to be negligible. Additional rents for a corner within a shopping center are probably not justified in most cases.

Although customer interchange between retail and non-retail facilities such as medical offices, theaters, and laundromats is rather low, most retailers like to have non-retail facilities in a center so long as they do not cause parking problems. The presence of non-retail facilities does affect location preferences within a center. Finally, stores which are open late and on Sunday (if the rest of the center is not open) should be located at the front of the center for good visibility and to minimize lighting and safety costs.

STRATEGY FOR RETAIL STORE LAYOUT

From considering factors dealing with where to locate a retail store, we now move our attention inside the store itself to consider factors dealing with the spatial relationships of things inside the store. In this move, we have purposely overlooked such areas as exterior and interior design, procedures for determining layout, and descriptions of various layout patterns such as "grids" and "free flows." Our attention is focused on strategic considerations. A popular definition of layout states: "The layout of a retail store

[12]Clifford M. Baumback, Kenneth Lawyer, and Pearce C. Kelley, *How to Organize and Operate a Small Business* (Englewood Cliffs, New Jersey: Prentice-Hall, Inc., 1973), p. 156.

[13]Barry Berman, "Location Analysis Within Regional Shopping Centers," *Retail Management Strategy: Selected Readings*, ed. David J. Rachman (Englewood Cliffs, New Jersey, Prentice-Hall, Inc., 1970), pp. 262–275.

[14]Berman, p. 266.

refers to the arrangement of equipment and fixtures, merchandise, selling and sales-supporting departments, displays, aisles, and check-out stands where needed in proper relationship to each other and in accordance with a *definite plan.*"[15] The phrase, *definite plan,* is the key to the concept of layout. We will therefore limit ourselves to factors underlying the layout strategy plan. Numerous retailing books are available, along with other sources, once the factors of the strategy plan are understood.

From a functionalist point of view, *form follows function.* We may therefore ask: What is the function(s) of layout or to what purpose or objective is layout directed? From the customer side, layout provides locational convenience, minimizes time and effort, and complements consumer buying habits and preferences in other ways to make shopping in that store a pleasant and worthwhile experience. However, in actual practice, layout involves compromise. From the retailer side, such considerations as keeping expenses (such as labor and shoplifting) to a minimum and increasing sales and profits in the available selling area are very important. For example, a major influence on layout and on the selection of store fixtures in recent years has been the switch from service type selling to self-selection (also known as simplified selling) and to self-service.

Our layout discussion is adapted from the "nine basic layout ideas that retail managers should remember when they make layout decisions."[16] These nine ideas are (1) value in space, (2) customer traffic flow, (3) impulse goods versus demand goods, (4) related merchandise departments, (5) good-looking and action-related merchandise, (6) high gross margin and high sales volume departments, (7) store image, (8) seasonal departments, and (9) other considerations.

Value in Space

As a major, limited, and costly resource of the SB retailer, space should be managed wisely. For our discussion, we will refer only to selling space. Thus we have assumed that the SB retailer has determined what space is necessary for nonselling activities and has reserved the more valuable and more appropriate space for selling. The SB retailer may divide the space allocation question into the following levels: (1) how much and which selling space for each department, (2) how much and which selling space for each product group or product category within a department, and (3) how much and which selling space for each individual item. The level(s) of analysis used and the amount of detail applied to each level depend on such factors as total store size, number of stores, number of departments, self-service versus self-selection, store image, and so forth. For example, some very small retailers may find their personal experience and close knowledge of customer preferences to be the best and only guide to use in space allocation. For most other retailers (both SB and BB), some indication of sales space productivity will be used. The productivity rationale may be expressed in a ratio of productivity, such as sales per square foot; or eventually it may result in a model stock plan or basic stock list based upon such a productivity ratio. For our purpose of determining space strategy, we will skip the calculations of such ratios, but we will examine some underlying principles of space management.

Space allocation problems differ by type of retailer. For example, the new and used automobile dealer, the men's wear store, and the supermarket are faced with somewhat

[15]Duncan, Phillips, and Hollander, p. 124.

[16]R. Ted Will and Ronald W. Hasty, *Retailing: A Mid-Management Approach* (San Francisco: Canfield Press, 1973), pp. 360–362.

different problems regarding selling space. Major attention to space allocation has been given by such mass retailers as supermarkets. Reasons for this attention are the use of self-service and the relative absence of personal selling, which places a heavy sales burden on the display factor. Such outlets carry many items or are offered more items than they can possibly carry, and mass retailers are often BB multi-store operations which stand to benefit from standardized operations based upon space allocation research. This last comment, however, does not exclude SB retailers from taking advantage of available knowledge concerning space management. This is especially true for SB retailers who are mass merchandisers.

The state of the art (not the science) of space allocation is reviewed in a comprehensive article which notes:

> Although shelf space manipulation is widespread, knowledge about the effects of shelf space allocation changes on product sales is fragmentary. Retail organizations have made countless trial-and-error changes, but have conducted few legitimate experiments. Those experiments that have been conducted have yielded very few results that can be generalized to classes of products. Academic researchers have conducted a number of well-designed experimental studies on the effects of shelf space changes on sales, but these studies have also involved only a relatively small number of products and frequently have yielded uncertain results. In general, reported experiments have had little impact on management practices.[17]

Most space allocation studies are conceptually based on space elasticity, that is, the ratio of relative change in unit sales to relative change in shelf space. From the findings of shelf-space allocation researchers reviewed by Curhan, such generalizations as the following might be stated:[18]

1. The impact of shelf space on unit sales differs among products. The relationship is not clearly understood, but once a threshold level of exposure has been received, staples are probably less responsive to increases than are so-called impulse items.
2. Space elasticity tends to be higher for private label and packer label brands than for "national" manufacturer brands.
3. Space changes tend to have greater sales effects in product categories having many brands rather than fewer brands.
4. Space changes tend to have greater sales effects (i.e., more space elasticity) for faster-selling items as opposed to slower-selling items.
5. Regular size (or best selling size) items tend to have more space elasticity.
6. Sales tend to be affected equally by *like* changes in shelf space on *different* shelf levels, although the space changes on shelves closer to eye level would have a greater impact on sales than would identical changes made on shelves above or below eye level.

The universality and strength of the above tendencies should not be overestimated. As Curhan states: "It may be concluded that there is a small positive relationship between shelf space and unit sales. This relationship, however, is uniform neither among products nor across stores or intra-store locations."[19]

The SB retailer may be more interested in what happens to sales of a total product

[17]Ronald C. Curhan, "Shelf Space Allocation and Profit Maximization in Mass Retailing," *Journal of Marketing*, 37, No. 3 (July 1973), p. 54.
[18]Curhan, pp. 54–60.
[19]Curhan, p. 56.

category as shelf space is variously distributed among the competing products and brands in that category. Such results are also of vital importance to SB and BB manufacturers whose products are sold through retailers. For example, if giving more space to Brand X spaghetti sauce at the expense or possible elimination of Brand Y spaghetti sauce will increase the total sales and profits on the spaghetti sauce category, should the retailer make such a change? He probably should (unless Brand Y has other advantages going for it), and he probably will make the change if he is aware of the expected outcome. This strongly suggests that the manufacturer of Brand X, even if he is a SB manufacturer, can receive advantageous space allocation for displaying his product if (and this is an important *if*) he can convince the retailer of the expanded sales of the total product category as opposed to merely brand-switching from Y to X. He may even be able to command more total space for spaghetti sauce as a product category.

In summary, the impact of space allocation on sales and profits does not operate in a vacuum. It interacts with other marketing variables such as price and promotion. Separating the importance of such interacting variables is most difficult.

Elaborate systems of space management such as COSMOS have been developed to utilize computers; however, costs versus benefits make such systems unavailable to most. Space allocations ". . . still are largely determined subjectively by merchandisers on the basis of their personal experience and historical aggregate product improvement data."[20] Two types of items seem to receive the major attention:

> At the present time, this discretionary manipulation is focused on items having high gross margins and/or thought to be purchased on the basis of impulse. Whether impulse purchasing is a spontaneous in-store decision or whether it is part of a preplanned shopping strategy, product exposure is essential if the process is to be triggered.[21]

Now we will consider the fact that not all space is equal in value; this is due primarily to customer traffic flows.

Customer Traffic Flow

Eye-level shelf space has a greater value for selling than does bottom shelf space. So also, the value of space varies from one portion of the store to another, usually according to the amount of customer traffic. Thus, large department stores may charge higher rents to departments located on or near the main floor. Layout both affects and is affected by customer traffic. Customer traffic within a store is somewhat analogous to automobile traffic within a city. Location of merchandise within a store should take advantage of potential customer traffic patterns in the same way that store location takes advantage of automobile traffic patterns. The one great difference is that the SB retailer has much more control over in-store traffic.

A major purpose of controlling customer traffic is to direct as many customers as possible past as much merchandise as possible in order to increase the total opportunities for purchasing. One strategy for accomplishing this is the placement of merchandise items or merchandise departments that are natural traffic generators. By locating these natural traffic generators in less accessible areas of the store, customers are forced to pass through

---

[20]Curhan, p. 59.
[21]Curhan, p. 60.

other departments and receive exposure to other items. The SB retailer using such a strategy should always remember that the customer may be slightly inconvenienced in order for the retailer to achieve maximum product exposure, but that if the inconvenience is too great the customer may be lost to a competitor. So-called impulse items are almost always displayed at high traffic locations such as ends of aisles and near check out counters. Among supermarket shoppers there is a definite tendency to shop the perimeter of the store. Thus, perimeter aisles receive nearly twice as much customer traffic as interior aisles. In large departmentalized stores, space along main aisles receives more traffic, and is therefore more valuable than interior departmental space. Elevators, escalators, and stairways are traffic movers and therefore affect space values of retailers located in large buildings. The above comments refer mainly to self-service and self-selection methods of operation. For a limited number of specialty shops operating with a high degree of sales assistance and service, customer traffic is far less important. For example, an exclusive women's store whose customers are always accompanied by a salesperson does not face the same customer traffic problems and opportunities as the supermarket.

Manufacturers recognize the value of customer traffic, and they have sometimes paid cash for preferred shelf location or for other known high-traffic locations. For example, cigarette marketers and magazine publishers have made payments for specific locations, such as those near checkouts. These payments are sometimes based upon the size of the display. Payments for special displays which are usually larger and at higher traffic locations are offered to retailers by many manufacturers. Whether or not the SB manufacturer should offer such payments depends on their effectiveness in terms of the rest of the marketing program. Also, a question of business ethics may arise, depending on to whom the actual payments are made.

Some retailers and writers advocate the practice of dividing the total store area into a grid and assigning "rents" or values to various sections of the store. Such a practice may be a useful technique for planning; but one should remember when using such generated data that layout and customer traffic interact, that is, each can affect the other. Cause and effect are not always clear. The actual charting of current customer traffic patterns can provide valuable data for anticipated changes in layout.

Impulse Goods Versus Demand Goods

Demand goods are those which customers have clearly in mind—perhaps they are on a shopping list—before going to a store. They can therefore be placed in somewhat less accessible locations. As noted earlier, impulse goods, seldom clearly defined, are a major subject of discussion in layout. Four broad classes of impulse buying can be identified:[22]

1. *Pure impulse buying* is truly unplanned in any way, and probably accounts for a very small portion of so-called impulse buying, since customers usually tend to act in other ways.
2. *Reminder impulse buying* occurs when a customer sees an item in the store and is reminded of a need and a previous decision to buy.
3. *Suggestive impulse buying* occurs when a customer sees a product for the first time while in the store and rationally visualizes a need without previous product knowledge.
4. *Planned impulse buying* occurs when the customer enters the store with some specific

[22]Hawkins Stern, "The Significance of Impulse Buying Today," *Journal of Marketing,* 26, No. 2 (April 1962), pp. 59–60.

purchase(s) in mind, but also with the expectation and intention of making some additional purchase(s), depending on appeals such as special price, coupon offers, and so forth.

Impulse buying indicates that customers are transferring at least a portion of the purchase planning function from the home to the store. In a sense, the store and its layout have, for many types of products, become a life-size visual shopping list. Thus, the changed consumer behavior of increased "impulse" buying makes the layout emphasis on "impulse" goods more important.

What goods are impulse goods? Nine factors, associated with increased ease of consumer buying, can be used as criteria for identifying impulse items. These nine criteria are guides only, since no impulse items exist *per se;* such goods exist only as items which, for most customers, are usually purchased on the basis of one of the four classes of impulse buying. The nine criteria or guides are: (1) low price, (2) marginal need for item, (3) mass distribution, (4) self-service, (5) mass advertising, (6) prominent store display, (7) short product life, (8) small size or light weight, and (9) ease of storage.[23]

The importance of impulse buying to the SB retail layout is obvious. The SB manufacturer can also benefit by adjusting the marketing mix to changed consumer behavior:

> As the nature of impulse buying changes, manufacturers should re-examine their merchandising strategies toward this type of buying. Although factors such as product size or price may be difficult, if not impossible, to modify, impulse buying can be favorably influenced through distribution, advertising, and store promotions. One relatively simple tactic, for example, is the establishment of a close tie-in between at-home and in-store advertising, to encourage reminder impulse buying.[24]

Related Merchandise Departments

A major objective in locating merchandise is to place complementary item in adjacent locations in order to increase sales. Studies have shown that increased sales do result. If merchandise is departmentized, within each department the generic product groupings are often displayed together. Either on a permanent basis, such as in a boutique, or on a temporary basis by using special displays, the grouping of merchandise by target market groups can sometimes be very effective. Although this may involve the duplication of merchandise in more than one department, sales increases will often more than justify the added investment in inventory. Another idea is, whenever possible, to locate departments with different seasonal sales patterns adjacent to each other. The seasonal exchange of selling space provides for more total sales at greater efficiency.

Good-Looking and Action-Related Merchandise

Not all merchandise has equal display potential. For example, fresh peaches in season have much greater display appeal than canned peaches; a refrigerator probably beats a hot water heater; and fashion items usually exceed staples. In self-service and self-selection merchandising, the display must create excitement on its own. The salesman is not there to do it. The right fixtures can help, but the fixtures are not for sale. Their function is to help display the merchandise.

[23]Stern, pp. 61–62.
[24]Stern, p. 62.

From the point of view of the SB manufacturer, packaging and the offering of point-of-purchase displays can be very beneficial in creating good-looking and action-related merchandise. Success here benefits both the manufacturer and the retailer. A product which illustrates the point is Tic Tacs, which are a fruit or mint flavored candy packaged in a small plastic container and usually displayed in an attractive display case near the cash register. At 25¢ for a ½ ounce package, consumers are paying $8.00 per pound for this product. In the absence of excellent packaging and prime display space, what sales success would this product enjoy at such a price?

High Gross Margin
And High Sales Volume Departments

Some items and/or departments command higher gross margins than others. High value, non-bulky products such as jewelry carry high margins and are thus able to pay the "rent" for valuable space. However, another factor to consider in layout decisions regarding which products or departments can support more valuable space is the rate of stock turnover.

Stock turnover, also known as rate of stockturn, is the number of times during a given period (usually a year) that the average amount of inventory is sold. As a profit planning tool, stockturn can be useful in both layout and merchandising decision areas. It is the combination of gross margin and stockturn that leads to profit.

Stockturn may be calculated on the basis of cost, selling price, or in units. The three should not be confused and the average inventory should be representative. On the basis of cost, stockturn equals, in our example:

Beginning inventory at cost	$10,000
+ Ending inventory at cost	14,000
= Sum, which divided *by* 2	$24,000
= Average inventory at cost	$12,000
which divided *into* a cost	
of goods sold of	$48,000
= STOCKTURN of	*4* times per period.

On the basis of selling price, stockturn equals, in our example:

Beginning inventory at selling price	$15,000
+ Ending inventory at selling price	21,000
= Sum, which divided *by* 2	$36,000
= Average inventory at selling price	$18,000
which divided *into* a	
Net sales of	$72,000
= STOCKTURN of	*4* times per period.

On the basis of units, stockturn equals, in our example:

Beginning inventory in units	5,000
+ Ending inventory in units	7,000
= Sum, which divided *by* 2	12,000
= Average inventory in units	6,000
which divided *into*	
Net sales in units of	24,000
= STOCKTURN of	*4* times per period.

Although increased profits may or may not result from increased stockturn (depending on how the increase is achieved), there are some advantages of higher stockturn. Some of these are reduced storage costs, less investment in inventory, and fewer markdowns.

The stock-sales ratio is another tool which the SB retailer can use for comparison and control of stock. This ratio is the beginning inventory at selling price divided by sales for the period (usually a month).

Store Image

The store image is affected by nearly everything the SB retailer does. Store layout is surely one of the more important influences of store image. The image the store is attempting to project should be immediately apparent to customers when they enter (and even before they enter) the store. A crowded layout with large bargain price signs may be appropriate for some stores, but not for others. Layout is but one of the elements of interior design used to create a store image. Others are color, light, texture, music, and virtually anything else that appeals to the human senses. Layout should add to the desired store image. This statement must, of course, be balanced with such hard productivity figures as sales and profits per square foot.

Seasonal Departments

Flexible layouts are becoming more popular in many types of retail stores. The merchandise which was the "new" merchandise at the beginning of a season is the "clearance" merchandise at the end of the season. Nearly everyone is familiar with the seasonal toy department expansion that later becomes the seasonal lawn and garden center. Other departments also expand and contract and this does affect layout and customer traffic patterns.

In addition to seasonal variation, other time variations, such as time of day, and day of the week or month, can be used by the SB retailer in order to bring about more effective layout. Portable displays may at times replace portable checkouts or other non-display fixtures and equipment, depending on the amount of customer traffic at any given time. The SB retailer should try to take advantage of his inherent flexibility.

Other Considerations

Examples of other considerations which affect layout are the following:

1. Use the least desirable space in the store for employee areas, stock areas, and customer service areas.
2. Place departments which require extensive stock requirements (such as a shoe department) close to stock areas.
3. Place departments which require refrigeration, cooking facilities, and heavy fixturing, and which sell large bulky items, on the perimeter of the store.[25]

[25]Will and Hasty, pp. 362–363.

PHYSICAL DISTRIBUTION AND SB

To the SBM, whether he is a manufacturer, a wholesaler, or a retailer, the management of physical distribution as an active ingredient in the marketing mix can be of strategic importance and value. Our limited discussion permits us to do little more than emphasize the importance of using physical distribution as a means of gaining a differential advantage over competitors.

Physical distribution, sometimes referred to as the "other half" of marketing because of the lack of attention it receives, probably receives less attention from SB than from BB. As a part of place strategy, physical distribution is a controllable part of the marketing mix. However, for many SB firms, certain physical distribution questions may be answered (i.e., controlled) by the supra-firm with which the SB firm is associated. In any case, the SBM should attempt to understand and appreciate the role of physical distribution as a part of the marketing mix. That is the purpose of our brief discussion.

The major activities of physical distribution are transportation and storage. Accompanying activities are materials handling, inventory management, and order processing. The purpose is the effective and efficient flow of products through the channel of distribution. Since the scope involves the entire channel of distribution rather than a single firm, a multi-level systems type of thinking is often employed concerning physical distribution. This means that the physical distribution strategy of the individual SB firm must take into account the needs of the rest of the channel.

Physical distribution is a two-edged marketing weapon, and the SBM should learn to use both edges. One edge is the supplying and servicing of demand created by marketing mix. This is the demand-servicing edge. The other edge is the demand-obtaining edge.[26] Physical distribution can be used both for satisfying demand and for generating demand. On the satisfaction side, such activities as transportation, warehousing, and order processing are all directed at servicing the demand for the firm's products. How well, or at what customer service level, this demand is serviced affects the future demand for the firm's products.

Physical distribution management grew from the necessity for centralizing control over the cost of servicing demand. Previous approaches to the cost of servicing demand were not total cost approaches. That is, they tended to reduce costs in one area of operations at the expense of either (a) increasing costs, possibly by more than the reductions in another area; (b) reducing the service level with such means as slower transportation; or (c) both. Prior to the total cost approach, some BB firms actually created markets for their competitors (some SB firms) by such mistakes. The key idea of the total cost approach to physical distribution is ". . . to *minimize the costs* consistent with constraints imposed by the desired level of customer service and other constraints imposed outside the firm's control by competitors."[27] Thus, the *selection of the service level* is the strategic decision for the SBM. He should actively make such a decision, not merely

---

[26]For an excellent basic discussion of physical distribution see Richard J. Lewis, "Physical Distribution: Managing The Firm's Service Level," *Readings in Basic Marketing*, ed. E. Jerome McCarthy, John F. Grashof, and Andrew A. Brogowicz (Homewood, Illinois: Richard D. Irwin, Inc., 1975), pp. 216–228.

[27]Lewis, p. 220.

imitate or attempt to imitate the service level of competitors. Due to the unique resources of the SB firm, the SBM can often provide a service level which is both desired by the target market and not easily duplicated by BB competitors. The result is, of course, a differential advantage. Thus, the strategic physical distribution problem for the SBM is selecting the right service level for the target market. The operational problem is achieving that service level at a least total cost of physical distribution.

What do we mean by customer service and level of service? *Customer service* does not mean the same thing here as when we were speaking of retail store customer services in the chapter on product. Our focus is on the supplying of the product itself as demanded by the customer. The customer can be an ultimate consumer, but the physical distribution concept is probably more often applied to the intermediate market. The dimensions of the service level are:

1. *Order cycle time*—the time the customer orders a product to the time of satisfactory product delivery.
2. *Percent of demand to be satisfied*—having the product available rather than out-of-stock.
3. *Quality control of order processing*—making sure that the ordered product (i.e., the right one) is delivered.
4. *Insuring acceptable physical condition of goods upon delivery*—getting the product there in good physical shape.[28]

The order cycle dimension of the service level is summarized as follows:

In a structural sense, customer service is measured by the performance around an order cycle measured from the time of customer commitment to the time of product delivery. Such measurements as level of service and speed of service are important in determining the basic capabilities of the system. However, consistency of service, which is a measure of how frequently the objectives of speed and level are accomplished, is the critical measure over time.[29]

Percent of demand to be saatisfied involves the balancing of inventory carrying costs against the possibility of losing sales (and possibly customers) due to out-of-stock conditions. Competitive conditions and product substitutibility affect the percent decision along with cost considerations. On 'he cost side, the SBM should remember that as his satisfaction percentage increases near the 100% range (i.e., no out-of-stocks), costs increase at an increasing rate. Thus, 95% satisfaction may cost considerably more in terms of inventory safety stocks, and so forth than 90% satisfaction.

Order processing quality control refers to delivering the right goods, and, when a mistake is made, being able to correct that mistake very quickly and to the satisfaction of the customer. Physical condition upon delivery means that the marketer, and not the purchaser, assumes the responsibility for proper packaging and transportation to insure that the products arrive in satisfactory condition.

Through the activities of physical distribution (i.e., transportation, storage, materials handling, inventory management, order processing, etc.), both the demand-generating and the demand-servicing purposes of physical distribution are accomplished. The SBM who can perform these activities well and who has carefully selected a level of customer service appropriate to his target market has a distinct advantage over competi-

---

[28]Lewis, p. 220.

[29]Thomas A. Staudt, Donald A. Taylor, and Donald J. Bowersox, *A Managerial Introduction To Marketing* (Englewood Cliffs, New Jersey: Prentice-Hall, Inc., 1976), p. 342.

tors. The concept of physical distribution is relatively new, but even so its implementation in marketing strategy planning has probably lagged unnecessarily. The SBM whose market approaches that of pure competition may be able to enhance his competitive position by incorporating physical distribution into his marketing strategy as follows:

> Significantly increasing service levels may be extremely profitable in highly competitive situations where the firm has relatively little to differentiate its marketing mix—for example, in pure competition or oligopoly. Here, simply increasing the service level—perhaps through faster delivery or wider stocks—may enable the firm to make significant headway in the market without altering prices or promotion. In fact, improved service levels can put a marketing mix across, and competitors may not fully realize what has happened.[30]

In summary, we might say that the incorporation of the physical distribution concept into the marketing strategy of the SBM is one more way in which the SBM can truly implement the marketing concept. To do so does not always require sophisticated Electronic Data Processing (EDP) and other resources unavailable to some SB firms, but it does require that decisions be made regarding appropriate customer service levels for the target market(s). This area of place strategy can and should be used by the SBM in order to create a more effective total marketing strategy.

BIBLIOGRAPHY

Books

BAUMBACK, CLIFFORD M., LAWYER, KENNETH, AND KELLEY, PEARCE C. *How to Organize and Operate a Small Business.* Englewood Cliffs, New Jersey: Prentice-Hall, Inc., 1973.

DUNCAN, DELBERT J., PHILLIPS, CHARLES F. AND HOLLANDER, STANLEY C. *Modern Retailing Management: Basic Con-Concepts and Practices.* Homewood, Illinois: Richard D. Irwin, Inc., 1972.

MARQUARDT, RAYMOND A., MAKENS, JAMES C., AND ROE, ROBERT G. *Retail Management: Satisfaction of Consumer Needs.* Hinsdale, Illinois: The Dryden Press, 1975.

MCCARTHY, E. JEROME. *Basic Marketing: A Managerial Approach.* Homewood, Illinois: Richard D. Irwin, Inc., 1975.

MCGUIRE, E. PATRICK. *Franchised Distribution.* New York: The Conference Board, Inc., 1971.

STAUDT, THOMAS A., TAYLOR, DONALD A., AND BOWERSOX, DONALD J. *A Managerial Introduction To Marketing.* Englewood Cliffs, New Jersey: Prentice-Hall, Inc., 1976.

WILL, R. TED, AND HASTY, RONALD W. *Retailing: A Mid-Management Approach.* San Francisco: Canfield Press, 1973.

Articles and Periodicals

APPLEBAUM, WILLIAM. "Guidelines for a Store-location Strategy Study," *Journal of Marketing,* 30, No. 4 (October 1966), pp. 42–45.

BERMAN, BARRY. "Location Analysis Within Regional Shopping Centers," in David J. Rachman, ed., *Retail Management Strategy: Selected Readings.* Englewood Cliffs, New Jersey, 1970, pp. 262–275.

BUCKLIN, LOUIS P. "Retail Strategy and the Classification of Consumer Goods," in Ben M. Enis and Keith K. Cox, eds., *Marketing Classics.* 2d ed. Boston: Allyn and Bacon, Inc., 1973, pp. 236–247.

CURHAN, RONALD C. "Shelf Space Allocation and Profit Maximization in Mass Retailing," *Journal of Marketing,* 37, No. 3 (July 1973), 54–60.

[30]E. Jerome McCarthy, *Basic Marketing: A Managerial Approach* (Homewood, Illinois: Richard D. Irwin, Inc., 1975), p. 381.

KINNARD, WILLIAM N., JR., AND MESSNER, STEPHEN D. "Obtaining Competitive Locations For Small Retailers In Shopping Centers," *Journal of Small Business Management,* 10 (January 1972), 21–26.

LaLONDE, BERNARD J. "The Logistics of Retail Location," in Ronald R. Gist, ed., *Management Perspectives in Retailing.* 2d ed. New York: John Wiley & Sons, Inc., 1971, pp. 198–203.

LEWIS, RICHARD J. "Physical Distribution: Managing The Firm's Service Level," in E. Jerome McCarthy, John F. Grashof, and Andrew A. Brogowicz, eds., *Readings in Basic Marketing.* Homewood, Illinois: Richard D. Irwin, Inc., 1975, pp. 216–228.

McKEEVER, J. ROSS. "Factors In Considering A Shopping Center Location," *Small Marketers Aids,* No. 143. Washington: Small Business Administration, 1970, pp. 1–8.

MERTES, JOHN E. "A Retail Structural Theory for Site Analysis," in Rom J. Markin, Jr., ed., *Retailing: Concepts, Institutions, and Management.* New York: The Macmillan Company, 1971, pp. 181–191.

NELSON, RICHARD LAWRENCE. "Principles of Retail Location," in Ronald R. Gist, ed., *Management Perspectives in Retailing.* 2d ed. New York: John Wiley & Sons, Inc., 1971, pp. 204–208.

STERN, HAWKINS. "The Significance of Impulse Buying Today," *Journal of Marketing,* 26, No. 2 (April 1962), 59–62.

13

Price Strategy for SBMM

THE PRICING QUESTION

Price is one of the five major elements in the SB marketing mix. Almost all firms, both SB and BB, have some discretion in setting the prices at which they sell their goods and services. However, a surprisingly small percentage of firms in all size categories have well-defined pricing strategies. Setting prices is *not* the same thing as having a pricing strategy. Even firms which do formally consider pricing as a topic at committee meetings are often not clear on what the pricing objectives are, or they may consider pricing as a non-marketing variable unrelated to the other "p's" of the marketing mix. Why is there so much neglect and confusion concerning pricing? The following selected quotes indicate some dimensions of the pricing question.

The gap between academicians and business practitioners accounts for part of the difficulty. Most authors tend to concentrate on a single dimension of the pricing problem, whereas the businessman ". . . must generally deal with price as one element in a multi-dimensional marketing program."[1] Thus, pricing practice is often not what the textbooks say.

The reader may then read the following good advice from the SBA and attempt to benefit from its "pragmatic value":

> The "best" price for a product is not necessarily the price that will sell the most units. Nor is it always the price that will bring in the greatest number of sales dollars. Rather the "best" price is one that will *maximize the profits* of the company.

[1]Alfred R. Oxenfeldt, "A Decision-making Structure for Price Decisions," Reprinted from *Journal of Marketing*, published by the American Marketing Association, Vol. 37, No. 1 (January 1973), p. 49.

The "best" selling price should be cost oriented and market oriented. It should be high enough to cover your costs and help you make a profit. It should also be low enough to attract customers and build sales volume.[2]

Management practice has also tended to neglect pricing. Speaking primarily to top marketing management, Oxenfeldt notes:

Pricing is among the most complicated functions entrusted to top marketing executives. Nevertheless, it is still not regarded as a specialized field—in the way that advertising and sales-force managements have come to be viewed—possibly because persons lacking any special training or experience can generally set a tolerable price. (Indeed, many, if not most, persons responsible for setting price have no special training or competence to do so.) From the standpoint of a firm's profitability, however, there is often an enormous difference between a tolerable price and the best one under the circumstances. Because of this great difference, top management must devise a practical program for the effective exercise of the pricing function.[3]

The availability of pricing strategy to the marketer and the difficulty of dealing with price are noted by the following remarks of Albaum and Oxenfeldt respectively:

The gap that exists between cost and value makes it possible to have a pricing strategy. Observation of pricing practices suggests that in many cases companies are not using price as an element in strategy by which they plan to attain certain defined objectives. To forego pricing as an element in a company's grand strategy is to forfeit the most powerful weapon available in a marketplace economy.[4]

Of all the areas of executive decision, pricing is perhaps the most fuzzy. Whenever a price problem is discussed by a committee, divergent figures are likely to be recommended without a semblance of consensus. Although unanimity in marketing decisions is a custom more remarkable in its occurrence than in its absence, agreement in pricing decisions is even more rare.[5]

Now that the reader is almost convinced of the impossibility of dealing with the difficult price element, let's look briefly at some general criteria for setting prices, as shown in Table 13–1.[6] There does seem to be some logic around which the SBM can begin to build his own pricing strategy. As noted in Table 13–1, the pricing criteria listed in the center column tend to indicate either a low price or a high price depending on the marketing characteristics involved. For example, a product with fast turnover tends to be priced low, and a product with slow turnover tends to be priced high. In the practical pricing situation, the SBM must simultaneously consider all pricing criteria.

---

[2]Victor A. Lennon, "What Is The Best Selling Price?" *Management Aids For Small Manufacturers,* No. 193 (Washington: Small Business Administration, 1972), p. 2.

[3]Alfred R. Oxenfeldt, *Pricing: For Marketing Executives* (Belmont, California: Wadsworth Publishing Company, Inc., 1961), p. 55.

[4]Gerald Albaum, *Price Formulation* (Tucson, Arizona: The University of Arizona, 1965), p. 21.

[5]Alfred R. Oxenfeldt, "Multi-stage Approach to Pricing," *Marketing Classics,* ed. Ben M. Enis and Keith K. Cox (2d Ed.; Boston: Allyn and Bacon, Inc., 1973), p. 387.

[6]Adapted from W. J. E. Crissey and Robert Boewadt, "Pricing in Perspective," *Sales Management,* June 15, 1971, p. 44. Reprinted by permission from *Sales & Marketing Management Magazine.* Copyright 1971.

Table 13-1   Criteria For Setting Prices

Low Price When	*Pricing Criteria*	*High Price When*
1. Little	1. Promotion	1. Much
2. Commodity	2. Product type	2. Proprietary
3. Mass-produced	3. Manufacture	3. Custom-made
4. Intensive	4. Market coverage	4. Selective
5. Long-lived	5. Product obsolescence	5. Short-lived
6. Slow	6. Technological change	6. Rapid
7. Capital-intensive	7. Production	7. Labor-intensive
8. Large	8. Market share	8. Small
9. Short	9. Channels of distribution	9. Long
10. Mature	10. Stage of market	10. New or declining
11. Long-term	11. Profit perspective	11. Short-term
12. Single-use	12. Product versatility	12. Multiple-use
13. Much	13. Promotional contribution to line	13. Little
14. Few or none	14. Ancillary services	14. Many
15. Short	15. Product life in use	15. Long
16. Fast	16. Turnover	16. Slow

Source: Adapted from W. J. E. Crissey and Robert Boewadt, "Pricing in Perspective," *Sales Management,* June 15, 1971, p. 44. Reprinted by permission from *Sales & Marketing Management* magazine. Copyright 1971.

What Is Price?

Simply stated, *price* is the amount of money paid by the buyer to the seller of a product (goods–services combination). It is the agreed-upon money value of a product in a market transaction. However, every market transaction also involves some other aspects of price. In Chapter 3, we stated that price is that which the SBM receives in exchange for the goods and services combinations he markets. The price variable probably most directly affects the profits of the SBM. Strategic questions in pricing are how much; in what form; when; with what variations, such as discounts, and so forth.

From the perspective of the buyer, price is not the same thing as cost, although price is usually a large part of the cost. The buyer will also experience other costs, such as convenience costs and psychological costs. For example, a buyer may be willing to pay a higher price in terms of dollars at a convenience food store in order to avoid a higher cost (but perhaps lower price in terms of dollars) at a crowded supermarket during the rush period.

From the perspective of the seller, that is, the SBM, price is not only an element of the marketing mix, but, as the only income-generating element, it is also a rather direct determinant of profitability. Unit price times volume of units sold equals total revenue. Even beyond total revenue, price also directly affects profits. The basic formula for profits states that units sold times price per unit, less costs, equals profits. Also, as a means of market cultivation, price is a determinant of quantity.

Pricing Problems and Decisions

An illustrative list of important pricing problems is given below to suggest that the setting of prices and the making of price changes have far-reaching effects. The specific pricing problems facing the individual SBM will, of course, vary in each situation. The following list does, however, represent some of the pricing problems that may be commonly found:

1. A decline in sales.
2. Prices are too high—relative to those charged by rivals, relative to the benefits of the product. (Prices might be too high in a few regional markets and very appropriate elsewhere.)
3. Price is too low, again in certain markets and not in others.
4. The company is regarded as exploitative of customers and not to be trusted.
5. The firm places excessive financial burdens on its resellers.
6. The price differentials among items in the line are objectionable or unintelligible.
7. Its price changes are too frequent—or do not take account of major changes in market circumstances.
8. The firm's price reflects negatively on itself and on its products.
9. The price is unstabilizing the market which had finally become stabilized after great difficulty.
10. The firm is offering its customers too many price choices and confusing its customers and resellers.
11. The firm's prices seem higher to customers than they really are.
12. The firm's price policy attracts undesirable kinds of customers which have no loyalty to any seller.
13. The firm's pricing behavior makes customers unduly price sensitive and unappreciative of quality differences.
14. The company has fostered a decline in market discipline among sellers in the industry.[7]

Another way of viewing the area of pricing is via ten key questions which illustrate the many dimensions of pricing strategy for the marketing executive. These strategy questions are the following:

. . .(1) What to charge for each product and service sold by the firm; (2) what to charge different types of customers (whether to give quantity and functional discounts and, if so, of what size; and at what volumes of purchase to make the breaking points); (3) whether to charge different types of distributors the same price—and how to distinguish distributors from retailers in borderline cases; (4) whether to vary price systematically over time—for instance, setting the price high on a new item and reducing it in planned steps, and having a regular seasonal pattern of price changes; (5) whether to give discounts for cash and how quickly payment should be required to earn them; (6) whether to invoke price maintenance powers, where legal or otherwise enforceable; (7) whether to suggest resale prices or only set the price charged one's own customers; (8) whether to price all items in the

[7]Oxenfeldt, "A Decision-Making Structure for Price Decisions," p. 51.

firm's line as if they were separate or whether to price them as a "team" (including promotional items, loss leaders, etc.); (9) whether to limit output on some items below what the market would absorb in order to push sales of other items in the line; and (10) how many different price offerings to have for each item and when to add and drop particular items.[8]

As Albaum has pointed out, the last two decisions in the above list serve to emphasize the role of price in product planning; and the first eight decisions can be classified into either of two categories: price determination or price administration.[9] We will make reference to the above list in our later discussion of price strategy formulation for the SBM.

The complexity and the multidimensional nature of pricing strategy is further illustrated by adding one more listing to the above lists. This is the list of the parties involved in the pricing process. A basic distinction between SB and BB, which will be discussed later, is the extent to which each of these parties is involved in the pricing process. According to Oxenfeldt, in most situations the parties include:

> . . . (1) The various individuals and departments within the executive's own firm who are directly and indirectly involved in pricing, sales, and sales promotion; (2) the ultimate customers for the product—who may be household consumers, or industrial, commercial, or government buyers; (3) rival sellers, including all firms *currently* selling a product or service that potential customers might be willing to accept in place of the seller's own; (4) potential rivals; (5) resellers, including individuals and businesses that buy his product for resale at a profit; (6) suppliers, including laborers and their unions, firms from which primary raw materials and components are purchased, and those who supply funds; and (7) the government.[10]

The pricing problems and decisions facing SB are similar in many ways to those facing BB. For example, the above seven parties may be involved to a different extent in the SB pricing process, but they are usually involved to some extent. SB firms usually do have some discretion in the pricing process, that is, they employ administered prices. Administered prices are not—and never were—the sole property of BB. Harper notes:

> The claim is sometimes made that administered prices are the prices of "big business" and that small business firms use some other kind of price making. This is, of course, false since, as we have seen, most prices in the United States are administered, and all kinds and sizes of industries and firms make use of administered pricing. The small retailer, wholesaler, or manufacturer practices price administration just as surely as does Standard Oil of New Jersey or General Motors. Indeed, even when the American economy was characterized chiefly by small business firms, administered pricing prevailed, as it does today.[11]

Scope Of Pricing Coverage

The scope of coverage in this chapter will necessarily be a less than complete investigation of pricing. Noticeably absent are: (a) the economic analysis of price,

[8]Oxenfeldt, *Pricing: For Marketing Executives,* pp. 19–20.
[9]Albaum, p. 2.
[10]Oxenfeldt, *Pricing: For Marketing Executives,* p. 22.
[11]Donald V. Harper, *Price Policy And Procedure* (New York: Harcourt, Brace & World, Inc., 1966), p. 21–22.

(b) geographic pricing practices, (c) ethical considerations, and (d) most of the legal aspects of pricing. These important subjects are covered extensively in other books and are beyond the scope of our SB perspective. For example, because of its size, SB is not often challenged on the legal aspects of its pricing. State and local laws and customs tend to be more important to the SBM than federal legislation. The Consumer Goods Pricing Act of 1975, which became effective in March, 1976, terminated all interstate utilization of "fair trade" or resale price maintenance.[12] The legal death of fair trade removed one of the federal laws which at one time directly affected the pricing strategies of many SB marketers.

Our plan for the remainder of the chapter is to show the role of pricing strategy in the SB marketing mix. In doing so, many practical aspects of pricing, such as pricing methods, policies, price changes, and discounts, will be considered. And a pricing strategy guideline for the SBM will be given.

Pricing Objectives

As an element of the marketing mix, pricing strategy should be directed toward the accomplishment of specific marketing objectives which lead to ultimate overall company objectives. Thus, a hierarchy of compatible objectives and strategies exists from price to marketing to total company. Which pricing objectives are meaningful for a particular SBM depends upon (a) overall company objectives and differential advantages, (b) target markets served, (c) the environment, and (d) the remainder of the marketing mix for that SB firm. Many firms, both BB and SB, do not have specifically stated pricing objectives. Table 13-2 is a partial list of feasible pricing objectives. Each SBM must determine for himself which objectives are appropriate for his firm and what the priorities are going to be when conflict arises among objectives. The list, as suggested by Oxenfeldt, has been marked with asterisks by the author in order to indicate objectives which have a high probability of being realistic objectives for the SBM.[13]

Room for some disagreement certainly exists regarding many of the objectives given (or not given) an asterisk in Table 13-2. However, differences generally do exist in the pricing objectives of SB and BB. One noticeable difference is in the area of those pricing objectives relating to profitability. Perhaps BB firms should aim for "satisfactory" or "level" profits, but profit *maximization* (and perhaps in both the short and long run) seems to be a meaningful price objective for most SB firms. SB firms which do not attract large amounts of public attention and which have successfully carved out desirable target markets are in a position to try for profit maximization. Other SB firms may seek a target return, such as a return on sales, investment, or time. For example, a small family-operated business may seek a fixed dollar amount of profit in order to cover living expenses. Other objectives listed in Table 13-2 relate more to pricing as a element of the marketing mix rather than to the profit which results from a successful marketing mix.

PRICE IN THE SB MARKETING MIX

Unlike the cheese in the nursery rhyme which "stands alone," price and the other elements of the SB marketing mix work together in a synergetic fashion to produce a

---

[12]James C. Johnson and Louis E. Boone, "Farewell to Fair Trade," *MSU Business Topics,* 24, No. 2 (Spring 1976), p. 22.

[13]Oxenfeldt, "A Decision-Making Structure for Price Decisions," p. 50.

Table 13-2   Potential Pricing Objectives

*1. Maximum long-run profits
*2. Maximum short-run profits
*3. Growth
 4. Stabilize market
 5. Desensitize customers to price
 6. Maintain price-leadership arrangement
 7. Discourage entrants
 8. Speed exit of marginal firms
 9. Avoid government investigation and control
*10. Maintain loyalty of middlemen and get their sales support
 11. Avoid demands for "more" from suppliers—labor in particular
 12. Enhance image of firm and its offerings
*13. Be regarded as "fair" by (ultimate) customers
*14. Create interest and excitement about the item
 15. Be considered trustworthy and reliable by rivals
 16. Help in the sale of weak items in the line
*17. Discourage others from cutting prices
*18. Make a product "visible"
 19. "Spoil market" to obtain high price for sale of business
*20. Build traffic

Source: Alfred R. Oxenfeldt, "A Decision-Making Structure for Price Decisions," Reprinted from *Journal of Marketing* published by the American Marketing Association, 37, No. 1 (January 1973), p. 50. Used with permission.

consistent unified effect. At least, that's the way it's supposed to be. In fact, some marketers, both SB and BB, tend to ignore price as one of the elements of the marketing mix. Even though the marketer may ignore price as a variable over which he has control, the effects of price are felt by ultimate consumers, resellers, suppliers, rivals, and so forth. Pricing cannot be done in a vacuum. It affects and is affected by the other elements (product, place, promotion, and people) of the SB marketing mix. A change in one element will often call for a change in the other elements. For example, should a physical product improvement be accompanied by a price increase? Does a substantial price change call for new types or numbers of retailers? Will very intensive advertising make feasible and necessary an increase in price in order to cover costs? Will a prestige price require prestige distribution employing prestige-type people?

An obvious and rather direct effect of price on the marketing mix is the use of low prices or price cuts. For the SBM, such pricing strategies should be labeled "Handle With Care." Only when the SB firm's volume can be increased substantially, and not at the expense of a more powerful competitor, does such a pricing strategy make much sense.

A less obvious way of incorporating price into the marketing strategy is by using various forms of psychological pricing. In some cases, prestige pricing may be used to indicate the high prestige of the product. Even at intermediate and lower levels, consumers tend to classify products according to their prices. Some SB firms may *purposely* attempt to downgrade or eliminate the importance of price as an element in the marketing mix. Uniform prices for a product among most retailers are an evidence of such a strategy. Price is an element of the marketing mix, but the importance of its role is often within the control of the SBM.

One study on the importance of pricing in competitive strategy reported the results shown in Table 13–3.[14] The researcher in this study does not imply that price is unimportant, but he does state that ". . .one-half of the respondents did *not* select pricing as *one* of *the five* most important policy areas in their firm's marketing success."[15] The relatively low ranking of pricing was attributed to the following factors: (a) Supply exceeds demand in today's competitive economy; (b) today's relatively well-to-do consumers are interested in more than just price; and (c) through successful product differentiation, a marketer is able to obtain some pricing freedom. Although the study covered some firms with annual sales of less than $50 million, the emphasis was definitely on BB. The significance of pricing may, or may not, vary according to size of firm.[16]

One author lists four general types of situations in which pricing decisions are of great importance. These are: (a) when a firm must set a price for the first time; (b) when circumstances lead a firm to consider initiating a price change; (c) when competition initiates a price change; and (d) when the company produces several products that have interrelated demands and/or costs.[17] Another author describes various roles for pricing in the marketing mix according to specific situations.[18] First, it is suggested that whether pricing is stressed or de-emphasized depends basically on the business philosophy of the firm. Second, price can be used to influence demand over time, such as with seasonal discounts. Third, pricing can be used to adopt to a geographic advantage or disadvantage.

Table 13–3 How Management Ranks The Factors Of Marketing Success

Rank	Policy Areas	% of Firms Selecting the Policy Area*
1.	Product research and development . . .	79
2.	Sales research and sales planning	73
3.	Management of sales personnel	59
4.	Advertising and sales promotion	56
5.	Product service	52
6.	Pricing	50
7.	Organizational structure	44
8.	Distribution channels and their control	41
9.	Marketing cost budgeting and control	17
10.	Financing and credit	14
11.	Transportation and storage	7
12.	Public relations	7

*Based on a tabulation of 135 usable questionnaires. Percentages here are rounded.
Source: Jon G. Udell, "How Important is Pricing in Competitive Strategy," Reprinted from *Journal of Marketing,* published by the American Marketing Association, 28, No. 1 (January 1964), p. 45. Used with permission.

[14]Jon G. Udell, "How Important is Pricing in Competitive Strategy," Reprinted from *Journal of Marketing,* published by the American Marketing Association, 28, No. 1 (January 1964), p. 45.
[15]Udell, p. 44.
[16]Udell, pp. 44–48.
[17]Philip Kotler, *Marketing Management: Analysis, Planning, And Control* (Englewood Cliffs, New Jersey: Prentice-Hall, Inc., 1972), p. 516.
[18]John M. Rathmell, *Managing The Marketing Function: Concepts, Analysis, and Application* (New York: John Wiley & Sons, Inc., 1969), p. 369–370.

Fourth, through the discount structure, pricing can be used to employ multiple channels of distribution effectively. Fifth, price deals are a timely means for meeting a rapidly evolving competitive situation. Finally, price adjustments can sometimes be made on a selective basis for individual customers. SB firms can sometimes do this more easily than their BB competitors.

The relative importance of pricing in the marketing mix is ultimately determined by the importance attributed to price by the target customers of the SBM. Their response to price, in combination with product, place, promotion, and people, is what counts. However, some other factors must be considered by the SBM. Among these are (a) cost, (b) administrative characteristics, and (c) effects.[19] Will an equally effective price cut cost more or less than additional promotion or more sales training? How does a price change compare with other possible marketing mix changes regarding speed of implementation, risk of poor implementation, and the precision of being directed at small groups of target customers? What are the various positive and negative effects of price changes on different customers, competitors, resellers, and so forth? Costs, administration, and effects must all be considered.

One may conclude that pricing does have a role to play in the marketing mix of the SBM. The magnitude of the role is probably overstated by economists, who tend to ignore nonprice competition. In fact, prices are probably not as important to most consumers as consumers think they are. It is important for consumers to be "smart" or to at least believe they are "smarter than other people." Getting a "good deal"—which means a good price— is one way that consumers "prove" they are smart. This perception (or perhaps it is a misperception) of self is very important. Most consumers, in fact, possess very limited price information. What all this means to the SBM is that a particular *price image* may be at least as important as, if not more important than, the actual price facts. However, consumers are not easily fooled. One study on consumer appraisal of retail price advertisements showed that consumers tend to be skeptical. Advertising reliability and price work together.

> For the retailer, the results emphasize the importance of image as a factor influencing the impact of advertisements, particularly at the lower discount levels. Two separate image components, advertiser reliability and price competitiveness, influenced consumer acceptance of the regular price and the sale price. The retailer must determine what "mix" of the two components is most beneficial for his operations.[20]

THE "HOW TO" OF PRICE STRATEGY PLANNING FOR SB

Adapted to the element of pricing, the eight-step "How To" of marketing strategy planning for SB results in the "How To" of price strategy planning for SB. The eight steps in this process are:

1. Record the current price strategy.
2. Identify strategic price problems.

---

[19]Alfred R. Oxenfeldt, *Pricing Strategies* (New York: AMACOM, 1975), pp. 18–34.
[20]Joseph N. Fry and Gordon H. McDougall, "Consumer Appraisal of Retail Price Advertisements," *Journal of Marketing,* 38, No. 3 (July 1974), p. 67.

3. Divide current strategic price problems into core strategy areas and supporting strategy areas.
4. Formulate alternative price strategies at both core and support levels.
5. Evaluate the alternatives in various combinations.
6. Choose the new price strategy.
7. Plan the details of implementation of the new price strategy.
8. Set performance standards and monitor feedback.

The above eight steps, similar to those used in Chapter 3, are used here with specific reference to the pricing element of the SB marketing mix. Our method of using this simple and practical framework for planning pricing strategy requires the conference room, note pads, good marketing leadership, and teamwork. Since price strategy is a part of our overall marketing strategy, we will assume that the SBM has already (a) defined overall company and marketing objectives in specific terms, (b) defined target markets, (c) delineated the differential advantages of the firm regarding both (a) and (b), (d) properly assessed the marketing environment, and (e) made at least some tentative decisions regarding the other P's of the marketing mix. Since price strategy planning and overall marketing strategy planning are interrelated, and since both are on-going processes, a consideration in pricing strategy may suggest changes in the overall marketing strategy. However, in this chapter, we'll focus our attention on the pricing element while bearing in mind that price both affects and is affected by the other elements (P's) which together form the overall marketing strategy. In other words, we are not going to attempt to formulate pricing strategy in a vacuum. The application of the following eight-step outline to a specific SB is the job of each individual SBM. The outline will give as much direction as possible. (The reader may, at this point, wish to review the eight-step outline used in Chapter 3 for overall marketing strategy planning.)

Step 1—Record the current price strategy. For each target market served, the SBM should have a current pricing strategy. However, if such a strategy does exist, the chances are pretty good that the strategy is quite fuzzy and rather incomplete. General statements such as: "Our pricing strategy is one of being competitive"; "We price in order to offer a good value"; or "Our price strategy is to maximize profits in the long run" are *not* of much value to the SBM at this point. What the SBM needs are some concise statements regarding exactly *what* it is that the firm is currently doing in making its pricing decisions, and *why*. For example, our core pricing strategy may currently be to follow the leader in the target markets where we are marketing. The *why* may be because (a) we have no other choice, (b) we have not taken the trouble to investigate any alternatives, (c) this core strategy has proven to be very successful, or (d) we really don't know why.

In many companies, both SB and BB, the attempt to record the current pricing strategy will probably result in the conclusion that the firm's pricing is done by formula rather than by strategy. For example, cost-plus seems to be the most common method of determining prices. The method is not necessarily applied in the absence of a pricing strategy, but this is often the case. Cost-plus means that the firm determines its cost (either total cost or some other cost figure) and then determines its selling price by adding a markup to the cost. It is a simple and direct method of determining prices; but unless the determination of how much markup should be added is based upon a realistic pricing strategy, such "formula" pricing can be quite dangerous. Making pricing decisions and having a pricing strategy are *not* the same thing. However, we must begin somewhere, so let's begin by recording what we have been doing and why we have been doing it. Right or wrong, it is a beginning. So let's record everything that describes the current pricing strategy. Using this record as a base, we are now ready to move to the next step.

Step 2—Identify strategic price problems.   If the current price strategy is not perfect, it is possible that some strategic (as well as tactical) pricing problems exist. Finding and properly identifying pricing problems (and opportunities) comprise the second step for the SBM. Caution must be used in order to differentiate between problems and symptoms of problems. For example, if a customer complains that the price is "too high," does he really mean that the price is too high or is that really a shorthand summary statement encompassing several forms of sales resistance? Strategic pricing problems may exist either in the core (relating to the differential advantage) or supporting price strategies.

How does the SBM seek out and find the strategic pricing problems? Some may have surfaced in Step 1 above. Others can be found by actively looking for them on a periodic or continuous basis. Our list of pricing problems earlier in this chapter (which actually contains symptoms as well as problems) suggests that a variety of problem types and information sources may be needed. Some system for monitoring feedback (as in Step 8 of our process) is essential for providing information to the SBM. Some data sources the SBM may wish to consider as part of a monitoring system are suggested by Oxenfeldt:

1. Sales—in units and in dollars
   a. Previous year comparisons
   b. Different markets/channels comparisons
2. Rival's prices
3. Inquiries from potential customers about the line
4. Company's sales at "off list" price
   a. Measured as a % of total sales
   b. Revenue as % of sales at full price
5. Types of customers getting the most and largest price reductions
6. Market shares—in individual markets
7. Marketing costs; production cost; production costs at nearly output
8. Price complaints
   a. From customers
   b. From salesmen
9. Inventories of finished goods at different levels
10. Customers' attitudes toward firm, prices, and so forth
11. Number of lost customers (brand-switching)
12. Inquiries—and subsequent purchases
13. Marketing costs[21]

In effect, the SBM should search everywhere to find potential pricing problems. However, he should be sure to confine his search to those target markets he is serving or planning to serve. Developing pricing strategies for other target markets will not pay off. His BB competitors may be involved with a large number of target markets, but the SBM

---

[21]Oxenfeldt, "A Decision-making Structure for Price Decisions," p. 51.

is likely to be in only a few. This may be to his advantage. He can concentrate his attention.

Step 3—Divide current strategic price problems into core strategy areas and supporting strategy areas. Here, the SBM determines whether the price problems are core or supporting. For example, if the core strategy was built around a differential advantage, such as a very high quality product at an equally high price, a decision to introduce a new product will present the SBM with this question: Can we duplicate this high quality and high price core strategy, or do we lack the same differential advantage regarding the new product? Perhaps the high quality would not be recognized by customers for the new product. Perhaps an entirely new core marketing strategy is appropriate for the new product, and that requires a new role for price and the other elements of the marketing mix.

Price strategy questions which will often be regarded as *core* price strategy questions by the SBM are: (1) How important a role is price to play in the overall marketing strategy? (2) What is the proper relationship among interrelated products of the firm? (3) How does the firm react to price competition from rivals? (4) Over time, when should the firm employ different pricing strategies, such as skimming or penetration? Core price strategy questions are those which deal very directly with the differential advantage. The core price strategy, taken together with core strategy in product, place, promotion, and people, is a main pillar of the overall marketing strategy. On the other hand, supporting price strategies are those which support either the core price strategy or some other core (or support) strategy.

Both core and support price strategy areas will require the time and effort of the SBM. Simply because supporting price strategy areas are not as crucial as the core areas does not mean that they are unimportant. Good planning and execution in support areas may make a big difference in the success of the SB firm. Also, problems probably occur more frequently in supporting rather than in core strategy areas. Thus, the number of opportunities for excellence is greater in the supporting area.

The SBM has (1) recorded the current price strategy, (2) identified strategic pricing problems, and (3) divided these price problems into core and support areas. In one sense, this has been an analysis of the past and present. On this base, the SBM can now begin to plan for the future.

Step 4—Formulate alternative price strategies at both core and support levels. Some of the alternative pricing strategies which may be used in various combinations with each other and with additional strategies and tactics are mentioned briefly below. The competitive strengths and weaknesses and the objectives of SB make some strategies more or less attractive for SB than they would be for BB. Other strategies seem to have equal attractiveness for both BB and SB. The alternative pricing strategies are: (1) price level strategies, (2) product line pricing strategies, (3) stability pricing strategies, (4) psychological pricing strategies, (5) discriminatory pricing strategies, and (6) other areas of pricing strategy.

1. *Price level strategies* can be employed by most firms. For established products, this may involve pricing at, above, or below the market target competitors. However, the comparison should always be within a single target market, because selling at different prices in different target markets gets into another consideration of pricing strategy. Extreme cases of price level strategy are skimming and penetration. These terms usually apply to the pricing of new products in relation to costs, desired market share, and potential competition. Skimming combines relatively high prices (often, all the traffic will

bear) with heavy promotion in the early stages of the product life-cycle. Price is progressively lowered in order to attract additional segments of the market and to meet competition. Penetration pricing results in new product prices being set only slightly above costs (smaller unit margins) in the hope of achieving mass market status in early stages of the product life-cycle. The strategy also includes the idea that the firm will gain a substantial (or at least a satisfactory) share of that mass market by discouraging competitive entry. Skimming and penetration are two extremes. A firm may also select a middleground. For the SBM, strategies which lean heavily toward the skimming side usually make more sense. SB usually does not have the power to limit entry or force exit. Skimming provides immediate dollars which can be used for promotion and/or taken as short term profits.

2. *Product line pricing strategies* attempt to take account of the interrelationships on both the cost and demand sides of the various products in the total product line of a multi-product firm. The extent to which products are complements, substitutes, or are neutral will affect pricing strategy. The question the SBM should ask himself when looking at pricing strategy for the total product line is: Are these products aimed toward the same target markets or are different products different enough so that they are generally aimed for different target markets? The general rule is that products for the same target market should bear meaningful price relationships, while products for totally different target markets need not do so. Regarding product line pricing, Oxenfeldt notes that special attention should be paid the "end items", that is, the lowest and highest priced items in a line.[22] The lowest priced item in a line affects sales very greatly, because it is most frequently remembered by consumers and is often used as a basis of price and quality comparison. As Oxenfeldt states:

> For these two reasons, and possibly there are others, reductions in the price of the lowest—priced item in a company's line are likely to have a highly stimulating effect on sales. Similarly, increases in that price are likely to reduce sales far more than would increases in the price of inbetween items.[23]

A term sometimes confused with product line pricing (the pricing of a full product line) is the somewhat different strategy of *price lining*. Price lining is the practice of selecting a few desirable ultimate selling prices for the products in the line. Quality is then determined by figuring necessary margins backwards to determine how much the product can cost to make. The product is produced to sell for a price. An example would be cookies that are produced to be sold on a "mix-n-match" basis of three bags for $1.00.

Not all SB firms have the opportunity or desire to employ product line pricing or price lining. For example, a firm such as Michelin may wish to compete against the Akron giants by offering only a first line tire. This is target marketing.

3. *Stability pricing strategies* once relied heavily on "fair trade," which is, for all practical and legal purposes, dead today. Other forms of resale price maintenance to keep prices relatively stable are used by many marketers. These include: limiting the number of resellers (distributors and dealers); consignment selling to maintain price and title until received by the ultimate consumer; restrictive contracts; cooperative promotional programs which limit participation to those following "suggested retail price"; preticketing of

---

[22]Alfred R. Oxenfeldt, "Product Line Pricing," *Managerial Marketing: Policies, Strategies, And Decisions*, ed. Eugene J. Kelley and William Lazer (Homewood, Illinois: Richard D. Irwin, Inc., 1973), pp. 392–393.

[23]Oxenfeldt, "Product Line Pricing," p. 393.

merchandise; extensive price advertising; and so forth. Practices such as notification of pending price changes and guarantees against price declines are given to resellers (and sometimes to consumers) in order to mitigate the effects of price changes. To the extent that the SBM wishes to stabilize prices, he may consider which of the above means are appropriate. Reasons for wishing to stabilize prices are to keep prices high, to avoid reseller resentment, and to create a price/quality image, as well as many others.

4. *Psychological pricing strategies* are the several forms in which the expression of a price uses the principles of psychology. For example, many marketers believe that $2.98 is a much better price than $3.00. Among the forms of psychological pricing strategy are: (a) prestige pricing, whereby the customer assumes that a high price means commensurate high quality; (b) leader pricing, in which a well-known and widely used low-priced product is given a "special" price in order to get customers into the store; (c) bait pricing, which is a somewhat questionable practice whereby an advertised low price is used to get the customer into the store where salesmen trade up the customer to better merchandise; (d) odd-even pricing, which refers to using prices ending in certain numbers, such as $2.98 or $29.95; and (e) customary pricing, as was once used on the extinct five-cent candy bars, cup of coffee, cigar, and so forth.

The SBM should be aware of the benefits of the various forms of psychological pricing in both his own pricing strategy and those pricing strategies of his competitors. The effects seem to be felt most at the retailer–consumer level of distribution, but this does have repercussions throughout the channel of distribution.

5. *Discriminatory pricing strategies* refer to the variability or lack of variability in the prices charged similar buyers for similar products under similar conditions. Discrimina-tory pricing, as with other forms of discrimination, is favored by those it discriminates *for* and opposed by those it discriminates *against*. A critical question for the SBM is: Do customers and potential customers know that our pricing strategy exists in order to discriminate among customers? The three major concepts of price variability are: (a) nonvariable price, (b) variable price, and (c) single price.[24] A *nonvariable* price policy does have price differences, but the terms and conditions which determine the applicable price are generally known and uniformly administered. Under a *variable* price policy, different prices would be charged to some buyers for the same product, at a given time for comparable quantities and conditions of sale, even though other buyers of the same class did not receive these "different" prices. A *single* price policy is the practice of charging all customers the same price regardless of their trade classification, size, or conditions of purchase.

Price discrimination in many forms, especially at the retail-consumer level, is legal. For example, some stores, such as retail paint stores, have a standard practice of charging shelf price but giving a discount of 10% or more to steady customers and to just about anyone else who is knowledgeable enough to ask for the discount. Marketing students don't pay list price (assuming they can afford to buy) for new cars or motorcycles, but some people do. Is that discriminatory pricing?

6. *Other pricing strategies* not yet mentioned are available to the SBM. Skimming and penetration referred to the early stages of the product life-cycle. The PLC has price strategy implications at all stages (see the appendix to Chapter 10). The SBM may wish to employ leasing as an alternate to outright sale. His pricing will be different if the leasing

---

[24]See D. Maynard Phelps and J. Howard Westing, *Marketing Management* (Homewood, Illinois: Richard D. Irwin, Inc., 1968), pp. 359–361.

strategy is used. Unit pricing may be actively promoted by a retailer in an attempt to sell larger sizes and private-label merchandise on which a greater profit can be made. Although we have briefly covered the main areas of pricing strategy alternatives, the number of combinations available to the SBM is very great. This is emphasized when one remembers that the pricing strategies selected will interact with the other elements of the marketing mix.

Step 5—Evaluate the alternatives in various combinations. The pricing strategy alternatives generated in the above step should now be evaluated by the SBM. In this step we are merely evaluating alternatives. We are not yet selecting an alternative. Each alternative and meaningful combinations of alternatives should be evaluated in terms of company goals and resources, marketing objectives, and price objectives. The effectiveness of alternative pricing strategies in helping to solve the current pricing problems identified in Step 2 above should be considered. Earlier we mentioned that pricing strategy affects various parties: others within the firm, ultimate customers, rival sellers, potential rivals, resellers, suppliers, and government. The SBM should ask: What are the desirable and undesirable effects of each pricing strategy alternative on each of these parties? He must also remember that what is being evaluated is alternative pricing strategies and *not* alternative prices. The SBM and his marketing management team should have some agreement among themselves as to what criteria are to be used, and the relative importance of each, in evaluating the pricing strategy alternatives. This is essential, particularly since price is possibly the element of the marketing mix about which so many intangible and diverse approaches can be taken.

Step 6—Choose the new price strategy. The time for making a choice has now arrived. The newly-selected pricing strategy will be a combination of core and supporting price strategies, consistent with the rest of the marketing mix, whose implementation will be adjusted from time to time by tactical moves. However, the basic pricing strategy should be one that will endure for some time. It will probably reflect the subjective value judgments of the SBM and his management team. Many portions of the new pricing strategy will be identical with or carried over from the previous pricing strategy. The SBM has now decided *what* the pricing strategy will be. He is now ready to spell it out in detail.

Step 7—Plan the details of implementation of the new price strategy. How, when, where, and by whom is the new price strategy to be implemented? The details of implementation are *planned* in this step in order that the actual implementation will occur smoothly. The details which the SBM fails to specify in this planning stage will probably also be neglected in the implementation stage. Involved here are such items as timing, discount schedules, cost calculations, projected sales estimates, the preparation and dissemination of pricing information, assignment of specific tasks, and so forth. For example, if the new pricing strategy of the SB retailer calls for a semi-annual 10% off regular price sale, are the cash registers and store personnel capable of handling the calculations in an efficient and effective manner? Such "nitty-gritty" tasks must be planned for in this step.

Step 8—Set performance standards and monitor feedback. In this step, we set the criteria by which we will later evaluate our success in accomplishing our pricing, marketing, and company objectives. Thus, we *plan* what the standards will be rather than actually use them, and we *plan* how feedback will be monitored rather than actually monitoring the feedback.

Execution and control of the pricing strategy formulated in the eight-step process above will succeed only to the extent that the pricing strategy is sound and is a solid element in an overall marketing strategy which is sound. The planning phase is essential for the successful execution and consequent control. "Copycat" pricing *strategies* (not the same as follow-the-leader pricing) do not make sense for either BB or SB. And having no pricing strategy at all amounts to the refusal to use one of the five important tools of the marketing mix. Setting prices and making other pricing decisions can be meaningful activities only within the framework of a pricing strategy. The individual SBM must determine his own strategy; no one else can do it for him.

SOME PRACTICAL PRICING ISSUES
OF SPECIAL INTEREST TO SB

Briefly discussed below are several issues about which the SBM often has a very practical interest. More complete discussions of these issues can often be found in basic and advanced marketing books. Current articles are also available on many of the topics.

Pricing Methods or Approaches

Approaches to pricing are either cost-oriented, demand-oriented, or a combination of the two. These approaches, and the limitations of each, are covered extensively in basic marketing texts. In practice, cost-oriented methods are what is used, in spite of the fact that many pricing experts suggest that this is one of the biggest mistakes a firm can make. Cost-oriented approaches such as cost-plus-markup may make sense, especially to wholesalers and retailers selling products that lack great exclusiveness. The simplicity of use is a definite advantage. However, the firm using a cost approach never knows how much the customer might be willing to pay.

In practice, cost-oriented approaches do dominate. Our point here is that the SBM should understand the limitations of all pricing approaches. Tools such as break-even charts and formulas may be helpful, but they do contain limiting assumptions: for example, not all costs are either fixed or variable. In cost-plus-markup pricing, how much markup should be added? Should the markup percentage be fixed or flexible? When should the SBM sell below full cost? The answers to these questions are not always as easy in practice as they are in theory. The theory is available in books. In practice, the SBM is often left with what amounts to a trial and error method of pricing which employs some concept of cost as the floor and some concept of demand as the ceiling for price. Hopefully, the ceiling is above the floor, and far enough above the floor for the SBM to achieve his profit objectives.

Price Cutting and Price Wars:
Competition and Collusion

The SBM is usually competitive, but he usually prefers to be competitive on a nonprice basis. He wishes to exercise control over the setting of his product's prices rather than to have his prices set by the competitive forces of the market. The same is generally true of BB. Experience suggests that collusion among SB firms is not uncommon in order to avoid direct price competition which might be ruinous. Price collusion among SB firms has different social implications than would collusion among BB firms since most SB firms, both as individuals and when in collusion with each other, do not exert much market power. For this reason, and because enforcement would be nearly impossible, price collusion is rarely a legal concern among SB firms. For example, one SB grocer can tell the SB grocer on the next corner that he is raising bread prices two cents a loaf in order to adjust for an increase in his cost of bread. Or, more likely, the truck driver for the bakery will be the communicator. In any event, before a day or two has gone by, both grocers will sell the bread for the same price. The necessity for price collusion among SB firms in many situations is pointed out in the following paragraph:

> The reason for such collusions is easy to understand. In most instances, the small businessman views his market as inelastic; there is only so much volume that can be done in the territory and lowering price does not increase it sufficiently to offset the loss of margin. So the businessman feels very strongly that he must protect the price structure for the goods he sells. He knows price cutting quickly leads to losses. Thus the price cutter becomes a hated foe. One must understand the strong emotions underlying this matter for they are not to be taken lightly. The businessman's entire life and the welfare of his family are tied up in his business. If it goes under, he is ruined. His life is a shambles.[25]

Price cutting as a marketing strategy (not the same thing as a price reduction) is not often associated with SB firms. And if price cutting is used, it is often secret rather than open price cutting. The simple fact is that most SB firms do not have the financial resources needed to give them staying power to survive the potential price war. SB firms, especially if they know what's good for them, usually don't start price wars. As is noted by Lynn, "When a small firm steps out of line by cutting price, and he is disciplined by larger rivals who match (or perhaps exceed) the cut, he will probably restore price. Price wars are more likely to occur in markets where rivals are more evenly matched."[26] Thus, the SBM may be forced to participate in a price war or suffer the loss of much of his sales volume. However, he should not knowingly "pick a fight with the big boys." What are his alternatives to a price cut by BB or to a price cut by a SB rival and a subsequent price cut by BB rivals? Besides closing the business for a two-week vacation, the SBM can participate but not undercut, let his rivals have the price sensitive share of the market, help to create a climate for ending the price war by the careful choice of public statements and actions, and attempt to determine the cause of the price war in order to arrive at a strategy. Causes may be oversupply, entry of new competitors, the desire of a competitor to increase market share, cost-cutting innovations, and so forth. Whatever the cause, the effects of price cuts and price wars are sometimes fatal to SB. Although a federal court may eventually punish a BB firm for its illegal acts in price cutting, the fatalities of a price war are usually SB firms.

New Product Pricing For SB

New products involve different degrees and kinds of newness. The more unique a new product is, the greater will be the pricing problem and the freedom of action regarding price. However, such freedom of action may be a disadvantage unless the SBM

[25]Richard H. Buskirk and Percy J. Vaughn, Jr., *Managing New Enterprises* (St. Paul: West Publishing Co., 1976), p. 322.
[26]Robert A. Lynn, *Price Policies And Marketing Management* (Homewood, Illinois: Richard D. Irwin, Inc., 1967), p. 64.

plans carefully. For example, pricing analysis should be undertaken in the early stages of product development with the analysis becoming more refined during the successive stages. Price strategy planning for new products will involve all parts of the SB firm. Production and finance executives should participate with marketing executives in order to arrive at the best strategy. New product pricing strategies may change the marketing performance of existing products in both positive and negative ways. It all depends on such factors as price lines, product complements and substitutes, competitive response, customer perceptions, and many others. The complexities of new product pricing may often vary directly with the degree of newness involved.[27]

In addition to the above suggestion, the SBM, especially the SBM who is new to the consumer goods industry, can benefit from applying the somewhat arbitrary "cost rule of thumb." This rule takes into account the chain of discounts between the manufacturing cost and the retail selling price. This rule of thumb, which is based upon experience, states that, ". . . unless a consumer product can be sold at retail for *at least* five times its direct production cost, the chances for making a profit on it are rather slim."[28] If the SBM has a new product and is planning to sell it through the traditional channels of distribution, he should investigate the channels to see what the expectations of middlemen are regarding markups and terms of sale. If the SBM has a very unique product and/or is appealing to a very specific target market through nontraditional channels of distribution, he still needs information on middlemen expectations. However, such information will probably be less specific and less reliable than it otherwise would be. Whatever the marketing program, its costs must be covered.

Pricing During Inflation

Inflation might be described as the 14 ounce box of cookies that used to be a one pound box selling for 39¢ now becoming a 12 ounce box selling for 69¢—and they don't taste as good as they used to. As the cost floor rises, the SBM must raise prices if profits are to continue. When and how he does this are important parts of his marketing mix during inflation. Some of the techniques are to eliminate deductions and discounts from the "book" or list price, eliminate deals, eliminate so-called "free" services, and eliminate price quotes in favor of deferred pricing systems based upon expected or actual future costs. Pricing at the time of delivery (rather than time of sale) has become more popular in the industrial market. Price reductions, if and when they do occur, are given a more temporary nature by being given as rebates which can be eliminated at any time. In the consumer market, today's special sale price is yesterday's regular price, and the consumer is urged to "buy now before anticipated price increases go into effect."

For the SBM, inflation means more funds needed to support the same amount of physical inventory, higher expenses, and a higher replacement cost for inventory that may show up as paper profits, depending on the inventory valuation method used. In many ways, inflation makes pricing a variable which deserves more of the time of the SBM. Individually, he cannot do much about inflation; but he can take its effects into account in planning his own marketing strategy, especially his pricing strategy.

---

[27]Stephen J. Welsh, "A Planned Approach To New Product Pricing," *Modern Marketing Thought* ed. J. Howard Westing and Gerald Albaum (New York: Macmillan Publishing Co., Inc., 1975), p. 377.
   [28]Buskirk and Vaughn, p. 315.

How To Make Price Changes

The key to making effective price changes is to properly identify the effects of such changes on each of the parties involved. Customers, resellers, rivals, suppliers, and others will be affected in different ways. The SBM must also assess the consequences of the price change in terms of the firm's objectives. Among the items which can be varied when making a price change are timing, publicity, and the form of the announcement.[29]

A price increase may be more acceptable when new models come out. On the other hand, a price cut may be reserved for later on when the newness has worn off a bit. The advance announcement of a price hike as of a certain date (e.g., January 1) will give different parties time to adjust. The timing of price changes for the SB retailer is especially critical with fashion and seasonal merchandise. Too early a markdown amounts to a price-cutting strategy. Too late a markdown is almost totally ineffective. The amount of the markdown is also critical. In general, the way to minimize the total dollar markdowns is to take a substantial markdown the first time in order to eliminate the need for further markdowns. Added markups should always be taken as soon as possible on the premise that if an added markup is warranted, the conditions that call for the added markup may not last forever.

Publicity, or the lack of it, regarding a proposed price change can alter the effects among the various parties involved. This is especially true if such practices as guarantees against price declines and advance announcement of price changes are common in an industry. Although a BB firm may utilize advance announcement of a price increase (or a forecast of a price increase) in order to see if competitors are willing to go along with the increase, this does not usually apply to SB, since SB is seldom a price leader. Trade relations, however, are extremely important for SB. Thus, letting the rest of the channel know what is going to happen does make a difference. At times, such as when a small increase is to be made or when a quiet price cut is desired, open publicity will be avoided. Of course, secrets are hard to keep. The chief merit of a secret price or deal may be that it doesn't remain a secret very long, at least not from everyone.

Among the forms of price change announcement, a change in discounts is among the easiest to implement successfully. Both the amount of the discount and the persons to whom it applies can be changed. Changing the prices of extras rather than the price of the basic product may also be very effective. Also, quantity and quality changes in the product itself have been a way of life, as most price changes have been in the upward direction. Whatever price changes BB makes usually affect many SB firms. The alert SBM can often anticipate such changes by paying attention to the trade press. This will give him the necessary time to plan the timing, publicity, and form of his own price changes.

Individualized Prices and Group Prices

Should the SBM attempt to individualize prices to very small market segments, and perhaps even to individual customers? With bidding and negotiated contracts, this is what takes place in both BB and SB. But what about the SB retailer? Should the SB retail

[29]Lynn, pp. 185–189.

furniture store, clothing store, paint store, drug store, and so on have so much price flexibility that very few customers pay the "marked" price and practically all customers get a discount, the amount of which depends upon individual bargaining power? Such discount schemes may be worked on a group basis as well. A major employer in a community, a student organization, a union, a bank, or any other organization representing a large group of consumers may form a group of merchants who agree to give discounts to the individual consumers of the organization. An examination of the participating merchants in these discount schemes usually reveals that most are SB. In fact, BB retailers are noticeably absent. They simply don't have the flexibility to administer such pricing programs even if such programs were compatible with their mass merchandising and one-price images. The SB retailer does have such flexibility. Whether or not he should use it is another question.

The key factor in successfully using both individual and group price concessions is to gain additional business by so doing, and, at the same time, to retain the loyal support of customers not receiving the price concessions. One way to do this is to maintain relative secrecy. Another is to be open but very selective as to what groups receive publicity about the discounts. A third method may be to give some kind of a deal to all customers and make them all think they got the best deal. Whatever method is used, the SBM should be certain to maintain a rather tight control over the administration of the program, and he should always take care to at least give the appearance of being fair to all in his pricing. Fairness is as much a part of America as apple pie. Price bargaining, if properly done, gives the customer an opportunity to *participate* with the SBM in the setting of price. Participation can be very important in building customer loyalty.

Changing Pricing Strategy Over The PLC

In an appendix to Chapter 10, the product life-cycle (PLC) was explained. Prices generally tend to decline over the PLC, at least until the decline stage of the product, when many competitors may exit. Cost reductions during the growth stage may make a large portion of a market very price competitive, especially in the maturity stage. Profits will also tend to be low for many firms in the maturity stage.

The SBM should consider the effects of the PLC when planning his pricing strategy. If he is unable to do a good job of target marketing by the time the product reaches the growth stage, pricing is likely to be a problem in the future.

Using Temporary Price Reductions

In addition to the normal discounts which may be available to the trade, and sometimes to consumers (such as cumulative and noncumulative quantity discounts, trade or functional discounts, seasonal discounts, and cash discounts), the SBM does have some other price-related tools which are of a more temporary or tactical nature. Among these are: (a) a direct price reduction for a limited period, (b) promotional and display allowances; (c) combination offers of an old and new product; (d) introductory price offers; (e) "free" deals, such as "buy ten and get one free"; (f) coupons; (g) premiums; (h) full-line bonuses; and so forth. The use of such temporary price incentives can be very productive or counterproductive, depending on how it is done. The cost-benefits ratio can vary considerably. The SBM should therefore use the above in a limited way, according to a definite plan that is consistent with the firm's overall pricing strategy.

Ten Suggestions For SB

To conclude this portion of the chapter, let us mention that the SBA publishes a pricing checklist which may be helpful to the SBM.[30] Another list which recognizes that several pricing differences exist between BB and SB is the following list of ten suggestions for the SBM:

1. Never assume that any price established on a product is necessarily correct, or that the product is priced "right."
2. Be willing to experiment with prices and to change them to an extent that is not inconsistent with company policy or likely to affect customer goodwill.
3. Try to avoid head-on price competition with larger companies or others who are better able to achieve a lower pricing structure.
4. Study markets, products, and people continuously and carefully to determine what will work, under what conditions it will succeed, and how such can be incorporated into the goals of the organization.
5. Be realistic as to price changes of products and services over time, and the necessity of setting a pricing structure which allows for reductions and the movement of the goods at the end of seasonal periods. Prepare to meet the pricing of competitors from time to time. Apply the idea of balancing or compensating over the entire range of products and services offered to develop and maintain some average gross margin figure which is consistent with the needs of the business.
6. Constantly utilize service to achieve competitive advantage. Nothing will support a price as well as having it accompanied with service. Many small business services can be provided with very little cost. In fact, a smile, knowing a customer's name, some conversation, and showing an interest in customers may be all the service that is needed to win and hold them.
7. Make use of the flexibility available to most businesses. React to changes and make adjustments. Capitalize on developing opportunties and fill voids that have been created, or in some other way prepare for new opportunities and move quickly when they present themselves. Later, if larger competitors move in, or "cutthroat" competition develops, the opportunist is mentally prepared to move out of his or her present operation into something else.
8. Examine all phases of the business constantly in regard to the effect that pricing has on the operation. Examine product sales by individual product, by departments, by seasons of the year, by customers and class, by amount of sales transactions, and any other yardstick that makes sense. In other words, be a leader and an innovator rather than a follower, who must do business on somebody else's terms.
9. Analyze the relationship that credit and installment selling have on the pricing structure. Many times a price is meaningless unless the item or service is available for sale over time or on credit terms.
10. Use your customers as a sounding board to find out what they think about your prices and also your competitors' prices.[31]

---

[30] Joseph D. O'Brien, "A Pricing Checklist For Managers," *Small Marketers Aids*, No. 105 (Washington: Small Business Administration, 1972).
[31] Donald P. Stegall, Lawrence L. Steinmetz, and John B. Kline, *Managing The Small Business* (Homewood, Illinois: Richard D. Irwin, Inc., 1976), pp. 418–419.

From personal experience, most of us are aware of differences in pricing practices of such SB firms as the bicycle shop versus the convenient food store or the furniture store versus a food vending machine. Somewhat less obvious to us as consumers are the different pricing practices that tend to exist among SB manufacturers, retailers, wholesalers, and service firms. Many of these differences also exist among BB firms of the same types. Despite such differences in actual pricing practices, the process of pricing strategy formulation outlined in this chapter is equally applicable to all SB types. The SB firm types are actually more similar than different once the surface is breached and the underlying pricing process is investigated.

In the next few paragraphs, we are looking at surface differences as reflected in the pricing practices of SB manufacturers, retailers, wholesalers, and service firms. A great diversity of pricing practices also exists within all four of these groups. Our examples above pointed out some of the diversity among SB retailers. The same is true for each of the other classifications of SB firm types.

SB manufacturers. As we have previously stated, all firms (right or wrong) tend to be cost-oriented in their pricing. This is true of SB manufacturers, many of whom will use some cost-oriented formula which incorporates materials cost, direct labor cost, overhead, and a profit. Transportation cost, whether absorbed directly by the manufacturer or his customers, will be a consideration in pricing if the SB manufacturer wishes to sell in more than local markets. Geographic market coverage by manufacturers, even SB manufacturers, is often much greater than the geographic market coverage of other SB types. The more opportunity the SB manufacturer has (and uses) to differentiate his products, the more discretion he has over prices. Generally, SB manufacturers tend to have more discretion than do other SB types. However, this is not always true, as the other types do have many opportunities to differentiate in the services rather than the goods portion of the total product.

SB retailers. Pricing practices of SB retailers are often influenced by the fact that the retailer carries a very large number of items. With hundreds or thousands of items being carried, the retailer often groups products for pricing decision purposes. Rather than make decisions about each item (of which only a small quantity of sales might be made), traditional markups are often applied to entire product groups. Competitively, retailers look only to local market price and service competition. Some common methods of pricing which the SB retailer may employ separately or in combination are: (a) using a standard or flexible markup which may be calculated on cost or selling price, but is usually cost-oriented in any event (see appendix in this chapter); (b) selling at the suggested retail selling price as suggested by the manufacturer or wholesaler; (c) following the leader pricing of other BB and SB retailers in the local market; (d) having very competitive prices on at least some products; and (e) using clearance prices to move otherwise slow-moving merchandise.[32]

---

[32]Hal B. Pickle and Royce L. Abrahamson, *Small Business Management* (Santa Barbara: John Wiley & Sons, Inc., 1976), pp. 371–374.

256

SB wholesalers.   Less freedom in pricing decisions is typical of SB wholesalers. One reason is that the manufacturers supplying the SB wholesalers may exercise, or at least attempt to exercise, quite a bit of control over the prices at which wholesalers sell to retailers. The amount of price control the manufacturer exercises over the wholesaler usually is proportionate with the exclusiveness of the distribution rights of the wholesaler for a given geographic market.

When a wholesaler does not have an exclusive on a product, he must be price competitive with other wholesalers in the geographic area. Those wholesalers who handle many products face the same problems as retailers, in that cost allocations and profit calculations for individual items are difficult and expensive. Standard group markup on cost often results. Specialized wholesalers serving SB manufacturers may sometimes have great flexibility regarding price due to the lack of involvement of the SB manufacturer in nearly all marketing activities.

SB service firms.   Pricing by SB service firms is often tied to an hourly rate based upon labor costs. Occasionally, as in the case of emergency service (such as automobile starting at inconvenient hours), an additional charge may reflect the "all the traffic will bear" philosophy. Normally, price is calculated by taking either the actual or standard time needed to perform the service, multiplying by an hourly rate, and adding to this a list price for materials used. From a competitive point of view, the SB service firms may feel compelled to adhere to prevailing price schedules in the locality. SB service firms which are franchisee members of a franchise organization may have little or no control over the prices they charge. A difficulty in service firm pricing is that customers do not understand the allocations (which are usually somewhat arbitrary) of indirect costs to each service job. Some service firms feel that flat rate pricing helps to solve this problem.

The above pricing practices show some diversity among SB types. It should be emphasized again that pricing practices are *not* the same thing as pricing strategy. The SBM may easily understand and follow one of the above pricing practices, even in the absence of a pricing strategy. What has been advocated in this chapter is that the SBM first formulate a pricing strategy as part of his overall marketing strategy. The selection of pricing practices in order to implement that strategy will then be a much easier and more meaningful activity.

BIBLIOGRAPHY

Books

ALBAUM, GERALD. *Price Formulation.* Tucson, Arizona: The University of Arizona, 1965.

BUSKIRK, RICHARD H., AND VAUGHN, PERCY J. *Managing New Enterprises.* St. Paul: West Publishing Co., 1976.

HARPER, DONALD V. *Price Policy And Procedure.* New York: Harcourt, Brace & World, Inc., 1966.

KOTLER, PHILIP. *Marketing Management: Analysis, Planning, And Control.* Englewood Cliffs, New Jersey: Prentice-Hall, Inc., 1972.

LYNN, ROBERT A. *Price Policies And Marketing Management.* Homewood, Illinois: Richard D. Irwin, Inc., 1967.

OXENFELDT, ALFRED R. *Pricing: For Marketing Executives.* San Francisco: Wadsworth Publishing Company, Inc., 1961.

——*Pricing Strategies.* New York: AMACOM, 1975.

PHELPS, D. MAYNARD, AND WESTING, J. HOWARD. *Marketing Management.* Homewood, Illinois: Richard D. Irwin, Inc., 1968.

PICKLE, HAL B., AND ABRAHAMSON, ROYCE L. *Small Business Management.* Santa Barbara: John Wiley & Sons, Inc., 1976.

RATHMELL, JOHN M. *Managing The Marketing Function: Concepts, Analysis, and Application.* New York: John Wiley & Sons, Inc., 1969.

STEGALL, DONALD P., STEINMETZ, LAWRENCE L., AND KLINE, JOHN B. *Managing The Small Business.* Homewood, Illinois: Richard D. Irwin, Inc., 1976.

Articles and Periodicals

BROOKS, DOUGLAS G. "Cost-Oriented Pricing: A Realistic Solution To A Complicated Problem," *Journal of Marketing,* 39, No. (April 1975), 72–74.

CRISSEY, W. J. E., AND BOEWADT, ROBERT. "Pricing in Perspective," *Sales Management,* June 15, 1971, p. 44.

FRY, JOSEPH N., AND McDOUGALL, GORDON H. "Consumer Appraisal of Retail Price Advertisements," *Journal of Marketing,* 38, No. 3 (July 1974), 64–67.

JOHNSON, JAMES D., AND BOONE, LOUIS E. "Farewell to Fair Trade," *MSU Business Topics,* 24, No. 2 (Spring 1976), 22–29.

LENNON, VICTOR A. "What Is The Best Selling Price?" *Management Aids For Small Manufacturers,* No. 193 Washington: Small Business Administration, 1972, pp. 1–8.

O'BRIEN, JOSEPH D. "A Pricing Checklist For Managers," *Small Marketers Aids,* No. 105. Washington: Small Business Administration, 1972, pp. 1–4.

OXENFELDT, ALFRED R. "A Decision-making Structure for Price Decisions," *Journal of Marketing,* 37, No. 1 (January 1973), 48–53.

——"Multi-stage Approach to Pricing," in Ben M. Enis and Keith K. Cox, eds. *Marketing Classics.* 2d Ed. Boston: Allyn and Bacon, Inc., 1973, pp. 387–402.

——"Product Line Pricing," in Eugene J. Kelley and William Lazer, eds. *Managerial Marketing: Policies, Strategies, And Decisions.* Homewood, Illinois: Richard D. Irwin, Inc., 1973, pp. 387–399.

UDELL, JON G. "How Important Is Pricing in Competitive Strategy?" *Journal of Marketing,* 28, No. 1 (January 1964), 45–48.

WELSH, STEPHEN J. "A Planned Approach To New Product Pricing," in J. Howard Westing and Gerald Albaum, eds. *Modern Marketing Thought.* New York: Macmillan Publishing Co., 1975, pp. 367–378.

APPENDIX
MARKUP:
A SIMULATED SELF-ADMINISTERED EXERCISE
IN PRICING FOR PROFIT*

*Kathleen Brannen is the co-author of this appendix.

PREFACE AND PURPOSE

The following simulation of retailing reality is a self-administered game which can be played with or without the use of a computer. If a computer is not used, the enclosed planning forms may be helpful. If a computer is used, the complete instructions for putting the game on the computer and for playing the game are given in the instructor's manual.

The purpose of the game is to provide the student with experience in using markups on cost and on selling price in order to determine what selling prices should be to earn a desired gross profit. The game deals at both the per item level and at the total department level. Simply stated, the markup for the total department is the per item markup weighted by the sales of each item.

Each player plays against himself. The game is divided into ten weeks. Each week is independent of all other weeks. Per item costs are given for each week but do often vary from week to week. For the purposes of the game, costs and selling prices do *not* vary within a given week. This is an assumption used for simplifying the structure of the game. Limiting the number of products to twenty is another simplifying assumption. One of the twenty items is featured each week as the "weekly advertised special" or (WAS). For this item (which is different each week), the sales at the regular price will be zero for that week. Expected weekly sales of each item vary according to such factors as total store sales, product quality, competition, holidays, weather, prices, and so forth. For the purposes of the game, all factors affecting sales (except price) will be incorporated into a figure called "expected weekly sales." The rationale for expected weekly sales will be given in the "Weekly Planning Report," which is a nonquantitative merchandising tool given to the player for each week. For the noncomputer players, "expected weekly volume" will vary according to selling price by a method given below. For computer players, "expected weekly volume" will vary inversely with price, but the formula for variation will not be given, since the computer player may test several selling prices before setting his price. Unit selling prices may be in pounds or by count and are given. This does not affect the computations. The selling price of the weekly advertised special must be at or near cost.

The discussion prior to the actual beginning of the game gives some of the flavor of the business. The game is a simulation of a produce department of a supermarket in a small midwestern community. Figures mentioned in the discussion are broad general guidelines.

BACKGROUND OF THE BUSINESS

Pat had just finished up his final exams for the Spring semester and was getting ready to load the car to take all his gear home for summer vacation. Of course, summer vacation was really not all vacation, since Pat was working his way through college by working summers in his father's supermarket. He had a summer job whether he wanted it or not.

As he was loading the car, he began wondering which part of the store he would work in this summer. It seemed that he always ended up managing the produce department. And since the produce department was a one-person department, managing the produce department meant managing the heads of lettuce, stalks of celery, bunches of grapes, and bags of oranges. It was a lot of hard work, but it was even more difficult to make a profit at it during the summertime. Pat often thought he should take a semester off during the winter months. Oh well, maybe he'd be lucky this summer and be assigned stocking shelves in the grocery department. It seemed that every summer, just as summer vacation was about to begin, something happened to the regular produce manager. One year he quit. Another year the produce manager was promoted to assistant store manager. Another produce manager ran off to California with a checker and never came back. It seemed that they always managed to leave about three days before summer vacation started. Pat knew the current produce manager quite well and could think of no reason that George would be changing from his current duties.

Pat and his roommate said goodby to each other after having made plans to get together at the lake over the fourth of July weekend. In a couple of hours he would be home. On the way home the thought crossed his mind that perhaps he should stop by the store just to make sure that George was still there. No, he decided, if I stop there this afternoon, I'll end up working tonight. I'll just go home and talk with Mom for awhile and then I'll rather leisurely unpack my stuff. That way maybe I'll even have the evening free to do something. I wonder who is back in town.

When Pat arrived home, nobody was there. There was a note on the kitchen table. It said: "Dear Pat, George quit to go into partnership with his brother-in-law in a small store in northern Iowa. Dad is really short-handed on help until school is out. I am at the store trimming lettuce. Grab yourself a quick sandwich and come on down. Love, Mom." As he ate his sandwich (without lettuce), Pat vowed, with the same kind of enthusiam with which Charlie Brown begins each baseball season, that this year was going to be different—this year he was really going to rack up those gross profit dollars.

It's Tough To Make A Profit In The Summertime

The grocery business is a very competitive business all the time, but it's especially tough to make a profit in the produce department during the summer months. Several factors account for this difficulty. Spoilage is higher during the summer. Sales of some products are reduced when the home gardener is harvesting his own crop. Prices tend to drift lower for many products as the season progresses. And more labor is required on some of the low unit value bulky products such as watermelons and potatoes.

Rules of Thumb
for Operating a Produce Department

Scientific management is often replaced by workable rules of thumb in the management of small businesses. Such is the case with the produce department in the supermarket owned by Pat's father. Here are some of the rules:

1. Department sales—the desired level of departmental sales as a percentage of total store sales is 7%. In other words, if total store sales were $30,000 per week, total sales for the produce department would, ideally, be $2,100 per week. For some reason, this ideal was not very often reached. Produce department sales as a percent of total store sales tended to run about 6% to 7%. Once in a while the seven percent goal would be reached or exceeded if a high volume produce item was on sale. For example, if watermelons were used as a loss leader, 500 watermelons at 79¢ each would boost sales by almost $400.00. Loss leaders however, did have an adverse effect on the gross margin percentage for the department.

2. Departmental expenses—the expenses of the department did not tend to vary significantly. In effect, as far as the department manager was concerned, expenses could be ignored in the pricing of products. This is not to say that expenses were not carefully watched, because they were. Expenses were simply rather constant and could therefore be taken as a given. For example, if very accurate records were maintained, labor expense could possibly be slightly higher during the summer months. However, in actual fact, labor expenses were approximately the same during the summer, but the produce manager simply had to work a little harder. On occasion, he would borrow a few hours of assistance from the grocery department in order to accomplish a major task such as unloading a truckload of watermelons. Charges were not assigned for such borrowing.

3. Markups—in order to achieve the desired net profit for the produce department, with its given expenses and a reasonable allowance for spoilage and markdowns, the rule of thumb for the average markup for the total department is a markup percentage of 33⅓% of the selling price. This is the same as a 50% markup on cost. Methods of converting markups from cost to selling price and from selling price to cost will be given later.

4. Spoilage—spoilage does vary according to the season of the year. The goal is to limit spoilage to no more than 3–5% of sales.

5. Markdowns for sale items—the department average gross margin of 33⅓% of the selling price is a weighted average of all items sold by the department. It includes a weighting for some items that are sold near or below cost as advertised specials. No separate accounting is kept of such advertised specials, and the lack of gross margin on

these items directly affects departmental gross margin. In other words, this lack of gross margin is not charged separately as an advertising expense.

6. Net profit—the desired net profit for the department is not a part of the game.

7. Physical inventory—a physical inventory is taken each Monday morning of all merchandise in the department. This inventory is taken at retail prices. The cost percentage is then applied to the physical inventory in order to determine the cost value of the inventory. By retail price is meant current retail selling price of that day on which the physical inventory is taken. Thus, if the new retail selling price for lettuce is now 19¢ per head rather than 25¢ per head as it was last week, when the retailer purchased the lettuce, the inventory price is 19¢ per head. In this way, inventory depreciation and inventory appreciation takes place from week to week according to changes in the market. By taking weekly physical inventories, changes in the inventory valuation are most closely reflected during the week in which market prices changed. Retail prices do, however, change at any time during the week, not just on Monday morning.

For our simulation game, some of the above rules of thumb will not be used, since the game begins anew each week. Thus, inventory valuations are not a part of the game. The game also assumes daily delivery, with no out-of-stock conditions and no excess inventory upon which markdowns need be taken. In the game, the player deals with the pricing of twenty products plus an advertised special. Costs are given. Prices do affect volume somewhat. The game can be played with or without a computer. Complete details of the game follow.

DISCUSSION OF MARKUP CALCULATIONS

Markup is the difference between the cost of a product and the selling price. It is a planning concept, as opposed to gross margin or gross profit, which reflect what actually happened after markdowns, shortages, spoilage, and so forth. Our concern here is with markup. Another way of describing *markup* is by stating that it is what the business adds to the cost in order to determine the selling price.

Markup is a basic pricing tool used in retailing. An understanding of markup is essential to successful merchandising. Although markup tables, markup wheels, and computers may be available to shortcut the computations, the need remains to understand what is behind the computations. Markup percentages and stock turnover are often inversely related. That is, the higher the markup percentage, the lower the rate of stock turnover; and conversely, the lower the markup percentage, the higher the rate of stock turnover. *Stock turnover,* or *turnover,* or *stock turn* may be defined as the number of times during a given period (usually a year) that the average inventory is sold. The stock turnover calculation, which can be made at cost, selling price, or in units, is not discussed here. Its link with markup in determining total dollar gross profit is most important. Simply stated, the more units of product we sell (a part of turnover) at a stated markup, the greater the total dollar markup will be. And if more units of produce are sold at an even higher markup, the total dollar markup will be even greater.

In our discussion, we will use some symbols, or abbreviations. They are:

$$C = Cost$$
$$SP = Selling\ Price$$
$$MU = Markup$$
$$\% = Percent\ or\ percentage$$
$$\$ = Dollar(s)$$
$$> = Greater\ than$$

As we stated above, by definition:

$$\$MU = \$SP - \$C$$

This could be stated in two other forms by moving the equivalent positions around. These two other forms are:

$$\$C = \$SP - \$MU$$

and

$$\$SP = \$C + \$MU$$

Markups are frequently stated in percentages. That is, the $MU is stated as a proportion or percentage of something else, such as $C or $SP. While MU may be expressed as a percentage of either or both C or SP, it is customary and conventional to express MU as a % of SP *unless specifically stated otherwise.* However, not everyone follows this convention.

It is sometimes desirable to convert % MU on C to an equivalent value expressed as % MU on SP. Conversely, it is sometimes desirable to convert % MU on SP to an equivalent value expressed as % MU on C. As mentioned above, such conversions can be performed by using tables, wheels, and computers. Conversion is also possible by the use of the following formulas. The choice of which formula to use depends on which items are known and which item (only one) is unknown.

In order to obtain % MU on SP, we use any one of the following three formulas, depending on the form of our known information.

By definition: % MU on SP = $MU/$SP
By substitution: % MU on SP = $MU/($C + $MU)
In percentages: % MU on SP = % MU on C/(100% + % MU on C)

The first equation is simply $MU as a proportion or percent of $SP. In other words, we divide $MU by $SP. In the second equation, we are merely substituting in the denominator, since we know from earlier consideration that $SP = $C + $MU. The third equation (which is analogous in its structured format to the second equation) is used if we have knowns that are percentages. This third equation is used in converting a % MU on C to a % MU on SP. In all three forms of the equation, the answer will appear as a fraction or a decimal. The percent form is attained by multiplying the answer by (100%/1). For example $\frac{1}{3}$ = .333 = 33⅓%.

In order to obtain % MU on C, we use any one of the following three formulas, depending on the form of our known information.

By definition: % MU on C = $MU/$C
By substitution: % MU on C = $MU/($SP - $MU)
In percentages: % MU on C = % MU on SP/(100% - % MU on SP)

As with our previous set of equations for converting the other way, the first equation above is simply $MU as a proportion or percent of $C. In the second equation, we are merely substituting in the denominator, since we know from earlier consideration that $C = $SP - $MU. The third equation (which is analogous in its structured format to the second equation) is used if we have knowns that are percentages. The third equation is used in converting a % MU on SP to a % MU on C. In all three forms of the equation, the answer will appear as a fraction or decimal. The percent form is attained by multiplying the answer by (100%/1). For example: $\frac{1}{3}$ = .333 = 33⅓%.

Try a few simple problems.

1. If a retailer buys a product for 50¢ and sells it for 75¢, what is:

A. $MU	A. 25¢
B. % MU on C	B. 50%
C. % MU on SP	C. 33⅓%

2. If a retailer buys a product for 48¢ and sells it for 75¢, what is:

A. $MU	A.	¢	You
B. % MU on C	B.	%	Answer
C. % MU on SP	C.	%	Here

3. What are the equivalents for the following percentages?

% MU on C		% MU on SP
A.	100%	%
B.	42%	%
C.	%	25%
D.	%	38%

The reasonableness (but not the absolute correctness) of your answers may be checked by remembering the following simple rules:

1. % MU on C can be > 100%.

2. % MU on SP *cannot* be > 100%.

3. % MU on C is > equivalent % MU on SP.

The following brief table shows, in fraction and percentage form, some widely used equivalents. Note that the numerator of all fractions is 1, and that for equivalent percentages the denominator of the fraction is always 1 greater for SP than for C. This is true because SP is greater than C.

INSTRUCTIONS FOR PLAYING MARKUP WITHOUT THE COMPUTER

MARKUP is actually ten games rather than one game. It is the same game played ten times, once for each week of the ten week summer. Costs and units sold vary from week to week, depending on the forces of supply and demand. Each week is independent from

Equivalents			
on C		*on SP*	
%	Fraction	Fraction	%
100%	1/1	1/2	50%
50%	1/2	1/3	33 1/3%
33 1/3%	1/3	1/4	25%
25%	1/4	1/5	20%
20%	1/5	1/6	16 2/3%
16 2/3%	1/6	1/7	14 2/7%
14 2/7%	1/7	1/8	12 1/2%

every other week. The player is faced with a new set of costs (given), a new demand for each product (a function of price and the environment), and a new environment on both the supply and demand sides. The environment is described briefly in the *Weekly Planning Report*. In playing MARKUP, it is anticipated that the player will learn more about markup from one week to the next, and that he will be able to use his increased understanding of markup in order to achieve better performance. However, the measure of performance is strictly judgmental. In other words, performance from one week to the next is not directly comparable. The main purpose is to *understand* how markup works with sales to produce item dollar markup and total markup dollars for the produce department.

Selling price (SP) is the principal input by the player into the game. This is, the player is to determine the selling prices for all items in the produce department. Selling prices are given in units such as pounds, dozen, per bag, and so on; and these units must be the same as those used for costs. The twenty products for our produce department are ten nonseasonal or staple products and ten seasonal products. An actual produce department would have many other products. The products are shown below with their code names and their units of measure.

In addition to this list of twenty items, one of the seasonal items each week will be designated (given) as the *weekly advertised special* (WAS). The price for the WAS must be at or only slightly above cost in order to avoid a severe penalty in terms of lower departmental sales. All prices, including the price of the WAS, should be above cost. All prices should also be reasonable in order to avoid penalties. *The Weekly Planning Report* suggests possible pricing strategies for various items for different weeks of the game. For ease of calculation, no price should exceed 99¢. (The 99¢ limit is imposed on the computer version of the game; and a price above 99¢ would be unreasonable for the present version also because of the units of measure used.)

In selecting prices, you may think in terms of different units (see PCH and CAN as used for the WAS in the *Weekly Planning Report* for weeks 7 and 9, for example), but, for the

Nonseasonal or Staple		
1. lettuce	LET	Head
2. cabbage	CAB	Lb.
3. carrots	CRT	1 Lb. Bag
4. celery	CEL	Stalk
5. oranges	ORA	Lb.
6. onions	ONI	Lb.
7. bananas	BAN	Lb.
8. radishes	RAD	Large Bag
9. peppers	PEP	Lb.
10. yams	YAM	Lb.
Seasonal		
1. tomatoes	TOM	Lb.
2. strawberries	STR	Pint Box
3. potatoes	POT	Lb.
4. watermelons	WAT	Lb.
5. sweetcorn	CRN	Ear
6. grapes	GRA	Lb.
7. peaches	PCH	Lb.
8. cantaloupe	CAN	Each
9. cucumbers	CUM	Each
10. apples	APL	Lb.

purposes of the game, your price-setting must be in the units given. For the sake of realism, you'll probably want to use psychological pricing, such as odd pricing—by selling for such prices as 29¢, 33¢, 35¢, 39¢, and so on, rather than for such prices as 30¢, 32¢, 36¢, and so on. However, the game will accept even or nonpsychological prices even if real consumers would not. But odd prices might make it more fun and challenging. From week to week, price consistency on some items such as staples adds realism. Look at cost trend information over the ten week period in order to see whether or not an item should have price consistency.

Expected weekly sales (EWS) is given in units each week for every product. This is the number of units of each product that will most likely be sold for the week. It is essentially the same thing as unit sales and may be regarded as *sales. Selling price* per unit, multiplied by the number of units sold, is equal to dollar sales for that product. The summation of dollar sales for all products is equal to total departmental sales for the week. EWS for each product depends on the selling price of each product and on how much markup (as a % of SP) that selling price contains. Generally, the higher the markup, the lower will be the EWS or unit sales for the product. In general the converse is also true. That is, the lower the markup, the higher will be the EWS or unit sales for the product. This inverse relationship between markup percentage and unit sales is, however, not necessarily proportioned. In other words, one does not necessarily go up as much as the other goes down. For each product, for each week of the game, five ranges of unit sales are given in the EWS table for that week. These five ranges of unit sales are for each of five ranges of markup percentages for each product. The markup ranges are 0% to 15%, 16% to 25%, 26% to 40%, 41% to 50%, and 51% or more. For purposes of the game, a %MU on SP greater than 66⅔% will equal zero sales. All these markups are in terms of %MU on SP. Quite often, selling prices with markups in the 25% to 40% range will be considered average or normal pricing policy. However, information from price testing and from the *Weekly Planning Report* may sometimes make other markup ranges more profitable.

Cost is given. It is given in cents per unit for every product. Cost does vary somewhat from week to week. For seasonal items, the variation tends to be greater and usually reaches a low point when the seasonal crop is at its peak of harvest, that is, when supply is greatest. Cost for all items is given for all ten weeks in the *Cost Table*. These are the only cost data to be used. We have ignored such problems as transportation and discounts, which in real life would figure into the calculation of cost. If it makes you more comfortable, assume that these items have been figured in to arrive at the costs in the *Cost Table*.

Steps to follow in playing the game are given below. As you become more familiar with markup, you may wish to rearrange the order to suit yourself. You may also wish to back up occasionally to repeat steps. You should begin with week #1 and proceed in chronological order through week #10. This makes the total game more interesting and permits you to look at cost trend information for products over the ten week period. However, remember that each week is independent of every other week. In other words, each week is a new game.

Step 1—Player forms. Before beginning the game for each week, make sure you have all the necessary materials. A scratch pad and/or a pocket calculator may prove to be very useful. In addition, you should have:

1. A blank player form* for each week
2. *The Weekly Planning Report* for the appropriate week
3. *The Cost Table*
4. *The Expected Weekly Sales (EWS) Table* for the appropriate week.

---

*Use a copy machine to make additional player forms. Other portions of this game may not be reproduced in any form without the expressed, written permission of the publisher.

Step 2—Cost.   From the *Cost Table*, enter the cost for each product on your blank player form. Cost data should be entered under the column titled cost (c).

Step 3—Weekly Planning Report.   Study this report to help you formulate your pricing strategy for the week. Look for clues in this report which will affect both prices and units sold.

Step 4—Pricing.   Begin to set prices for each of the products. You may experiment with different prices or you may simply follow a rule of thumb, such as marking all items up by 33⅓% of SP (except for the WAS, which is at or near cost). In any event, after you have recorded your selling price on the player form, *STICK WITH IT* for the weekly game. Record your price for each item on the player form in the "SP" selling price column.

Step 5—$MU Per Unit.   You should now calculate the dollar (cents) markup per unit. This easy calculation for each produce item is simply $MU = $SP − $C. Record the $MU per unit in the column called $MU per unit.

Step 6—%MU on SP.   You are now ready to calculate the percentage markup on selling price for each item. Be sure you use the correct formula. By looking at the %MU on SP for each item, and for all items, you should begin to get the idea that some items are going to produce more markup dollars than other items. If you established your prices in step 4 above by using %MU on C (since you didn't know selling price before you established it), you may be able to check your %MU on SP figures by using approximate conversions.

Step 7—EWS.   Estimated weekly sales (in units) can now be obtained from the *EWS Table.* Be sure you enter the correct EWS figure in the EWS column of your player form. Also, be sure you have the *EWS Table* for the correct week.

Step 8—Sales.   Sales for each product can be determined for the week. Sales is equal to $SP × EWS. Record sales in the column called Sales. Do this for all products, including the weekly advertised special (WAS). Total this column. This total is your departmental sales for the week. Record this total at the bottom of the sales column.

Step 9—$MU per product.   For each of the products, you are now able to calculate the total dollars of markup. This calculation can be done by at least two methods: (a) Multiply the %MU on SP for each product by the total sales of each respective product; or (b) Multiply the $MU per unit for each product by the number of units (EWS) of each respective product sold for the week. Enter the answers after each product in the $MU per product column. The total of this column is the total $MU of the produce department for the week. Enter this total.

Step 10—Departmental %MU on sales.   The percentage markup for the overall produce department for the week is a weighted average of the products sold. We have already done this weighted averaging in the above steps. Calculate the departmental %MU on sales by dividing total departmental sales (bottom of sales column as determined in step 8) *into* total $MU of the department (bottom of $MU per product column as determined in step 9). The resulting percentage is %MU on sales for the entire department for the week. Be careful not to reverse your figures when dividing.

Step 11—Follow-up.   Reread the *Weekly Planning Report*, evaluate your pricing, and then record your comments under #4 on the *Weekly Planning Report*. Your evaluation is as important as what you actually did.

Week___   **PLAYER FORM**

Code	Cost	SP	$MU per Unit	%MU on SP	EWS in Units	Sales in $	$MU per Product
LET							
CAB							
CRT							
CEL							
ORA							
ONI							
BAN							
RAD							
PEP							
YAM							
TOM							
STR							
POT							
WAT							
CRN							
GRA							
PCH							
CAN							
CUM							
APL							
WAS							

Column total
Dept. %MU on Sales___ %

Week # 1 Weekly Planning Report

1. *Weekly advertised special* (WAS) should be tomatoes. After a period of poor supply, tomatoes are now in good supply at much lower cost from our southern growing regions. Cost is 28¢ per pound. Advertise them at 29¢ per pound for almost no profit (or some loss

after spoilage). Look for complementary salad items to make up for the lack of profit on tomatoes.

2. *Crop report* from wholesaler shows lettuce quality to be excellent at a cost of 20¢ per head. In a special display with tomatoes, we may be able to get some real profit on lettuce this week. What would be the best combination of selling price and expected volume? Celery cost is also fairly low for excellent quality. Check costs on other salad vegetables. Strawberries are in good supply, but will be even better next week. It is too early for most summer fruits.

3. *Other items of interest.* The grocery department is advertising salad dressing. This should help the sales of our department. Total store sales should be about average— $30,000. Our sales goal, at 7% of $30,000, is $2,100. This will probably be difficult to reach this week.

4. Follow-up comments after close of week:

Week #2 Weekly Planning Report

1. *Weekly advertised special* (WAS) is California strawberries at a cost of 38¢ per box. Our competition will probably also advertise these at or near cost. Quality is supposed to be excellent, and the bakery department is featuring shortcakes at a special price. How can we best merchandise strawberries in order to enhance our own departmental sales?

2. *Crop report* from wholesaler shows higher costs on some regular (nonseasonal) items. How should we handle this? As supplies increase, seasonal items are coming down, but only slightly. Bananas are still costing 20¢ per pound this week, but are expected to arrive very green from the warehouse, due to a four day strike in New Orleans. This will cut banana sales considerably.

3. *Other items of interest.* Expected total store sales are about average. Department sales are estimated to be down somewhat due to bananas.

4. Follow-up comments after close of week:

Week #3 Weekly Planning Report

1. *Weekly advertised special* (WAS) is potatoes. Long white (California shafter) potatoes are at the peak of harvest, and probably at their lowest price of the season. We'll have to be careful not to order too many because they certainly don't keep very long in the summer. For all size bags sold, we may be able to cover our cost of 6¢ per pound. Bagging them is certainly a lot of work. Perhaps we should also have a large bulk display with a big sign.

2. *Crop report* shows apple quality to be steadily declining; strawberry prices continue low with quality excellent; watermelons decline with increasing supplies; sweet corn is of excellent quality but the price is not yet near bottom; peaches are beginning to come down as supplies increase; and, most importantly, the banana crisis is definitely over.

3. *Other items of interest.* The storewide advertising theme is built around dairy products this week. This probably won't help or hurt many of our items very much. It should be about an average week if the weather is good.

4. Follow-up comments after close of week:

_____

_____

_____

_____

Week #4 Weekly Planning Report

1. *Weekly advertised special* (WAS) is watermelons for the July 4th week. This traditional special will really bring the crowd into the store. Departmental volume will also be up due to (a) increased store traffic and (b) high sales of watermelons. Unfortunately, watermelons won't increase our profits. In fact, they'll make it harder for us to get a good overall departmental markup percentage. However, increased sales will help total departmental profit dollars if we plan carefully. It's also a lot of hard work handling all those melons; but we did get a good buy on them by getting half a truck load on a drop shipment basis.

2. *Crop report* from wholesaler shows extremely high priced lettuce with poor quality and good supplies; and fairly stable prices on most other staples (nonseasonal items); lower cost and more plentiful supplies of good quality on seasonal items such as tomatoes, sweet corn, grapes, peaches, and so forth.

3. *Other items of interest.* Watermelons will receive about one half page in the weekly newspaper ad and will be featured over the radio. Total store weekly sales should be about $40,000. If we get 7% of that we'd have a big week, with sales of $2,800. Watermelons will help on volume, but we must work on other items for profit.

4. Follow-up comments after close of week:

_____

_____

Week #5 Weekly Planning Report

    1. Weekly advertised special (WAS) is sweet corn—with a "homegrown" sign on it, even though most of it is probably shipped in from Florida. We'll figure a selling price of 49¢ per dozen or six ears for 25¢. This a pretty good special for our area, since the real "homegrown" crop in our locality won't be ready for a week or two yet.

    2. *Crop report* from wholesaler tells us that watermelons are becoming more plentiful, as are most other seasonal items. Lettuce is in very plentiful supply, and quality is excellent at a much reduced price.

    3. *Other items of interest.* Peaches are now getting down far enough in price that one of our competitors may advertise them on a per pound basis. If this happens, do we meet their price or keep our profit in peaches? Expected store sales will be down this week as many customers begin vacation trips. Estimated total store sales are $27,000 to $28,000.

    4. Follow-up comments after close of week:

Week #6 Weekly Planning Report

    1. Weekly advertised special (WAS) is table grapes. At 19¢ per pound, we'll barely break even; but at least there is no strike or boycott against grapes this year. It's great to be able to give away grapes at cost without offending union members or college students. Marshmallows are featured by the grocery department as a complementary item.

    2. *Crop report* from wholesaler didn't say much of anything this week. The head produce buyer is on vacation, and the assistant buyer must have been told not to go out on a limb. He sounded more like a stockbroker.

    3. *Other items of interest.* Total store sales should be about the same as last week. Even though the wholesaler didn't mention it, we notice from our cost sheets that watermelons and sweet corn are still low in cost. Quality is usually best when cost is low. Maybe we can pick up some profit on these two items. The grape promotion won't cost us too much, because most people buy only about two pounds of grapes.

    4. Follow-up comments after close of week:

Week #7 Weekly Planning Report

1. *Weekly advertised special* (WAS) is a big one this week. We're selling freestone peaches at an average selling price that we hope will cover cost. By the lug (a 17 lb. box), we are selling at $1.69, which is two cents below cost. By the pound, we are selling at two pounds for 29¢. Thus (for purposes of the game), we'll program our selling price at 13¢ per pound, because we plan to sell slightly more by the pound than by the lug. If sugar prices weren't so high, we would probably sell more by the lug for canning.

2. *Crop report* indicates that the wholesale head produce buyer is back on the job. Information is that lettuce continues to be a bargain with excellent quality, bananas are down slightly with superb quality, and cantaloupe are approaching bottom. Potatoes, watermelon, and corn are beginning to go up in price, as their seasons have peaked.

3. *Other items of interest.* This week is usually pretty slow, what with warm weather and many customers away on vacations. Total store sales of $26,000 are expected. Departmental sales may exceed 7% of store sales if we sell well on other seasonal items in addition to peaches.

4. Follow-up comments after close of week:

Week #8 Weekly Planning Report

1. *Weekly advertised special* (WAS) had been cantaloupe from Arizona at a cost and selling price of 29¢ each. That was the plan until these two guys came by in their pickup truck from St. Joseph, Missouri. After much hard bargaining, and after giving the two truckers time enough for lunch and a cool beer or two, the entire load of homegrown cantaloupe was bought at an average cost of slightly less than 29¢ each. This was a great buy because of the excellent quality and because these homegrown cantaloupes averaged twice the size of the Arizona product. This should really create some traffic.

2. *Crop report* showed tomatoes at a season low in cost, but this was of little interest to us since many of our customers (and their neighbors) grow tomatoes that are now ripe. Some price trends of last week continued, and cucumbers reached a new low in cost due to plentiful supplies.

3. *Other items of interest.* Total store sales should be up this week—probably at about $30,000—due to the community-wide back-to-school days promotion. This event, combined with our cantaloupe deal, should give us a good week in the department if we don't give away anything but cantaloupe.

4. Follow-up comments after close of week:

Week #9 Weekly Planning Report

1. *Weekly advertised special* (WAS) is cucumbers, suggested at 9¢ each. If every customer buys one (or even two), our overall department markup won't be affected very much because of the low unit value of cucumbers. It's not the same as heavy watermelons on sale. This should be a good profit week if spoilage on soft fruits is not too high and we don't start giving the profits away.

2. *Crop report* from wholesaler shows cucumbers as a best buy, with the suggestion that cukes be used to stimulate sales of other salad vegetables. Radishes are of top quality. Strawberries are of poor quality, but are expected to be better next week. New apples are beginning to come in; but quality is only fair to poor depending on the growing area.

3. *Other items of interest.* Total store sales should be about $30,000. Advertised prices on canning jars and lids may stimulate sales of peaches and other items. However, many canners are also home gardeners.

4. Follow-up comments after close of week:

Week #10 Weekly Planning Report

1. *Weekly advertised special* (WAS) is apples from the pickup duo of St. Jo, Missouri. Maybe they are giving us another good buy, or maybe they're trying to make up for last time. It's for sure that the only time they come this far in their little truck is when the St. Jo market is overstocked. At half the price we buy from our regular wholesaler, we can't go too far wrong, even if these apples are "windfalls." Windfalls are apples that are picked from the ground rather than from the tree. They fall from the wind or from a good shaking of the tree branches. Bruises result; but if we figure our cost on the basis of getting four pounds of good apples for every five the St. Jo guys are selling, we'll give our customers a good quality apple at an average cost of 10¢ per pound. Ten cent apples are great for the back-to-school lunches.

2. *Crop report* from wholesaler shows top quality apples scarce and expensive but due within a week or two; lettuce quality is medium; strawberries are good; sweet corn is somewhat high and somewhat dry; and grapes have climbed considerably.

3. *Other items of interest.* This is your last week as produce manager, so you'll want to make a good profit. You are training your replacement, so be sure to do things as well as you know how. Your replacement catches on fast. By using his added labor, the produce department should be in great physical shape this week. Good appearance always stimulates sales.

4. Follow-up comments after close of week:

_____

_____

_____

_____

Cost Table

Week #:	1	2	3	4	5	6	7	8	9	10
Regular Products										
Product:*										
LET	20	22	24	29	18	18	17	22	24	24
CAB	11	11	11	10	10	9	10	11	12	12
CRT	19	20	20	19	19	19	18	19	20	19
CEL	28	28	29	29	30	30	31	30	29	29
ORA	12	12	13	13	12	12	12	12	12	12
ONI	16	17	16	16	16	15	15	14	14	14
BAN	20	20	20	20	19	19	19	19	19	19
RAD	22	22	22	20	20	20	19	19	19	19
PEP	30	30	31	32	34	34	34	34	35	35
YAM	18	20	20	18	18	20	19	21	19	19
Seasonal Products										
TOM	28	29	29	24	20	20	20	18	18	24
STR	42	38	38	38	41	42	42	44	44	44
POT	10	9	6	7	7	8	8	9	9	9
WAT	11	10	8	5	5	4	6	6	6	6
CRN	8	8	7	6	4	4	6	7	8	8
GRA	40	40	38	28	24	18	18	18	20	27
PCH	30	26	20	18	15	15	12	13	15	16
CAN	40	38	37	37	34	34	33	29	28	27
CUM	15	15	14	14	12	12	10	9	9	10
APL	25	25	25	25	26	28	28	20	20	10
WAS	28	38	6	5	4	19	12	29	9	10

*All cost figures are in cents per unit.

EWS
Week #1—Demand Schedule of Expected Weekly Sales (in units)

Products:	*If %MU on SP =* *0%–15%*	*16%–25%*	*26%–40%*	*41%–50%*	*51%–67%*
LET	900	850	800	650	300
CAB	500	450	400	250	150
CRT	400	340	300	270	150
CEL	280	250	200	200	100
ORA	600	550	500	400	250
ONI	400	350	300	200	100
BAN	900	800	700	400	100
RAD	300	280	250	150	100
PEP	180	150	100	50	30
YAM	200	200	150	100	50
TOM	0	0	0	0	0
STR	300	240	200	80	40
POT	1,800	1,500	1,300	900	600
WAT	600	400	300	200	50
CRN	550	500	400	300	100
GRA	200	150	100	50	20
PCH	400	200	120	100	50
CAN	350	200	150	100	50
CUM	300	220	200	150	80
APL	200	180	150	100	50
WAS	800	300	200	100	50

EWS
Week #2—Demand Schedule of Expected Weekly Sales (in units)

	If %MU on SP =				
	0%–15%	*16%–25%*	*26%–40%*	*41%–50%*	*51%–67%*
Products:					
LET	700	600	550	450	300
CAB	500	450	400	250	150
CRT	400	340	300	270	150
CEL	275	250	220	180	100
ORA	600	550	500	400	250
ONI	400	350	300	200	100
BAN	550	500	400	250	100
RAD	300	270	250	150	100
PEP	180	150	100	50	30
YAM	200	175	150	100	50
TOM	450	425	400	250	100
STR	0	0	0	0	0
POT	1,800	1,500	1,300	900	600
WAT	800	500	400	200	100
CRN	550	500	400	300	100
GRA	220	150	120	100	50
PCH	400	220	150	100	50
CAN	350	200	150	100	50
CUM	300	220	200	150	80
APL	200	180	150	100	50
WAS	700	300	250	200	50

EWS
Week #3—Demand Schedule of Expected Weekly Sales (in units)

	If %MU on SP =				
	0%–15%	*16%–25%*	*26%–40%*	*41%–50%*	*51%–67%*
Products:					
LET	700	550	450	350	250
CAB	500	450	400	250	150
CRT	400	340	300	270	150
CEL	280	240	200	150	100
ORA	550	500	450	300	150
ONI	400	350	300	200	100
BAN	900	800	700	400	100
RAD	350	320	300	150	100
PEP	180	150	100	50	30
YAM	200	175	150	100	50
TOM	400	375	350	225	100
STR	450	400	350	200	50
POT	0	0	0	0	0
WAT	1,000	850	700	300	150
CRN	650	550	450	300	100
GRA	240	200	150	100	50
PCH	425	350	300	120	50
CAN	350	200	150	75	50
CUM	300	220	200	150	80
APL	180	140	100	50	50
WAS	4,000	2,000	1,500	900	600

EWS
Week #4—Demand Schedule of Expected Weekly Sales (in units)

	If %MU on SP =				
	0%–15%	*16%–25%*	*26%–40%*	*41%–50%*	*51%–67%*
Products:					
LET	450	425	400	250	150
CAB	570	550	500	300	150
CRT	480	450	400	300	200
CEL	300	280	250	210	120
ORA	550	500	450	300	150
ONI	450	425	400	250	100
BAN	900	850	800	500	150
RAD	450	425	400	250	100
PEP	200	175	150	100	50
YAM	200	175	150	100	50
TOM	450	425	400	225	100
STR	450	400	350	200	50
POT	2,000	1,700	1,500	900	600
WAT	0	0	0	0	0
CRN	700	550	500	350	100
GRA	260	240	200	100	50
PCH	500	475	400	200	50
CAN	350	250	150	75	50
CUM	300	250	250	150	80
APL	140	120	100	50	50
WAS	9,500	4,000	2,000	800	200

EWS
Week #5—Demand Schedule of Expected Weekly Sales (in units)

Products:	*If %MU on SP =* *0%–15%*	*16%–25%*	*26%–40%*	*41%–50%*	*51%–67%*
LET	850	800	700	400	150
CAB	420	400	350	240	150
CRT	350	320	270	220	125
CEL	275	250	200	180	100
ORA	500	450	400	250	100
ONI	400	350	300	200	100
BAN	800	700	600	350	100
RAD	275	250	250	175	100
PEP	180	150	100	50	30
YAM	200	175	150	100	50
TOM	400	375	350	225	100
STR	350	300	250	125	50
POT	1,800	1,400	1,200	800	500
WAT	4,800	4,500	4,000	800	200
CRN	0	0	0	0	0
GRA	260	240	200	100	50
PCH	500	475	400	200	50
CAN	400	250	200	100	50
CUM	275	250	200	150	80
APL	140	120	100	80	40
WAS	1,200	700	400	300	100

EWS
Week #6—Demand Schedule of Expected Weekly Sales (in units)

	If %MU on SP =				
	0%–15%	*16%–25%*	*26%–40%*	*41%–50%*	*51%–67%*
Products:					
LET	850	800	700	400	150
CAB	500	450	400	250	150
CRT	350	320	270	220	125
CEL	275	250	200	180	100
ORA	500	450	400	275	125
ONI	400	350	350	200	100
BAN	800	700	600	350	100
RAD	275	250	250	175	100
PEP	180	150	100	50	30
YAM	200	175	150	100	50
TOM	350	300	300	225	100
STR	280	240	200	100	40
POT	1,800	1,400	1,200	800	500
WAT	4,800	4,500	4,000	900	300
CRN	800	600	500	300	100
GRA	0	0	0	0	0
PCH	525	475	400	200	50
CAN	350	250	200	100	50
CUM	200	175	150	100	50
APL	140	120	100	80	40
WAS	700	300	250	200	100

EWS
Week #7—Demand Schedule of Expected Weekly Sales (in units)

	If %MU on SP = 0%–15%	16%–25%	26%–40%	41%–50%	51%–67%
Products:					
LET	850	800	700	400	150
CAB	450	425	400	220	120
CRT	350	320	270	220	125
CEL	260	240	200	180	100
ORA	500	450	400	250	100
ONI	425	375	350	225	100
BAN	950	800	750	500	200
RAD	250	225	200	150	75
PEP	180	150	100	50	30
YAM	200	175	150	100	50
TOM	340	320	300	200	80
STR	280	240	200	100	40
POT	1,800	1,500	1,300	900	600
WAT	2,800	2,400	2,000	600	200
CRN	450	375	300	200	100
GRA	475	450	400	200	100
PCH	0	0	0	0	0
CAN	350	300	250	140	80
CUM	250	225	200	100	80
APL	140	120	100	80	40
WAS	2,000	700	400	100	50

EWS
Week #8—Demand Schedule of Expected Weekly Sales (in units)

	If %MU on SP =				
	0%–15%	*16%–25%*	*26%–40%*	*41%–50%*	*51%–67%*
Products:					
LET	700	650	650	300	150
CAB	450	425	400	220	120
CRT	400	340	300	270	150
CEL	300	270	250	180	120
ORA	500	475	450	250	125
ONI	425	375	350	225	100
BAN	900	800	750	400	100
RAD	250	225	200	150	75
PEP	180	150	100	50	30
YAM	200	175	150	100	50
TOM	400	375	350	225	100
STR	200	175	150	100	40
POT	1,800	1,500	1,200	800	600
WAT	2,500	2,200	1,800	500	200
CRN	275	250	200	100	50
GRA	500	475	450	200	100
PCH	900	800	800	300	100
CAN	0	0	0	0	0
CUM	400	325	300	200	100
APL	375	325	300	100	50
WAS	800	350	200	100	100

EWS
Week #9—Demand Schedule of Expected Weekly Sales (in units)

	If %MU on SP =				
	0%–15%	*16%–25%*	*26%–40%*	*41%–50%*	*51%–67%*
Products:					
LET	650	625	600	300	150
CAB	450	425	400	220	120
CRT	425	375	350	300	150
CEL	300	270	250	180	120
ORA	500	450	400	250	100
ONI	425	375	350	225	100
BAN	850	720	650	375	100
RAD	300	275	250	200	100
PEP	200	160	150	75	50
YAM	200	175	150	100	50
TOM	475	425	400	225	100
STR	150	125	100	50	25
POT	1,800	1,500	1,200	800	400
WAT	2,200	1,800	1,500	500	200
CRN	275	250	200	100	50
GRA	500	475	450	225	125
PCH	950	900	900	350	100
CAN	275	225	200	100	50
CUM	0	0	0	0	0
APL	800	700	600	200	100
WAS	750	250	100	50	50

EWS
Week #10—Demand Schedule of Expected Weekly Sales (in units)

| | *If %MU on SP =* | | | | |
	0%–15%	*16%–25%*	*26%–40%*	*41%–50%*	*51%–67%*
Products:					
LET	775	750	700	350	150
CAB	450	425	400	240	140
CRT	400	340	300	270	150
CEL	300	270	250	180	120
ORA	650	625	600	400	180
ONI	425	375	350	225	100
BAN	850	720	650	375	100
RAD	275	250	200	150	75
PEP	200	160	150	75	50
YAM	200	175	150	100	50
TOM	340	320	300	200	100
STR	250	225	200	100	50
POT	1,800	1,600	1,400	900	500
WAT	1,200	1,000	900	300	100
CRN	200	175	150	75	75
GRA	400	375	350	150	100
PCH	800	750	700	300	100
CAN	160	140	120	120	50
CUM	280	240	200	100	50
APL	0	0	0	0	0
WAS	1,500	600	400	150	100

14

Promotion Strategy For SBMM

STRATEGY PLANNING FOR PROMOTION

The fourth point of our five-pointed star model is *promotion.* Promotion is the variable used by the SBM to communicate information and to persuade the target customers concerning the total product offering of the firm. Through promotion, the SBM must effectively communicate to target customers that the right product is available, in the right place, at the right price, from the right people.

Is promotion really necessary for the SBM? In our competitive society, the answer is always YES. The competitors of the SBM are going to promote. Even though the costs may seem high or appear to be wasted, the SBM must also promote through such means as advertising, personal selling, sales promotion, and/or publicity. Some promotion is necessary simply to replace the customers who are lost over time. If the SB firm wishes to grow by adding new customers and by selling more to present customers, promotion is essential. If the SBM could gain one new customer each day while retaining all his other customers, the cumulative effect on sales would be as surprising as the compound interest the SBM pays to his banker. Promotion is a must for sustaining the life of a business.

Promotion encompasses all forms of communication which originate with the seller, are ultimately geared to the profit objective, and are directed to target customers for the purpose of bringing about some intended response. Promotion may be divided into the following major areas: (a) advertising, (b) personal selling, (c) sales promotion, and (d) publicity (and public relations). The AMA defines these terms as follows:

> *Advertising*—Any paid form of non-personal presentation and promotion of ideas, goods, or services by an identified sponsor. . . .
> *Personal selling*—Oral presentation in a conversation with one or more prospective purchasers for the purpose of making sales. . . .

284

Sales promotion—(1) In a specific sense, those marketing activities, other than personal selling, advertising, and publicity, that stimulate consumer purchasing and dealer effectiveness, such as display shows and exhibitions, demonstrations, and various non-recurrent selling efforts not in the ordinary routine. . . .

Publicity—Non-personal stimulation of demand for a product, service, or business unit by planting commercially significant news about it in a published medium or obtaining favorable presentation of it upon radio, television, or stage that is not paid for by the sponsor.[1]

The basic objective of promotion is to promote. Promotion is somewhat unique among the five "P's" in that its major purpose is to call attention to and generate interest in one of more of the other "P's" of the SB marketing mix. Promotion may be said to inform, persuade, or remind. Or the five general objectives of promotion may be stated as: providing information, stimulating demand, differentiating the product, accentuating the value of the product, and stabilizing sales.[2] Within the framework of such general objectives, the SBM will formulate specific promotional objectives for each portion of, and for the overall promotional program.

Effective promotion, in whatever form, relies on the communications process. This process is often pictured in a diagram similar to that in Figure 14–1. For our purposes, the SBM is the information source who is attempting to communicate a promotional message to the target customer (receiver). The "noise," which may occur at any point in the process, could be lack of attention, misunderstanding, interference from competitive messages, and so forth. Encoding by the source and decoding by the receiver are the symbolic means by which ideas are expressed for effective transmission via the message channel. The degree to which the source-encoder and the decoder-receiver have common frames of reference and fields of experience determines whether or not the message symbols have the same meaning for both. The message channel (or medium) used by the SBM to communicate his message also affects the success of the communication process.

A second communications concept of importance to the SBM is called the two-step flow of communications. Briefly, this concept suggests that mass media are effective in

Figure 14.1 The Communications Process

KEY:

MESSAGE →
NOISE XX

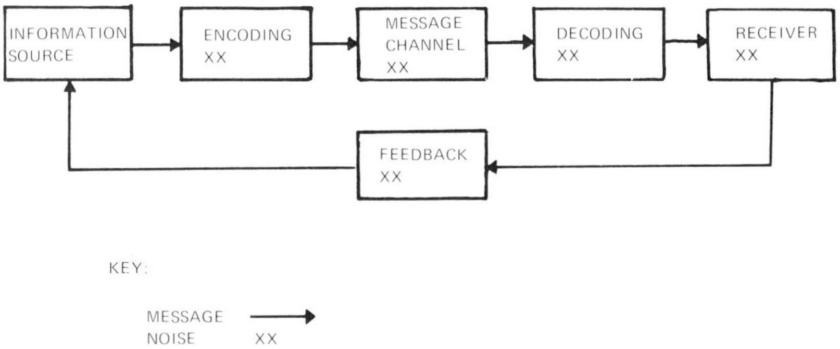

[1]Committee on Definitions, Reprinted from *Marketing Definitions: A Glossary of Marketing Terms* published by the American Marketing Association, Chicago, 1960, pp. 9–20.

[2]Louis E. Boone and David L. Kurtz, *Contemporary Marketing* (Hinsdale, Illinois: The Dryden Press, 1974), p. 271.

reaching opinion leaders, who in turn may influence target customers through word-of-mouth advertising. The SBM who intends to rely heavily on word-of-mouth advertising should further study the adoption process and the two-step flow of communications. These topics are covered in most books on consumer behavior.

The field of promotion offers the SBM many opportunities to either excel or make mistakes. Probably the most basic (and perhaps the worst) promotion mistake the SBM can make is to have no promotion strategy at all, but simply to be led in several different directions at the same time by the various media salesmen and others who are always there to fill the vacuum partially. Other common promotion mistakes among SB are: (a) advertising over too large a geographic area; (b) spreading the promotion effort too thin to reach a threshold level; (c) using an "on-again, off-again" approach to scheduling; (d) not integrating the various elements of the firm's promotion mix in order to achieve the synergetic effect; (e) using poor timing, such as advertising a new product before sufficient distribution has been built up; (f) poor allocation of the promotional budget; (g) occasional use of promotional gimmicks that conflict with the desired image; and (h) amateur production of promotional messages. This list is probably far from complete, but it does give an indication of the range of opportunities facing the SBM in the area of promotional strategy. In order to succeed in promotion, the SBM will often require the assistance of outside expertise. Such expertise can best be utilized in the execution phase if a sound strategy has been planned. Strategy planning for promotion is mainly the task of the SBM and his marketing team.

PROMOTION AS A PART OF THE SB MARKETING MIX

In both SB and BB, the promotion element seems to be a very important part of marketing strategy. The author was unable to find studies which dealt with SB firms exclusively, so the following remarks should be regarded as generalizations to which some SB exceptions may be found. *Promotion* is sometimes used synonomously with *selling* or *sales efforts.* The term *sales promotion,* as previously defined in this chapter, is a part of promotion. Other parts of promotion are advertising, personal selling, and publicity. However, in some retailing circles, the term *sales promotion* is used in place of *promotion* to mean ". . .all methods of stimulating consumer purchasing, including personal selling, advertising, and publicity."[3] But whatever the terminology used, the importance of promotion is apparent. Promotion is that informative and persuasive communication by which the SBM makes the target market aware of the rest of the marketing mix. In terms of expenses, promotion often accounts for the largest portion of the total marketing expenses.

A study among successful manufacturers of established, successful products rated promotion (i.e., sales effort) as the most important facet of the marketing mix. As Udell stated, "The facets perceived to be the most important in the marketing success of the selected products were sales effort or marketing communications—sales management, advertising, and other promotional programs."[4] The relative rankings and percentages of the elements of the marketing mix for manufacturers were: (1) sales effort, 41.1%; (2) product effort, 27.8% (3) pricing, 18.4%; (4) distribution, 12.2%, and (5) other, 0.5%.[5] The

[3]Committee on Definitions, p. 20.

[4]Jon G. Udell, "The Perceived Importance of the Elements of Strategy," Reprinted from *Journal of Marketing* published by the American Marketing Association, 32, No. 1 (January 1968), p. 35.

[5]Udell, p. 35.

study did not include wholesalers and retailers. However, the study did show the variations in the importance of sales efforts among manufacturers of (a) industrial goods, (b) consumer durables, and (c) consumer nondurables. The respective percentages for sales efforts are 40.9%, 37.5%, and 44.7%.[6] The perceived importance of the elements of marketing strategy among wholesalers or retailers (especially SB) is an area for further study.

THE SB PROMOTION MIX

We have discussed the importance of promotion as an element in the SB marketing mix. Now, let us discuss the promotion mix itself—composed of advertising, personal selling, sales promotion, and publicity. In general, advertising and personal selling are the two most important components of the promotion mix. However, this is not always so. Also, among SB firms, we will note that so-called supplementary forms of advertising may take on major roles, while mass media may be less important. The optimal promotional mix varies from firm to firm, according to such factors as product type, target customers, company image, channels of distribution used, retail store location, funds available, and so forth.

In general, advertising tends to be most important in the promotional mix of consumer marketers, while personal selling tends to be most important for industrial marketers. Sales promotion is usually considered to be of equal (but lesser) importance in both markets. Publicity usually plays an equal (but even lesser) role in both markets. These statements are generalizations, and many successful promotional mixes can be found which do not conform to the generalizations. The promotional mix should be uniquely suited to the target market at which it is directed. It will be the result of building up a blend around the specific tasks and overall objectives the SBM wishes to accomplish. Both experience and good judgment are helpful in arriving at the optimal mix. The percentages in Table 14–1 are taken from the Udell study of 485 manufacturers cited earlier in this chapter.[7] The table shows the perceived importance of the elements of marketing communication which comprise the promotional mix.

The conditions under which the marketer is operating influence the relative importance of advertising and personal selling in the promotional mix. These may be summarized as follows:

It may be useful to summarize the points that relate to when certain forms of promotion should be used. Personal selling is most important under the following circumstances: (1) when the firm may have insufficient financial strength to carry out an adequate advertising program, (2) when the market is concentrated, (3) when the salesman himself is needed to establish rapport and create confidence, (4) when the product has high unit value, (5) when demonstration is required, (6) when the product must be fitted to the customer's needs, or (7) when a trade-in is involved.

On the other hand, advertising becomes a major ingredient when the following conditions exist: (1) When the primary demand for the product tends to be increasing. (2) When there is considerable opportunity to differentiate the product from others that are available on the market. In effect, we are only saying that this

---

[6]Udell, p. 35.
[7]Udell, p. 38.

Table 14–1   Relative Importance of the Elements of Marketing Communication*

	Producers of:		
Sales Effort Activity	*Industrial Goods*	*Consumer Durables*	*Consumer Nondurables*
Sales Management and Personal Selling	69.2	47.6	38.1
Broadcast Media Advertising	.9	10.7	20.9
Printed Media Advertising	12.5	16.1	14.8
Special Promotional Activities	9.6	15.5	15.5
Branding & Promotional Packaging	4.5	9.5	9.8
Other	3.3	.6	.9
Total	100.0	100.0	100.0

*The data are the average point allocations of 336 industrial, 52 consumer durable, and 88 consumer nondurable goods producers. Nine responses are excluded because of point allocations which did not equal 100.

Source: Jon G. Udell, "The Perceived Importance of the Elements of Strategy," Reprinted from *Journal of Marketing* published by the American Marketing Association, 32, No. 1 (January 1968), p. 38. Used with permission.

condition provides the advertiser with something to say. (3) When the product has what might be termed "hidden properties." Thus the objective will be to inform and educate the public about these characteristics through the advertising. (4) Where powerful emotional buying motives exist for the product. Buying action is thus motivated through the stimulation of these motives. (5) Where the company has adequate funds to carry out such an advertising program. Thus, if a firm is in the position of meeting all or most of these conditions, then advertising may be the most effective promotional approach.[8]

The optimum promotional mix is one which does not suboptimize by having the optimum amount of one element at the expense of others. The elements of the mix work together to get the total promotional task done in the optimum way. For a specific promotional task, one element, such as consumer coupons (a form of sales promotion), may appear to be an optimum choice. However, when viewed from the perspective of the total promotional task and objectives, coupons may be considerably less than optimum. Or the optimum promotional mix may involve coupons of a lesser value combined with the other elements of the mix.

Promotion tasks can be assigned to the elements of the mix according to the strengths of each of the elements. Advertising can create an awareness of new products and brands (or established products being introduced to new markets); can create an interest

[8]George L. Herpel and Richard A. Collins, *Specialty Advertising In Marketing* (Homewood, Illinois: Dow Jones-Irwin, Inc., 1972), pp. 60–61.

in products and product features; can help to identify prospects by employing return message devices; can reinforce confidence in the buyer; can help to increase loyalty; can create a favorable image; can make the salesman's call better received and more productive; and so forth. Personal selling can handle complaints and clear up misunderstandings; meet objections and overcome competitive claims; provide service; give aggressive sales push; and get immediate feedback. Sales promotion, with its less structured format, tends to be used for short term enhancement of the promotional mix. It may be directed at the channel of distribution or the ultimate consumers, or both. Publicity performs the promotional function of providing news (hopefully favorable) about the marketer and his products.

The optimum promotional mix for SB often involves a different combination than that for the BB competitor. This is to be expected, since the SBM will be directing his promotion to different target markets in some cases; since the SB product offering will be different; since the channel of distribution which includes the SBM is likely to be different, and so forth. In terms of a generalization, the promotional mix differences are shown in Figure 14–2. The point of Figure 14–2 is that the SBM is likely to rely more heavily on target types of promotional elements and to rely less on mass elements, such as major media advertising. Remember, this is only a generalization; exceptions are numerous.

In addition to size of the firm, other factors not yet mentioned affect the promotional mix. The time element, both in terms of the individual transaction and the product life-cycle, can be important. The market can be viewed as having a pretransactional, a transactional, and a posttransactional phase. The relative importance of advertising and personal selling varies by phase. Advertising may be pictured as a U-shaped curve which is most important in the pretransactional phase, least important in the transactional phase, and which then rises to become somewhat more important in the posttransactional phase. Personal selling complements advertising by being least impor-

Figure 14.2 The Promotional Mix Continuum for BB and SB

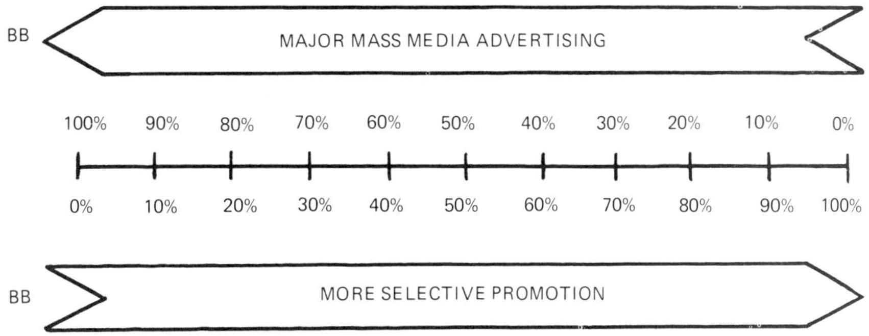

EXAMPLES OF MAJOR
MASS MEDIA ADVERTISING

1. Network Television
2. Magazines
3. Large City Newspapers
4. Local Television
5. Public Relations

EXAMPLES OF MORE
SELECTIVE PROMOTION

1. Personal Selling
2. Sales Promotion
3. Supplementary Advertising
   Such As Direct Mail,
   Specialty, Directory,
   Packaging, Etc.

tant, then most important, and then of medium importance in the same three phases. Again, these are generalizations.[9]

The product life-cycle (PLC) may be viewed in the four stages of introduction, growth, maturity, and decline. During *introduction,* the promotional mix will be aimed at stimulating primary demand by making potential customers aware of the product's existence. Important in the promotional mix for the introductory stage will be introductory mass advertising, publicity, and sales promotions, such as trade shows and conventions. During the *growth* stage, attention turns to the creation of selective demand for the company's own brand. Heavy use of mass media is employed by many competitors in order to gain brand preference among both trade and final consumers. In the *maturity* stage, the promotion message may be either of a reminder type or of a very persuasive type. Intensified competition often results in the heavy use of mass media and the heavy use of deals for both the trade and ultimate consumers. The *decline* stage often brings a substantial reduction in total promotional effort. Advertising is cut; salesmen no longer give much effort to the product; publicity is almost impossible to get; and if sales promotion is used, it is likely to be in the form of deals.

The channel of distribution employed also affects the promotional mix. If the SBM uses other than a direct channel, he may choose a push, a pull, or a combination push-and-pull strategy. These strategies have special meaning during the introductory stage when distribution is being built up. Push strategy directs promotional effort to the channel members, who in turn market to the ultimate consumer. Pull strategy is directed at the final consumer who "demands" the product from the retailer—and so on back through the channel. Advertising and sales promotion are emphasized in pulling, while personal selling of an aggressive "order getter" type is associated with pushing strategy. However, the basic difference is that the targets of promotion are different in push and pull strategies.

In order to illustrate some alternative promotional mixes, the following examples are given. The first example, taken from a popular marketing text, notes that even though a small budget for promotion may place some restrictions on the SBM, the range of alternatives from which to choose is still great:

> A small budget, however, need not limit a firm to personal selling. Sales promotion, public relations, and direct mail are attractive possibilities. A small tire manufacturer who wanted to tell potential dealers about his product and was not in a position to compete with the big tiremakers' promotion programs decided instead to use direct mail. His carefully targeted campaign was extremely successful, yielding $196 in new business for every dollar invested. A direct-mail expenditure of $1,861 brought in 101 new dealers and more than $360,000 of new business.[10]

The second example, taken from a popular small business management book, shows how sales doubled in two years by a change in the promotional mix combined with a change in the distribution system:

> The manufacturer of a line of good-quality costume jewelry sold to retail jewelry stores. The owner wanted his company to grow faster. The company had been advertising in monthly trade magazines, using no sales representatives but employ-

---

[9]Harold C. Cash and W. J. E. Crissy, "Comparison Of Advertising And Selling," *Managerial Marketing: Policies, Strategies, And Decisions,* ed. Eugene J. Kelley and William Lazer (Homewood, Illinois: Richard D. Irwin, Inc., 1973), p. 446.

[10]E. Jerome McCarthy, *Basic Marketing: A Managerial Approach* (Homewood, Illinois: Richard D. Irwin, Inc., 1975), p. 400.

ing order-takers, attending trade shows, and having good services, pricing and packaging.

Owner's Study: Company sales volumes for each area of the country were examined over a three-year period. The southeastern area sales were lagging.

New Marketing Mix: Advertising outlays were reduced in the southeastern area. A sales representative was hired for this area.

Results: Sales in the southeastern area began growing more rapidly than in any other area of the country. The sales representative concentrated her efforts on retail jewelry stores that had the largest growth potentials.

Next Phase: Different types of point-of-purchase displays and advertising mats for retailers were developed. More sales representatives were hired.[11]

Our final example is based upon promotional strategy in a high technology industry—the peripheral data processing equipment manufacturing industry. It is an industry rather than a single firm example and is taken from an article by Schlissel:[12]

In 1970 the industry was composed of about 650 SB firms, most of whom considered IBM (with about 75% of the market) as their primary competitor. Product innovation (compatible with IBM equipment) was the major competitive strength of most of the SB firms. A promotional strategy encompassing the marketing concept was absent in many SB firms. A comparison of the promotion activities of the more successful firms with those of the less successful firms suggests a preferred promotional strategy for the SB firms of the industry. An analysis of successful versus unsuccessful firms, as defined by market segment share, resulted in the following conclusion:

> Inasmuch as Group 1 appears on the whole to have a larger share of the market, it suggests that similar strategies of promotion to theirs may be better for firms in this industry to follow and possibly for firms in like industries. The strategy of Group 1 may be summed up. Personal selling is employed as the major promotional tactic, with an allocation of 80 percent of the promotion budget. The sales force is organized along product lines so that salesmen may develop skill in selling a highly technical product. Advertising, trade shows, and publicity are used in minor supporting roles, probably with the objective of stimulating market awareness. Product quality is used as the major customer appeal, with price in a secondary position, and new product development and service in supporting roles.[13]

HOW TO FORMULATE PROMOTIONAL STRATEGY FOR SB

Our familiar eight-step process for the "How to" of marketing strategy planning can easily be adapted to become a framework for SB promotional strategy planning. This strategic planning framework is presented below.

The eight steps given below are for the overall SB promotion strategy. As substrategies, the SBM will probably have an advertising strategy, a media strategy and a message strategy for advertising, a personal selling strategy, and so forth. Also, our systems view of marketing suggests that the SBM must coordinate the promotion strategy with strategies in the areas of product, place, price, and people. Finally, the SB promotion

[11]Curtis E. Tate, Jr., Leon C. Megginson, Charles R. Scott, Jr., and Lyle R. Trueblood, *Successful Small Business Management* (Dallas: Business Publications, Inc., 1975), p. 230.

[12]Martin R. Schlissel, "Promotional Strategy In A High-Technology Industry," *Journal of Economics And Business*, 26, No. 1 (Fall 1973), pp. 67–73.

[13]Schlissel, p. 72.

strategy must be a compatible integral part of the overall marketing strategy of the SB firm. We therefore will assume that the SBM has already fairly well defined (a) overall company and marketing objectives, (b) target market(s), (c) the differential advantage upon which strategy is based, (d) the SB environment, and (e) a tentative strategy for at least some of the other five "P's." The application of the eight step framework to a specific SB is properly the duty of the SBM for that business.

The eight steps in the formulation of promotion strategy for SB are:

1. Record the current promotion strategy.
2. Identify strategic promotion problems.
3. Divide current strategic promotion problems into core strategy areas and supporting strategy areas.
4. Formulate alternative promotion strategies at both core and support levels.
5. Evaluate these alternatives in various combinations.
6. Choose the new promotion strategy.
7. Plan the details of implementation of the new promotion strategy.
8. Set performance standards and monitor feedback.

As noted in previous chapters, our simple practical method of SB strategy formulation is merely a framework or skeleton. The conference method involving the SBM and his marketing management team is used to put life into the framework. The familiar tools are a pad and pencil, good leadership, and hard (and smart) work.

Step 1—Record the current promotion strategy. The model of the communications process presented earlier in this chapter (Figure 14–1) may serve as a stimulus for thinking about the current promotion strategy. We are assuming that if a current promotion strategy does exist, it is not yet recorded. Remember, making promotion decisions and having a promotion strategy are not the same thing. Strategy implies the existence of a rationale behind the current promotion practices.

Items to be recorded in the current promotion strategy are answers to such basic questions as:

1. What are the target audience(s) to which our promotion is directed? Possible answers are current users, potential users, influencers, family or industrial purchasing agents, opinion leaders, trade channel members, and so forth. These audiences are the receivers in our communications model.

2. What are the responses which the promotion of the SB firm is seeking from each of the audiences? These are the objectives of the promotion strategy. Some possible objectives (i.e., intended responses) might be: (a) to make a target market aware of the existence of our product, (b) to build brand preference in the target market, (c) to get X% of the desired retailers to stock a product, (d) to bring new customers into a store, or (e) to get X number of target customers to purchase and use a product. More is said about promotion objectives below.

3. What specific promotion tasks have been assigned to advertising, personal selling, sales promotion, and publicity? Some overlap probably exists. However, the SBM should know what the current promotion strategy has assigned to each area and to individual instruments within each area. These areas involve the message channels.

4. What is the overall importance or magnitude of promotion as a part of the current marketing mix? This is not necessarily the same thing as the promotion budget, but it is closely related to budget size.

5. In what ways (especially regarding message) does promotion relate to other marketing strategy areas? For example, the current promotion strategy could be based upon a positioning strategy which interfaces directly with the extent of the current product line offered. Or an image identification strategy may currently be employed which ties in directly with current product quality and pricing strategies.

Once the above questions and other questions pertinent to the particular current promotion strategy have been answered, the recording job is a relatively easy but essential task. The SBM should make certain that the current promotion strategy (including all its omissions and weaknesses as well as its strengths) is recorded in a usable manner.

Step 2—Identify strategic promotion problems. In this step, the SBM attempts to locate and identify problems (and opportunities) in the current promotion strategy. If the current promotion strategy was a bit confusing at points when the SBM attempted to record it in Step #1 above, chances are that these points of confusion involve problems. Some of these problems may be strategic, while others are tactical. Problems are found early by actively looking for them and attempting to analyze the symptoms which are received in the feedback system (Figure 14–1). The failure to recognize such problems and opportunities in the promotion strategy may be an indication that a problem exists with the feedback system itself. The SBM must ask such questions as: Are the promotion objectives being met? Are the promotion objectives what they should be? Are the elements of promotion (advertising, personal selling, sales promotion, and publicity) performing their respective assigned tasks in an efficient and effective manner? What environment changes (such as new competition, a new television station in the area, or some recent legislation) have taken place that affect the current promotion strategy? What changes have taken place in the target market of the SBM that will affect promotion strategy? How will changes in other marketing mix elements create promotion problems? The SBM is looking for the strategic (not tactical) problems of the promotion strategy. For example, selecting radio station A or B is a tactical decision that can more easily be made after a promotion strategy incorporating an advertising strategy has properly defined the expected role of radio as a message channel to reach a specified target market.

Step 3—Divide current strategic promotion problems into core strategy areas and supporting strategy areas. Some of the potential core strategy areas of promotion have already been suggested by the questions posed in Steps #1 and #2 above. The core promotion strategy areas are usually some of the following:

1. How important a role promotion is to play in the overall marketing strategy.
2. Which and how important are the roles each of the promotional elements (advertising, personal selling, sales promotion, and publicity) is to play in the overall promotion strategy.
3. The determination of the promotional objectives in terms of desired responses.
4. The promotion message to be communicated in order to accomplish the promotion objectives.
5. Planned changes in basic promotion strategy over time, for example, the PLC.

Supporting promotion strategies are those which support either the core promotion strategy or some other core (or supporting) strategy. For example, a core promotion strategy calling for increased product identification by consumers may call for a shift in media and message strategy which includes more visualization of the product package via more showings on highly visual media such as television, point-of-purchase displays, and advertising specialties. A quite different example, as a supporting strategy, would be using sales engineers as a personal selling message channel for an overall marketing objective of increasing use among present product users. This supporting strategy could, in turn, be supported by industrial advertising directed at increasing customer requests for engineering assistance.

Having recorded the current promotion strategy, identified strategic promotion problems, and divided these into core and support areas, the SBM now has the basis for beginning to plan for the future.

Step 4—Formulate alternative promotion strategies at both core and support levels. The formulation of alternative promotional strategies is logically guided by beginning with the determination of promotion objectives. The setting of promotional objectives is itself a core promotion strategy decision. Once alternative objectives are considered, other core promotional strategy areas can be considered for fruitful alternatives. Remember that in this step of our eight-step process we are merely formulating alternatives. We are *not* evaluating or selecting an alternative at this point. Comprehensive lists of promotion objectives (or more commonly, advertising objectives) frequently appear in advertising and promotion books. We will not repeat such a list here. The objective is the desired response behavior of the target audience of the promotional effort. Ideally, promotion objectives should be specific by stating exactly what is to be accomplished, when, by whom, and how success is to be measured.

The scope of realistic promotional objectives faced by BB and SB is not the same. For example, if General Foods brings out a new product, it may budget several million dollars into the introductory promotion campaign. Hence a promotion objective such as "80% of nationwide distribution in supermarkets within a one-year period" may be realistic for GF. (However, this is an incomplete statement of a promotion objective, because it does not state exactly what is to be accomplished, when, by whom, and how success is to be measured.) For the SB firm, the stating of promotion objectives is perhaps more difficult if realism is to be achieved. Being specific on the four points just mentioned should add some realism. The experience of the SBM and the statement of overall company and marketing objectives are the basic guidelines.

The number of alternative promotional strategies available to the SBM is almost endless. Many of these alternatives, for SB especially, will revolve around the tasks the SBM assigns to advertising, personal selling, sales promotion, and publicity. It is suggested that the SBM might be wise to individualize his promotion according to the availability (to him) of specific good performers in each of the elements. For example, if the SBM has a very good sales force, he may wish to build the entire promotion campaign around that sales force in much the same way that a small college football coach might gear his entire defensive strategy around an outstanding linebacker. The SBM must take advantage of whatever excellence will be available to him when the time comes to execute the strategy. Creative strategy seeking at this stage never hurts.

Step 5—Evaluate these alternatives in various combinations. Once a group of promotion strategy alternatives, encompassing both core and support levels, has been generated, these alternatives should be evaluated in various combinations. In this step we are evaluating; in the next step we will make a selection. Evaluation involves assessing the risks of competitive reactions, the chances for success in reaching the objectives, and the costs of different alternatives. The SBM will ask: To what extent will this promotion strategy alternative help solve the promotion problems identified in Step #2 above? The SBM should also remember that at this point he is evaluating alternative promotional strategies. He is not evaluating alternative promotional campaigns, themes, or individual promotions. These items are parts of the execution phase of the promotion strategy, which will be selected later. As with the evaluation of other marketing mix elements, the SBM may find it helpful to have agreement on the explicit criteria to be used in evaluating alternative promotional strategies.

Step 6—Choose the new promotion strategy. At this point, the SBM should be prepared to make a choice among the proposed alternative promotion strategies. This choice will be a combination of core and supporting promotion strategies. Its implementation should be flexible enough, both in structure and in budget, to allow for tactical adjustments as desired. Assuming that several good alternatives were proposed, the promotion strategy selected will very likely be one which best meets the promotion needs of the SB firm and one which is also compatible with the subjective value judgment and company philosophy of the SB firm. In short, the promotion strategy will be unique in some ways. A major portion of the new promotion strategy will be very similar, if not identical with, the current promotion strategy which it replaces.

Step 7—Plan the details of implementation of the new promotion strategy. This step involves the how, when, where, and by whom or by what means the new promotion strategy is to be implemented. Such details must be planned in this step in order to insure their smooth implementation. Just as "nothing happens until somebody sells something," we might also state that smooth implementation (or even mediocre implementation) in the absence of planning is probably wishful thinking. Involved in this step are such details as: (a) the assignment of various promotional tasks and responsibilities among the various promotional media, such as specific major advertising media (i.e., newspapers, radio, television, magazines, etc.), supplementary advertising media (directories, advertising specialties, etc.), the personal sales force (territorial salesmen, channel of distribution, sales engineers, etc.), the sales promotion methods (contests, coupons, premiums, etc.), and publicity; (b) the exact nature of the message to be said and the manner in which it will be presented to the target audience(s); (c) the coordination of the promotion schedule; and (d) the necessary cooperation with parties outside the SB firm, such as the advertising agency, media representatives, shopping center promotion managers, and others.

Step 8—Set performance standards and monitor feedback. Here, the SBM sets the criteria by which he will later evaluate the ways (qualitative) and degree (quantitative) to which the selected promotion strategy has been successful. He also plans for a constant flow of feedback on the promotion strategy in order that tactical changes can be used during the execution phase of management to make slight adjustments. In practice, the SBM will find that measuring the effectiveness of promotional activities is very difficult and that both methods of measurement and actual results are almost always controversial. In spite of such limitations, the SBM will want to have some grasp of how well he is doing in the important area of promotion. More is said about this later in the book.

One last thought on promotion strategy is this: If the SBM is to have a promotion strategy, he and his marketing management team must devise it; however, if he wishes only to have promotional effort in the absence of a promotion strategy, numerous media sales representatives stand ready and willing to help him find a place to spend his promotion dollars.

As has previously been stated, promotional strategy becomes operative through four major instruments or elements. These four are advertising, personal selling, sales promotion, and publicity. In the remainder of this chapter and in much of the following chapter, we will look at promotion strategy in each of these four instruments as employed by the SBM.

PROMOTIONAL STRATEGY IN SB ADVERTISING

In beginning the discussion on advertising, I cannot resist the temptation to repeat for you the supposedly anonymous "formula for business success" that was clipped from a magazine and hung for many years on the bulletin board in the backroom office of my father's SB retail store. This formula (the latter three portions of which were followed rather religiously by my successful SB father) stated that the key to success is:

Early to bed,
Early to rise,
Work like hell,
And advertise.

Our discussion will examine the promotion tasks which advertising can perform for the SBM. Appropriate message strategy for SB is described. Then each of the advertising media is examined from the perspective of SB.

The Nature Of Advertising

One of the most successful advertising books ever written gives the following conditions favorable to the use of advertising:

1. A good product.
2. The product should have a significant differential.
3. The product should be identifiable by a trademark.
4. The standard of quality must be maintained.
5. The price should fit into a market price bracket.
6. The product can be sold impersonally to a mass market.[14]

Other conditions under which advertising can be favorably used are: when sufficient funds are available, when emotional motives are important, when the product has hidden qualities, and when the demand trend is favorable. It is rather obvious, from the above conditions, that the SBM does not always find himself in the ideal circumstances to employ advertising. What, then, can the SBM expect from advertising? The following lists of what advertising *can* and *cannot* do give the SBM a realistic idea of what to expect:

Advertising has two top objectives: to draw in new customers, and to help hold the old ones.

[14]Otto Kleppner, *Advertising Procedure* (Englewood Cliffs, New Jersey: Prentice-Hall, Inc., 1973), pp. 51–53.

Advertising can also identify a business with the goods or service it offers.

It can build confidence in a business.

It can create good will.

It can increase sales and speed turnover.

It can reduce your expenses by spreading them over a larger volume.

However, there are a number of things advertising *cannot do.*

Advertising can't make a business prosper if that business offers only a poor product or an inferior kind of service.

Advertising can't lead to sales if the prospects that it brings in are ignored or poorly treated.

Advertising can't create traffic overnight, or increase sales with a single ad. (Unfortunately, many smaller businesses follow this kind of touch-and-go advertising policy.)

Advertising that is untruthful or misleading will not build confidence in the business that sponsors it. [15]

The strategic decision areas within advertising are essentially those same ones discussed earlier in the chapter for promotion. That is, the strategic (both core and supporting) decision areas for promotion apply to advertising and the other forms of promotion. However, different promotion tasks may be assigned to the different forms of promotion. Tasks which SB advertisers assign to advertising vary according to type of business, promotion objectives, and other factors. For example, the SB industrial advertiser may advertise in order to generate leads, to pave the way for the sales force, to announce new products, to create an image, and so forth; whereas retail advertising may be done to bring customers into the store, to help sell the promoted product, to create an image (often called institutional advertising), and to let the customer know where the product is available. Whatever the differences, two major areas of concern for the SBM will be message strategy and media strategy.

Advertising Message Strategy

The planning and execution of the message strategy is largely a creative endeavor. Although some broad guidelines (such as the twenty items we quoted from Britt near the end of our consumer behavior chapter) may be available to the SB advertiser, exceptions can always be found. The determination of what to say and how to say it is more an art than a science. Nevertheless, the SBM and his "creative" people from the advertising agency or wherever should use the basic principles of communication as much as possible. Our communications model presented at the beginning of the chapter can serve as a useful framework. Beyond that framework, the SBM may wish to use the so-called AIDA checklist. The AIDA checklist reduces message strategy to the four major points of a good advertisement: (a) get Attention through such devices as size, color, headlines, and so forth; (b) arouse Interest by employing an interesting (to the intended audience) theme; (c) create a Desire on the part of the audience by showing that the product can meet needs; and (d) get Action—such as, the person goes to the store or asks for the advertised product. It is through the message that the SB advertiser lets the audience know, in an appropriate manner, the objective(s) of the advertising communication.

[15]Robert E. Karp, "On Developing Good Advertising Practices," *Journal of Small Business Management,* 12, No. 2 (April 1974), p. 2.

Advertising Media Strategy

Advertising media are the vehicles or message channels through which the advertising messages reach the target market(s) of the SBM. Since the SBM is very often a target marketer rather than a mass marketer, he will often be quite selective in making media choices. From a strategy point of view, a media selection program which results in satisfactory, though not necessarily optimum, media selection may be most appropriate for SB. The added cost to approach the optimum may outweigh the benefits of doing so. A four-step media approach in which each of the steps represents one of the strategic media questions faced by the SB advertiser, is proposed by Nylen:

1. The first step is to define the specific requirements of the media program.
2. The second step is to select the medium or combination of media that best fit these requirements.
3. The third step is to select a vehicle or vehicles (e.g., a specific TV station or a specific newspaper) within a chosen medium.
4. The fourth step is to schedule insertions within the vehicle and to determine the size or length of time of the message.[16]

Briefly, determining media requirements is the first step of what turns out to be a matching process between the target market audience and the available means for reaching that target effectively with the advertising message in order to accomplish the advertising objectives. Creative requirements, such as a need to display the product in color, may limit the media strategy. However, the major requirements are those of the target market(s) of the product and the budget limits for advertising media.

The media strategy will call for some combination of message impact in terms of media reach, frequency, and continuity. *Reach* is the total number of people to whom the message is delivered. *Frequency* is the number of times the message is delivered during a given time period (often a four-week period). *Continuity* is the total length of time over which the schedule runs. Decisions regarding these concepts also relate to our list of twenty items on consumer behavior near the end of Chapter 6.

Our principle of market dominance (discussed in Chapters 3 and 4) suggests that the SBM will want to limit the number of vehicles used within each medium to such a point that the threshold level of impact will be achieved. In other words, the SBM should be a target advertiser as well as a target marketer. The advantages and disadvantages of many of these media are given below from the perspective of the SB marketing program. Advertising agencies employ specialists in media buying. The SBM may find it advantageous to get some expert advice, especially as the size of the media budget increases.

Newspapers.   More advertising money is invested in newspaper advertising than in any other advertising medium. Newspapers come in such varieties as large city and small town dailies, Sunday, weekly, national, neighborhood, shopping, and special interest. Because they tend to overestimate the geographic size of the market area they serve, SB retailers sometimes advertise in large city newspapers whose circulation, for the SB retailer, is

---

[16]David W. Nylen, *Advertising: Planning, Implementation, And Control* (Cincinnati: South-Western Publishing Co., 1975), p. 261.

mostly wasted. Using suburban or zoned editions can partially negate this problem. Major advantages of newspapers are that the short lead time provides flexibility to the SBM for scheduling and for changing copy, that the cost is often relatively low, and that they provide broad coverage of most persons within a geographically limited market. Disadvantages for the SBM can be the short life span of the newspaper, wasted circulation, and discount structures which favor larger advertisers. Most media have discount structures based upon total usage, number of insertions, and so on that give the quantity user of the medium a discount. For this reason as well as for implementing the principle of market dominance, the SBM should limit the number of media used and should select only those media where dominance, in some form, can be achieved. If shopping and special interest newspapers are used, the SBM should take care to distinguish between claimed and actual circulation and between circulation and the audience which actually read such newspapers. If properly used, such newspapers can be very effective at a lost cost.

Magazines. Today, most magazines are very selective in the audiences which they reach. Magazines exist for nearly every special interest group. If the SB manufacturer produces products for special interest group target markets (e.g., archery equipment, bilge pumps, supermarket supplies, professional equipment, or religious goods), magazines will be available whose circulations are good matches of such target markets. Many magazines and services, such as the Starch Readership Service, provide audience characteristic data for magazine readers. Other advantages attributable to some magazines are their prestige, which "rubs off" on the advertiser, and the good quality of color reproduction possible. Magazines are usually not a SB retailer medium.

Radio. The audience of a radio station can sometimes be determined by sampling its music. For example, a "pop" or "top 40" station may have a large but very young audience. Formats and audiences vary from AM to FM, from station to station, and according to the time of day. Ease of changing the message and relatively low cost make radio a good medium for many SB local advertisers. A major disadvantage of radio is that the nonvisualized message is very short-lived. Slogans and musical jingles are often used to increase message effectiveness. Also, many "listeners" of radio are quite often "tuned-out," especially to advertising messages. Local radio is often very helpful in creating commercials if the SB advertiser does not use an agency.

Television. Sight, sound, color, and motion combine in this very effective medium. For the SBM, these advantages are somewhat offset by high time and production costs. The SBM who can afford to use television (and many can and should) must be certain to employ professionals for producing commercials if the medium is to be used most effectively. In the author's opinion, the local TV commercial which shows the SBM himself giving a sales pitch is not among the most effective commercials. Local television "spots" or spot announcements are often used by SB retailers. SB manufacturers who market on a regional or local basis may also use television if their products and target markets can be adequately matched with an audience. For example, a regional manufacturer of vitamins may sponsor local wrestling shows. Local specials such as golf matches, basketball games, bowling tournaments, and so forth will be good programs for certain SB target marketers.

Outdoor. Posters or billboards are most often used to convey brief messages. For the SB retailer or service firm, the sign designates the place of business and the name of the business. Unusual signs are sometimes used to convey a store's image. Although many legal and ecological considerations must be taken into account, outdoor advertising can be a very effective low-cost medium, especially for firms catering to the travel market. Who would want to travel across South Dakota without the company of the signs from the Wall Drug Store?

Transit. Advertising on the interior and exterior of city buses and other transportation vehicles can reach a geographically selective audience which is, to some extent, captive. The SBM who plans to use transit should ask such questions as: Are the bus exteriors kept clean in bad weather; how often is the copy changed, and does the transit user comprise a part of our target market?

Specialty advertising. In this medium, the SB advertiser has his advertising message imprinted on a useful object such as a calendar, a book of matches, a pen, a ruler, a key chain, a tote bag, a hot pad, and so forth. For the SBM, specialty advertising has the advantage of being tailor-made to fit his advertising needs. It is limited only by the creativity of the representative that serves him. Advertising specialties have a long life, with repeated use and repeated exposure of the ad message. A high unit cost per item of a relatively short message may thus prove to be very economical. An additional benefit for the SBM is that the total cost of a specialty campaign can be fairly small when compared to some other media. Figure 14–3 is an example of the successful use of specialty advertising by SB.

Direct mail. Even with higher postage rates, direct mail is an economical medium for the SBM because of the extreme selectivity of its audience. It can and should be a very

Figure 14.3   An Example of Successful Use of Specialty Advertising by SB

personalized medium. Direct mail advertising has been developed to a rather fine art by some marketers who test direct mail programs to figure costs in terms of coupons returned, inquiries, sales, and so forth. If direct mail is to be a major portion of the SB media mix, the SBM should study the materials of the Direct Mail Advertising Association (DMAA) intensively.

Directories. Like it or not, the SBM would often be wise to plan an effective campaign for the "yellow pages" of the telephone directory. This medium reaches the active shoppers who are in the market to buy. Of course, in order to use this medium effectively, the SBM must have courteous, trained people answering the telephone. Firms selling shopping goods, specialty goods, and services often rely heavily on telephone directories. Industrial directories used by purchasing agents can be important in the industrial market.

Catalogs. Catalog sheets prepared by manufacturers for insertion in wholesaler catalogs and for use by salesmen are very important for some marketers. Catalogs may also be used as a direct mail piece to be sent to consumers. Good detail and color reproduction are important. In addition, catalogs are printed by large retailers who may request the cooperation of the SB manufacturer who supplies an item. Arrangements vary according to whose name appears on the product. Catalog selling has been on the increase.

Point-of-purchase. This medium is sometimes considered sales promotion rather than advertising. It includes the placing of display materials and signs inside the store where the product is sold. Common forms of P-O-P are floor displays, racks, counter displays, window displays, over-the-wire banners, shelf talkers, and permanent displays (e.g., Timex watches or a clock with the name of a brand of beer displayed in a bar). P-O-P is selective in reaching and reminding people when and where they are shopping for a product. The message is usually limited to a short reminder. A major difficulty with P-O-P is getting the materials used, since mass merchandisers receive more materials than they can possibly use. P-O-P is a good medium for the SB manufacturer if his own sales force or some other responsible party is going to perform installation. For example, a P-O-P rack can be designed to properly display a complete line of small products which otherwise may be partially available and poorly displayed.

Handbills. Low cost to the SBM is a major advantage of this medium. Distribution may be at the SB retail store, on cars, or at places of residence. The selection and supervision of reliable people to distribute the handbills is a major problem. Some customers may consider handbills to be a nuisance and act accordingly.

Other media. Not all varieties of media available to the SBM have been specifically discussed above. Should the SBM advertise in religious, fraternal, high school, and college newspapers? For many, the answer would be: If it is charity, call it charity; if it is a good ad medium, use it. Motion picture theater advertising may be good for reaching some target audiences.

For planning his media strategy, the SBM may wish to employ a media matrix. The same device could be used for individual vehicles available within the media. The matrix is simply a two-dimensional picture of all media employed by or available to the SBM and the strength of specific characteristics of each. Within each box, a number or letter system is used to rate strengths and weaknesses. For example, the SBM may use 1–10 or A–F. The

Figure 14–4   Media Matrix For SB (Illustrative Only)

Characteristics / Media									
Daily Newspaper									
Shopping Newspaper									
Local AM Radio									
Local FM Radio									
Specialty Ad									
Direct Mail									
Handbills									
Etc.									
Etc.									

matrix in Figure 14–4 is for illustrative purposes only. Each SBM should construct his own. A second device which is often used for planning is the promotion calendar. We will not illustrate this common device, which can be found in many retailing and advertising books.

Our discussion of the implementation of promotional strategy through advertising is now concluded with the reminder that both the advertising media and the message should be chosen with reference to the promotion objectives of the SBM. In the next chapter, our discussion of promotion strategy continues. We first consider the remaining three implements: personal selling, sales promotion, and publicity.

BIBLIOGRAPHY

Books

BOONE, LOUIS E., AND KURTZ, DAVID L. *Contemporary Marketing.* Hinsdale, Illinois: The Dryden Press, 1974.

HERPEL, GEORGE L., AND COLLINS, RICHARD A. *Specialty Advertising In Marketing.* Homewood, Illinois: Dow Jones-Irwin, Inc., 1972.

KLEPPNER, OTTO. *Advertising Procedure.* Englewood Cliffs, New Jersey: Prentice-Hall, Inc., 1973.

McCARTHY, E. JEROME. *Basic Marketing: A Managerial Approach.* Homewood, Illinois: Richard D. Irwin, Inc., 1975.

NYLEN, DAVID W. *Advertising: Planning, Implementation, and Control.* Cincinnati: South-Western Publishing Co., 1975.

TATE, CURTIS E., JR., MEGGINSON, LEON D., SCOTT, CHARLES R., JR., AND TRUEBLOOD, LYLE R. *Successful Small Business Management.* Dallas: Business Publications, Inc., 1975.

Articles and Periodicals

CASH, HAROLD C., AND CRISSY, W. J. E. "Comparison Of Advertising And Selling," in Eugene J. Kelley and William Lazer, eds. *Managerial Marketing: Policies, Strategies, And Decisions.* Homewood, Illinois: Richard D. Irwin, Inc., 1973, pp. 439–450.

KARP, ROBERT E. "On Developing Good Advertising Practices," *Journal of Small Business Management,* 12, No. 2 (April 1974), 1–6.

SCHLISSEL, MARTIN R. "Promotional Strategy In A High-Technology Industry," *Journal of Economics And Business,* 26, No. 1 (Fall 1973), 67–73.

UDELL, JON G. "The Perceived Importance Of The Elements of Strategy," *Journal of Marketing,* 32, No. 1 (January 1968), 34–40.

Reports

Committee on Definitions. *Marketing Definitions: A Glossary of Marketing Terms.* American Marketing Association. Chicago, 1960.

15

More Promotion Strategy For SBMM

This chapter continues the discussion of promotion strategy from the previous chapter. Topics covered include personal selling, sales promotion, publicity, the promotion budget, measuring promotional effectiveness, and the effective use of advertising agencies by the SBM.

PROMOTION STRATEGY IN SB PERSONAL SELLING

In the marketing of consumer nondurables, there is a saying that "personal selling gets the merchandise on the shelves and advertising moves them off." Although this is somewhat of an overstatement, the saying does point up one of the important roles of personal selling even where mass retailing and mass media advertising are so dominant. That role is to sell to the trade. The roles of personal selling are many and varied, and when taken altogether, they represent the largest portion of promotion.

Our purpose in this chapter is to briefly examine personal selling as a tool for the SBM to use in carrying out promotional strategy. In our SB perspective, we will look at strategic decision areas. Such strategic questions as the following face the SBM: What should be the role and importance of personal selling in the promotional mix? What types of selling tasks are to be performed? Who is going to sell? To whom is the selling to be directed? What selling approaches and processes are appropriate? And how is personal selling to be integrated with other portions of the promotional mix and the overall marketing mix?

The role and importance of personal selling in the SB promotion mix is, first of all, a function of the strengths of personal selling as a communications medium. Is it redundant to state that personal selling is personal? In some cases, the salesman may be the only personal contact the customer has with the company. In effect, the salesman is the company to the customer. (We will use the term *salesman* rather than *salesperson* to include both men and women involved in selling.) Personal contact enables the salesman to make each sales situation unique by adapting the sales message to the message receiver. Personal selling can also be rather effective in providing two-way communication, that is, salesmen can bring information back to the company. Personal selling can operate at the pretransaction and posttransaction phases of the selling process even though its most obvious role may be during the transactions phase. Sometimes other marketing activities, such as physical distribution, implementation of sales promotion, and credit and collections are combined with personal selling activities.

Personal selling tends to play a more important role in the promotion mix under such conditions as the following:

1. The management philosophy of the company has, by choice and over a long period of time, preferred personal selling (e.g., door-to-door selling).

2. The nature of the product favors personal selling because of complex features, installation, customization, need for demonstration, natural sales resistance, infrequent purchase, service requirements, and so forth.

3. The transaction process itself, because of trade-in valuations, price bargaining, and so forth, favors personal selling where interaction is possible.

4. The sale is at a sufficient margin and of a sufficient dollar magnitude to support the high expenses involved in the personal selling.

5. The needs of the buyer are not well defined in the buyer's mind, or perhaps not even present in the buyer's mind; therefore, aggressive personal selling is necessary in order to create desire in the buyer and confidence in the seller.

6. Other situations, such as a very small number of potential buyers, the lack of good advertising media, and the use of "push" oriented channels of distribution, may favor personal selling.

Beyond determining the relative importance of personal selling in the promotion mix, the SBM must determine what promotion tasks are to be performed by personal selling. Specific sales tasks are usually a blend of various types in actual practice, but for purposes of classification they are sometimes grouped into such categories as order-getting order-taking, and support. Order-getters, of whom there are not very many, use creative selling to sell both tangibles and intangibles to industrial, trade, and consumer markets. Order-takers perform service-selling for regular customers on a routine basis, but they certainly may employ some creativity in their work. These salesmen may be either inside or outside, and may serve any of a number of customer types. Supporting salesmen are missionary salesmen or technical specialists who usually do not write orders themselves. For example, sales engineers are often employed in industrial selling.

Whatever classification of selling tasks the SBM arrives at is likely to be a result of the overall promotion and sales objectives of the firm. Ideally, individual salesmen will then set their own objectives, in cooperation with the sales manager, and each salesman will in effect become a sales strategist for the target market he is covering. Of course, the effective execution of that sales strategy is the major task of the individual salesman.

Who performs the selling tasks for the SBM? Here, a major difference may exist between BB and SB. As we have noted in earlier chapters, the SB firm may find it more necessary or at least more beneficial to use a series of middlemen in the channel of distribution. Many times, these middlemen (e.g., sales agents, manufacturer's agents, food brokers, etc.) are used because they provide the strong personal selling support needed by the SB manufacturer. The pay-as-you-go advantage of using commission middlemen (as opposed to the fixed costs involved in one's own sales force, even if a commission compensation plan is employed) may be very important to the SBM. In effect, it lets him know that sales expense will vary almost directly with sales.

To whom the sales effort should be directed is also a strategic question. Sales effort may be directed at consumers, retailers, wholesalers, manufacturers, other industrial buyers, and at various combinations of these. Sales objectives and sales message will vary from audience to audience.

We have already noted that sales situations vary considerably. The SBM is faced with developing a program of effective sales communications in order to transmit the need-satisfying capabilities of his product to the target market. Is there a theoretical basis upon which the SBM can build such a communications framework? Not one, but four basic selling theories have been put forth as the basis for sales strategy formulation. These four theories are (1) stimulus-response theory, (2) mental-states theory, (3) need-satisfaction theory, and (4) problem-solving theory.[1] The SBM must decide for himself which theoretical base is appropriate for the selling situations his firm faces. Once this has been done, he may combine this answer, along with his answers to the previous questions, to formulate a personal selling program that will suit the needs of his overall promotional strategy.

Stimulus-response theory, the simplest of the four forms, is based upon the principle that there is a response for every sensory stimulus. It is Pavlov's dog applied to personal selling. The result is often a completely standardized or "canned" sales presentation which the salesman memorizes. This selling method is limited to very simple selling situations where product price is low and time utilization is critical.

Mental-states theory ". . . is based on the idea that a buyer's mind passes through several successive stages during the course of a sales presentation."[2] This is also known as the selling formula theory or the AIDA theory of selling (attention, interest, desire, action). Although this approach encourages the salesman to plan his sales presentation, the salesman may experience difficulty in identifying the buyer's specific mental state at any given time. The method is applied in industrial selling. It is used when the product is complicated and difficult to understand, when repeat calls are made on a long-run basis, and when a multi-product line is being offered.

Need-satisfaction theory is based upon the idea that products are purchased in order to satisfy needs. In using this customer-oriented theory as a basis for sales strategy formulation, the salesman identifies the prospect's need, makes him aware of that need, and then shows how the product offered will satisfy the need. The SBM who has adopted the marketing concept will feel comfortable with this customer-oriented approach. However, the approach requires highly trained salesmen with a professional attitude and with the time to analyze customer needs. Costs must be weighed when considering this strategy.

Problem-solving theory is the extension of need-satisfaction theory via the scientific method. Here, the salesman helps the buyer identify needs, analyze alternative solutions, evaluate advantages and disadvantages, and select a solution. This is also a customer-oriented approach. In effect, the salesman becomes a recognized authority in the area of the problem. Time and talent are the major restrictions to using this approach. This lengthy process is described as follows:

> The application of the problem-solving process in personal selling involves the use of a scientific, systematic approach in the development of an effective buyer-seller

[1]This discussion of theory is based on Robert F. Gwinner, "Base Theory in the Formulation of Sales Strategy," *MSU Business Topics,* 16, No. 4 (Autumn 1968), pp. 37–44.
[2]Gwinner, p. 39.

relationship. Planning, therefore, becomes an integral part of the selling situation. Prior to the initial interview, the salesman studies the prospect, his business, the industry, and the existing economic and business conditions that may have a bearing on the problem analysis. Backed with this information, he is in an excellent position to offer his service to the prospect as a true business consultant. He completely de-emphasizes his product or service offering, and concentrates his total attention on the prospect and his problem areas.[3]

The selection of sales strategy should be done by the SBM. If it is not done by management, each salesman will do it for himself; and under such circumstances, the various sales strategies chosen are not likely to blend well with the promotion mix and the overall marketing mix. Four factors which the SBM will consider when determining whether or not a given selling theory can be useful to the firm in formulating sales strategy are: (1) the creation of satisfied customers, (2) the resources and capabilities of the firm, (3) the nature of the market, and (4) the nature of the product offering.[4]

Personal selling in retail stores is of interest to many SB retailers, wholesalers, and manufacturers. In recent years a substantial shift has taken place in many lines of merchandise. This shift has been away from personal selling in favor of preselling through advertising supported by retail display and consumer promotions. The nature and extent of the shift can be seen most readily in mass retailing, but the shift may have far-reaching effects. A noted retailing book reports:

> During recent years some observers have contended that the era of informed, creative personal selling in stores has passed and that we are now in the age of impersonal selling. As a discount house operator has said within the hearing of one of the authors: "We don't want salesmen in our organization. Our people are educated order-takers. . . . Our clerks are trained to be courteous, to answer his (customer) questions, and give him what he wants, but not to waste time trying to sell him anything. I believe this is the coming pattern of retailing—for every kind of merchandise—cars, motor-boats, everything. Selling has become an unnecessary vocation."[5]

What are the implications of this thinking for the SB retailer? First of all, a very subtle distinction may be made between heavy emphasis on personal selling as a method of promotion, and *people* as an element of the marketing mix of the SBM. To illustrate, in a midwestern city of medium size are located a national supermarket chain, a regional supermarket chain, and a local supermarket chain. All are mass marketers in this city, employing self-service, mass display, mass advertising, and mass merchandising. However, only the local chain operates with the SB people concept. It does this even though it has a larger share of the local market than either the regional or national chain. None of these three mass marketers employs personal selling as an important part of the promotion strategy, and all three employ people; but only the local chain has a people strategy as a part of its marketing mix. Just as the gasoline companies once told consumers of the personal service they could expect (and usually never received), so also the two BB firms in our supermarket example were telling a people story in their mass media advertising. Maybe the top executives even believed it. But the potential customers didn't because it simply wasn't true at the store level. This may be an indication that it wasn't true at any

[3]Gwinner, p. 42.
[4]Gwinner, p. 43.
[5]Delbert J. Duncan, Charles F. Phillips, and Stanley C. Hollander, *Modern Retailing Management: Basic Concepts And Practices* (Homewood, Illinois: Richard D. Irwin, Inc., 1972), p. 479.

other level in the case of the two BB chains. Our point is that a people strategy (discussed in detail in the next chapter) can and should be a part of the SB marketing mix regardless of whether or not personal selling is important in the SB promotion mix.

A second major point is that personal selling, even if it is simply a really good job of order-taking by a retail clerk, represents an opportunity for the SB retailer. It is an opportunity for the SB retailer to differentiate himself. In fact, personal selling may represent the single best device by which many SB retailers are able to differentiate themselves.

PROMOTION STRATEGY IN SB SALES PROMOTION

Sales promotion represents an opportunity for the SBM to do something different from what his competitors are doing. Sales promotion supplements the rest of the promotion mix. It cannot do the job alone, but it is that "something special" which is communicated via advertising and/or personal selling. Sales promotion can be used by SB manufacturers, wholesalers, retailers, and service firms. It can be directed to three major audiences: consumers, the middlemen of the trade, and the firm's own sales force.

Usually, the nature of sales promotion is to call for a quick response from the audience. That is, the objective may be one or more of the following: (a) to build up (load) dealer stocks prior to the heavy selling season; (b) to encourage special dealer selling effort; (c) to gain distribution during the introduction of a new product; (d) to get new users to try the product; (e) to combat a competitive sales promotion effort; (f) to stimulate the sales force; and so forth. These objectives may suggest that sales promotion is a tactical rather than a strategic decision area of the SB promotion mix. It is true that sales promotion may be viewed as a group of tools or gimmicks that may be tactically employed by the SBM on rather short notice. However, this is not a complete view of sales promotion. In fact, such a view may even be dangerous to the overall promotion and marketing strategies of the SBM. Sales promotion devices are powerful communicators of the firm's image. For example, a price appeal store with a heavy promotional image can use well-planned special sales and other sales promotion tools to help fortify that image. On the other hand, a store of high fashion and quality appealing to a restricted clientele may lose more than it gains if it attempts to stimulate sales during a temporary lag through the use of certain types of sales promotion. Our point here is that individual sales promotion tools, because of their quick response, can be employed tactically by the SBM. However, this employment of tactics should be within a strategic planning framework that has properly defined the roles and objectives of sales promotion. Thus the SBM should plan sales promotion as a regular part of his promotion strategy.

In using sales promotion, the SBM must remember that it is not all advantages and no limitations. Whether or not a promotion is borrowing sales from the future rather than actually creating new sales can be a problem. Although such a borrowing effect may sometimes be reduced by narrow targeting of the promotion, such is not always the case. Another problem is that competitive retaliation and too frequent use of promotions may make them standardized, thus negating much of their effect. SB firms have a particular advantage here if they select promotions which are not easily duplicated by BB competitors. For example, a local contest, such as picking team winners of a local football "pool," would not be duplicated by a chain store competitor.

Having the right promotion at the right time is important. The effectiveness and popularity of promotional devices seem to run in cycles. And many promotions seem to be most effective at some point before they reach the height of popularity. From a retail perspective, the following lessons may be learned regarding the use of promotional techniques:

1. The use of promotional techniques that are readily available to other retailers cannot replace sound retailing/merchandising strategies and planning.
2. Consumer preferences and response to promotional techniques may shift in short periods of time, so that what was in vogue last year is the villain the next.
3. The first retailers to use new promotional techniques may easily capture larger market sales and gain greater profits in the short run; however, once the technique becomes widespread, they may easily be in a worse competitive condition than other, more powerful retailers who adopt the same technique.
4. Dependency upon a promotional technique overlooks the fact that strong new retailers and retailing concepts may emerge while the other retailers are engaged in a competitive promotional battle.
5. It is evident that a particular market segment is attracted to stores that offer particular promotional techniques such as stamps and games. As a result, it may be possible for certain retailers, particularly independent stores and chains, to use these techniques as long as large competitors do not adopt the practices. This is particularly true after larger competitors have tried and discontinued the techniques.[6]

We will now briefly examine the sales promotion forms listed in Table 15–1. These are divided into promotions directed to consumers, the trade, and the sales force. Sales promotion is also used in industrial markets. Point-of-purchase and specialty advertising were discussed previously as forms of advertising. In spite of their possible dual classification, we will not discuss them again here.

Sales Promotion Directed Toward Consumers

Coupons. In recent years, the consumer has almost been forced to read the Wednesday newspaper with a pair of scissors in hand. In addition to issuing coupons in their own advertisements (often in cooperation with a manufacturer), SB retailers may stimulate sales by redeeming manufacturer coupons. One SB grocer started a coupon exchange box in his store. On the honor system, customers could deposit coupons they didn't want and take coupons they wished to use to make purchases in the store. Handling costs and misredemption are major problems in using coupons. In order to reduce misredemption, the SB manufacturer may follow a policy of redeeming coupons only up to the amount of merchandise purchased over the period. The SBM does have some control over the number of coupons issued, the value of each, and the timing. The rate of redemption is affected by the method of distribution. Neilsen figures show the following redemption rates by method of distribution: newspapers, 4%; magazines, 7%; Sunday supplements, 4%; in-on pack, 20%; direct mail, 16%.[7] Of course these percentages could vary considerably, especially for a product of a popular SB manufacturer marketing in a local area. Couponing may be especially effective for the SBM who has a small share of market

---

[6]From *Retail Management: Satisfaction of Consumer Needs* by Raymond A. Marquardt, James C. Makens and Robert G. Roe. Copyright © 1975 by The Dryden Press, A Division of Holt, Rinehart and Winston. Adapted by permission of Holt, Rinehart and Winston, pp. 268–269.

[7]Reported in Don L. James, Bruce J. Walker, and Michael J. Etzel, *Retailing Today: An Introduction* (New York: Harcourt Brace Jovanovich, Inc., 1975), p. 339.

Table 15–1   Some Forms Of Sales Promotion

A. *DIRECTED TOWARD CONSUMERS*
1. Coupons
2. Sampling
3. Premiums and gifts
4. Trading stamps
5. Contests and sweepstakes
6. Demonstrations
7. Deals, price-offs, and so forth
8. Special promotional events
9. Shows and exhibitions
10. Point-of-purchase displays
11. Advertising specialties
12. Others

B. *DIRECTED TOWARD THE TRADE*
1. Cooperative advertising
2. Sales contests
3. Deals and allowances
4. Push Money (P.M.)
5. Trade shows and exhibitions
6. Premiums and gifts
6. Others

C   *DIRECTED TOWARD SALES FORCE*
1. Bonuses
2. Contests
3. Premiums and gifts
4. P.M.
5. Sales aids
6. Sales meetings
7. Others

and wishes to increase that share. This is so because the cents-off coupon can reach many non-users rather than simply acting as a price reduction for current users. Local groups such as the Junior Chamber of Commerce may also sponsor "coupon books" in order to raise money for the organization. SB retailers using such books should plan the coupon offer to fit the intended audience.

Sampling.   The distribution of a "free" or "trial size" sample of the actual product enables the potential customer to actually use the product at a negligible cost. However, this may be an expensive form of promotion for the SBM. Production and distribution of samples can be costly. Sampling usually works best for low unit value products of small size which are frequently purchased. However, the sampling approach can be used for other products by allowing their use for a limited trial period. Food product samples distributed at the store are especially effective in stimulating impulse sales for tasty products whether new or old. Sampling may be used in conjunction with other promotional means such as couponing. SB manufacturers operating in local markets may find that they are in a good competitive position to use sampling, especially if they back up the sampling with local advertising. As far as SB retailers are concerned, sampling can be very effective, low-cost promotion for certain firms. The author is reminded of the nut shop whose major means of promotion was to give a few free nuts to every passerby in front of the store.

Premiums and gifts. Something for nothing is the basic appeal behind gifts and premiums. As the parent of any cereal-eating child can readily tell you, both the "something" and the "nothing" may be quite illusory. However, these same parents can also attest to the effectiveness of these premiums in making sales. Gifts may be outright to all takers, along with the purchase of a product, or as a self-liquidating premium offer which may require a payment at a "good value" price by the consumer. They may be included in or on the package, or they may require the consumer to save several "proofs of purchase" to mail in. This latter type, along with "dish deals" where a set of glassware or stoneware is completed over a period of time, have the advantage of keeping the customer coming back. Gifts are also sometimes given to current customers for providing leads to new customers for door-to-door selling. Gifts and premiums which have some relationship to the product and are not easily purchased elsewhere or duplicated by competition are often most effective.

Trading stamps. This is an excellent example of a sales promotion tool that became so common a few years ago that many retailers, both BB and SB, felt that it lost its effectiveness. Unlike some other forms of sales promotion, trading stamps tend to be a long-term commitment on the part of the retailer. Stamps are still popular in many areas. The SBM who is considering the use of stamps should consider what other complementary and competing stores in his area offer the same stamps or competing stamps, the cost at two to three percent of sales, stamp saving patterns in the area, and the availability of redemption facilities.

Contests and sweepstakes. Contests in which the entrant must perform some active participation, and sweepstakes in which "pure chance" decides which entrant(s) win, have been popular in recent years. Even after government investigation of the "gas-station games" of a few years ago, these forms of sales promotion are still very popular. However, from the SB point of view, contests must take on a somewhat different flavor. For example, the SB firm cannot give away a million dollars. Perhaps even a thousand dollar prize may be out of the question for many SB firms. Because of legal aspects and because contest planning is quite an art, the SBM who is planning to use a contest which involves either much money or complexity should seek some professional assistance. Sales promotion firms are available to assist with many of the forms of sales promotion mentioned in this chapter. Otherwise, the excitement created may be among the many losers (perhaps former customers also) rather than among the few winners.

Demonstrations. Products such as farm equipment and major household appliances may be too expensive to sample and too complex to sell in the absence of a personal or group demonstration of the product in use. Manufacturers often supply the trained demonstrator, and the SB retailer is expected to supply the audience. Although expensive, demonstration can be very effective if the characteristics of the product so dictate.

Deals, price-offs, and so forth. Deal merchandise; price-offs, such as a cents-off deal; price packs; "free" deals, such as buy three—get one free; one cent sales; and so on are price promotions to consumers which offer a special price for a limited time period. The art is in selecting the best form in which to express the price deal, the amount of the price cut, and, especially for multiproduct manufacturers and retailers, the right product(s) on which to offer a special price deal. A version of the price deal which has become popular among some food processors in recent years is the money refund offer. This offer states: "We'll pay you $2.00 to try our _____." The consumer is encouraged to buy the product, enjoy it, and then send a proof of purchase in order to receive the refund. Obviously, not all consumers will get as far as the final step.

Special promotional events.   Among the special events used by retailers are fashion shows, schools, seasonal displays, local celebrations, and so forth. The test of the promotional value of special events is sales to customers or some other defined promotional objective.

Shows and exhibitions.   For certain product lines, such as recreational vehicles, automobiles, boats, sporting equipment, and hobbies and crafts, shows have become very popular in recent years. Municipal auditoriums with spacious display areas and "live entertainment" have combined to attract large crowds. Persons attending such shows are much better than average prospects for the merchandise and services on display. Quite often, manufacturers and their local retail dealers will cooperate in promoting at such shows. For reaching prime prospects, this is a good promotional tool for certain types of SB firms.

Sales Promotion Directed Toward the Trade

Cooperative advertising.   As explained earlier in the book, allowances for cooperative advertising are payments from a manufacturer to a retailer to cover a portion (usually half) of the retailer's cost for advertising the manufacturer's product. From a sales promotion point of view, cooperative advertising may also result in a mass display, special price, and increased sales. The SB manufacturer should be sure to get performance from cooperative monies spent. The SB retailer should be sure to collect cooperative monies due.

Sales contests.   Contests for dealers and their salesmen are sometimes offered as special incentives for exceeding quotas or for other outstanding performances. Many prizes—with a grand prize, such as an expensive paid trip—are usually awarded.

Deals and allowances.   Many forms of deals, such as "free goods," an additional discount for a limited time, display allowances, and so forth, are offered to the trade. If offered too frequently, such deals become part of the standardized way of doing business, and large buyers especially will buy only when a deal is on. The SB manufacturer should attempt to make his deal distinctive from that of his BB competitors.

Push money.   Push money (P.M.) is offered to the salesmen of the trade through which the firm sells. Some trade members may object to their salesmen receiving push money from suppliers, as it tends to undermine their own merchandising plans and employee relations.

Trade shows and exhibitions.   For the SBM with a very limited sales force, such trade shows and exhibitions represent an opportunity to establish a large number of contacts in a very short period of time. The display booth at a trade show, along with hospitality suites and other trade show activities, can be a major sales tool for the SB firm. The selection of the one best, or three or four best, trade shows to participate in is, for many SB manufacturers, a very important sales promotion decision. For example, the SB manufacturer who does not have national representation may be able to secure a high percentage of national distribution by doing an outstanding job at a national trade show.

Premiums and gifts. Business customers also like to receive premiums and gifts. For example, the author can remember that, when stocking shelves in his father's supermarket, a close watch was kept for the premium certificates in one brand of food flavorings and one brand of spaghetti products. Incidentally, both of these were products of SB manufacturers. The value of these premium certificates was not great on a per case basis, but grocer's wives enjoy spending them very much if the stock boys don't throw them away. The certificates could be spent like cash in a gift catalog. The SB manufacturer contemplating the use of business gifts and premiums will find many "premium houses" ready to assist him in this sales promotion program.

Sales Promotion Directed Toward the Sales Force

Many of the same sales promotion tools that are directed toward the trade may, in slightly different form, be directed toward the sales force of the SB firm. Among these are contests, premiums and gifts, and push money. Other sales promotion devices are bonuses, helpful sales aids, and meaningful sales meetings.

PROMOTION STRATEGY IN SB PUBLICITY

Publicity is an indirect but very important supplement to the rest of the promotion mix. In terms of the communications process, publicity differs, especially in the eyes of the audience or receiver. Even though the SB firm may influence publicity, the actual sender-encoder is the news media. This fact tends to have a favorable effect on the credibility of the message in the eyes of the receivers. This fact also allows the message to get past the selective perception of the receiver, which sometimes filters out advertising and personal selling messages. In one sense, publicity also tends to extend beyond the promotional mix of the firm into other areas, such as employee morale. For example, a news release stating that several employees have received a certificate of achievement for completing a special training school will boost morale among the employees. It will also get the name of the company in front of the public in a favorable light.

Publicity differs from other promotion methods in that it is nonpaid communication over which the SB firm has little control. However, most SB firms are probably doing some worthwhile things for the community which are newsworthy and could, if properly handled, result in good publicity. Examples of such activities in which SB firms may be involved are sponsoring athletic teams, contributing prizes to local organizations, actively participating in civic affairs, and so forth. Other newsworthy items are the introduction of a new product, the grand opening of a store, the addition of new services, installation of energy-saving devices or techniques, professional and trade awards to employees, trips to conventions or fashion markets, speeches given, and so forth.

In many SB firms, publicity may be an unassigned responsibility or may be one of the many responsibilities of the chief executive. In such cases, many publicity opportunities may be missed or poorly handled. While very few SB firms can afford to hire a PR man to handle public relations and publicity, a specific assignment of the task within the firm or to the firm's advertising agency may be a very worthwhile move. The Small Business Administration publishes *Management Aid* # 165 entitled *Publicize Your Company By Sharing Information.* This will help the SBM who is beginning to use publicity.

THE PROMOTION BUDGET FOR SB

A strategy for managing the promotion budget, once that budget is determined, is needed by the SBM. First, how should the SBM determine how much to spend for promotion? The determination of (a) how much to spend for promotion and (b) how to allocate those promotion funds among advertising, personal selling, sales promotion, and publicity are not the same things as (c) the strategy decision of determining the role of promotion in the marketing mix and (d) the strategy decision of determining the roles of advertising, personal selling, sales promotion, and publicity in the promotion mix. Items (c) and (d) are basic marketing and promotion strategy decisions of a "core" nature. Items (a) and (b) are operational decision areas for implementing those strategies. As such, the SBM will be seeking decision criteria or decision-making approaches to the budgeting process in promotion. Promotion budgeting is the process of allocating resources (dollars) to (1) promotion; (2) the four elements (advertising, personal selling, sales promotion and publicity); and further (3) to the specific media and vehicles within each of these elements. Our concern here will, however, be limited to level # 1, with the notation that many marketers of all sizes often consider personal selling outside the promotion budget.

Factors To Be Considered

Whether the SBM is dealing with the size of the total promotion budget or the size of the advertising budget, the economic principle of marginal analysis would apply in theory. However sound marginal analysis may be in theory, it is pretty much ignored in practice. The necessary data is not available. Therefore businessmen are left to arbitrary rule of thumb methods of promotional budgeting—if they plan the promotional budget at all. Each SBM may wish to examine the several methods given below for the purpose of constructing his own budgeting method based on the factors most important to him. Among the factors to be considered are such items as the following:

1. What is the minimum amount of promotion (and each form of promotion) needed to attain a threshold level of impact for the target market(s)?
2. What economies of scale can be realized at different levels of promotion?
3. How much promotion is "too much" in terms of decreasing and negative returns?
4. What effects do the strengths and weaknesses in the remainder of the marketing mix have on the desired level of promotion expenditure? For example, specific items—such as a good or poor location for a retail store, an established reputation and loyal customer following versus a new product or a new store, and so forth—all must be considered.
5. What is the competitive climate and how is it changing?
6. What promotional tools are available to the SBM which may be especially advantageous? For example, the SBM may raise both prices and the advertising budget if he decides that a new promotional medium (e.g., trading stamps, shopping newspaper, etc.) will be extremely successful.

7. What environmental changes are taking place? For example, right or wrong, many businessmen decrease promotion when entering a recession and increase promotion during the upswing of the recovery.

Approaches To Promotion Budgeting

Four basic approaches will be discussed here. Other approaches, as well as combinations of these four, are possible. The four widely used approaches are percentage of sales, competitive parity, available funds, and objective task.

Percentage of sales. This method is easy to understand and apply. It is, therefore, quite popular among SB. Here, the promotion budget is set at some fixed percentage of sales. The sales base may be past sales, expected future sales, or some combination of these. The expected future sales is probably the most logical base. The rationale for determining the percentage is usually past experience. Thus, if two percent worked last year, the SBM budgets two percent for the coming year. A variation of this method is to use a fixed sum per unit or per case.

Since sales are one (if not the major) of the intended responses to promotion, it seems somewhat backwards to assume a sales level and then determine how much promotion will be used to cause that effect. However, as a base or starting point, the percentage method does have merit. From this starting point, adjustments may be made for such factors as new competition, the introduction of a new product, the opening of new territories, changing business conditions, and so forth.

Competitive parity. Under this approach, competition sets the promotion budget. This may be a possible method for BB to employ for the mass media portion of promotion, but the application to SB or to the rest of the promotion budget is limited. Competitive parity means that the firm monitors what competitors spend for promotion and act accordingly by budgeting the same dollar amount, the same percentage of sales, an industry average, or some other competitor-based guideline. The method assumes (a) that share of market and promotion expenditures are directly and/or proportionately related, (b) that the SBM knows what competitors are doing, (c) that the competitors know what they are doing, (d) that what would be a good mix for competitors would also be good for the SBM, and (e) that the SBM can afford to match competitive promotion budgets. Any and all of these assumptions may be incorrect. Whatever the case, competitive parity considers only the competitive variable. As such, it is lacking as a comprehensive budgeting device.

Available funds. The budgeting of "all you can afford" may result in too little or too much. The method involves allocating to promotion the residual (if there is any) after planned expenses for all other items and a planned profit have first been established. Although this method has been used successfully to promote a new product during the introductory phase, in general the method is not recommended.

Objective task. In this approach, the SBM (a) defines all the specific tasks that are to be accomplished via promotion, (b) assigns a cost to each task, and (c) totals up the costs. In effect, the total is a series of task budgets. This problem-oriented approach probably appeals to marketing students because it seems to be scientific. Tasks can be rank-ordered as to importance if funds are not available to accomplish all tasks. From a practical view, what this approach does is to break the budgeting problem down into several small budgeting problems. The question then must be asked: Is the SBM in a position to properly define and accurately cost each of these smaller problems (tasks)? Whether or not the objective task method is used for budgeting, the SBM can and should set promotional objectives early in the planning of his promotional strategy. The promotion tasks necessary to accomplish these specific objectives should be spelled out in detail as a part of the promotion strategy plan.

The above approaches are basically each dealing with a single variable (sales, competition, availability, costs). None is a comprehensive approach, but each does have something to offer the SBM. Percentage of sales probably receives the most emphasis from SB. The SBM is well advised to, first of all, be more concerned with promotion strategy then with the budgeting process. To the extent that budgeting is necessary and useful, the SBM should determine the promotion budget and its allocation by using a combination of the above approaches. Some small portion of that budget should be reserved for experimentation. In that way, trial and error will be more than "doing the same thing we did last year."

Cost Per Response

Promotion activity of all kinds is communication carried on in order to elicit some sort of response from the intended receivers. There are many possible intended responses and many ways of measuring costs. In fact, there are so many combinations of response and measurement method that comparisons are difficult. The SBM should be cautious when making comparisons among advertising media and vehicles, and when comparing costs among advertising, personal selling, sales promotion, and publicity. A few of the cost per unit measures are:

1. Cost per thousand of (a) circulation or (b) audience. This is figured by dividing the total amount of money by the number of people (in thousands).
2. Direct mail may use cost per inquiry and cost per sale.
3. Cost per column inch or page is used by print media.
4. Cost per time unit is used by broadcast media. The numbers and methods used by rating services to show numbers of sets on, listeners, or viewers can be confusing.
5. Traffic counts are used by outdoor advertising.
6. Specialty advertising uses cost per campaign, cost per item, and cost per impression.
7. Personal selling measures cost per call, cost as a percentage of sales, selling cost per unit, and so forth.

The point of the above listing is that costs are not easily compared in the promotional area. The "apples and oranges" problem is further complicated by the fact that, in a good promotion mix, all the elements blend together in such a way that the synergetic effect results—that is, the whole is greater than the sum of its parts. Evaluating promotional effectiveness is even more difficult than comparing promotional costs.

MEASURING THE EFFECTIVENESS OF PROMOTION

In the opinion of the author, the overall effectiveness of promotion cannot be accurately measured. Likewise, the overall effectiveness of advertising, personal selling, sales promotion, or publicity cannot be accurately measured. These concepts are rather inclusive of many activities and objectives. They are complex and have interrelated cause-effect patterns. The effectiveness measurement task is simply overwhelming. In essence, if the marketing program is working well in achieving company goals and objectives, the promotion portion is probably working well, along with product, place, price, and people. If the marketing program is not working well, this may or may not be due to the promotion program.

What, then, can be measured in the promotional sphere? And what can and should be measured by the SBM? Again, in the opinion of the author, individual advertisements, individual layouts, individual media choices, the performance of individual salesmen, and the effectiveness of an individual sales promotion are examples of promotion that are capable of being measured. These individual parts, along with other individual parts, of the promotional effort are definable, are manageable, and should be measured by the SBM. Thus, while the only way the SBM may be able to find out if his advertising is doing any good is to discontinue all advertising, less drastic and more meaningful measures are available for evaluating individual advertisements. The SBM can and should use such available measures. Our discussion of effectiveness measure will be limited to advertising and personal selling.

Measuring Advertising Effectiveness In SB

Parts of the advertising campaign may be evaluated by using various marketing research techniques. Our listing below is incomplete, but is illustrative of SB application. Advertising is usually classified as immediate response or image-building. Likewise, advertising effectiveness research is sometimes classified according to the sales effect or the communications effect. A measure of the communicating ability is a more direct measure, since so many factors affect sales. However, the SBM who is advertising for a direct sales reponse may be more interested in a measure of the sales effect. Direct mail advertisers have the best opportunities to measure sales effectiveness. Retailers also have some opportunities which are easy to use and not very costly. Among these opportunities are:

Coupons brought in. Usually these coupons represent sales of the product. When the coupons represent requests for additional information or contact with a salesman, were enough leads obtained to pay for the ad? If the coupon is dated, you can determine the number of returns for the first, second, and third weeks.

Requests by phone or letter referring to the ad. A "hidden offer" can cause people to call or write. Include—for example, in the middle of a paragraph—a statement that on request the product or additional information will be supplied. Results should be checked over a 1-week through 6-months or 12-months period because this type ad may have considerable carry-over effect.

Split runs by newspapers. Prepare two ads (different in some way you would like to test) and run them on the same day. Identify the ads—in the message or with a coded coupon—so you can tell them apart. Ask customers to bring in the ad or coupon. When you place the ad, ask the newspaper to give you a split run—that is: to print "ad A" in part of its press run and "ad B" in the rest of the run. Count the responses to each ad.

Sales made of particular item. If the ad is on a bargain or limited-time offer, you can consider that sales at the end of 1 week, 2 weeks, 3 weeks, and 4 weeks came from the ad. You may need to make a judgment as to how many sales came from display and personal selling.

Check store traffic. An important function of advertising is to build store traffic which results in purchases of items that are not advertised. Pilot studies show, for example, that many customers who were brought to the store by an ad for a blouse also bought a handbag. Some bought the bag in addition to the blouse, others instead of the blouse.[8]

Measuring Personal Selling Effectiveness In SB

Call reports of salesmen and company sales records provide data for measuring the effectiveness of individual salesmen and sales supervisors. The personal selling effort can be evaluated both quantitatively and qualitatively on both the input and output sides. Although selling conditions, competition, potential, customer concentration and composition, and so on vary from one territory to another, such factors as the following are suggestive of the ways in which the performance of personal selling may be measured and evaluated:

Output—quantitative factors:
1. Sales Volume
   a. By product groups (such as equipment vs. sundry sales)
   b. By customer type (such as laboratory sales vs. sales to dentists)
2. Market share—percentage of total sales in an area
3. Sales volume against a reasonable quota (scientifically established)
4. Gross profit earned
5. Average Sale—total sales divided by the number of sales

Input—quantitative factors:
1. Number of days worked
2. Number of calls made in a specified period
3. Miles driven
4. Direct selling expense
5. Leads or prospects generated
6. Number of detail calls

Combination of output and input quantitative factors:
1. Batting average—(number of orders divided by the number of calls)
2. Routing Efficiency—(miles traveled divided by the number of calls)[9]

SB AND THE ADVERTISING AGENCY

A major promotion decision for many SB marketers is whether to use an advertising agency or to make advertising (and other promotion activities sometimes performed by ad agencies) a do-it-yourself project. For the do-it-yourselfer, the danger of costly amateurish mistakes is present. However, outside assistance, short of using an advertising agency, is available. The SBM may choose to work through an agency for the media portion of his advertising while performing some of the other portions in-house.

[8]Elizabeth M. Sorbet, "Measuring The Results Of Advertising," *Small Marketers Aids,* No. 121 (Washington: Small Business Administration, 1972), pp. 2–3.
[9]Ross M. Trump et al., *Essentials Of Marketing Management* (Boston: Houghton Mifflin Company, 1966), p. 72.

For The Do-It-Yourselfer

The suggestion has been made that the SBM who is going to manage his own advertising program and supervise its execution might think of himself as a general contractor who hires sub-contractors with various specialized skills and expertise in advertising. Among the subcontractors would be printers, graphic artists, media salesmen, suppliers, and so forth. One SBA publication lists the following four sources of help to the SB retailer, in addition to the advertising agency:

1. The advertising departments of newspapers offer assistance in copy preparation, art work, and layout. They are often willing to advise the retailer on his general merchandising and sale promotional planning.
2. The firms that supply the retailer with his merchandise often provide advertising materials free of charge; grant advertising discounts; and participate cooperatively in the retailer's advertising by sharing a portion of the cost.
3. Direct-mail agencies compile specialized mailing lists which can be used by the retailer to contact selected customer groups. These agencies also assist in the preparation of the mailing literature.
4. The trade newspapers and magazines of his particular field of retailing often provide useful information to the store manager concerning the advertising practices of his fellow retailers. Trade associations, Chambers of Commerce, and Better Business Bureaus also frequently provide information on advertising and advertising ethics.[10]

Financial resources and the size of the advertising budget may determine whether or not an ad agency is used. Depending on individual circumstances, such as the number of media employed, the advertising capabilities of the SBM as measured by someone whose ego is not involved, and the time costs and opportunities available, the SBM should consider the use of an advertising agency if his firm is spending one or two thousand dollars a month for advertising. The alternative is to hire someone as a company employee to handle the advertising. For a local advertiser receiving local media rates not subject to agency discounts from media, this may seem to be an economical and effective method. For the SB national advertiser such as the SB industrial firm, an advertising agency specializing in the industry may do a better job. In addition, the cost may be lower due to the discounts (usually a 15% commission) media allow to agencies but not to direct placement by the advertiser.

Using An Advertising Agency

When an advertising agency is used, the SBM is still responsible for working with the agency to formulate the overall promotion strategy. In addition, the SBM must make sure that the advertising efforts of the agency are properly coordinated wat te personal selling and other promotion efforts of the firm. The role of the advertising agency may vary from full service to the writing and placing of advertisements. Full service might include

---

[10]J. Wade Rice, "Advertising—Retail Store," *Small Business Bibliography,* No. 20 (Washington: Small Business Administration, 1973), p. 2.

such services as creating a campaign theme, package design, logo design, creating a slogan or jingle, writing copy, doing layouts, copy testing, audience and readership measurement, sales promotion, and publicity.

In order to use an agency to best advantage, the SBM must first find the right agency. To do so, he must know what he is looking for. The SBM should therefore determine what he expects from the agency *before* he begins the search for a particular agency. The SBM should look for three things in an agency:

> You should look for three things in an agency: (1) Does the agency have experience in selling to the kinds of customers who make up my market? If not, does it have the ability to adapt its experience to my type products? (2) Will it assign some of its most skilled people to my account? and (3) Is it financially responsible?
>
> You can get an answer to the first question fairly easily. You ask the agency for samples of its past and present work with your type of products.
>
> You can answer the second question by asking for experience resumes of the people who will do the day-to-day planning and creative work on your advertising.
>
> Financial responsibility is important because the agency will represent you in financial dealings with media.[11]

The basic goals and philosophy of the SB firm are a background against which any advertising agency will be measured before a relationship is established. In fact, the selection of an agency is an excellent opportunity to use the total marketing strategy plan of the firm. A review of the strategy plan should indicate to the SBM what to look for in an agency. The agency will become a part of the marketing management team. In effect, the agency is a diversity of advertising specialists available to the SBM at an economical cost because other clients are sharing the cost of supporting such a collection of expertise. In selecting an agency, the SBM must know what he expects the agency to do for him in order to know what areas of expertise the selected agency should possess in strength.

The agency selection process may begin by simply finding out who is available in the geographic area or industry involved. The size of the agency is important. Of course, the SBM wants the agency to have expertise and specialization. But caution should be taken *not* to select an agency that is too large. If the account of the SBM is not an important part of the agency's business, the performance on the account is not likely to be first-rate. A smaller agency, especially one that is interested in growth through the growth of its clients, may be best for SB.

At some point the SBM and one or two advertising agencies will mutually select each other for more serious consideration. At this point, the SBM would be wise to spend a few hours at the agency in order to become familiar with the people who will do the actual work on his account. Being able to work well together is very important for a successful campaign. The one or two "finalist" agencies may be asked to prepare a presentation which outlines the ideas the agency has for doing the advertising job for the firm. In the case of an SB firm, advertising agencies may not wish to invest in a presentation until they have a reasonable assurance that they have the account, or that presentation costs will be covered. The SBM should at least be willing to limit the number of agencies from which he requests a presentation. Otherwise, presentations will be rather vague and meaningless.

In order for an agency-client relationship to last over a period of time, the

---

[11]Harold Marshall, "Effective Industrial Advertising For Small Plants," *Management Aids For Small Manufacturers*, No. 178 (Washington: Small Business Administration, 1971), p. 4.

relationship must be profitable for both the agency and the advertiser. How should the agency be compensated? It depends. A commission, a fee, or a combination of commission and fee may be used. Whatever is mutually agreeable between the SBM and the agency can work well so long as the SBM is not paying for more than he is receiving and the agency feels that the account can be profitable for the agency.

BIBLIOGRAPHY

Books

Duncan, Delbert J., Phillips, Charles F., and Hollander, Stanley C. *Modern Retailing Management: Basic Concepts And Practices.* Homewood, Illinois: Richard D. Irwin, Inc., 1972.

James, Don L., Walker, Bruce J., and Etzel, Michael J. *Retailing Today: An Introduction.* New York: Harcourt Brace Jovanovich, Inc., 1975.

Marquardt, Raymond A., Makens, James C., and Roe, Robert G. *Retail Management: Satisfaction of Consumer Needs.* Hinsdale, Illinois: The Dryden Press, 1975.

Trump, Ross M., *et al. Essentials Of Marketing Management.* Boston: Houghton Mifflin Company, 1966.

Articles and Periodicals

Gwinner, Robert F. "Base Theory in the Formulation of Sales Strategy," *MSU Business Topics,* 16, No. 4 (Autumn 1968), 37–44.

Marshall, Harold. "Effective Industrial Advertising For Small Plants," *Management Aids For Small Manufacturers,* No. 178, Washington: Small Business Administration, 1971, pp. 1–4.

Rice, J. Wade. "Advertising—Retail Store," *Small Business Bibliography,* No. 20, Washington: Small Business Administration, 1973, pp. 1–7.

Sorbet, Elizabeth M. "Measuring The Results of Advertising," *Small Marketers Aids,* No. 121, Washington: Small Business Administration, 1972, pp. 1–4.

16

People Strategy for SBMM

The significance of the people variable as a means of differential advantage to the SBM is perhaps best pointed out by the attempts of BB to duplicate this advantage for themselves. In an article to which we will again refer, Tinsley correctly perceives the nature of such attempts at the retail level:

> Such obvious problems as inflation, capital shortages, and recessions make the survival of small retailers increasingly difficult. However, the most serious future threat to small retailers could well be found in the increasing efforts of large retailers to seize for themselves the traditional advantages of small businesses. Two examples are the popular practice by large retailers of establishing boutique departments with personalized services and the increasing tendency of franchisors to substitute direct company operation of retail units for conventional franchising arrangements.[1]

Throughout this book we have made occasional references to PEOPLE as a marketing variable in the SB marketing mix. It is not found as a part of the BB marketing mix. In our SBMM model, people works along with product, place, price, and promotion to comprise the SB marketing mix. In this chapter we will investigate the people variable in detail. First, we will discuss exactly what people is and is not. People differences between SB and BB will be shown, and the resulting problems and opportunities will be noted. The role and importance of people as a variable in the SB marketing mix will be investigated. The SB people mix itself will be described. Important strategic decision areas of people strategy in SB will precede the eight-step process of people strategy formulation for SB. Upon completion of this chapter, the SBM should be ready to use people effectively as one of the controllable variables in his SB marketing mix.

[1]Dillard D. Tinsley, "Competition, Consultants, And Completeness: Strategy In The Small Retailer's Future," *Journal Of Small Business Management*, 14, No. 3 (July 1976), p. 12.

WHAT PEOPLE IS AND IS NOT AS A MARKETING VARIABLE

The importance of people and the interpersonal relationships among the members of the work group grew out of the now famous Hawthorne experiments of the 1920s. There, the focus was on the resulting productivity from worker attitudes toward management, the work, and the work group. Our emphasis is slightly different. First of all, the Hawthorne Works of Western Electric is certainly not an example of SB. More fundamentally, however, we are looking at people as a part of the marketing mix rather than from a managerial perspective such as human relations or personnel. Although the people involved are a very important ingredient in the success of a business of any size, a special significance may be attached to people in SB. The lack of an elaborate hierarchy, as with a large and formal bureaucratic organization, enables the SBM to use people as a controllable variable in the SB marketing mix. The result may often be a very significant differential advantage to the SB firm. This may happen but it does not necessarily happen. In fact, many SB firms have no people strategy at all. Other SB firms may have personnel policies and strategies, but they are not employed as a part of the SB marketing mix. In this author's opinion, the lack of a people strategy as an important part of the SB marketing mix is an unnecessary self-imposed disadvantage for the SBM. The right people are every bit as much a part of the SB marketing mix as the right product, place, price, and promotion.

By *people*, we mean all the people of the SB firm. All can and should be a part of the marketing mix of the successful SB firm. The SBM who has both adopted and implemented the marketing concept has permeated the marketing philosophy throughout the firm. People includes the SBM; other managers; all employees, whether salesmen or otherwise; outside consultants and advisors; the advertising agency; and possibly members of the channel of distribution. As we stated in Chapter 1, people strategies include such areas as investment in people and their development, organization, motivation, and other "personnel" matters that can, if viewed as a part of marketing strategy, give the alert SBM a differential advantage.

Can we find evidence in research studies which shows that SB firms which have "good" people strategies tend to be more successful than SB firms which have "zero" or "bad" people strategies? To the author's knowledge, such evidence is not available. However, casual observation of successful SB firms does suggest that such an hypothesis could be supported. The more potential customers of the target market that know the SBM and his people in a positive and personal manner, the more customers the SBM will have. The people variable of the SB firm is a part of the reason behind the patronage motives of its customers. For example, the customer who deals with the "top man" in the SB retail firm may receive certain psychic benefits unavailable to him from the BB retailer. BB cannot easily duplicate the SBM's advantage of being his own top management. As Tinsley notes:

> Interaction of this type is increasingly important for retailers because of the customer's increasing search for self-actualization through consumption. Interpreted as the expression of individual priorities and preferences reflecting different life styles and going beyond those related to satisfying basic wants and needs, self-actualization implies a highly individualized approach to need-satisfaction which requires a high level of personal sales efforts. The selling efforts of the independent

firm's top management should be more effective than those of the larger retailer's sales personnel, who are usually far removed from their own top managers and often unmotivated.[2]

Before looking at what people strategy is *not*, let us look at one more example of people strategy in SB. Amazing as it may seem, Johnny Carson, in his monologue on the "Tonight Show" reported on a bank that used the fact that there are two sexes as a basis of market segmentation. A California bank, owned and operated by women, recently opened for the purpose of serving a specific target market: women.

Here are some of the things that people strategy in the SB marketing mix is not:

1. People strategy is *not* simply the personal selling element of the promotion mix. Although the people variable may (or may not) surface in personal selling, people is a larger concept as a separate "P" in the marketing mix of SB.
2. People strategy is *not* viewed here as a part of broad management strategy, but it is viewed as a part of marketing strategy.
3. People strategy is *not* the people of the target market, that is, customers. Indeed, customers are usually people also; but we are using the term to mean the people of the SB firm.
4. People strategy is *not* concerned primarily with personnel as an end in itself, but only as one means to accomplish the people marketing objectives. That is, the nuts and bolts of personnel administration supports but is not the same thing as the people variable in SB. Our perspective is that of the SB marketing mix, not the staff function of personnel or the management function of human relations. However, these can be important means to our end.
5. People strategy is *not* people tactics.

PEOPLE DIFFERENCES IN SB

In Chapter 1 we discussed the differences between BB and SB. From these differences, certain advantages and disadvantages were said to be inherent in SB. Some of these were listed in Chapter 1. Also listed in Chapter 1 were the 24 summarized conclusions of Cohn and Lindberg on how management is different in small companies.[3] A review of these 24 conclusions at this time will reveal that approximately half of these conclusions deal with people. The reader is invited to refer to Chapter 1, where complete details of the following conclusions regarding people can be noted:

2. Focus on achieving managerial excellence.
3. Adapt rather than adopt BB methods and practices.
4. Don't skimp on management staff.
11. Can afford less to be a specialist.
12. Board of directors with outside membership.
13. Consensus decision making.
14. Natural habitat for entrepreneur.

[2]Tinsley, p. 13.
[3]Theodore Cohn and Roy A. Lindberg, *How Management Is Different in Small Companies,* An AMA Management Briefing, 1972, pp. 2–3.

15. Offset personal deficiencies and utilize strengths.
16. Seek to employ high potential people.
17. Attract and keep effective people.
18. People skilled in handling a high volume of detail.
21. Not make a fetish of keeping organization as simple as possible.
24. More problems in creating sales than managing people.

The most basic people difference between BB and SB is the necessary presence of a bureaucratic hierarchy in BB and the absence of such a bureaucracy in SB. In the BB bureaucracy, people are fitted into slots. In SB, the simple organization is built around the people. An analogy from the world of sports would contrast the strategies of a coach from a large football university and a small football college. Although both coaches will attempt to get the most from their players, their approaches will vary. The big school coach with a large squad (and perhaps a number of "redshirts" waiting in the wings) will utilize players as they fit in with his style of football. On the other hand, the small college coach with a smaller squad will build his style of football around the people available to him. Our example is somewhat extreme in order to make the point that the SB philosophy and practice begins with people and builds the organization around them.

The people differences which exist in SB present a whole host of problems and opportunities which are unique in many ways in the SB setting. These problems and opportunities deal with the four "people" of SB: the SBM himself, other SB managers of the firm, nonmanagerial employees, and SB people outside the firm itself. In one sense, these problem areas may be regarded as personnel problems. However, in our view, they are marketing problems, because we are concerned with the right people as a part of the marketing mix. We are controlling the people variable as a part of our marketing strategy. Personnel tactics and techniques, and even personnel strategies, will be used to support our marketing strategy. Below are brief discussions of some of the major people problems found in SB. It will become more apparent later on in the chapter how these problems fit into marketing strategy rather than being simply personnel or general management problems.

Management succession. It would seem reasonable to assume that a successful SBM would want to be actively interested in providing for his own (and other top managers') successful successor. This is often not the case. Thus, SB may have a continuity of top management over a long career of the SBM, but a sudden break may result if the SBM retires, starts another business, and so forth. The marketing importance of this people area is tied to the people image of the firm as perceived by loyal customers. In effect, the personality of the SBM is the company image of the SB firm.

The paradox of management succession in SB may stem from the fact that the SBM possesses characteristics and habits which were key elements in achieving success but which make it more difficult for him to pass control of the firm gracefully to a successor. Perhaps it is difficult to think of one's own replacement. One writer notes: "It is interesting that concern for survival occupies so much time of many of these executives, but always under the assumption that they will be around to implement whatever policies are established."[4] Whatever approach is used to provide for top management succession (e.g., heir apparent, internal management struggle, bringing in an outsider), it is obvious that the people portion of the marketing mix will be directly affected.

---

[4]Parks B. Dimsdale, Jr., "Management Succession—Facing The Future," *Journal Of Small Business Management,* 12, No. 4 (October 1974), p. 42.

Family business problems.   Many SB firms are family businesses. This has both advantages and disadvantages for people strategy in the marketing mix. Greater concern and involvement of family members in the people strategy is probably the greatest advantage. On the other hand, such involvement, especially if emotional, can cause many problems. The following advice on how to make your family business more profitable is summarized from one article:

1. Cash in on increased flexibility in order to gain an edge in the marketplace by being able to increase or decrease resources rapidly.
2. Keep emotions outside the business.
3. Make objectivity a fetish.
4. De-personalize key business decisions.
5. Make employment attractive to non-family candidates in order to attract and keep outstanding people.
6. Apply businesslike financing techniques.
7. Personalize your approach with customers, suppliers, employees, and so forth, but don't do everything yourself.
8. Put man-woman roles in perspective.
9. Make hereafter plans for your business.[5]

The above advice is certainly sound if it can be followed. Experience tells us that "blood is thicker than water." For the SB family business, this means that when family and business goals come into conflict, family will quite often take first place before business. This is a fact of family-business life which is so, even though some authors say it should not be so.

The SBM himself.   Although he is certainly a part of the solution, he may also be a part of the problem. Since the personality of the SBM is the image of the SB firm, the firm's image may be difficult to control or change. Several potential problems exist here. For example, the strong ego of the SBM may keep him from using or listening to consultants. BB employs consultants on a regular basis. The SBM may fail to delegate. The SBM must be able to have others work "with" him rather than simply "for" him. One writer contends:

> It is the contention of this writer that if there is any one most important key to small business survival and growth, it lies in the ability of the entrepreneur or chief executive officer to lengthen his own shadow through the recruiting, selecting, and motivating of the types of managerial and executive talent necessary to achieve this objective.[6]

Through effective leadership, the SBM may be able to get more out of his people than his BB counterparts. If so, this will be reflected in productivity as well as in the people element of the marketing mix. That phenomenon which makes it possible, but not automatic, for the SBM to get more from his people could be called the leveling effect. The leveling effect is usually present in a bureaucracy where people are fitted into slots. Here,

[5]Robert E. Levinson, "How To Make Your Family Business More Profitable," *Journal Of Small Business Management,* 12, No. 4 (October 1974), pp. 35–41.
[6]O. G. Dalaba, "Lengthening Your Shadow—The Key To Small Business Growth," *Journal Of Small Business Management,* 11, No. 3 (July 1973), p. 17.

the person knows the requirements of the job slot and may do a poor, mediocre, or excellent job of performing these requirements. However, due to structuring and interrelationships within the bureaucracy, it is almost impossible, even when an excellent job is done, for the person to exceed the predetermined contribution of that job slot in contributing to the success of the firm. Thus, until he is promoted to a higher job slot in the bureaucracy, the leveling effect prevents him from making a maximum contribution to the success of the firm. In SB, the organization can be, and often is, built around the people. Fiedler has suggested that BB could also benefit from building the job (job engineering) around the man; however, in practice little of this has been done:

> To get good business executives we have relied primarily on recruitment, selection, and training. It is time for businessmen to ask whether this is the only way or the best way for getting the best possible management. Fitting the man to the leadership job by selection and training has not been spectacularly successful. It is surely easier to change almost anything in the job situation than a man's personality and his leadership style. Why not try, then, to fit the leadership to the man?[7]

Recruiting and selection. A major distinction between BB and SB is that the ". . . small firm typically lacks internal sources of specialized knowledge in all the diverse areas of personnel management."[8] The SB firm should therefore develop personnel strategies (e.g., recruiting, training, and motivating) that are compatible with its resource capabilities and which will effectively support its people strategy in the marketing mix. SB firms do have attractive things to offer people, such as greater chance for involvement, growth opportunities, broader responsibilities, more freedom of action, an informal and friendly atmosphere, and so forth.[9] Even though most business school curricula have traditionally been geared toward preparing people for BB, one study revealed the following generalizations:

1. The large firm is viewed by students in colleges of business as offering the best opportunity for monetary reward.
2. The smaller firm is viewed by these students as offering the best opportunity for non-monetary, or intangible, rewards.
3. Student employment preference is clearly in the direction of the smaller firm when salary and benefits are comparable to those of the larger firms.
4. The typical student is unaware of job opportunities in the smaller firm.
5. The vast majority of students expect to take a job with a large firm after completing college.
6. Hiring of recent graduates from colleges of business is practiced only by large and medium size businesses. Furthermore, most small businesses are likely to continue to ignore this source of management trainees.[10]

---

[7]Fred E. Fiedler, "Engineer The Job To Fit The Manager," *Harvard Business Review,* 43, No. 5 (1965), p. 115.

[8]John B. Miner, "Personnel Strategies In The Small Business Organization," *Journal Of Small Business Management,* 11, No. 3 (July 1973), p. 13.

[9]Ronal G. Borgman, "Winning The Recruiting Battle In Small Business," *Journal Of Small Business Management,* 11, No. 3 (July 1973), p. 23.

[10]A. Thomas Hollingsworth, Lawrence A. Klatt, and Thomas W. Zimmerer, "An Untapped Resource For Small Business: Business School Graduates," *Journal Of Small Business Management,* 12, No. 1 (January 1974), p. 45.

Another major source of people which has not been utilized to the best extent by both BB and SB is women. The business world has only recently begun to devote substantial attention to the recruiting and selection of women. In January, 1973, for example, the *Journal of Small Business Management* devoted an issue to this topic. In conclusion, SB cannot afford not to actively recruit and select the "right" people.

Developing people.   There is an axiom which says: You pay for a training program whether you have one or not. Many SB firms have under-invested in people development. The marketing implications are most readily seen in the area of training sales personnel. However, the people development problem extends throughout all the SB people: the SBM, management, other employees, and outside people. Due to lack of specialized training resources, the SB firm must rely heavily on outsiders such as schools, seminars, supplier training programs, short courses, and trade associations. Another alternative may be to participate in cooperative training programs.[11]

Motivating and working "with" people.   If you want to know if the employees of a firm are highly motivated to do a good job, ask the customers. They know. No one comes right out and tells them in so many words, but they know. "Actions speak louder than words." The fact that customers do know is of major significance in the SB marketing mix.

Because personnel administration in BB, however good and humane it is, tends to be impersonalized or non-personal, it is most difficult for the employee to fulfill such high level needs as self-actualization. Most BB firms lack the ability to personalize their personnel and their management. Human motivation in SB can be personalized or humanized. One article notes:

> Humanizing the organization means that the company will know its employees and what they are seeking in their jobs, and thus be able to support them in their search for life satisfaction. Here the smaller enterprise has a decided advantage—it can get to know its employees, their needs and their desires much more easily than a firm employing thousands.[12]

The SBM may, in a sense, regard employees as customers. Thus the act of the SBM in properly handling and not neglecting a minor employee grievance becomes similar to the handling of a minor customer complaint. Many items discussed in the chapter on consumer behavior (such as the hierarchy of needs) are borrowed directly from the behavioral sciences and apply equally to company personnel and consumers. The SBM should use the behavioral sciences along with SB management education and experience to develop his own philosophy or approach to motivating employees in SB.[13]

Outside people.   In previous chapters we have discussed using advertising agencies, marketing researchers, consultants, and so forth. Outside representation on the board of directors was mentioned earlier in this chapter. These outside professionals are part of the people mix of the SB firm. Their influence on the rest of the marketing mix may in some

[11]D. L. Howell and W. Randy Boxx, "The Reduction Of Small Business Failures Through Cooperative Training," *Journal Of Small Business Management,* 12, No. 3 (July 1974), pp. 1–6.
[12]Robert A. Sutermeister and Borje O. Saxberg, "Human Motivation In The Smaller Enterprise," *Journal Of Small Business Management,* 11, No. 3 (July 1973), p. 9.
[13]Burt K. Scanlan, "Motivating Employees In The Small Business," *Journal Of Small Business Management,* 11, No. 3 (July 1973), pp. 1–6.

cases be greater than that of some "insiders." For example, the SB manufacturer who has selected an exclusive distributor in a geographic area has gained all the people problems and opportunities of that distributor.

SOME EXAMPLES OF PEOPLE DIFFERENCES IN BB AND SB

The problem areas discussed in the previous section are mainly personnel areas in support of people as a marketing mix element. It is sometimes possible to become so involved in the personnel support problems that we forget the marketing focus. Some examples may be helpful at this point in order to further illustrate the people element as a part of the marketing mix.

For our first example, let's pose the question: Can people be a part of the BB marketing mix; or are people in the marketing mix restricted to SB? Robert J. Eggert, Staff Vice President-Chief Economist for RCA, (certainly BB) says that people are the most important part of a high productivity marketing plan. He notes: "There is no substitute for able people who are creative, confident, and courageous. The ideal person is one who uses the factual approach (along with good judgment) for solving marketing problems."[14] Did Eggert mean the same thing we mean when we refer to people in SB? Let's look at a nonmarketing example of people (employee relations) in another BB firm. The "friendly skies of United" (UAL) became a bit cloudy when two workers sued, claiming that the company stole their ideas via the employee suggestion system.[15] With an informal suggestion system in SB, would such people differences be likely to be settled in a court of law? Finally, let's look at the supra-firm organization such as the franchisor-franchisee arrangement which is often a combination of BB and SB. Do franchise firms use the people variable in the marketing mix?—and if so, are people used as an effective variable? Does the franchisor or the franchisee typically determine the people element in the marketing mix? Or is some combination of planning and implementation of the people element shared by the franchisor and franchisee? The reader should have his own opinions. In the opinion of the author, to the extent that people can be a part of the BB marketing mix, it is a less personalized and more generalized meaning of the term *people* than is used in SB marketing. The following examples will further illustrate this.

In the large and somewhat automated commercial bakery, the bread, cakes, cookies, and everything else that is baked all seem to be pretty much the same regardless of who does the baking. The specific baker is not a major ingredient in the mix. This is a BB bureaucracy. However, SB is somewhat analogous to the daughter-in-law who, even though her mother-in-law may give her the recipe to her son's favorite dish, finds it most difficult to come up with exactly the same thing that mother had been making for many years. Thus the major ingredient here, as in SB, is people, that is, specific people.

The differential advantage that can be gained by SB through the people element (plus a parrot and no computer) is illustrated by an Alexandria, Virginia bank. The bank has a parrot and does not use a computer. Apparently customers can better relate to

---

[14]Robert J. Eggert, Staff Vice President, RCA Corporation, "Improving Marketing Productivity—Or Else!" (Speech before Omaha-Lincoln Chapter, American Marketing Association, May 13, 1975).

[15]"Unfriendly Skies: Employees' Suggestion Erupts in Legal Fight For United Airlines," *Wall Street Journal*, February 23, 1976, p. 1.

parrots than to computers. The bank is prospering by being different, as noted in *The Wall Street Journal:*

> Unlike many banks that pride themselves on their size, Burke & Herbert likes to point out how small it is (Assets: $41 million). While other banks boast of free checking, plastic credit cards and 24-hour mechanical banking units, Burke & Herbert is proud of its old-fashioned ways. ("Computers have never saved anybody any money," asserts Mr. Burke.) Tellers make a point of greeting depositors by name, and loan negotiations are considered something of a family affair.[16]

Another example of people in SB was given in a previous chapter on promotion. There we discussed in detail the key to success of a local supermarket chain in competing against a regional and a national chain. The customers of the local chain were very much aware of the importance of people in the marketing mix of the local chain. Both the regional and national chains were unable to convey such a message even through the use of extensive institutional advertising. The message carried almost no credibility among many potential customers.

Certainly we know that each person is important to the success of the SB firm. For example, a firm with ten total people must place approximately ten percent of its success on the efforts of each person. It does make a difference! Is the "fifth P"—that is, people—really a necessary and integral part of the SB marketing mix? Some persons may suggest that people in the SB marketing mix is about as useless as a fifth wheel would be on an automobile. An examination of other vehicles shows unicycles, bicycles, tricycles, and so forth with varying numbers of wheels and varying degrees of effectiveness, depending upon use and conditions. Our contention here is that conditions are such in SB that the "fifth P" is a necessity for successful marketing. An individualized personalized people variable is to SB what a well-organized people bureaucracy is to BB.

ROLE AND IMPORTANCE OF PEOPLE
IN THE SB MARKETING MIX

As a controllable variable of the SB marketing mix, people is influenced by the target market(s) served and by the environment in which it operates. It also interacts in several different ways with each of the other controllable variables. People is an important ingredient in serving the target market at a profit to the SBM. Planning, execution, and control of the people variable can contribute to the success of the SBM. The SBM should not be willing to leave to chance, or to the decisions of low-level employees, what happens in the people areas.

An explanation of the interaction of people strategy and target market(s) is facilitated by referring to our two principles described in detail in Chapter 4: the principle of market simplification for SB and the principle of market dominance for SB. Simplification tells the SBM not to copy BB methods if they are not appropriate in defining SB target markets. The SBM should be more concerned with a share of target market rather than with a share of total market. And, according to dominance, the SBM

---

[16]"It Lacks Computer And Cairo Branch—But Bank Has Parrot," *Wall Street Journal,* March 11, 1976, p. 1. Reprinted with permission from *The Wall Street Journal,* © Dow Jones & Company, Inc. 1976. All Rights Reserved.

should have some means and some degree of dominance in the target markets he serves. People is one means for achieving an effective (or optimum) degree of dominance in *some* target markets. In which market segment types can people be an important means for achieving that desired degree of dominance? The consumer behavior of individual market segments suggests the answer. In Chapter 4, we suggest that target markets for which the people variable is very important include those in which the personal treatment received by customers as affected by the personalities of employees is important. Such personal treatment can be more easily managed and controlled by SB. Examples of close customer contact businesses are taverns, ice cream parlors, restaurants, and service firms. In consumer behavior terms, the bank with the parrot and no computer, cited earlier in this chapter, may be serving a large number of late adopters and laggards as a market segment. Or, due to its location near the nation's capitol, persons who are forced to be part of the bureaucracy in their work lives may find the bank especially appealing in their private lives. Life style, social class, and other consumer behavior concepts could be used to match the people strategy of the bank (or some other SB firm) to specific target markets. Another example is the SB retailer who is involved in fashion merchandising, either for men or women. By the target market customers, he is regarded as an opinion leader. If he is wrong, the customers are wrong. He must dress both himself and his customers according to fashion correctness which will symbolize the desired images.

The uncontrollable or environmental variables affect the role of people in the SB marketing mix. For example, a decline in economic activity may influence customers to seek fewer personalized services. An increased level of technology may force the SB firm to go along with changes by decreasing the emphasis on people. Or, in some cases, the SBM may decide to place more emphasis on the people variable because technology has (at least temporarily) eliminated the people role in the marketing mix of competitors. The SBM must assess the effects of environmental variables on both the target market and the variables of the marketing mix.

Product and people interact together in the SB marketing mix. How does people affect product and how does product affect people? The same question may be asked for place, price, and promotion. The SBM may plan variations in people strategy throughout the stages of the product life-cycle. People strategy may vary according to the extent of the product line. Product image and people image must be compatible. The goods-services proportions of the product will influence the role of people strategy. The choice of family versus individual brands may be influenced by people strategy.

The people relationship with place is evident in channel of distribution decisions and in decisions regarding desired customer service levels. Channel members are often regarded as part of the people mix of the SB firm. For example, the people strategy of a small retailer will be heavily influenced by the people policies of his major wholesaler. In fact, the effect on people strategy may in some cases be more noticeable than the effect on the product mix. The customer service level is directly related to the number and quality of people the SBM employs. This is, his people inventory and his product inventory are tied together.

The interrelationships of people and price strategies are less obvious. Psychological pricing may be an attempt to match price and people variables. Individualized pricing and price image relate closely to people. Prices may be varied from target market to target market according to the personalized service desired by each segment. The people element may be an effective means for the SBM who wishes to avoid direct price competition, especially during periods of oversupply, price cuts, and price wars.

Promotion and people relate most directly in the image of the firm and its people.

The communication of the desired people image is extremely important to SB. Unless communicated through advertising, personal selling, sales promotion, and publicity, the people image may just as well not exist. In fact, it doesn't exist for those target customers to whom it is not communicated. The common background of experience and frame of reference between the people of the SB firm and the people of the target market is essential to effective marketing. In discussing advertising in a previous chapter, the author suggested that a TV sales pitch by the SBM may not be the most effective form of commercial. A retraction of that statement is not being made here, but the statement is being qualified to include the notion that the personality (but not necessarily the physical person) of the SBM and his people should be present in all communications, including TV commercials.

In order to achieve the desired synergetic effect of the SB marketing mix, the SBM must have the ideal combination of the right product, at the right place, at the right price, with the right promotion, by the right people. How important a role people plays in that mix will vary according to such factors as (a) whether the SB firm is a manufacturer, a wholesaler, a retailer, a combination, or a service firm; (b) the roles assigned to other variables; (c) the target market(s); (d) the environment; (e) the desires and philosophy of the SBM; and (f) other factors.

STRATEGIES IN THE SB PEOPLE MIX

The major strategy areas of the SB people mix include: (a) the SB people–target market matching strategy, (b) SB people organization strategy, (c) SB people image strategy, (d) the optimum SB people–machine combination strategy, (e) SB personnel support strategies, and (f) strategies for the utilization of "outside" people in the SB people mix. In addition to these strategies within the people area, the SBM must decide the role and importance of people in the SB marketing mix.

The SB People–Target Market Matching Strategy

In the chapters on product, we discussed the product-market matching strategy of the SBM. From his study and experience with consumer behavior in the target markets the SBM is serving or is contemplating serving, the SBM should be fairly knowledgeable about the dimensions of the people that comprise his markets. He knows his market. He also knows that effective people to people relationships and communications depend on the common frames of reference and common experiences of message sender-encoders and receiver-decoders. These two people groups are the SB people and the target market people. The SBM will therefore attempt to match the SB people with the target market people. For example, the SB operator of a clothing store for big and tall men will probably employ big and tall men as salesmen. Although the match is not always quite so obvious, the common frame of reference is very important.

In attempting to formulate the right SB people–target market matching strategy, the SBM will be seeking that strategy which best relates people to the overall marketing strategy of the firm, to other marketing mix strategies, and to other people strategy areas. He will ask questions such as: Should we be serving this target market? If so, should we be using these people to do so? In what ways, such as better penetration within present target markets, could our people better serve at a profit? What other target markets, if any, should we consider serving with the present people mix or with a new people mix? Is our people–market matching strategy compatible with our goals and differential advantage?

The ideal people composition (both quantitative and qualitative) of the SB firm has many dimensions. Some of these are: young and old, male and female, temporary and permanent, part time and full time, and so forth. In effect, all the demographic and psychographic factors that can be used to segment the people of markets can also be used to segment and describe the people of the SB firm. The SBM should think in such terms when determining his people mix. A strategy of designing and using a people mix which meets the needs of, but which does not necessarily match in characteristics, the target market, can play an important role in the success of the SB.

The SB People Organization Strategy

The organization and management of people is less difficult in SB than BB. However, this does not mean that it takes care of itself. A strategy for effectively organizing the various people of the SB firm into a meaningful whole is needed. As the SB firm grows from perhaps one person or one manager to many people, the need for a marketing-oriented formal organization structure increases. The best structure will vary from firm to firm. We will not suggest "typical" organization structures here. Such charts and their underlying rationale are found in SB and BB management books. Our point is to emphasize that all the people of the SB firm must know what is expected from them in performing the various marketing functions in order to deliver the desired utilities to the target market. As a size guide to departmental organization, Cohn and Lindberg found that "departmental organization is seldom found in companies with annual sales below $100,000. Companies with annual sales above $1 million but less than $3 million usually have two or three formalized departments; those with sales from $3 million to $6 million, three to five departments; and those with sales from $6 million to $20 million, from five to eight departments."[17]

Basic organizational guidelines, such as clear lines of authority, written statements of comparable responsibility and authority, reporting to only one boss, keeping levels to a minimum, span of control, flexibility, simplicity, and so forth, should be followed when organizing the people. However, unique capabilities of SB people and innovative ways of organizing work accomplishment rather than the people themselves may be more important in SB. The SBM should be reluctant to give up unnecessarily the people advantages of SB firms such a close personal rapport, direct communications, person-to-person motivation, and so forth. His strategy for organizing his people should always take into account that in SB people is a part of the marketing mix and the customers of the target market are often well aware of this.

The SB People Image Strategy

All the controllable variables of the SB marketing mix contribute to the image of the SB firm and its product offering. People image is just as real and important as brand image, advertising image, and so forth. In fact, for SB, people image may be more

---

[17]Reprinted by permission of the publisher from Theodore Cohn and Roy A. Lindberg, *How Management Is Different in Small Companies,* An AMA Management Briefing, © 1972 by American Management Association, Inc., p. 12.

important, since a good people image is not easily duplicated by competitors. The SBM must decide: What exactly is the people image we are trying to create? The SB people image is the perception that someone has regarding the reality of the people of the SB firm. The perception and the reality may differ. Also, the perception may vary depending on who is doing the perceiving. In addition to the reality of the SB people, there may be the "ideal" people image in the mind of the SBM; the actual people image in the perception of the SBM; the perceptions of customers, potential customers, employees, competitors; and so forth. For example, one study found that images of stores do vary when it compared the profiles of images of six retail stores as these existed in the minds of (a) the owner-manager, (b) present customers, and (c) potential customers.[18]

Images can be more important than reality, since people act as they perceive. The SB people image is formed by a variety of things. Those things which tend to influence present and potential customers most are those which are easily perceived by them. Such items are friendliness, manner of dress, speech patterns and mannerisms, cleanliness, knowledge, poise, general appearance, personal interest, courtesy, and so forth.

People image is but one part of the total image of the SB firm. Images are also generated from product (e.g., brand and package), place (e.g., store image), price (e.g., low-price), and promotion (e.g., advertising image). Consistency in all these image forms with each other and with reality are usually desired by the SBM. To the extent that the SBM himself is heavily involved in all these phases of the marketing mix, such consistency is likely. It is also likely that the resulting total image will be a projection of the personality of the SBM. Building the desired favorable image may take a long time and much hard work. Changing an established image to another favorable image is also difficult and costly. However, changing a favorable image to an unfavorable or "fuzzy" image is not too difficult. A little neglect is all it takes.

Every SB firm employing people will project some kind of people image. In the absence of a people image strategy, this is likely to result in a weak and ineffective image or possibly even in a negative image. The SB people image is projected (i.e., can be controlled) by the SB firm and is perceived by the market. It is the personality of the SB firm as demonstrated through the SBM, his management team, other employees, and his outside people. A major people strategy decision for every SBM is to take a positive management approach in deciding what the people image should be.

The Optimum SB People–
Machine Combination Strategy

Throughout the discussion of the SB marketing mix we have made several references to combinations of people and/or things along a continuum. We suggested that the product mix of SB will tend to be more toward the services end of the goods-services continuum than would be true for BB. We suggested that the SB promotion mix would tend to have less major mass media advertising and would favor more selective promotion, such as personal selling, than would BB. What we are suggesting regarding the SB people–machine combination is this: The optimum people–machine combination strategy for SB will tend to favor more of the people element and less of the machine element than would be the case for BB. This is a tendency which will be true in general, but to which numerous

---

[18]Carter Grocott, "Newspaper Advertising And The Small Retail Store's Image," *Journal Of Small Business Management,* 12, No. 2 (April 1974), pp. 7–15.

exceptions may be found. An example of people–machine combination strategy used previously in the discussion of customer services would be whether the SB supermarket should have young men and women carry out groceries to its customers' automobiles (more people and less machine) or have customers pick up their groceries at the end of a conveyor belt at a pick-up station (more machine and less people). Another example is our Virginia bank without a computer. The SBM, in making his people–machine decisions, cannot afford to totally ignore costs. However, in the opinion of the author, cost would rank second after the desires of the target market regarding the right amount of the people variable. What's the point in reducing costs if you are no longer providing what the target market wants? For the SBM, the optimum should be determined by the target market rather than by dollars and cents efficiency.

The SBM should also be attentive to what is going on in the target market. Markets do change. The SBM whose business is down because, as he diagnoses it, "customers just don't appreciate good personal service any more," may be making excuses for his own failure to invest in new machines to serve the new and changed needs of the target market. It all depends on the target market. For example, few of us consider food from a vending machine to be "gracious dining." However, there are times to eat in a hurry and times to dine. The optimum people–machine combination varies accordingly.

The SB Personnel Support Strategies

Under this category are included all the recruiting, selection, developing, and motivating activities directed toward all people of the SB firm. Unlike some of the other people strategy areas mentioned above, this area is a supporting rather than a core strategy when viewed from the marketing rather than the personnel perspective. What we are saying is that a good overall personnel strategy in SB and the parts of that personnel strategy can be viewed as major supporting strategies for the SB people strategy in the marketing mix. Our discussion of personnel support strategies is purposely very limited.

Strategies For Utilization of Outside SB People

In order to gain expertise and specialized skills, it is often necessary and advisable for the SBM to use people who are not regular managers or employees of the SB firm. In effect, these outside people do become a part of the people mix of the SB firm. As such, the above people strategy areas do apply, in a certain sense, to these outside people. For example, if the customer of a retailer is insulted by a manufacturer whose products are sold by that retailer, when attempting to secure repair service under the warranty, who does the customer blame even if the retailer had nothing to do with the factory warranty repair service? Certainly, the retailer at least shares in the blame. The retailer may also share in the praise (by association and future patronage) if there was courtesy and excellent service in repairing the item.

People strategy questions extend beyond the borders of the SB firm to include suppliers, distributors, dealers, service contractors, delivery services, finance companies, consultants, attorneys, accountants, marketing researchers, advertising agencies, and so forth. These outsiders both affect and are affected by the people strategy of the SB firm. Some strategy questions which concern the utilization of outside people in the SB marketing mix are: To what extent do we use outside people rather than inside people? For what purposes do we use them? What is the longevity of our relationship? In what ways do outsiders interface with insiders and with target market customers? And there are, of course, others.

In bringing this section to a close, we should note that we have by no means exhausted the list of people strategy questions in the above discussion. For example, we did not show how the SBM might vary people strategy in the marketing mix according to the stage of the product in the product life-cycle. How might people strategies be used in connection with market segmentation? The list can go on and on. We have concentrated our attention on the major people strategy areas.

THE "HOW TO" OF PEOPLE STRATEGY FORMULATION

In Chapter 9 we stated: "Within the entire field of product strategy, there is one strategy area that is a core strategy. All other product strategy areas are supporting strategies. The core strategy area is the one which we have already discussed: the product–market matching strategy." A very similar situation exists in the SB people strategy area. Here, we may say that the SB people–target market matching strategy is almost always the core people strategy. SB personnel support strategies have already been identified as supporting rather than core strategies. Likewise, the remaining SB people strategies tend to be supporting rather than core strategies. Some exceptions may be found. For example, if the SBM is not a target marketer, this may not be true.

The exact nature of people strategy for an individual SBM will depend on company and marketing goals and objectives, target market(s) served, the marketing environment, the differential advantage of the firm, and the relative roles of people and the other controllable variables in the SB marketing mix. By now, the reader should have ready the pad, pencil, conference room, and the SB marketing management team. The familiar eight-step process of strategy formulation can be adapted to SB people strategy formulation as follows:

1. Record the current people strategy.
2. Identify strategic people problems.
3. Divide current strategic people problems into core strategy areas and supporting strategy areas.
4. Formulate alternative people strategies at both core and support levels.
5. Evaluate the alternatives in various combinations.
6. Choose the new people strategy.
7. Plan the details of implementation of the new people strategy.
8. Set performance standards and monitor feedback.

At this point, the SBM should be ready to use this eight-step process as a framework for organizing his own experience and knowledge into an effective people strategy for his firm.

Step 1—Record the current people strategy. This first step is probably the first time the SBM has recorded, or perhaps even recognized the existence of, his people strategy. The possible absence of a current (and past) people strategy will complicate things somewhat. The SBM facing such a situation has plenty of company, because many firms have failed to recognize people as a controllable strategy variable in the marketing mix. However, that may be of little comfort. The SBM may wish to review the previous material of this chapter as a guide to specific questions he might ask about how the people variable has been operating in his business. What should the SBM record? The answer is that he should record everything of significance (right or wrong) that the firm *is* or *is not* doing regarding its people. In as complete a form as possible, the SBM should record the people strategy for each target market served. He should record something regarding each of the people strategy areas identified earlier in this chapter. In addition to *what* the firm is doing regarding people, some reasons *why* should also be noted.

Step 2—Identify strategic people problems.   In this step the SBM attempts to identify problems and opportunities in the current people strategy. Of course, one basic problem may be that no people strategy existed as a part of the marketing mix. In such a case, the SBM has identified the need for a people strategy framework. Undoubtedly some problems emerged in Step #1 above. Many of these will be tactical problems, but some may be or may indicate the existence of strategic problems. Active search for people problems and the analysis of symptoms from the feedback system should reveal some problems. People problems may be uncovered by asking such questions as: Are customer complaints and customer turnover too high? Is employee turnover too high? In what ways is our people strategy similar to and different from that of competitors? Which similarities and differences are desirable and undesirable? What are our people objectives and how are they being met? What changes have occurred in the target market and the environment? What changes have taken place in the rest of the marketing mix and how do these changes affect people?

Step 3—Divide current strategic people problems into core strategy areas and supporting strategy areas.   We have suggested above that the people–market matching strategy will be a core strategy area and that all other strategic (not tactical) problem areas will tend to be supporting people strategy areas. Whether a problem is core or supporting depends on its significance to the firm. Core people problems usually are the result of a major change, such as a loss of a differential advantage, a shift in the composition of the target market, an environmental change, or a change in firm goals. Specific examples would be the loss of a key executive (perhaps the SBM) whose personality heavily influenced the people mix and image, the entry of younger persons into the market, changes in laws regarding part-time employees, or a change from a conservative to a growth-oriented goal for the firm. These, and similar changes, can result in core strategy problems. Although core people strategy problems are likely to occur less often than supporting people strategy problems, the core problems often call for more radical strategy revisions than do supporting problems.

Supporting people strategies should not be neglected. They enhance the chances for success by giving support to the core strategy. For example, the personnel supporting strategies of recruiting, selecting, developing, and motivating the right people for the target markets served are key factors without which success would be unlikely. The SBM has now recorded the current people strategy as best as it could be determined, identified strategic people problems, and divided these into core and support areas. He is now prepared to begin planning the future people strategy.

Step 4—Formulate alternative people strategies at both core and support levels.   The process of formulating alternative people strategies begins with a reappraisal of the firm's differential advantage, then proceeds first to core strategies, and then to supporting strategies. Core people strategies may vary in three basic ways. These are: (a) the redefining of target market dimensions and the people of those markets to which the SB people mix is to be matched; (b) calling for different levels of people in the marketing mix; and (c) calling for different levels of support from supporting people strategies.

Formulating alternative people strategies is (or at least should be) a creative process in which the SBM is not inhibited by the careful evaluation which is to come in the next step. A new people strategy may or may not involve new people. The formulation of new people strategies takes place at both core and support levels, even though problems may have been identified at only one level. People strategies work in combination with each other, in combination with the other P's, and in combination with the overall marketing mix. People also relates to nonmarketing areas of the SB firm.

Care should be taken in attempting to copy people strategies from other firms. Successful strategy ideas always travel fast, and the temptation to imitate may be very great. However, unlike some of our other marketing variables, people is much less tangible. Individual people tend to be unique, and although there is a great difference between people and a people strategy, the copying of a people strategy (which may have taken some time to perfect) would be most difficult. Even if it were not difficult, the desirability of doing so may be questioned, since what is a good people strategy for one target market may not be for another.

Step 5—Evaluate the alternatives in various combinations.   The people strategy alternatives generated in the above step should now be evaluated by the SBM. We are merely evaluating, not yet selecting an alternative. Each alternative and combinations of alternatives should be evaluated according to company goals and resources, marketing objectives, and the objectives of the firm's people mix. The effectiveness of alternative people strategies in helping to solve the current people problems identified in Step #2 above should be considered. Also to be considered are the effects various alternatives will have in reducing people problems and other marketing problems in the future. Both the advantages and disadvantages of alternative people strategy combinations should be taken into account. For example, a people strategy which employs a people–machine combination that involves heavy expenditures must be weighed in terms of investment in some other marketing or nonmarketing variable. As noted in the product chapter, a consensus or agreement among the marketing management team as to what the important criteria of evaluation are to be may produce a more meaningful evaluation. The people strategy evaluations should be on a positive tone, and should be restricted to evaluating alternative people strategies rather than to evaluating alternative individual people.

Step 6—Choose the new people strategy.   The new people strategy selected by the SBM should be one that he plans to live with for some time to come. During that time, tactical adjustments will be made. The new strategy may not vary too greatly from the former one, but at least some changes in the supporting areas are likely. Under the assumption that several good alternatives are available, the people strategy selected is likely to be the one that (a) capitalizes most on the unique people advantages of the SB firm, and (b) which is compatible with the values and business philosophy of the firm. A choice must be made in this step. And that choice must be one that is realistic in terms of the resources of the SB firm. The final choice is likely to be a compromise between what would be ideal and what can realistically be accomplished. Realism is a necessary prerequisite to implementation.

Step 7—Plan the details of implementation of the new people strategy.   This stage involves not only *what* is going to be done in order to implement the new people strategy, but also the details of *how, when, where,* and by *whom.* In other words, at this point a program outlining the specific details of implementation is called for. Details which are not specified will probably not be accomplished; or if they are, they may be performed in such a way as to be ineffective, or less effective than desired. For example, if the new people strategy calls for a training program to correct some people problems, the details must be laid out. In the absence of such detailed planning, one of the following courses of action is likely: (a) nothing happens at all; (b) a token training effort is made for a short period of time; (c) an extensive training program is given, but it does not concentrate on the right problems; or (d) a training program is given with the assumption that (in the absence of program evaluation) the problem will vanish as a result of the program. In effect, if the SBM does not plan the details of strategy implementation, the implementation of *his* strategy will probably be replaced by chance, neglect, or the ideas of a lower-level employee.

Step 8—Set performance standards and monitor feedback.   As a planning step rather than an actual control program, this step involves the setting of quantitative and qualitative criteria by which the SBM will later evaluate the success of the people strategy. Later, in the control phase of our PEC marketing management process, the criteria will be used for the actual evaluation. A second question to be addressed in this final planning step is to make a provision for constant feedback on how the people strategy is doing in order that tactical adjustments may be made in the people strategy from time to time.

In conclusion, as mentioned in earlier chapters, strategy formulation (for people or for any other controllable variable) is a do-it-yourself project for the SBM. Personalized implementation under the direct leadership of the SBM is also important. There is no substitute for meeting and greeting each customer by name and having him return the same. With the discussion of SB people strategy, our coverage of the five controllable SB marketing mix variables is now complete.

BIBLIOGRAPHY

Articles and Periodicals

BORGMAN, RONAL G. "Winning The Recruiting Battle In Small Business," *Journal Of Small Business Management,* 11, No. 3 (July 1973), 22–26.

DALABA, O. G. "Lengthening Your Shadow—The Key To Small Business Growth," *Journal Of Small Business Management,* 11, No. 3 (July 1973), 17–21.

DIMSDALE, PARKS B., JR. "Management Succession—Facing The Future," *Journal Of Small Business Management,* 12, No. 4 (October 1974), 42–46.

FIEDLER, FRED E. "Engineer The Job To Fit The Manager," *Harvard Business Review,* 43, No. 5 (1965), 115–122.

GROCOTT, CARTER. "Newspaper Advertising And The Small Retail Store's Image," *Journal Of Small Business Management,* 12, No. 2 (April 1974), pp. 7–15.

HOLLINGSWORTH, A. THOMAS, KLATT, LAWRENCE A., AND ZIMMERER, THOMAS W. "An Untapped Resource For Small Business: Business School Graduates," *Journal Of Small Business Management,* 12, No. 1 (January 1974), 42–46.

HOWELL, D. L., AND BOXX, W. RANDY. "The Reduction Of Small Business Failures Through Cooperative Training," *Journal Of Small Business Management,* 12, No. 3 (July 1974), 1–6.

"It Lacks Computer And Cairo Branch—But Bank Has Parrot," *Wall Street Journal,* March 11, 1976, p. 1.

LEVINSON, ROBERT E. "How To Make Your Family Business More Profitable," *Journal Of Small Business Management,* 12, No. 4 (October 1974), 35–41.

MINER, JOHN B. "Personnel Strategies In The Small Business Organization," *Journal Of Small Business Management,* 11, No. 3 (July 1973), 13–16.

SCANLAN, BURT K. "Motivating Employees In The Small Business," *Journal Of Small Business Management,* 11, No. 3 (July 1973), 1–6.

SUTERMEISTER, ROBERT A., AND SAXBERG, BORJE O. "Human Motivation In The Smaller Enterprise," *Journal Of Small Business Management,* 11, No. 3 (July 1973), 7–12.

TINSLEY, DILLARD D. "Competition, Consultants, And Completeness: Strategy In The Small Retailer's Future," *Journal Of Small Business Management,* 14, No. 3 (July 1976), 12–15.

"Unfriendly Skies: Employees' Suggestion Erupts in Legal Fight For United Airlines," *Wall Street Journal,* February 23, 1976, p. 1.

Reports

COHN, THEODORE, AND LINDBERG, ROY A. *How Management Is Different in Small Companies.* An AMA Management Briefing, 1972.

Unpublished Material

EGGERT, ROBERT J. , Staff Vice President, RCA Corporation. "Improving Marketing Productivity—Or Else!" Speech before Omaha-Lincoln Chapter, American Marketing Association, May 13, 1975.

THE PEC MANAGEMENT
PROCESS IN SBMM

The dynamic SB marketing management process is composed of planning, execution, and control. Up to this point, our perspective has been from the planning portion of this ongoing process. In the one chapter of the final part of the book, execution and control join planning to complete the discussion of our SBMM model.

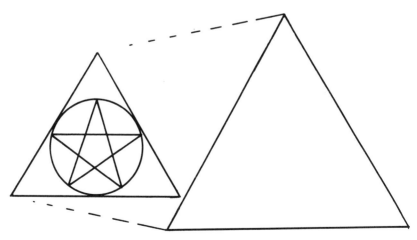

PART V—THE PEC MANAGEMENT PROCESS IN SBMM

17

Managing SB
Marketing Programs

In previous chapters, we have noted that management and marketing are different in SB. We examined SB markets, the environment of SB, and the five elements of the SB marketing mix. Our major emphasis has been on marketing strategy planning related to product, place, price, promotion, and people. References have been made occasionally to the execution and control of each of these five elements. References have also been made concerning the overall marketing strategy of the SBM. In both areas, such references were far from complete. Our purpose in this chapter is to shift our attention to a more concentrated discussion of the management (i.e., planning, execution, and control) of the total SB marketing program. This chapter will also focus more on execution and control, since planning has been given much more attention in previous chapters.

A review of some ideas concerning the PEC (planning, execution, and control) process of management in SB seems to be a good place to begin. Now that the SBM (you) has put some "meat" on the skeleton SBMM model in the last several chapters, an integrated SB marketing program, which will be both profitable and consumer-oriented, is possible.

In Chapter 3, a triangular path was used in Figure 3–1 (page 31) to depict the revolving motion of the PEC marketing management process in SB. This management process takes place not only for each of the five P's but also for the overall marketing mix for each target market (if more than one target market is served) and for the total marketing program of the SBM. The SBM must continuously manage the SB marketing program. Because the SB marketing system is a subsystem of the total SB firm, the specification of company objectives is a first step in the PEC process.

In this chapter, we will assume that this first step has been accomplished. Our starting point will therefore be to *plan* the total integrated marketing program for SB by examining the role or importance of marketing in the SB firm. SB marketing programs are *executed* through organizing and directing. Even though such organizing does not result in a bureaucracy in SB, there are certain principles which seem more likely to produce success for the SBM. Likewise, the *control* function in SB tends to differ from its BB counterpart. After the PEC process of SB marketing management has been discussed, management by objectives (MBO) in SB marketing is treated briefly. We then gaze at the "crystal ball" in order to speculate about what the future holds for SB marketing.

PLANNING SB MARKETING PROGRAMS

Marketing programs result from integrating the marketing plans for all of the five elements of marketing for all of the target markets served by the SBM. Ideally, such a program should be in a written form. The time dimension of the marketing program may be one year, or either longer and shorter programs may be used. Forms for writing out the marketing program are suggested in some marketing books. However, the author suggests that the SBM design his own written format tailored to his own needs. At least some portions of the marketing program need to be communicated to the various people of the SB firm.

The marketing concept implies an integrated marketing program in which the "ideal" mix of each of the five "P's" is included. (This was discussed at length in Chapter 3.) In other words, a compromise may be advisable. For example, what may have been the "best" price strategy may have to be adjusted in order to provide resources for accomplishing the place strategy or the promotion strategy, and so forth. Stern refers to this type of trading off as the result of functional and time-sequential interactions:

> It should be recalled that integration is necessary because interactions among the several marketing functions exist and require that trade-offs be made in order to maximize the total effectiveness of the marketing plan. There are two fundamental types of interactions to be considered: *functional* and *time-dependent* interactions.[1]

Functional interactions have been discussed earlier (Chapter 3) regarding the ideal mix. A major point that should be reemphasized here is that the SBM should seek a consistency among the elements of the marketing mix in such a way that the elements reinforce the effects of each other to create the synergetic effect. Time-sequential interactions remind us that the marketing mix is a dynamic rather than a static system. We cannot assume a static equilibrium (or disequilibrium) for the rest of the marketing system as we examine one element at a time. Time leads and time lags occur between the implementation of a marketing strategy, decision, or effect and the results in the form of a market response. For example, a new salesman should become more productive as time goes on; a new channel of distribution or a new outlet (after initial stocking) may have slow sales at first but gradually build into an effective means of distribution; or increased advertising may take time to produce results.

In addition to planning an integrated marketing program, the SBM must plan how important a part marketing is to play in the total of his SB firm. In previous chapters, we have strongly advocated the marketing concept. We are certainly not saying here that the marketing concept is not of great importance to the SBM. Rather, we are asking a question within the framework of the marketing concept: How much marketing is exactly

---

[1]Mark E. Stern, *Marketing Planning: A Systems Approach* (New York: McGraw-Hill Book Company, 1966), p. 105.

the right amount for a particular SBM serving a particular target market(s)? Each SBM must answer this question for himself. Knowing his target markets and the likely response functions, along with knowing and asking himself the right questions, should produce reasonably good answers. Some questions the SBM may wish to consider in planning the overall marketing program design are suggested by Willett. Without the accompanying discussion, the questions are:

1. What is the productivity level or dollar return on dollar investment in any single marketing input offered to the market?
2. What is the elasticity or rate of market response to changes in any input in the total marketing program over moderate ranges of variation of expenditure on the input?
3. At what level of input for any marketing variable is the threshold of effectiveness reached, as evidenced by an increase in the marginal productivity of marketing dollars spent?
4. How is the impact of a change in an input in the marketing program propagated throughout the market in time; and how much lag time is associated with the input's ability to induce an initial market response?
5. What are the economies and diseconomies of scale associated with the different kinds of marketing activities to be designed into the total program?
6. What is the decay rate of market response to any input in the total marketing offering?
7. What inputs in the marketing program can be effectively substituted for one another?
8. What inputs in the total marketing program tend to produce the greatest joint impact in the market, or in effect tend to reinforce each other?
9. What inputs in the total marketing program offer the greatest resistance to competitive ability to counter with a similar or new offering?
10. What inputs in the total marketing program are linked in sequence so that the greatest effect in the market is attained when a particular pattern of application of efforts in sequence is followed?[2]

So much for planning the SB marketing program. The reader seeking more detail on marketing planning is invited to review Chapter 3, especially the section dealing with the "how to" of marketing strategy planning for SB. In so doing, one will note that Steps #7 and #8 of our eight-step process of marketing strategy planning were concerned with planning for *execution* and planning for *control.*

EXECUTING SB MARKETING PROGRAMS

SB marketing programs are executed or implemented by implementing each and all of the parts of the marketing program to the full extent of the marketing plans. In the execution phase of the PEC management process, the planned strategies are implemented as adjusted at the time by marketing tactics. Execution is accomplished by *organizing* and *directing* work tasks to be performed in cooperation with other people. Our discussion will therefore be in three areas: organization, directing, and tactical adjustments.

Execution in SB marketing management is using the strategy plans to (a) make marketing decisions and (b) put those decisions into effect through actions. Such decisions

[2]R. P. Willett, "A Model for Marketing Programming," *Journal of Marketing,* 27, No. 1 (January 1963), 42–44.

and actions will take place throughout the marketing mix. For example, changing costs or competitive environmental factors may suggest the need for a price change. The SBM, with his current pricing strategy in mind, may decide to change the price of certain items by some amount. He will then either physically change such prices himself or communicate a directive to a clerk to execute the appropriate price change. Thus, the process he followed was: (a) review strategy, (b) make a decision, and (c) put the decision into effect.

Generalizations Regarding SB Marketing Execution

Prior to the main discussion of organizing, directing, and tactics, some observations concerning execution by SB marketers seem appropriate. These brief remarks further emphasize the management differences between SB and BB. First, a major strength of many SB firms has been in the execution rather than the planning or control phases of marketing management. Although strategy planning is extremely important, the mark of success may well be determined by how good a job the SBM does in executing a rather standardized or common marketing strategy. As your favorite sports announcer has said more than once, "Ball games are won on the field." Only well-executed plans pay off. The possibility of good execution (perhaps at lower costs) is an advantage which SB cannot afford to ignore. Mediocre performance in SB can only be avoided by SB management working with people who really want to work to do a good job. Many SB firms are built on doing a job and on getting that job done. Quite often, the SBM himself is physically involved in much of this doing. BB uses layer upon layer of management, each checking on the layer just below, in order to make sure the work gets done. On the other hand, in SB, the management layers are very few. Either the SBM and his people do the work or it doesn't get done.

Work tasks are usually less divided in SB than in BB. The problems of organizing both people and work tasks are different in SB. BB utilizes bureaucracy; SB does not. However, the absence of bureaucracy in SB does not mean that organization is not needed in SB. Organization is needed. The principles of organization are much the same, but the application of the principles varies. That is, the principles of organization must be properly adapted for use in SB. Remember, the principles of navigation apply to both aircraft carriers and rowboats, but not in quite the same ways. Much of the execution task in marketing management of the SB firm is concerned with what may be called rather "cookbook" or "how-to-do-it" ideas for getting lower level tasks accomplished. Knowledge of the industry, the market, marketing practices, and so on make up a major portion of the management skills of the SBM. This knowledge permits, but does not insure, good execution. The SBM himself must do that. The following brief discussion may be regarded as a "how to execute the tasks" for the SBM. However, our discussion is quite brief. The SBM may therefore wish to get additional ideas on organizing and directing from SB management books.

Organizing

Both the SB and the marketing orientations to organizing are important for the success of the SBM. From the SB marketing perspective, we will examine the need for organizing, organizing principles, forms of organization, size-related organization questions, and, finally, marketing-related organization questions.

The need for organization is expressed very vividly in Heskett's marketing text:

Many residents of communal living experiments, attracted by the potential for individual freedom that such arrangements promise, will tell you that the most frequent reasons for the failure of such organizations are disputes over responsibilities for doing the dishes and carrying out the garbage for the group. This inability to delineate jobs in such a way that they get done without unnecessary duplications of effort and with a reasonable level of morale is often experienced by more formal organizations. It suggests several of the most important reasons for organizing: (1) to differentiate between jobs and allow for specialization of effort, (2) to provide for coordination between tasks and people, (3) to define responsibilities and authority held by members of an organization, and (4) to reflect and support over-all strategies.[3]

Many SB managers do in fact have no clear understanding about who is to "take out the garbage" or perform other more desirable tasks. Pleasant duties are perhaps performed too well, while unpleasant ones are neglected. Time is wasted, arguments result, leadership is not what it should be, customers are not properly served, and so on. What principles of organization can the SBM employ in order to avoid such pitfalls and insure the successful execution of his marketing program? Organization principles adapted to the SB organization are for the purposes of dividing and grouping the work and for determining interrelationships among jobs. Lists of principles to be followed may vary from author to author. The following list of principles seems to well represent the thoughts of most SB management writers:

1. A good organization is designed to accomplish specific purposes.
2. There should be unity of command, with only one person responsible for any given activity.
3. Authority must be clearly spelled out.
4. Decision-making should be accomplished at the lowest level possible.
5. Communication is, desirably, a two-way street, working both from the top man down and from the bottom man up.
6. Employee performance in the organization is monitored and controlled.
7. The limits of control of any individual within the organization must be made clear.[4]

By surveying several marketing and SB management sources, we will now use the above list of seven principles as a framework for our discussion. The SBM may say to himself, "That makes a lot of sense," as he reviews the principles of organization. The important question is whether or not he continually employs such principles in organizing to execute the marketing program. It is probably easier, although not any more advisable, to ignore such principles in the somewhat autocratic SB organization than in the bureaucratic BB organization.

Accomplishing specific purposes. The management organization principle that *form follows function* means that the structure of an organization should be determined by the function or purpose for which the organization is formed. Thus, if a high priority is given to the accomplishment of marketing purposes, organization structure should facilitate the accomplishment of such marketing purposes. The formal organization structure of the SB firm may be grouped using a combination of the following methods:

[3]James L. Heskett, *Marketing* (New York: Macmillan Publishing Co., Inc., 1976), p. 440.
[4]Donald P. Stegall, Lawrence L. Steinmetz, and John B. Kline, *Managing The Small Business* (Homewood, Illinois: Richard D. Irwin, Inc., 1976), p. 152.

1. *Function.* Like skills are grouped together to form an organizational unit, such as *production* or *marketing.* The lowest level of the organization should probably be structured on this basis.
2. *Product.* Production or sales activities may be grouped by product, such as *men's wear, ladies' wear,* and so forth.
3. *Process.* Small companies often base their organization upon manufacturing processes, such as *welding* and *painting.*
4. *Geographic area.* If your company requires a strong, local marketing effort, organizing the sales force by areas or territories can be appropriate.
5. *Type customers.* A firm's customers may be classified as *industrial, commercial,* or other designation.
6. *Project.* To illustrate, a small public accounting firm may be organized on the basis of its clients' projects.
7. *Individual abilities of subordinates.* You may assign work to people according to their particular talents. However, a limitation is that the organization structure tends to change whenever a key employee is replaced.[5]

Whichever combination of methods the SBM uses to organize his firm could be a means of differentiating his offering from that of competitors. Increased size of firm usually calls for the use of two or more of the above methods. The SBM will therefore not use as many methods, but he can differentiate. First, he can examine the organization of his BB competitors in order to determine their strengths and weaknesses in serving specific target markets. His own structure can then be determined accordingly. Secondly, item #7 in the above listing is very practical for the SBM if he so desires, but it is not practical for BB. Third, the SB firm may be able to change its organization very rapidly in order to adapt to changing conditions.

Unity of command. This principle means that one person is charged with getting a job done and that each employee reports to only one boss to whom he is directly responsible in certain matters. This principle is probably most often violated in the SB family business where one family manager tells the employee to do one thing while another family manager tells the same employee to do something else. The dual commands result in employee frustration and low morale. Another time when this principle may be violated is when staff people (acting in an advisory capacity) give directions which, to the employee, seem to be in conflict with the directions received from line managers.

Clearly defined authority. Clearly assigning work responsibilities and the commensurate *authority* for accomplishment is the essence of this principle. Judgment is involved here. Responsibilities should be specific enough so as not to be vague or lead to jurisdictional conflicts, but they must also be stated in such a way that things which are not specifically stated do get accomplished. Written definitions are advisable. Putting it in writing may also help the SB manager to delegate responsibility. The failure to delegate is a major shortcoming of many SB managers. As the SB grows from very small to not-quite-so-small, the SB manager, whether in marketing or some other part of the business, must gradually shift from being a doer to being a manager of other people.

[5]Curtis E. Tate, Jr. et al., *Successful Small Business Management* (Dallas: Business Publications, Inc., 1975), pp. 159–160.

Lowest level decisions. SB firms do not have many levels of management. Therefore, the adherence to this principle should not be too difficult. The communication of strategies to all appropriate levels of management via clear policies, practices, and procedures enables decisions to be made at the lowest possible level. This does not necessarily always mean that decisions are made at the absolute lowest level; it means that they are made at the lowest possible level for decisions of that magnitude and type. This is management by exception put into practice. The advantages are that top SB executives have more time for more important matters and lower-level SB managers are able to use their first-hand knowledge of the situation in making decisions. An example may be that the SB marketing manager may reserve to himself the pricing and other decisions regarding a major account while allowing the salesmen considerable freedom with other accounts.

Two-way communication. Communication should flow freely both up and down (and across) the organization. Communication tends to be less formal in SB. Sometimes it is even too informal to be most effective. Communication channels should be established, kept open, and used. Short-circuiting or going around a manager is a communication problem sometimes found in SB.

Monitor and control. Sometimes referred to as the principle of accountability, we are speaking here of simply checking up to see that work gets done in the way it should be done. More is said about control later in our discussion of the PEC management process.

Span of control. There is a limit to the number of people that a manager can effectively manage. Although that number is finite, it is not necessarily the same for all managers. Managers who manage several subordinates, all of whom are performing very similar work, may be able to effectively manage ten, twenty, or even more direct subordinates. On the other hand, when less similarity exists among the work of subordinates (which is the case as we move up the organization), the span of control must necessarily narrow. The optimum span of control for the SBM himself may be from three to ten subordinates, for example. This, of course, will also depend upon other factors, such as geographic distances, staff assistance, individual capacities, and so forth. For example, the SB sales manager who supervises fifteen field salesmen may employ an assistant-to-the sales manager when expansion calls for the addition of five more field salesmen.

Other management guides, such as keeping the number of levels of management to a minimum, keeping the organization as flexible as possible, keeping the organization simple, and so forth, can be found. We now look at organization structure in SB while keeping in mind that the organization chart is not the organization. It is simply someone's perception of the organization at a given time. Although organizations are said to change before the ink dries on the chart, the SBM may find the chart to be very helpful in communicating organizational relationships to his people. It is suggested here that the SBM construct a chart of his own organization.

Organizations are usually some combination of the following pure types: functional, line, line and staff, and informal. *Functional* organization is an authority concept in which each manager is responsible for a specific function and subordinates report to several managers—one for each function. In this extreme form, functional organization violates the principle of unity of command. In practice, although organizations may be divided along functional lines, a line and staff organization is usually superimposed on the functional division. In a very small firm, such as a new business, functional organization may work. Even here, however, the implicit line authority of the top manager is present.

Line organization is a command authority relationship among superiors and subordinates. Although it also may exist in very small firms, the need for some staff assistance is often present. *Line and staff* organization combines the command authority of line organization with the advisory role of staff. This form tends to be very popular, especially as the SB firm grows.

Whether the formal organization is functional, line, line and staff, or (more likely) some combination of these, an *informal* organization will also exist. All social organizations, such as work groups, tend to develop informal organizations. The informal organization is made up of the structure and relationships resulting from group interaction. Friendships and rivalries develop, informal group leaders emerge, the grapevine communication system carries messages, and so forth. The SBM who is to be an effective manager must recognize the existence of the informal group and learn to use the informal group in accomplishing firm objectives. For example, the attitudes of one or two key salesmen who are regarded by their peers to be group leaders may be critical in the success of a proposed sales campaign.

Committees, whether temporary or permanent, represent an organizational supplement which brings group thinking to a problem area. Those who have served on committees are well aware of the saying: "A committee never did anything." We have suggested earlier in this book that marketing strategy formulation could best be done by a commiteee or marketing management team under the leadership of the SBM. The provision for communication relatively free from barriers is perhaps the greatest benefit from the use of committees. Even though most committees are strictly advisory, they do provide a forum for idea exchange.

SB management books have suggested that the stage of growth of the SB firm will be a major determinant of its form of organization. [6] Stages of growth may be identified as: (a) the direct supervision stage, (b) the supervised supervisor's stage, (c) the indirect control stage, and (d) the divisional organization stage. In the opinion of the present author, the last stage may be considered SB or BB, depending on the extent to which the people factor has been replaced by bureaucracy. In fact, this question might even arise in the third stage. One book briefly describes the four growth stages as follows:

> In the *direct supervision* stage you usually have less than 25 employees and you directly supervise all their work.
>
> In the *supervised supervisor's* stage, you have a first-line supervisor who reports to you. You analyze results through the supervisor's reports.
>
> If your compₐ ιy has 250–300 employees, you enter the *indirect control* stage and will need to supervise managers who, in turn, supervise first-line supervisors. Also, you will have staff people to establish policies and procedures, while you depend on reports.
>
> If your company grows to 1,000 employees, the *divisional organization* stage is entered and you have other managers in charge of certain product lines.[7]

Directing

Some people can tell a joke and others can't. Likewise, the ability to direct others in work activities seems to be unevenly distributed. Concepts such as leadership, motivation, and communication are too complex to cover adequately here. It is up to each SBM to

[6]See Stegall, pp. 149–151 and Tate, pp. 156–157.
[7]Tate, p. 157.

attempt to understand these concepts and to use them effectively in directing the SB organization. Such an understanding will better enable the SBM to guide, supervise, and actuate the performance of others toward the firm goals.

Regarding leadership and the SBM, this concept applies to a relatively few people in the typical SB firm—and the people themselves are often a given in many SB firms. That is, the leaders are the owner/managers, and so on. Since the leaders are a given and the leadership styles are likely to change slowly over time, the best use of given leadership may be to (a) define the leadership style with its weaknesses and strengths objectively, and then (b) attempt to build the organization around that leadership style by seeking employees who work well under such circumstances.

The complexity of motivation was discovered earlier when consumer motives were discussed in the chapter on consumer behavior. Worker motivation is no less complex. McGregor's "theory X" and "theory Y," Maslow's hierarchy of needs, Herzberg's hygienic factors, and others have all investigated the subject. The SBM interested in motivation is advised to read the management literature from the perspective of the SB firm. He is also reminded to employ people who really *want to* work, not simply those who are *willing* to work.

Communications among the management and other employees in SB is another area of directing. Our general communications model presented in the promotions chapters tells us that communications among SB people will be most effective when a common frame of reference and background of experience exist. SB firms probably have too little rather than too much communication. The reverse is probably true in BB. Each time a task is not performed, or is performed poorly, the SBM should ask himself whether or not the employee received proper communications to permit him to know exactly what was expected from him. Only then should he question his own leadership or the motivation of his employees.

Tactical Adjustments

In addition to organizing and directing the efforts of the workforce along with his own efforts, the SBM and his marketing team can execute the SB marketing program by making tactical adjustments to (a) the overall marketing program; (b) the marketing mix of a single target market; (c) an element of the marketing mix, such as product, place, and so on; and (d) an element component, such as the timing of the advertising component of the promotion element. These tactical adjustments could be viewed in terms of the above four levels. However, such a view may be somewhat arbitrary, since each level is a subsystem of another system, and so on. In any event, let's briefly examine a few examples of tactical adjustments being used to expedite the execution of the SB marketing program. These tactical adjustments may occur quite frequently. They should be broadly planned for, but not specifically programmed in the SB marketing program. By way of analogy, a television receiver has fine tuning buttons which may be used to make minor corrections in the reception. The proper use of these buttons can considerably enhance the quality of reception. However, when major adjustments are needed, the TV repairman must be called. Likewise, tactical adjustments have their place and their limitations.

Some examples of tactical adjustments to the SB marketing program follow. Although these are grouped under the five P's, they interact, and many of them may take place simultaneously.

Product examples. Within the present product strategy, (a) the SBM emphasizes a substitute product while a product is in short supply; (b) the SB wholesaler or retailer stops carrying a particular brand of a product; (c) the SBM adds an "economy" size of a fast-selling product; (d) a customer service which was formerly "free" is now available at a slight charge; (e) the SBM implements new procedures for check cashing or for some other customer service; or (f) a small improvement is made in the package or label.

Place examples.   Within the present place strategy, (a) the SBM signs up a new dealer or distributor; (b) a distributor's territory is made slightly larger; (c) a new supplier is secured by the SB wholesaler or retailer; (d) routine delivery day for a customer is changed from Tuesday to Wednesday; or (e) the SB manufacturer drops a dealer for failure to perform up to the standards of the franchise dealer agreement.

Price examples.   Within the present price strategy, (a) the SBM marks down the price of seasonal or perishable merchandise; (b) selling prices on the shelf are adjusted up or down to reflect changes in the cost of merchandise; (c) the SBM uses a "cents off" coupon to compete temporarily with a competitor's lower price; (d) the SB manufacturer offers a seasonal discount to a retail buyer; (e) buyers are notified in advance that the SBM will soon increase the price; (f) the SBM offers a temporary price reduction in the form of a rebate; (g) prices for a special sale are marked with "red tags" rather than regular tags; or (h) the SBM dramatically raises the price of an item to test the effect on sales.

Promotion examples.   Within the present promotion strategy, (a) the SBM tests responses from different layouts, competing newspapers, competing radio stations, and so forth; (b) the SBM adjusts the boundaries of a few sales territories; (c) the SBM switches part of the advertising to smaller but more frequent advertisements; (d) more emphasis is given to a part of the advertising message, such as the slogan; (e) the packaging of the SB reatiler is imprinted with an advertising message; (f) at a sales meeting, the sales manager explains to the salesmen how to use a new sales aid; or (g) sampling is carried on by the SB manufacturer in a retail store.

People examples.   Within the present people strategy, (a) the SBM takes a three-day course in management development; (b) people from the advertising agency, attorney's office, and so on are invited to the company picnic; (c) a major supplier is invited to participate in a meeting of the SB sales force; (d) after a trial period, the SBM hires on a permanent basis a clerk who has good rapport with the customers of the target market; (e) an employee who projected the wrong image for the SB firm through the wrong treatment of a target customer is made aware of the mistake; or (f) the SBM knows all his employees on a first-name basis.

The list of tactics that any SBM may use is almost endless. Specific tactics seem to be associated with different industries. In determining which tactics to employ for the fine tuning of the marketing program, the SBM should pay special attention to the target markets he is serving. He should not necessarily copy BB, but he should seek tactics which uniquely fit his own marketing program and which BB and SB competitors will find difficult to duplicate or render ineffective.

CONTROLLING SB MARKETING PROGRAMS

In Chapter 3, the final step in the eight step process of marketing strategy planning was to set performance standards and monitor feedback. In that chapter, we were formulating the plan for controlling the SB marketing program. In the present chapter, we are speaking not of planning but of the actual marketing control process itself. This is the third side of our PEC marketing management process triangle. We must answer the question: In what ways (qualitative) and to what extent (quantitative) has the SB marketing program been successful in accomplishing its objectives? These marketing objectives have been stated broadly and specifically in terms of both customer satisfaction and resulting profitable sales. Another way of stating the above question may be: In terms of the five controllable variables of the SB marketing program and the target market(s) to which this marketing effort was directed, how can the SBM minimize the gaps between planned and actual performance?

The Nature of Marketing Control

The control function in marketing management is the systematic comparison of the actual results of marketing effort with predetermined standards and plans in order that corrective action (if needed) can be taken to insure that the objectives are met. Control is a process rather than a one-time thing. For example, a steering system may control the direction of an automobile or a thermostat may control the operation of a heating/cooling system. The steering wheel and the thermostat are working all the time, not simply at the beginning or end of a trip or once a day. Likewise, marketing control should be an active, continuous, ongoing process of management rather than something which occurs once a year at budget time. Sales supervisors, salesmen, distributors, dealers, advertising agencies, and many others are constantly in the process of executing parts of the marketing program. Constant control of such performance is therefore required in order to insure success in reaching stated marketing objectives. The SBM needs control to know how things are going and how future plans may be affected.

Levels of Marketing Control

The PEC management process is an endless process which recycles again and again, with both external and internal changes taking place all the time. Insofar as the marketing system of a firm is composed of different levels of subsystems, we may say that the control process operates at various levels within the marketing system. Our SBMM model shows the PEC marketing management process operating at the overall strategy level for each target market and at the level of each of the five controllable marketing variables. At what other levels does marketing control exist in SB? Marketing control may be viewed from the following levels:

1. The total marketing program of the firm, composed of all target markets, marketing objectives, and overall company objectives.
2. The marketing plan for each target market served.
3. The effectiveness of product, place, price, promotion, and people as elements of a marketing mix.
4. The effectiveness of components of each of the five marketing mix elements, for example, the effectiveness of advertising as a component of the promotion mix.
5. An operational level of control, for example, the effectiveness of a particular advertisement, a particular salesman, a particular distributor, a particular price, and so forth. Also included at the operational level of control in marketing are such items as cash and credit control during marketing transactions, inventory control to protect from shoplifting and employee pilferage, and other control items relating to market-

ing, accounting, and other areas of the firm. The above five levels will be discussed briefly from the SB perspective.

The total marketing program level of control requires the SBM to ask: For our firm, are we serving the correct target markets? Do we have the right marketing objectives for these target markets—in light of our firm's objectives? Does marketing effort properly relate to other areas of our firm, such as production, finance, and so forth? This first level of control is really beyond the normal appraisal and evaluation of the marketing control process. It is infrequent at best in both BB and SB firms. This level may be comparable to appraising the core marketing strategy of the firm over the long run. An approach to this level of control which has found some favor in recent years is known as the marketing audit. The marketing audit, probably best performed with the help of outsiders, is a future-oriented endeavor geared toward new marketing opportunities. The comprehensive marketing audit, including the analysis of objectives, policies, organization, methods and procedures, and personnel, is probably beyond the scope of most SB firms. However, an infrequent audit employing the same basic idea may be warranted. Kollat notes the basic difference between the marketing audit and the marketing control process:

> The marketing audit differs from the control process in a very significant way. The control process is concerned with operations on a short-term basis and asks primarily: "Are we doing things right?" A marketing audit includes this question but goes well beyond it to ask: "Are we doing the right things?"[8]

Control of the marketing plan for each target market served is the second level. This is the third side of our large PEC triangle in the SBMM model shown in Chapter 3. Such control is the direct responsibility of the SBM. For each target market, the SBM has a marketing strategy plan which is executed. The SBM must determine how closely and how effectively that execution followed the plan in attaining the marketing objectives. He must then decide what changes (both strategic and tactical) should take place from time to time in the marketing plan for each target market. Decisions at this level of control will interact with the other levels of control.

The third level of control concerns the five controllable elements of the SB marketing mix: product, place, price, promotion, and people. Here, the SBM uses the standards of Step #8 in the strategy planning process of each of these five controllable variables. For example, the performance standards and routine monitoring of feedback regarding the effectiveness of product strategy as executed in actual practice is compared to the objectives (marketing and product) and expectations for product in the formulation of the product strategy plan.

The fourth level of control deals with the submix components of each of the five controllable marketing variables. Some of these control questions were raised in previous chapters. For example, we discussed whether or not advertising effectiveness could be measured. At this level of control, the SBM in the SB firm which is not extremely small will possibly be evaluating the managers responsible for these functions along with the functions themselves. In addition to advertising effectiveness, we may look at comparative media effectiveness, message effectiveness, sales force effectiveness, and so forth. Effectiveness of product components such as branding, packaging, new product development, goods-services combinations, and so on are also included here. Likewise for place, price,

[8]David T. Kollat, Roger D. Blackwell, and James F. Robeson, *Strategic Marketing* (New York: Holt, Rinehart and Winston, Inc., 1972), p. 500.

and people; the SBM controls the actual versus the planned for all the core and supporting strategies under each of these variables.

Level five, as indicated above, deals with individual and operational level specifics. It asks: How well is Joe doing in terms of selling expense control, dollar sales per call, and so on in terms of the expectations of the plan for Joe? We have not discussed this level because it is virtually impossible for anyone but the SBM himself to give meaningful answers for his firm. However, the fourth and fifth levels, when analyzed together, do comprise the bulk of the control process, at least in terms of volume of effort. Many control techniques have been developed to measure effectiveness at these levels. Most of these techniques (e.g., distribution cost analysis, expense control analysis, advertising effectiveness measures, performance analysis for other marketing functions) are explained at length in functional area marketing books such as those on sales management, advertising, physical distribution, and so forth. Although the use of such techniques may be less frequent or less complex in SB than in BB, the control techniques are essentially the same. A description of these operational level control techniques is beyond our present scope. However, it should be noted that in all such techniques, as well as in control at the other levels of the marketing system, the control process is essentially the same.

The Marketing Control Process in SB

Although the process may be broken down into any given number of steps, the following listing seems to be meaningful. The marketing control process in SB consists of the following three steps *after* planning for control has taken place. In planning for marketing control, the SBM determines (a) exactly what aspects and levels of marketing strategy, tactics, and operations are to be controlled and (b) what standards are to be used against which actual performance will be measured. The steps are: (1) gathering information by measuring actual performance, (2) management appraisal of performance in terms of deviations from predetermined standards, and (3) making decisions and taking corrective actions.

The information which results from measuring and recording actual marketing performance should be about key areas of marketing at the appropriate levels, as indicated previously in the chapter. When the performance measures involve the performance of people (and they usually do), the people being measured should have some participation in setting the standards of performance. The degree of participation depends upon the management philosophy of the SBM regarding participatory management. In any event, the performance measures should be clearly understood in advance and the rules should not be changed in the middle of the game. It is also important that performance appraisal is based only upon those factors that are within the control of the person or unit being evaluated. In BB marketing performance, information may be via an elaborate marketing information system (MIS). As discussed in Chapter 7, such is not likely to be the case in SB. Reports of routine recurring activities prepared by the accounting portion of the SB firm are likely to be the backbone for recording actual marketing performance in SB. Special marketing research reports may also be used. This suggests the importance to the SBM of reviewing the present system of reports to see that, wherever possible, such reports give adequate and usable marketing data as well as accounting and financial data.

The second step in the marketing control process is management appraisal of performance in terms of deviations from predetermined standards. By comparing the performance information gathered in the first step with the predetermined standards, the SBM can isolate deviations. In fact, his reporting system may be set up according to the exceptions principle in order to highlight deviations beyond a certain tolerable limit. Deviations may be either positive or negative. A positive deviation, that is, overperformance, may occur less frequently than negative deviations. Although overperformance may seem to be desirable at first, the SBM should not assume that no further action is required when overperformance is detected. Perhaps the marketing objectives should be revised. Or it may be that such overperformance in one activity area can be used to offset inadequate performance in another. The two may even be causally related. Analysis of both positive and negative deviations may point out new marketing opportunities for the SBM. Negative deviations present the SBM with the task of determining causes or reasons for lack of adequate performance. If such reasons are determined, and they are controllable, some type of corrective action will follow in the next step. If such reasons are not within the control of the firm (e.g., a recession, strike, or other environmental cause), the SBM will adjust the marketing program to take account of such factors. Whatever the causes, negative deviations tend to be compounding in such a way as to make the synergetic effect operate in reverse. Prompt attention and continuous monitoring are therefore essential to "keep the dominoes from beginning a chain reaction."

The third step is using what has been learned thus far in the control process to make decisions and to take corrective action where appropriate. Such corrective actions may be aimed at any of the levels of the marketing system identified above. If corrective action is needed at the marketing strategy level, the SBM may consider going to his alternate or back-up marketing strategy. Or, if the problem seems to be with the operational level of implementation, the SBM may tighten up on expense control where expenses were out of line. Corrective action often involves people whose performance was deemed to be lacking in some way. In the SB firm, discipline begins with the self-discipline of the SBM himself. Good personal example and positive reinforcement for others will decrease the need for discipline. However, in a small number of situations, the need for discipline is apparent. In administering discipline, the SBM should:

1. Know the rules.
2. Move promptly on violations.
3. Gather pertinent facts.
4. Allow employees an opportunity to explain their positions.
5. Set up tentative courses of action and evaluate them.
6. Decide what action to take.
7. Apply the disciplinary action, observing labor contract procedures.
8. Set up and maintain a record of actions taken.[9]

Marketing Control in SB

In what ways is marketing control different in SB? Size does make a difference. Earlier in this chapter, we identified four growth stages: (a) the direct supervision stage, (b) the supervised supervisors stage, (c) the indirect control stage, and (d) the divisional organization stage. Control will vary according to stage. The first stage will be mostly self-control of the SBM and his direct control of others. Some indirect control through reports will be necessary and desirable, especially in the case of outside salesmen. Both the need for control and control problems seem to increase as the size of a business increases. The

[9]Tate, p. 166.

inability to initiate adequate control procedures has prevented the successful expansion of many SB firms which had excellent direct control at the first stage of growth. Many readers are undoubtedly familiar with the small retailer who was extremely successful in operating one store but could not make money in either store when he opened a second store. Among the control problems were employee and management theft, high marketing expenses, less productivity per employee, lack of corrective actions, and so forth. At the second stage of growth and beyond, the SBM must rely on the reports of others. One small business management book notes:

> For example, under the first supervision stage of growth, the small businessperson can take immediate corrective action to remedy troublesome situations. However, in the supervision of supervisors stage of size, the small businessperson must have some way in which he or she might be apprised of (1) the fact that things are getting out of control and (2) what is being done (as opposed to what he or she should do) to get them "back in control." Therefore, the small businessperson must recognize that the larger and more successful the business becomes, the more necessary it becomes to be able to control the organization from a remote position. *This means, in essence, that the manager must be able to maintain control of operations by the use of reports which subordinate managers submit rather than by direct observation.* [10]

USING MBO IN MANAGING SB MARKETING PROGRAMS

Throughout this book, our approach to marketing management by the SBM has stressed the benefits of a systems approach. It seems natural, at this point, to raise the question of whether or not the SBM should use management by objectives (MBO) in managing SB marketing programs. Our brief answer to this question can be summarized: The MBO philosophy has much to offer the SB marketing managers. On the other hand, the formal implementation of MBO as a management process requires a substantial investment of resources and management time before benefits are realized. Therefore, for many SB firms, the formal MBO process may not be warranted. Each individual SBM must do his own investigation in order to determine whether to adopt MBO as a philosophy, as a management process, or not at all.

My position is that if the MBO philosophy is compatible with the management philosophy and style of the SBM, then the SBM will probably be well advised to adopt MBO as a philosophy. With this in mind, the following brief comments are intended to introduce MBO. A succinct description of MBO follows:

> MBO is probably the most widely recognized and used modern management technique. Within the last fifteen years, practically all organizations of any size have implemented MBO to various degrees. The basic MBO format presently comes in a variety of hybrid forms and is sometimes given different labels; however, it generally involves setting objectives and appraising by results. The overriding assumption is that mutual participation between subordinates and superiors in the determination of objectives leads to commitment, which in turn leads to improved performance. Appraising by results is an effective control technique because it leads to self-control, which in turn also leads to improved performance.
> Depending on the size of an organization, an MBO approach may take four or five

[10]Stegall, p. 165.

years to become an effective management system. At various stages, MBO may simply amount to a goal-setting process to improve short and long-range planning or an employee appraisal technique. When fully developed, MBO is supposed to provide a systematic method of giving feedback on specific and overall performance and matching rewards with contributions.[11]

MBO is further described by listing the three generally accepted steps of the MBO process. These steps are:

1. Meaningful organizational objectives are developed by top management.
2. Superiors and subordinates jointly develop objectives for the subordinate that are consistent with the organizational objectives.
3. Superiors and subordinates at some later specified time assess the subordinate's performance.[12]

The four tenets of MBO are objectives, time, participation, and motivation.[13] This means that specific objectives to be accomplished according to a specified time schedule are set for a subordinate with his significant participation in the process in order to gain the subordinate's commitment to the achievement of results. Although MBO has been most often associated with production rather than marketing, several areas of marketing application may be beneficial. Etzel and Ivancevich note, in the conclusion of their article:

Table 17–1   A Brief Summary of the PEC Process in SBMM

1. Determine company goals and objectives.
2. Determine marketing goals and objectives.
3. Identify the differential advantage.
4. Define target markets.
5. Recognize the environment.
6. *Plan* marketing strategy (Steps 1–8).
   A. Plan product strategy (Steps 1–8).
   B. Plan place strategy (Steps 1–8).
   C. Plan price strategy (Steps 1–8).
   D. Plan promotion strategy (Steps 1–8).
   E. Plan people strategy (Steps 1–8).
7. Integrate marketing strategy plans into an overall marketing program.
8. *Execute* strategic marketing program.
   A. By organizing.
   B. By directing.
   C. By tactical adjustments.
9. *Control* strategic marketing program.
10. The result is SUCCESS in terms of customer satisfaction at a profit for the SB firm.

[11]Fred Luthans and Robert Kreitner, *Organizational Behavior Modification* (Glenview, Illinois: Scott, Foresman and Company, 1975), pp. 193–194.

[12]Michael J. Etzel and John M. Ivancevich, "Management by Objectives in Marketing: Philosophy, Process, and Problems," *Journal of Marketing*, 38. No. 4 (October 1974), p. 49.

[13]Etzel and Ivancevich, p. 48.

There are several areas in marketing in which the benefits of a successfully implemented MBO program can be achieved. Among the most obvious are sales management, advertising, market research, new product development, and physical distribution.

Given the overview provided by this article, it should be clear that MBO is not a panacea for managing a marketing unit nor is it a common sense process. It is an approach that some firms have used successfully and others have had to discard as a failure. The success stories associated with MBO revolve around an appreciation of formal training, top management commitment, evaluation, modification, patience, and reinforcement. On the other hand, many of the failures can be attributed to the assumptions that MBO is simplistic and easy to implement, and requires only minimal attention from participants.[14]

From the above brief encounter with MBO, it may be concluded that MBO does work for some managers and does have marketing applications; however, the question of SB marketing application was not addressed. The answer to such a complex and important question will require each SBM to search further. A comprehensive answer to the question could fill an entire volume. Whether or not MBO as a *process* has SB marketing application, this author strongly suggests that MBO as a *philosophy* may have very important SB marketing implications. In a sense, MBO is a marketing-oriented approach to management. Table 17–1 briefly summarizes the PEC process in SBMM.

FUTURE OUTLOOK FOR SB MARKETING

The future outlook for SB marketing is a three-part question involving the future outlook for SB, the future outlook for marketing, and the future outlook for marketing in SB. Added to the general question, each individual present and prospective SBM must ask: What is the future outlook for this particular SB? This latter question must be answered individually. The answer to the first question, in the one-word opinion of the author, is BRIGHT!

The future is really anybody's guess. We may plan for the future by considering the futurity of present plans and by making educated guesses about the environment the SBM will face in the future. We may pay lip service to the future by such anonymous and common phrases as: "The future is where we all will spend the rest of our lives"; or that the future is "Something that comes one day at a time." Whatever our approach, most of us are not content simply to ignore the future.

The importance of SB in the American society was pointed out in Chapters 1 and 8. In an article written a few years ago, the following questions were posed:

What is the role of small business in American society today: Is its role the same as it was before the advent of the corporate giants? Will rapidly changing technology force small business to the wall because of its inability to compete with large, well-managed, and adequately financed firms? Does the urban society, with its growing interdependence, rapid transportation and communication, and increasing social services, provide an environment in which small business can take root and grow?

[14]Etzel and Ivancevich, p. 55.

Would the demise of small business endanger the maintenance of basic American political freedoms?[15]

To the above list may be added such questions as: What will be the future impact of multinational corporations on SB? How will future energy situations affect SB? How will shortages affect SB? What continued effects will inflation have on SB? The environment will continue to change. One popular SB management text reflects optimism for the future largely by looking at the opportunities for SB created by changes in the past:

> The long-range trend in American business history has been favorable to small business, especially in terms of new opportunities and the number of concerns. Each new industry, although it may eventually be dominated by large concerns, brings in new opportunities for small firms and results in a great increase in the total number of establishments. Electronics and semiconductors are recent examples. In whole-saling, the trend has been toward a larger number of small concerns. Nearly the entire field of service businesses was unknown a century ago. Only in farming has there been a decline in the number of small enterprisers relative to either population or the total number of businesses in operation. In fact, it is primarily the rise of many large industries and a steady increase in the use of capital goods and modern technology that have made it possible for us to have an ever-increasing number of small business units in operation.[16]

What about the future of marketing? Trends in marketing indicate that the scope of marketing continues to be extended into new areas of activity. Marketing ideas and concepts are being extended to the nonprofit sector.[17] Although this may be of little direct concern to SB, the indirect implications are tremendous when the SBM considers the increases in resources being channeled through the so-called "nonprofit" sector of our economy. The future of many SB firms may be tied to direct marketing cooperation with such nonprofit marketing institutions.

An area which bears directly on the future of marketing and its future in SB is the question of prejudice against marketing. A recent article began with the following words: "Society honors those who build better mousetraps but suspects those who market mousetraps better."[18] Such prejudice or antimarketing bias is nothing new, as Steiner notes:

> Hence, by the fall of the Roman Empire, the major foundations of the antimarket-ing bias had been sunk deep into intellectual soil. To wit:
>
> 1. Form utility occupations are productive and natural. Trade is inferior and unnatural.
>
> 2. The markups in trade, unlike those applied in agriculture or crafts, reflect the returns to chicanery rather than a true value added.
>
> 3. Farmers and craftsmen, especially the former, are noble and strong. Merchants are weak and slippery.[19]

---

[15]Harold K. Charlesworth, "The Uncertain Future of Small Business: Can This Picture Be Changed?" *MSU Business Topics,* 18, No. 2 (Spring 1970), p. 13.

[16]Clifford M. Baumback, Kenneth Lawyer, and Pearce C. Kelley, *How To Organize And Operate A Small Business* (Englewood Cliffs, New Jersey: Prentice-Hall, Inc., 1973), p. 536.

[17]See Shelby D. Hunt, "The Nature and Scope of Marketing," *Journal of Marketing,* 40, No. 3 (July 1976), 17–28.

[18]Robert L. Steiner, "The Prejudice Against Marketing," *Journal of Marketing,* 40, No. 3 (July 1976), p. 2.

[19]Steiner, p. 3.

The fact that the antimarketing bias is not new and that it undoubtedly will continue is somewhat disturbing. The fact that some of this bias is directed toward SB is also disturbing. However, the most disturbing fact, to this author, is that some SB managers and other SB people actively or passively support such prejudice against marketing. This book has attempted to bring something new to the SB. That "something new" is to put at the disposal of the receptive SBM the tools of marketing strategy in a form which is usable by the SBM. Acceptance and use of the tools of SB marketing strategy are up to each SBM. We know from our familiarity with the adoption process that there will be innovators and early adopters as well as laggards. The acceptance and implementation of the marketing concept in SB along with the maintenance of a success attitude will overcome many obstacles, as the following story illustrates so vividly:

> Of course, there are obstacles. Like sandbars hidden in the Mississippi River. You've heard about the steamboat owner who wanted to take his boat down to New Orleans for the first time. So, he interviewed a prospective pilot who was supposed to know the course of the river.
>
> The prospective pilot assured him, "I know where every sandbar is in the whole Mississippi River." So, he was hired. Sure enough, he knew where the sandbars were, because he ran the boat aground on one of them within the first three miles.
>
> Then the boat owner, having finally gotten his boat afloat again, interviewed another prospective pilot. This pilot told him confidently, "I may not know where every sandbar is, but I know exactly where the channel is." And so he did.[20]

Like the riverboat pilot, the SBM may not know everything about the environment, but he should know exactly the tools he has to work with. Product, place, price, promotion, and people are those tools by which a successful course can be charted. He should be able to plan, execute, and control a marketing program that both satisfies the target customers and achieves the profit objectives of the firm. Each SBM is unique. Equally unique marketing mixes will therefore be used by each successful SBM.

BIBLIOGRAPHY

Books

BAUMBACK, CLIFFORD M., LAWYER, KENNETH, AND KELLEY, PEARCE C. *How To Organize And Operate A Small Business.* Englewood Cliffs, New Jersey: Prentice-Hall, Inc., 1973.

HESKETT, JAMES L. *Marketing.* New York: Macmillan Publishing Co., Inc., 1976.

KOLLAT, DAVID T., BLACKWELL, ROGER D., AND ROBESON, JAMES F. *Strategic Marketing.* New York: Holt, Rinehart and Winston, Inc., 1972.

KOPMEYER, M. S. *Success Is As Easy As ABC/C.* Los Angeles: Sherbourne Press, Inc., 1968.

LUTHANS, FRED, AND KREITNER, ROBERT. *Organizational Behavior Modification.* Glenview, Illinois: Scott, Foresman and Company, 1975.

STEGALL, DONALD P., STEINMETZ, LAWRENCE L., AND KLINE, JOHN B. *Managing The Small Business.* Homewood, Illinois: Richard D. Irwin, Inc., 1976.

STERN, MARK E. *Marketing Planning: A Systems Approach.* New York: McGraw-Hill Book Company, 1966.

TATE, CURTIS., *et al. Successful Small Business Management.* Dallas: Business Publications, Inc., 1975.

[20]M. R. Kopmeyer, *Success Is As Easy As ABC/C* (Los Angeles: Sherbourne Press, Inc., 1968), pp. 130–131.

Articles and Periodicals

CHARLESWORTH, HAROLD K. "The Uncertain Future of Small Business: Can This Picture Be Changed?" *MSU Business Topics,* 18, No. 2 (Spring 1970), 13–20.

ETZEL, MICHAEL J., AND IVANCEVICH, JOHN M. "Management by Objectives in Marketing: Philosophy, Process, and Problems," *Journal of Marketing,* 38, No. 4 (October 1974), 47–55.

HUNT, SHELBY D. "The Nature and Scope of Marketing," *Journal of Marketing,* 40, No. 3 (July 1976), 17–28.

STEINER, ROBERT L. "The Prejudice Against Marketing," *Journal of Marketing,* 40, No. 3 (July 1976), 2–9.

WILLETT, R. P. "A Model for Marketing Programming," *Journal of Marketing,* 27, No. 1 (January 1963), 40–45.

Index